HARNESSING QUALITY FOR GLOBAL COMPETITIVENESS IN EASTERN EUROPE AND CENTRAL ASIA

HARNESSING QUALITY FOR GLOBAL COMPETITIVENESS IN EASTERN EUROPE AND CENTRAL ASIA

Edited by
Jean-Louis Racine

Europe and Central Asia Region

THE WORLD BANK

©2011 The International Bank for Reconstruction and Development / The World Bank
1818 H Street NW
Washington DC 20433
Telephone: 202-473-1000
Internet: www.worldbank.org

1 2 3 4 14 13 12 11

This volume is a product of the staff of the International Bank for Reconstruction and Development / The World Bank. The findings, interpretations, and conclusions expressed in this volume do not necessarily reflect the views of the Executive Directors of The World Bank or the governments they represent.

The World Bank does not guarantee the accuracy of the data included in this work. The boundaries, colors, denominations, and other information shown on any map in this work do not imply any judgement on the part of The World Bank concerning the legal status of any territory or the endorsement or acceptance of such boundaries.

Rights and Permissions
The material in this publication is copyrighted. Copying and/or transmitting portions or all of this work without permission may be a violation of applicable law. The International Bank for Reconstruction and Development / The World Bank encourages dissemination of its work and will normally grant permission to reproduce portions of the work promptly.

For permission to photocopy or reprint any part of this work, please send a request with complete information to the Copyright Clearance Center Inc., 222 Rosewood Drive, Danvers, MA 01923, USA; telephone: 978-750-8400; fax: 978-750-4470; Internet: www.copyright.com.

All other queries on rights and licenses, including subsidiary rights, should be addressed to the Office of the Publisher, The World Bank, 1818 H Street NW, Washington, DC 20433, USA; fax: 202-522-2422; e-mail: pubrights@worldbank.org.

ISBN: 978-0-8213-8509-8
e-ISBN: 978-0-8213-8510-4
DOI: 10.1596/978-0-8213-8509-8

Cover illustration: Romain Falloux
Cover design: Naylor Design, Washington, D.C.

Library of Congress Cataloging-in-Publication Data
Racine, Jean-Louis
   Harnessing quality for competitiveness in Eastern Europe and Central Asia / Jean-Louis Racine, editor.
      p. cm.
Includes bibliographical references and index.
ISBN 978-0-8213-8509-8 (alk. paper)
ISBN 978-0-8213-8510-4 (ebook)
   1. Quality of products—Europe, Eastern. 2. Quality of products—Asia, Central. 3. Competition, International. I. Racine, Jean-Louis.
HF5415.157.H368 2011
658.4'013—dc22
                              2010044598

Contents

Figures

Maps

Photographs

Contributors

Maurício Nogueira Frota is the head of the postgraduate metrology program of the Catholic University of Rio de Janeiro, Brazil. He serves as a consultant for the World Bank, the U.S. Agency for International Development (USAID), and European agencies in quality infrastructure–related projects. He is the founder and first president of the Brazilian Metrology Society, a former Director of Scientific and Industrial Metrology of Brazil, the former President of the Inter-American Metrology System (SIM), and the former Vice-President of the International Measurement Confederation (IMEKO). He has a PhD from Stanford University.

John Gabriel Goddard is an economist in the Europe and Central Asia Region for the World Bank, where he focuses on lending operations and analytic studies that can contribute to improving competitiveness, innovative capacity, and access to finance. He has also worked in the Africa Region's Energy Group in projects to develop power generation and promote energy efficiency. Prior to joining the World Bank, he worked as a researcher at Dauphine University and the Cournot Centre in Paris and as a consultant for the United Nations Economic Commission for Latin America and the Caribbean (ECLAC) and UK-based firms. He has a BA in Economics from Centro de Investigación y Docencia Económicas, Mexico, and earned an MPhil and DPhil in Economics from the University of Oxford.

Martin Kellermann is an international consultant in standardization and technical regulation with a decade of experience primarily in Africa and Central Asia, where he advises governments on optimizing their national quality infrastructure and establishing effective technical regulation frameworks compliant with the World Trade Organization (WTO)

Agreement on Technical Barriers to Trade (TBT Agreement). Previously, he was the vice president of the South African Bureau of Standards and represented his country in the International Organization for Standardization (ISO) Technical Management Board and the WTO TBT Agreement Technical Committee.

Manfred Kindler is a former head of the German Accreditation System of Testing (DAP) and a member and peer evaluator of the European cooperation for Accreditation (EA). For the past 15 years, he has been active in multiple projects of TRANSFORM, PRAQ III, Phare, TACIS, and MEDA and German projects in Eastern Europe; Central, South-East, and East Asia; and Latin and Centro-America, the Caribbean, and Africa. His specialties include International Laboratory Accreditation Cooperation (ILAC) and International Accreditation Forum (IAF) mutual recognition arrangements (MRAs); proficiency testing schemes; accreditation of conformity assessment bodies, including medical laboratories; and quality and risk management.

Jean-Louis Racine is an innovation specialist in the Europe and Central Asia Region for the World Bank. At the World Bank, his work focuses on policies and programs to support industrial upgrading, technology diffusion, and innovation. Prior to his current position, he worked in a private consulting practice where he advised regional governments and businesses on technology-based competitiveness strategies. He draws from a combined background in engineering and policy, with a PhD in Mechanical Engineering from the University of California at Berkeley, an MIA in Technology Policy for Economic Development from Columbia University, and an MSc in Mechanical Engineering from Stanford University.

Prathima Rodrigues has been at the World Bank for four years, working on policy issues in both the private development and the education sectors. She is a graduate of Columbia University, where she specialized in economic development. Her global experience includes working with the United Nations Children's Fund (UNICEF), the United National Industrial Development Organization (UNIDO) in Vietnam, and the International Institute of Rural Reconstruction in the Philippines. She is also the founder of Skills for Kids—an initiative that teaches entrepreneurial skills to middle-school children. She is a native of Mangalore, India.

Clemens Sanetra is a consultant on the different components of national quality infrastructure systems, with a main focus on metrology. He works in technical cooperation projects all over the world, mainly in Asia and Latin America. He has a PhD from the Institute for Fatigue Analysis and Plant Engineering at the Technical University of Clausthal,Germany, and professional experience in various areas, including material testing, environmental management, metrology in chemistry, and quality assurance in value chains.

Alexandra Schleier works for an industry association in the field of technical regulation and standardization. She is an expert in quality infrastructure and has a background in development cooperation in which she collected extensive regional experience in the countries of Europe and Central Asia.

Susanne Sieber is an economist at the Austrian Institute of Economic Research (WIFO) in the department Industrial Economics, Innovation, and International Competition. Her research interests focus on international trade and foreign direct investment. In addition, she teaches industrial policy at the Vienna University of Technology. Prior to joining WIFO, she worked at the Austrian Regulatory Authority for Broadcasting and Telecommunications (RTR).

María Teresa Silva Porto Díaz is a graduate from Universidad de las Américas Puebla who worked at the Austrian Institute of Economic Research (WIFO). After additional work experience at the European Commission, she joined the Centro de Estudios Económicos del Sector Privado in México City. Her various research fields include foreign trade, international trade relations, industrial economics, industrial policy, public finance, and public policy.

Hüseyin Ugur has been an independent consultant since 2004, after working in Turkey's National Metrology Institute (UME) as the founding director for 12 years. He is involved in the preparation and supervision of World Bank quality infrastructure projects in Europe and Central Asia. He has a PhD in Physics from the University of Chicago. His areas of specialty are metrology, accreditation, conformity assessment, quality infrastructure, innovation, and research and development policy and management.

Acknowledgments

This book benefited from the valuable inputs, contributions, and support of people in many countries. Policy makers throughout Eastern Europe and Central Asia provided critical advice on their needs for this book covering policy options for reform and modernization of quality systems. Quality infrastructure development practitioners provided unique insight from their experience working throughout the region. In particular, we are very thankful to Physikalisch Technische Bundesanstalt for their collaboration on this book and in other World Bank activities. We are also indebted to the many firms, business associations, and consumer groups that volunteered their time during the case studies developed for this book.

At the World Bank, we are most grateful to Fernando Montes-Negret for his encouragement from the beginning, to Gerardo Corrochano for his continued support and to George Clarke, Paulo Correa, and Donato De Rosa for their advice and comments on the various drafts. Additional research and contributions were provided by Victor Burunsus, Olivier Cattaneo, Doina Cebotari, Lorenzo Costantino, Donato De Rosa, Evgeny Evgeniev, Sorin Krammer, Andrej Popovic, Gordana Popovik, Gale Raj Reichert, and Chris Uregian. The team would like to thank Karl-Christian Goethner for his photograph contributions. Paul Holtz and Mary-Ann Moalli provided valuable editing support, Paola Scalabrin and Aziz Gokdemir provided support with the production, and Romain Falloux of El Vikingo Design, Inc. designed the book.

The team is grateful for comments received from peer reviewers, including José Guilherme Reis, Philip Schuler, and John Wilson. Comments on the concept note were given by Vinod Goel, Seven Jaffee, Suzanne Troje, and John Wilson. The team expresses its appreciation to Sylvie Bossoutrot, Marianne Fay, Indermit Gil, Pradeep Mitra, Lalit

Raina, Sophie Sirtaine, and Willem Van Eegehn for their support and guidance. Finally, we would like to acknowledge Zenaida Kalinger who generously supported us during the production of the book.

The authors alone take responsibility for the content of the book and the views expressed here, which do not necessarily reflect the views of our colleagues in the World Bank Group.

Acronyms and Abbreviations

APEC	Asia Pacific Economic Cooperation
APLAC	Asia Pacific Laboratory Accreditation Cooperation
ARSO	African Organization for Standardization
BERIS	Business Environment Reform and Institutional Strengthening
BICRO	Business Innovation Center of Croatia
BIPM	International Bureau of Weights and Measures
BP	British Petroleum
BSI	British Standards Institution
CAC	Central Asian Cooperation
CE	conformité Européenne, or European comformity
CEE	Central and Eastern Europe
CEE5	Czech Republic, Hungary, Poland, the Slovak Republic, and Slovenia
CEN	European Committee for Standardization
CENELEC	European Committee for Electrotechnical Standardization
CIPM	International Committee for Weights and Measures
CIS	Commonwealth of Independent States
CMC	Calibration and Measurement Capability
COMECON	Council for Mutual Economic Assistance
COOMET	Euro-Asian Cooperation of National Metrological Institutions
COPANT	Pan American Standards Commission
CT	Cambodia Trust
DIN	Deutsches Institut für Normung
DSME	Daewoo Shipbuilding and Marine Engineering

DZM	State Office for Metrology (Croatia)
EA	European co-operation for Accreditation
EAAB	East Africa Accreditation Board
EAC	East African Community
EA CT	Executive Agency for Certification and Testing (Bulgaria)
EASC	EuroAsian Interstate Council for Standardization, Metrology, and Certification
ECA	Eastern Europe and Central Asia
EFQM	European Foundation for Quality Management
EFTA	European Free Trade Association
EMS	environmental management system
ETSI	European Telecommunications Standardization Institute
EU	European Union
EURAMET	European Association of National Metrology Institutes
EurAsEC	Eurasian Economic Community
FDI	foreign direct investment
GDP	gross domestic product
GL	Grubel-Lloyd (index)
GMP	Good Manufacturing Practices (United States)
GOST	Gosudarstvennyy standart, or state standard
GOST-R	Standards of the Russian Federation
HACCP	Hazard Analysis and Critical Control Points
IAAC	InterAmerican Accreditation Cooperation
IAF	International Accreditation Forum
ICAITI	Central American Institute of Research and Industrial Technology
IEC	International Electrotechnical Commission
IFC	International Finance Corporation
IIT	intraindustry trade
ILAC	International Laboratory Accreditation Cooperation
ILNAS	Luxembourg Institute for Standardization, Accreditation, and Security
ISO	International Organization for Standardization
ITU	International Telecommunication Union
KOLAS	Korea Laboratory Accreditation Scheme
KONCRO	Productivity and Quality Facility (Croatia)
KRISS	Korea Research Institute of Standards and Science
LMD	legal metrology department
MEC	Manufacturing Extension Center
MEP	Manufacturing Extension Partnership
MLA	multilateral recognition arrangement
MNC	multinational corporation
MRA	mutual recognition arrangement

MSTQ	metrology, standards, testing, and quality
NAB	national accreditation body
NACE	Nomenclature Statistique des Activités Économiques dans la Communauté Européenne (Statistical Classification of Economic Activities in the European Community)
NGO	nongovernmental organization
NISM	National Institute for Standards and Metrology (Kyrgyz Republic)
NIST	National Institute of Standards and Technology
NMI	national metrology institute
NQI	national quality infrastructure
NSB	national standards body
OECD	Organisation for Economic Co-operation and Development
OIML	International Organization of Legal Metrology
PAC	Pacific Accreditation Cooperation
PASC	Pacific Areas Standard Congress
PQF	Productivity and Quality Facility (Croatia)
QMS	quality management system
R&D	research and development
RQE	Revealed Quality Elasticity
RTBET	Reducing Technical Barriers for Entrepreneurship and Trade (Kyrgyz Republic)
RUV2	relative unit value 2
RUV3	relative unit value 3
SADCA	South African Development Community Accreditation
SI	International System of Units
SIQ	Slovenian Institute of Quality and Metrology
SME	small and medium enterprise
SRAC	Romanian Society for Quality Assurance
TBT	technical barrier to trade
TNC	transnational corporation
TÜV	Technischer Überwachungs-Verein, or Technical Inspection Association (Germany)
UKAS	United Kingdom Accreditation Services
UkrCEPRO	Ukrainian Certification of Products
UME	Ulusal Metroloji Enstitüsü, or National Metrology Institute (Turkey)
WDI	World Development Indicators
WELMEC	European Cooperation in Legal Metrology
WTO	World Trade Organization

Definitions of Country Groups and Comparisons

For facilitation of comparisons, countries in Eastern Europe and Central Asia (ECA) and comparator countries are split into three country groups and one subgroup (see table below). The ECA country groups are constructed using findings from Broadman (2005), who identifies two trade blocs on the rise in ECA.

Country Groups

One group includes new European Union (EU) member states, while the other comprises the 11 full, participating, or associated members of the

Country Groups and Subgroups

Group		Subgroup	Countries
Eastern Europe and Central Asia (ECA)	Commonwealth of Independent States (CIS) and Georgia		Armenia, Azerbaijan, Belarus, Georgia,[a] Kazakhstan, Kyrgyz Republic, Moldova, Russian Federation, Tajikistan, Turkmenistan, Ukraine, Uzbekistan
		The Caucasus and Central Asia	Armenia, Azerbaijan, Georgia,[a] Kazakhstan, Kyrgyz Republic, Tajikistan, Turkmenistan, Uzbekistan
	Balkan countries and Turkey		Albania; Bosnia and Herzegovina; Croatia; Macedonia, FYR; Montenegro; Serbia; Turkey
	New EU members		Bulgaria, Czech Republic, Estonia, Hungary, Latvia, Lithuania, Poland, Romania, Slovak Republic, Slovenia
Comparator countries			Brazil; China; Germany; Korea, Rep.; Ireland; Spain; United Kingdom

a. Georgia stopped being a member of the CIS in August 2009.

Commonwealth of Independent States (CIS) defined as "Russia-centric." Broadman also defines countries in less polarized positions, such as southeastern European countries. The countries in each group share geographic, historical, social, or economic features. This book uses these country groups when they help with interpretations of results and when it seems sensible to aggregate indicators of quality.

World Bank Survey of National Quality Infrastructure

When noted, country-specific information was obtained through a World Bank survey of national quality infrastructure institutions. Survey information was collected through questionnaires circulated to the relevant institutions and through public information available on their Web sites. Survey data was collected for the following years: Albania, 2008; Armenia, 2008; Bosnia and Herzegovina, 2008; Brazil, 2007; Bulgaria, 2007; Croatia, 2008; Georgia, 2008; Germany, 2008; Hungary, 2007; Kazakhstan, 2008; Kyrgyz Republic, 2008; Macedonia, FYR, 2008 (metrology and accreditation), 2009 (standardization); Moldova, 2008; Montenegro, 2008; Poland, 2007; Republic of Korea, 2009; Romania, 2007; Serbia, 2008; Slovenia, 2008; Spain, 2007; Tajikistan, 2008; Turkey, 2009; United Kingdom, 2007; Ukraine, 2008; and Uzbekistan, 2009. Financial data refers to the year prior to the survey.

Reference

Broadman, H. G., ed. 2005. *From Disintegration to Reintegration: Eastern Europe and the Former Soviet Union in International Trade*. Washington, DC: World Bank.

In many countries in Eastern Europe and Central Asia (ECA), the national quality infrastructure (NQI) does not support business competitiveness, though this is one of its functions in Organisation for Economic Co-operation and Development countries. In most of the Commonwealth of Independent States (CIS) countries, it even impedes competitiveness.

In most CIS countries, the NQI needs to be restructured and its governance improved to eliminate conflicts of interest and provide technically credible services to the economy.

ECA countries can support business competitiveness by abolishing mandatory standards, streamlining technical regulations, and harmonizing their NQI with regional and international trade partners.

Most ECA governments need to make investments to upgrade their NQI—but they must ensure that this effort is cost-effective, does not replicate services available in neighboring countries, and is accompanied by efforts to stimulate demand for quality.

Standards are everywhere, yet invisible to most. Standards define how products, processes, and people interact with each other and their environments—assessing their features and performance, conveying information, and providing means of communication. Under the appropriate conditions, standards have important benefits for trade, productivity, and technological progress. Standards also support government efforts to protect consumers—including their safety and health—and the environment. This book defines standards as models or examples established by authority, custom, or general consent.

Most standards serve several purposes and cannot be neatly classified in simple categories. Still, the following categorizations have been used:

- Information and reference standards that establish a common language for comparing physical attributes and conveying technical information

- Variety-reducing (or interchangeability) standards that define common characteristics of two or more entities

- Compatibility and interface standards that define physical or virtual relationships between independent entities for the purpose of interoperability or communication

- Minimum quality and safety standards that allow users or consumers to assess the quality or safety of a product before buying it (Swann 2000)

Quality and standards are inherently linked. Quality is the degree to which the innate characteristics of a product, process, or person fulfill stated and unstated customer requirements and expectations; comply with stated norms, regulations, and laws; or both. Quality and standards are inherently connected because standards are often used to codify technical requirements expected by customers or governments. Moreover, standards are an essential element of efforts to upgrade quality.

Support by the National Quality Infrastructure of a Country's Global Competitiveness

The most common economic benefits of adopting standards include increased productive and innovative efficiency. Standards lead to economies of scale, allowing suppliers to achieve lower costs per unit by producing large, homogeneous batches of products. Standards spur and disseminate innovation, solve coordination failures, and facilitate the development of profitable networks.

Participation in world trade increasingly requires that suppliers comply with standards determined by lead buyers in global value chains. The nature of participation in the global economy has changed dramatically over the past two decades. Rarely do producers turn raw materials into final products and sell them directly to customers. Rather, research and development, design, production, marketing, and sales involve a chain of contractual relationships between firms—the global value chain. In parts of the chain, standards are used to lower transaction costs, create interchangeable and modular parts, and ensure that the lead buyer has control over the quality of goods produced throughout its entire supply chain. Decentralization extends the reach of quality standards through a vast network of independent suppliers to a much larger extent than vertical production ever did. Lead buyers who govern global value chains request that standards be met by their first-tier suppliers as well as those lower on the chain (Humphrey and Schmitz 2000; Kaplinsky 2000).

Improving the quality of goods and services and diversifying into sectors where quality matters can be a sustainable source of global competitiveness. Some of the productive tasks associated with high-quality goods have high learning and technological externalities. In those sectors, producers tend to form tight relationships with global buyers who transfer their knowledge and support the producers' quality-upgrading processes. Diversifying into a broad range of sectors also reduces macroeconomic volatility, but quality upgrading becomes necessary to enter new sectors that compete on quality. Standards are among a number of important factors that help support this quality-upgrading process.

Firms' ability to fully exploit the benefits of standards depends on a supportive NQI. The term *national quality infrastructure* denotes the complete chain of public and private institutions required to establish and implement the standardization, metrology, inspection, testing, certification, and accreditation services needed to ascertain that products and services meet defined requirements, whether demanded by authorities or the market (box 0.1).

The national quality infrastructure (NQI) can promote competitiveness by helping firms produce goods and services that meet the quality specifications of global markets. Inspection, testing, and certification lower information and search costs, enabling buyers to quickly assess whether products and services meet needed standards or requirements. Third-party testing and certification allow buyers on one side of the globe to trust the quality of suppliers on the other side, making it easier for firms to compete on the basis of quality, creating transparency in the market, and promoting quality. Such conformity assessments also facilitate innovation, enabling firms to test new products before launching

Components of the National Quality Infrastructure

The national quality infrastructure has the following components:

- **Inspection bodies and testing laboratories.** Inspection and testing help show that a product or process satisfies technical requirements—determining its features and performance. A firm can contract independent testing laboratories or inspection bodies to prove that a product or process conforms to certain characteristics.
- **Certification bodies.** Third-party certification is assurance by an independent certification body that a product, service, system, process, or material conforms to standards or specifications. Manufacturers and service providers can have their products or management systems certified to certain standards to distinguish themselves from less reputable suppliers.
- **Calibration laboratories.** Calibration involves determining the relationship between an instrument's input and the magnitude or response of its output. Calibration laboratories can be internal, serving only the needs of a firm, or commercial. In commercial labs, calibration serves industrial producers, testing laboratories, inspection bodies, research laboratories, universities, and other final users.
- **National standards bodies.** Standards provide the basis for evaluating conformity assessment bodies and define the requirements for such assessments. National standards bodies bring together public and private stakeholders to develop official national standards. Standards bodies usually adopt standards through consensus and publish them to make them available to industry, public institutions, and consumers.
- **National accreditation bodies.** Accreditation is the procedure by which an authoritative body (the accreditation body) gives formal recognition that an organization is competent to conduct specific tasks. Conformity assessment bodies—such as certification bodies, inspection bodies, and testing and calibration laboratories—can seek accreditation on a voluntary basis as proof of competence in a given area. The accreditation body evaluates the personnel and management of candidates for accreditation and can request practical tests for laboratories when relevant. Most countries have a single national accreditation body responsible for all areas of accreditation.
- **National metrology institutes.** A national metrology institute establishes the national measurement system used to maintain, develop, and diffuse measurement standards for basic units and to diffuse metrological expertise throughout the economy. These institutes operate in the primary calibration market: they disseminate measurement standards by providing calibration services to independent calibration laboratories and other organizations responsible for regulations and standards. Countries often have a single national metrology institute. But when there are several, each is responsible for distinct measurement areas.

Source: Authors' elaboration.

them and to obtain rapid feedback if the products do not meet customer requirements. Conformity assessments show that specified requirements for a product, process, system, person, or body have been—or have not been—fulfilled.

An effective NQI gives firms opportunities to import the latest technologies when technology standards between trading partners are shared. It also allows firms to export to global markets more easily—without retesting and recertifying goods in each country—when conformity assessment procedures are harmonized across borders. Measurement standards and their supportive metrology infrastructure play an important but often invisible role in industrial competitiveness. Measurement errors can lead to either the acceptance of poorly manufactured products or the rejection of good products, both of which are undesirable outcomes.

The NQI can also help the government protect consumers and safeguard human health, security, and the environment. Leaving product choice entirely to consumers when uncertainty exists about a product's technical characteristics, or when information about quality is asymmetric between producers and users, can cause serious harm.

Though their systems are far from perfect, Organisation for Economic Co-operation and Development countries have mostly harmonized their approaches to and building blocks for their NQI to reflect best practices of transparency, openness, consensus, impartiality, technical credibility, and the voluntary nature of standards. In addition, international organizations have been established to help countries harmonize their NQI to facilitate trade.

Many other factors influence the diffusion of quality and standards in an economy. Most are linked to a country's basic economic framework and include business regulations, trade barriers, market competition, and macroeconomic conditions. Others are linked to workforce skills, demand-driven knowledge institutions, and market structures that affect sectors with potential for quality upgrading.

The Government's Role in the National Quality Infrastructure

The government has a role to play in supporting the national quality infrastructure. Many Eastern Europe and Central Asia (ECA) countries have had difficulty developing goods and services considered worthy of import by global markets. Or when they do export, the goods tend to compete on price rather than quality and to not meet international standards. Many ECA countries have also found it difficult to diversify beyond a narrow range of exports.

There is scope for, at minimum, broad policy measures to facilitate quality upgrading and the diffusion of standards in an economy. Although there are market imperfections in quality upgrading, there are also positive externalities for the economy and society, and many supportive aspects of quality—such as metrology, accreditation, and standardization—incorporate strong elements of public goods. Small and medium enterprises are particularly affected by market imperfections in quality upgrading. They face financial, knowledge, and expertise barriers when upgrading their products, processes, and services. Another rationale for government support for the NQI is that government relies on a well-functioning NQI to conduct regulatory functions and implement trade policy.

No country has developed a well-functioning NQI without government support. Even in a large, high-income country with strong business associations and demand for quality services, such as the United States, the government provides extensive financing for metrology. And in most countries, accreditation to international standards is not profitable. Thus, it must be financed by government or government must recognize or attract foreign accreditation bodies. Some standardization bodies are self-financed, but this income is usually derived from activities other than standardization, such as certification.

In most countries, metrology, accreditation, and standardization institutions are government owned. In countries where they operate as foundations or nonprofit entities, governments support them by providing official legal recognition of their monopoly areas or promoting their coordination functions. Though conformity assessment services are typically provided by private entities, their success depends on public support for the upstream activities of metrology, accreditation, and standardization. In addition, when domestic markets are underdeveloped, governments can support public conformity assessment services to solve coordination failures in industry. But this approach is not always justifiable if such services are available in neighboring countries or demand prospects are limited.

Business Competitiveness and the National Quality Infrastructure

In much of ECA, the national quality infrastructure does not support business competitiveness, and in most of the Commonwealth of Independent States (CIS), it even impedes competitiveness. ECA systems for NQI remain underdeveloped and unharmonized with those of their trade partners. As a result, standards remain important contributors to trade costs in ECA and play a critical role in the region's export performance (Broadman 2005).

Most ECA transition economies had some type of NQI before the transition. But the systems were designed on the basis of the logic of a planned economy. Accordingly, two features inherited from central planning still distinguish the NQI of most ECA countries:

- In most CIS countries, trade barriers limit competitive pressures for technological upgrading on domestic producers and raise export costs. Moreover, consumers in developing countries tend to be less demanding when it comes to quality than those in high-income countries, so producers are more likely to compete on cost than quality in domestic markets. In non-European Union (EU) ECA countries, the intensity of competition is also limited and markets are captured by large domestic firms with few incentives to improve product quality or meet international standards.

- To be sure, various differences exist among ECA countries' NQIs. Some ECA countries are in various stages of accession as EU members (such as Romania), candidate members (such as the former Yugoslav Republic of Macedonia), or aspiring candidate members (such as Albania), and they have taken steps to integrate their NQI with the EU model and international norms. Others (such as Kazakhstan) remain torn between maintaining Soviet systems of standards and technical regulations and adopting international models that conform to international treaties such as the World Trade Organization's Technical Barriers to Trade Agreement. Although some ECA countries started to build technical expertise and capacity in their national quality institutions in the mid-20th century (such as Bulgaria), others did not inherit any such institutions after their recent independence and must build them from the ground up (such as Croatia). Though some larger or better-off ECA countries can use economies of scale to invest in an NQI to support the needs of a broad range of economic sectors (such as the Russian Federation), smaller or lower-income ECA countries remain bound by tight fiscal constraints (such as Armenia).

Restructuring and Improved Governance of the National Quality Infrastructure

In most CIS countries, the NQI needs to be restructured and its governance improved to eliminate conflicts of interest and to provide technically credible services. Well-governed institutions—lacking conflicts of interest—are crucial for an effective and internationally recognized NQI. To achieve them, some ECA countries need to restructure their NQI and create independent, transparent institutions that hear the voices of all stakeholders.

Conformity assessment is no longer a burden for firms in ECA's EU and Balkan countries, where compulsory product certification is mostly a relic of the past. These countries have restructured their conformity assessment organizations and liberalized their certification and testing markets. Investments by foreign conformity assessment bodies have led to dynamic, competitive markets in most of these countries.

But some ECA countries, particularly CIS countries, would benefit from transitioning from conformity assessment systems based on state ownership and control of the NQI to systems based on public and private ownership and cooperation. Some countries need to consider closing state entities that offer services not aligned with the needs of the economy or not necessary after a transition to voluntary standards. In other cases, when there is market demand, the state can consider privatization. But in all cases, liberalizing the market for conformity assessment to voluntary standards and enabling any entity to compete—domestic or foreign—will lower costs and improve services. Effective national accreditation systems, based on local or foreign accreditation, will be needed for such markets to function well.

Removing political interference and conflicts of interests requires providing more autonomy to institutions that support an effective NQI. Countries should, at the very least, adopt the following:

- Accreditation bodies must be independent from other NQI institutions.

- Metrology, accreditation, conformity assessment, and standardization bodies should not be involved in developing technical regulations, mandatory standards, or other regulatory activities.

- Metrology, accreditation, and standardization bodies should be free from political interference and be able to respond to market needs and represent their countries in relevant international organizations.

More Competitive ECA Countries

ECA countries can become more competitive by abolishing mandatory standards, streamlining technical regulations, and harmonizing NQI with regional and international trade partners. As ECA countries implement or upgrade their NQI, they must decide how to cater to technological needs; mitigate environmental, health, and safety concerns; and avoid unnecessary technical barriers to trade. Although the mandatory standards used in many ECA countries theoretically serve this purpose, they are too numerous and overly prescriptive, with most developed in a top-down fashion by national standards bodies. Quality upgrading can be improved if mandatory standards are replaced by voluntary standards and technical regulations.

Many ECA countries need to strengthen the capacity of ministries and agencies to develop technical regulations. A national standards body should not play any role in this process. But standards should be used as the basis for all technical regulations developed by all ministries or agencies given the authority to develop and implement them—not just the ministry responsible for trade. ECA countries can develop effective technical regulations by introducing regulatory impact assessments and establishing interdisciplinary and interministerial working groups to elaborate and implement priority technical regulations. Standards should be developed through open, consensus-based processes involving a broad range of stakeholders.

Harmonizing national standards with regional and international trade partners is the next step to supporting global NQI integration, though this step can be highly technical and does not happen overnight. National standards bodies should use three closely linked strategies to harmonize their standards: adopting international standards, influencing international standardization activities, and coordinating with trade partners to adopt regional standards appropriate to the region's needs. All ECA countries will face the challenge of adopting standards over which they have little influence. Whether EU members or not, ECA countries will need to increase their participation in regional and international standardization activities—so that they benefit from international knowledge spillovers and can push for standards that reflect their national conditions.

As a next step toward global integration, ECA countries can ensure that their conformity assessment systems are harmonized with international standards. Accreditation is the last level of quality control in conformity assessment services because it can provide credibility to certification, testing, inspection, and calibration bodies, so that their services are recognized and respected throughout the economy and abroad. For full recognition, national accreditation bodies must comply with international requirements; join regional or international accreditation organizations; and through them, participate in mutual recognition arrangements based on peer evaluations. Membership in a mutual recognition arrangement (also called a multilateral recognition arrangement) is required to guarantee the credibility of domestic certificates and test reports in importing countries. Although all ECA countries have achieved or are moving toward mutual recognition of their accreditation systems, CIS countries still have some way to go—products need to be retested and recertified when they cross borders, creating unnecessary barriers to trade.

Finally, recognition of the NQI requires international metrological traceability. An internationally recognized metrology system relies on modern equipment and sound technical skills, but these are only part of the story. For recognition abroad, measurements must be conducted using similar procedures across borders. Countries must also participate in international comparisons of their measurement equipment. A national metrology institute's measurement accuracy and precision must reach commercial laboratories and industry through an unbroken chain of measurement traceability.

This concept of measurement traceability has been implemented in ECA's EU countries and some of its Balkan countries. But it is not widespread in many CIS countries—particularly in the Caucasus and Central Asia—so there is no way of knowing whether a measurement taken by one economic actor is equivalent to that taken by another, with obvious detriments for product quality. Moreover, metrology in CIS countries largely follows the same guiding principle as conformity assessment.

Upgrading of the National Quality Infrastructure

Most ECA governments need to upgrade their national quality infrastructure, but they must ensure that this is cost-effective, does not replicate services available and accessible in neighboring countries, and is matched by measures to stimulate demand for quality. When institutions have been reformed on the basis of international norms, capacity building and technology upgrading can be targeted to individual aspects of NQI to achieve "quick wins," provide demonstration effects, and avoid repeating mistakes. Any upgrading should be done in the context of harmonization with international norms for NQI, including the adoption of relevant management processes. The goal should be an internationally harmonized NQI that responds to the needs of society without duplicating the role of the private sector.

Metrology is expensive, and CIS countries have struggled to build, equip, and staff their national metrology institutes. As a result, they often rely on obsolete, uncalibrated equipment. Equipment and infrastructure will need to be upgraded, but such efforts will be fruitless unless human resources are improved, quality systems are implemented, and international traceability is achieved.

Small ECA economies without language or geographic barriers should leverage the internationally recognized quality infrastructure of neighboring countries as much as possible. This practice avoids spending scarce public resources on building a comprehensive NQI that cannot draw on a critical mass of demand.

A first step toward achieving mutual recognition of accreditation is to establish a national accreditation system that conforms to international standards and guidelines. But most national markets are too small to make accreditation an attractive investment for the private sector. Thus, financing is a challenge for small ECA economies that do not have critical mass in their markets to sustain self-funded accreditation bodies.

Most ECA countries can build solid accreditation systems only through regional cooperation. CIS countries must address their lack of a regional accreditation body. To reduce operating costs, small ECA economies can join forces to develop and share complementary calibration capabilities. ECA's EU member states also need to continue strengthening their national accreditation systems while supporting regional collaboration.

In many ECA countries, a supply-side approach alone is insufficient to develop a market for quality services. Firms in many of these countries are unaware of their quality needs, face financial barriers, and are reluctant to approach NQI institutions because for decades they have been associated with state control, rent-seeking, and corruption. Government financial and technical support can help upgrade quality, particularly in small and medium enterprises. ECA countries can also leverage support for these efforts from international institutions. These goals are best achieved when national quality strategies put stakeholders in the driver's seat.

The road to an internationally recognized NQI is long, but the experiences of new EU member states show that no obstacle is too large. ECA policy makers face decisions about what type of NQI will best enable their countries' further engagement with the globally integrated economy. Policy makers also face challenges about both how and how quickly to transform the systems they have inherited and about how to restructure conformity assessment infrastructure. These efforts must reflect the varying economic, political, and historical contexts of ECA countries.

Finally, although an effective NQI is necessary for upgrading quality and diffusing international standards, it is no substitute for a supportive business environment, stable macroeconomy, and skilled workforce. ECA countries must address these factors in parallel.

References

Broadman, H. G. 2005. *From Disintegration to Reintegration: Eastern Europe and the Former Soviet Union in International Trade*. Washington, DC: World Bank.

Humphrey, J. and H. Schmitz. 2000. "Governance and Upgrading: Linking Industrial Cluster and Global Value Chain Research." IDS Working Paper 120, Institute of Development Studies, University of Sussex, Brighton, United Kingdom.

Kaplinsky, R. 2000. "Spreading the Gains from Globalisation: What Can Be Learned from Value Chain Analysis?" Working Paper 110, Institute of Development Studies, University of Sussex, Brighton, United Kingdom.

Swann, G. M. P. 2000. "The Economics of Standardization." Final Report for Standards and Technical Regulations Directorate, Department of Trade and Industry, Manchester Business School, University of Manchester, United Kingdom.

CHAPTER 1

The Role of Quality and Standards
for Competitiveness and Trade

*"It is the quality of our work which will please God
and not the quantity."*

—Mahatma Gandhi, *Young India* (April 30, 1925)

▶ **Improving the quality of goods and services and diversifying into sectors where quality matters can be a sustainable source of international competitiveness.**

▶ **Standards are among a number of factors that help support quality upgrading and participation in global value chains.**

▶ **Safety and other standards that regulate potentially dangerous products can help protect consumers and the environment.**

▶ **International harmonization of standards and technical regulations can reduce barriers to trade.**

Standards are everywhere—yet they are invisible to most. Standards define how products, processes, and people interact with each other and their environments. This book defines standards as models or examples established by authority, custom, or general consent. Most standards serve several purposes and cannot be neatly classified into simple categories, but the following categorizations have been used (Swann 2000):

- Information and reference standards that provide a common language for comparing physical attributes and convey descriptive technical information

- Variety-reducing (or interchangeability) standards that define common characteristics of two or more entities

- Compatibility and interface standards that define physical or virtual relationships between entities to foster interoperability or communication

- Quality and safety standards that allow consumers to assess products before buying them

Standards allow, for example, the large-scale use and sale of mobile phones across countries, thereby increasing demand for innovation. They allow automotive engineers to select standardized parts from a wide range of global suppliers, knowing that the parts will withstand required mechanical loads without having to measure and test each one. They allow hospitals to diagnose diseases and governments to monitor drinking water when using equipment with known characteristics.

Quality and standards are inherently linked. *Quality* is the degree to which the characteristics of a product, process, or person fulfill stated and unstated customer requirements and expectations; comply with stated norms, regulations, and laws; or both. Standards and quality are connected because standards are often used to codify technical requirements expected by customers or governments. Moreover, standards are an essential element of efforts to upgrade quality.

Opportunities and Risks of Supporting Quality Upgrading

This chapter discusses why countries should consider improving the quality of their exports, diversifying into sectors where quality matters, and adopting standards. In recent years, a vibrant debate has sought to establish whether the goods that countries produce and export matter for growth. This chapter does not aim to resolve this debate but draws on the literature to show that externalities warrant, at minimum, horizontal measures to support quality and promote standards. Whether public measures should target quality upgrading for specific goods or promote sectors with opportunities for quality upgrading will be left to other studies.

Measures to support quality upgrading are not easy to implement. Quality improvements are a function of numerous factors, such as investments in human resources; machinery and equipment; production processes; restructuring; innovation; and the infrastructure for quality upgrading developed by firms, governments, and individuals. The sum of quality-enhancing investments determines the speed at which a country moves to a higher level of production possibilities and whether it faces a narrowing or widening gap relative to the global quality frontier. Increasing competitiveness requires advancing faster than one's competitors. The 21st-century challenge is that while some emerging markets are catching up to or even leapfrogging technological leaders in record time, the bar is being raised for other developing countries.

A range of environmental and institutional factors can catalyze or impede investments in quality. Product, manufacturing, and other standards—and certification processes to verify that standards are met—are double-edged swords when it comes to prioritizing quality. If properly designed and implemented, standards are a source of quality improvements and send a powerful signal to customers. Standards can also increase trade when harmonized between countries. But standards can also lead to the entrenchment of inferior products, inefficient firms, and low-value-added industries. This chapter describes the opportunities and risks of introducing standards.

Perspectives on Export Quality and Development

The literature presents a range of views on whether export quality matters for growth. Lederman and Maloney (2010) review the theoretical and empirical evidence on whether the structure of countries' exports matters for their development. This chapter draws heavily on that study, which highlights multiple streams of sometimes opposing and sometimes complementary perspectives. Although there is some debate on the link between export quality and growth, little evidence indicates that countries should avoid competing on quality. An argument could be made that shifting from high- to low-quality exports using unskilled labor could have pro-poor outcomes in developing countries. But development of low-quality sectors is no more likely to face market failures than is development of high-quality sectors. This situation weakens the rationale for pursuing shared growth through sector-specific support rather than other pro-poor measures such as education and health. Traditional trade theory, which argues that countries should specialize in goods that reflect their static comparative advantages, ignores the complex dynamics of learning and technological trajectories revealed in the literature on national innovation systems.

Lederman and Maloney (2010) identify a large body of recent literature that argues that what countries export does matter for development. Some goods are associated with greater positive externalities and higher rents. But the authors also show that this is not the end of the story and that many factors are involved in making a country's exports relevant for growth.

At one end of the spectrum, the argument is that high-quality exports are desirable because they are associated with higher rents, increased market access and technology transfers, and lower market volatility. As wages rise, competing on price alone is no longer a sustainable export strategy. Some also argue that countries should produce goods with the greatest potential for quality upgrading—that is, goods that present many opportunities for increasing prices and profits as a result of quality improvements. Similarly, others argue that a developing country's exports should aim to reflect what rich countries produce—which typically includes a high share of quality-competitive goods—or goods that facilitate a transition to new industries.

FIGURE 1.1

Policy Guidance Based on Different Schools of Thought on Export Quality

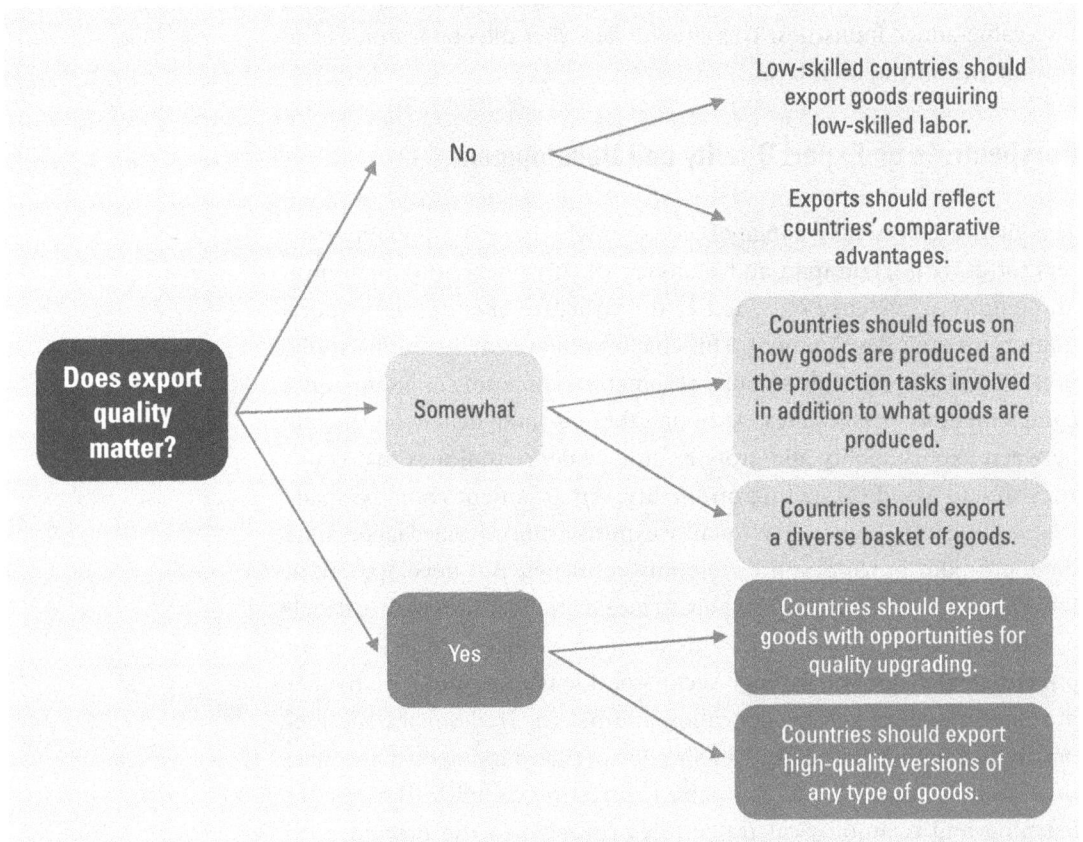

Source: Authors.

Lederman and Maloney's (2010) insights suggest that although export quality is probably good for development, what matters most is not the actual goods exported but the composition of the export basket, the way those goods are produced, and the production tasks that a country is involved in. Figure 1.1 draws on their study as well as others mentioned in this chapter to reflect some of the current debate on export quality.

Viewpoints

The sections that follow present some of the viewpoints that have emerged from this debate.

Viewpoint 1: Rather than competing on quality, countries can use their comparative advantages to compete on the basis of price in global markets and reduce macroeconomic volatility through diversification.

Although some goods compete on the basis of their quality, others (such as commodities and raw materials) compete on the basis of other factors, such as price.[1] The relative preponderance of these two types of goods varies significantly even across high-income economies (Baldwin and Ito 2008). Aiginger (2000) divides industries in individual countries into groups depending on (a) whether they are dominated by price competition or quality competition and (b) whether the country is successful in the prevailing type of competition. *Price competition industries* are those in which low costs lead to high exports and high costs lead to low exports. In industries dominated by quality competition, a higher unit value of exports (relative to imports) leads to a trade surplus (in terms of quantity of units traded), while a low relative unit value results in a trade deficit.

In other words, Aiginger (2000) finds that some categories of goods, such as isolated wires and cables, are fairly commoditized, and regardless of quality improvements, the market will not buy more of these goods. The market simply does not value improvements in the durability, flexibility, or conductivity of isolated wires and cables enough to pay higher prices for them. Moreover, producers can export more of these goods by competing on price. By ranking industries in accordance with the number of bilateral trade flows in which quality competition prevails, Aiginger created a taxonomy of Revealed Quality Elasticity (RQE) based on high, medium, and low RQE (see table 1.1 and appendix A).[2]

---

1. Other factors include supplier flexibility, functionality of the product, or simply intangible items such as brand.
2. The Aiginger RQE taxonomy uses European Union countries as reporters and 30 industrial and developing countries as partners.

TABLE 1.1
Examples of Product Classifications Based on Revealed Quality Elasticity

Two-digit NACE	Low RQE	Medium RQE	High RQE
15	Fruits and vegetables	Grain-mill products and starches	Dairy products
17	Made-up textile articles	Textile fibers	Textile weavings
24	Basic chemicals	Detergents, cleaning and polishing products, perfumes	Pharmaceuticals
28	Steam generators	Structural metal products	Tanks, reservoirs, central heating radiators, boilers
31	Isolated wires and cables	Lighting equipment, electric lamps	Electricity distribution and control apparatuses

Source: Aiginger 2000.
Note: NACE = Nomenclature Statistique des Activités Économiques dans la Communauté Européenne, or the Statistical Classification of Economic Activities in the European Community.

Some, however, argue that goods that compete on price are subject to greater market volatility. Primary and fabricated metals illustrate a supposed advantage of producing products with higher value added—namely, producers face a lower price elasticity of demand, which is especially important in the current downturn. In 2009, price declines caused by dropping demand were much larger for primary metals, such as nonferrous metals and electrometallurgical products, than for fabricated metal products, such as plumbing fixtures, fittings, and heating equipment (figure 1.2). Annual price variations for primary metals reached 15 to 30 percent, compared with at most 7 to 9 percent for fabricated metals. Sophisticated products with high steel content, such as vats used in the chemical and beverage industries, wheels in the automobile industry, and ball bearings, have more stable prices. Prices are more stable because fewer producers have the necessary high-quality manufacturing technology, which limits overcapacity, and because buyers have fewer available substitutes.

Lederman and Maloney (2010) explore the literature on goods that compete on price from the perspective of the so-called natural resource curse. This curse is often evoked as a reason countries should aim to develop industries associated with more sophisticated, higher-quality goods. Although the authors find numerous studies from the 1990s showing that countries with natural resources suffered slower growth, they find that further investigation on this topic weakens this argument and that the negative effects of natural resource exports are more likely

FIGURE 1.2

Metal and Metal Product Prices, 2005–10

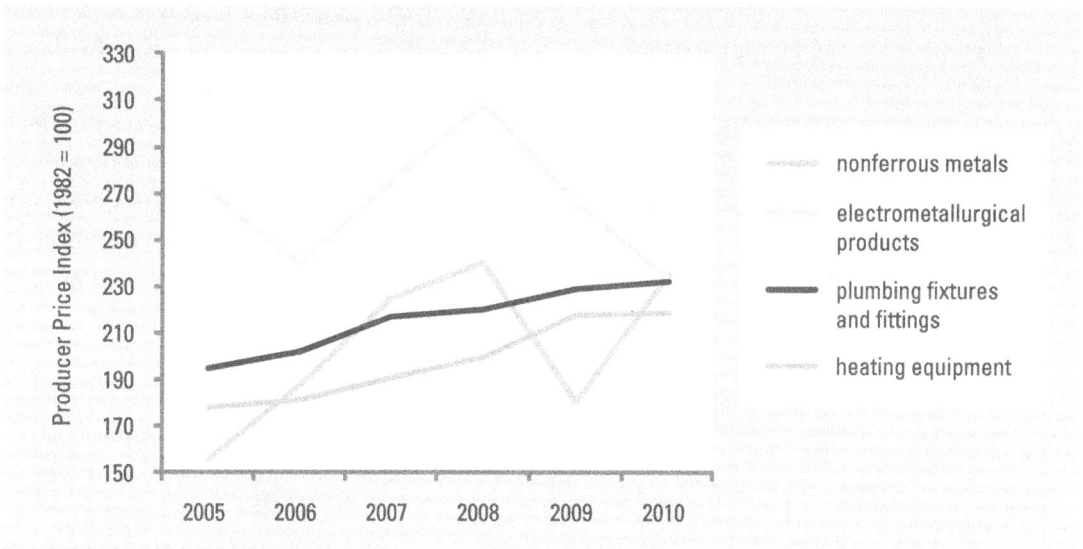

Source: U.S. Bureau of Labor Statistics, Producer Price Index database. http://www.bls.gov/ppi/#data.

due to extensive exports from resource-rich economies. Hence, countries need only diversify their export portfolios to protect against macroeconomic volatility—which need not imply a sole focus on high-quality goods.

Viewpoint 2: Competing on price alone is not a viable long-term export strategy when labor costs rise.

Manufacturing firms in high-income countries have recognized the futility of competing on price in the face of emerging competitors from countries with lower labor costs and strong comparative advantages. Competing on costs is often associated with competing on low wages and expendable labor, neither of which yields continued competitive advantage. High or rising labor costs in many countries in Eastern Europe and Central Asia (ECA) will make it difficult for firms in the region to compete on costs alone much longer. Costs can be lowered in the face of rising labor costs by investing in process innovation, but the decline of manufacturing in many high-income countries—facilitated by offshoring—suggests that this strategy is not always sustainable in the long run.

An alternative strategy is to focus on significant investments in technology and skills to spur the product and process innovations that allow countries to move up the value chain and to find or create niches with lower price elasticity of demand. There is evidence that firms from developing countries are also moving to higher-quality products. Competing on the basis of quality can sustain growth in wages and improvements in living standards as countries progress to middle- and high-income levels.

In an empirical study on the dynamics of trade quality, Krishna and Maloney (2010) find significant differences in the quality of exports across regions. But they also find significant differences in quality within regions. Even in Organisation for Economic Co-operation and Development (OECD) countries, many exports are of relatively low quality. A model developed by Chioveanu (2010) allows for simultaneous price and quality competition, showing that firms will adopt a mixed strategy to be profitable across multiple markets. This strategy raises the question of whether rich countries really compete only on the basis of quality.

Viewpoint 3: Quality allows countries to penetrate new export markets, sell goods at higher prices, and earn higher profits.

Empirical research shows that quality differences in similar products can lead to significantly different prices when traded between different countries.[3] The relationship between quality and consumers' willingness to pay allows higher-quality producers to more easily access import markets of wealthier economies. Empirical analyses by Hallak (2006) support the idea that rich countries tend to import more from countries that produce high-quality goods. Schott (2008) finds that U.S. consumers are more willing to pay for similar products made in the OECD than those made in China. Fontagné, Gaulier, and Zignago (2008) analyze product quality in 200 economies and find that products from developing economies do not compete directly with those from high-income economies because of differences in quality. By improving the quality of their exports, developing countries can hence open up new trade opportunities with high-income economies.

Some streams of economics relate the quality of manufactured goods and services produced by a country to its development path and growth perspectives in both theory and empirics (Grossman and Helpman 1991; Kremer 1993; Rodrik 2006; Hidalgo and others 2007). Game theory models show that price competition among companies offering similar products tends to erode an industry's profitability—limiting the scope for investment even when the market has relatively few rivals.[4] When com-

---

3. This price difference even holds true at very fine levels (6 and 9 digits) of product classification.
4. For a description of the models in question, see chapter 7 on oligopoly competition in Cabral (2000), and for a more technical account, see chapter 5 (short-run price competition) of that volume.

panies sell heterogeneous products, price competition leaves an economic rent to the highest-quality producers, and this rent is an important source of comparative advantage. Solid cash flow and profitability are self-reinforcing because they facilitate new investments in product differentiation and innovation, which are needed to maintain and widen the quality differentials between leaders and followers. One can also argue that climbing the quality ladder yields benefits for domestic labor markets, increasing employment, output, and income (Leamer 2007; Verhoogen 2008; Manova and Zhang 2009)—in contrast to decreasing revenues that are due to continuous price reductions dictated by competitiveness requirements (Pietrobelli and Rabellotti 2006).

Still, Lederman and Maloney (2010) find that some of the goods—such as electronics—associated with a measure of high quality defined by Hausmann, Hwang, and Rodrik (2007) actually had relatively low value added. This discrepancy calls into question the conventional logic of high-quality goods being associated with higher income and profits.

Viewpoint 4: Higher-quality exports increase technology transfers.

Suppliers competing on costs remain superficially integrated with global production networks and benefit little from technology transfers from buyers. One reason is that arm's-length transactions on a spot market—the most common market mechanism for low-value-added products with minimal or no differentiation (such as steel coil or plate)—do not generate knowledge-intensive interactions among suppliers and buyers. In contrast, advanced products made to order for a global supply chain based on long-term contracts (such as steel engine blocks used in trucks) must be manufactured to an agreed quality standard and meet constantly changing design requirements. To meet these standards, manufacturers have to work closely with buyers and users on product specifications and deliveries, invest in their production processes, and sometimes license new technology.

Firms that compete on quality typically benefit from long-term relationships with global buyers, resulting in the absorption of foreign technologies and the development of a domestic supplier base that can attract knowledge-intensive foreign direct investment (FDI) with high spillovers (Kaplinsky and Readman 2001) (box 1.1). Thus, although competing on the basis of cost may provide a quick and short-term solution for developing nations, competing on quality leads to more sustainable long-term growth.

Viewpoint 5: Exporting goods with greater potential for quality upgrading leads to faster economic convergence.

As discussed in viewpoint 1, Aiginger (2000) finds that some goods have more potential for quality upgrading than others. This means that increasing the quality of those goods results in greater exports. A related concept is proposed by Hwang (2006) whereby some goods lend themselves to greater quality differentiation than others—that is, they have longer "quality ladders." Hence, although limited opportunities arise to vary the quality of cement, there is an enormous quality differentiation in the market for watches, from Casio to Rolex.

Hwang (2006) argues both theoretically and empirically that countries specializing in goods with longer quality ladders will grow faster than those producing less differentiated goods. In other words, a country producing cement cannot expect to reap much growth by improving the

---

BOX 1.1

The Possibility of Industrial Upgrading through the Virtuous Circle of High-Quality Exports

A footwear company in Moldova that is partly owned by the government employs more than 1,000 people. From 2003 to 2006, sales grew by 20 percent a year, and in 2006, net profits rose 13 percent, reaching almost US$1 million. The firm's sales have been almost exclusively export oriented since the collapse of the local market, and 80 percent of its exports go to a single Western European partner (one of Europe's largest footwear companies) with whom it has been working since 2001. The firm's remaining exports go to a variety of Italy-based distributors, to whom the firm has been exporting since 1995.

The company's main competitors are from China and Vietnam, but the Moldovan firm has an advantage because of its proximity to the European Union and its higher-quality product relative to Vietnam. Finding foreign partners was initially difficult, but is now much easier because the company has a strong reputation among footwear distributors in Western Europe.

Exports have enabled the company to become more productive and to move up the value chain, because a foreign partner transferred high-quality equipment and knowledge on improving processes. The firm's clients have sent a permanent representative to the company to monitor production quality. As a result, the company has been able to obtain the design and technological information to produce new, higher-quality footwear, driving new demand and raising profits. Given current market conditions and company equipment, the company's management envisages remaining competitive, with exports growing consistently for another five years.

Source: World Bank Moldova case studies.

quality of its cement because there is little quality differentiation in the cement industry, and the country most likely already finds itself fairly close to the quality frontier of cement. But a country producing cheap watches can reap faster growth by bridging the large gap with high-quality luxury watches. Similarly, Hausmann, Hwang, and Rodrik's (2007) empirical work argues that a country's growth rate can be predicted by the extent of overlap between its export basket and goods exported by high-income countries.

Through their empirical work, Krishna and Maloney (2010) find that goods with lower initial quality levels experience faster growth in quality than do other goods, but only in specific regions. They find that poor countries are not improving quality faster than richer countries, as one would expect if larger quality gaps implied faster quality convergence.

Viewpoint 6: What matters is not what goods are exported, but how the goods are produced and what production tasks are involved.

Although Lederman and Maloney (2010) recognize that certain goods provide more opportunities for quality upgrading, they challenge the view that exporting such goods leads to unconditional growth. First, they argue that a diverse range of technologies can be used to produce seemingly identical goods across countries. Countries that use more sophisticated production technologies (such as robotic assembly of computers in the Republic of Korea) are likely to benefit from far more knowledge externalities than countries that do not (such as hand assembly of computers in the Philippines).

Second, the authors argue that because production processes are increasingly fragmented along global value chains that cross multiple borders, countries can specialize in different tasks in production processes, some of which can remain unsophisticated and with little value added regardless of the quality of the final product. Lederman and Maloney (2010) cite the emblematic case of China, which exports iPods but contributes only 1 percent of their value added.

Standards and Development

This section discusses how standards are one of the factors that can promote quality upgrading. Standards also have several features that can contribute to industrial competitiveness, help the government protect the public and the environment, and foster international trade.

The Role of a Number of Economic Factors in Quality Upgrading

Many factors, including size and income level, affect a country's ability to produce higher-quality goods and exports. In an influential paper, Hummels and Klenow (2005) show that high-income countries export a greater variety and higher quality of goods (as proxied by prices) than do small economies. A possible explanation is that large developed countries have industries with significant research bases, dense links and clusters, and large intrasectoral and international spillovers. Moreover, technological specialization and economies of scale favor the production of high-quality products. In addition, consumers in higher-income countries are more demanding, and, thus, their domestic industries are expected to produce higher-quality products. As a result, high-quality exports are often associated with high wages. But an important issue that plagues many of these findings remains moving from correlations between various factors (wages, income levels, and trade barriers) and product quality to causal inferences that are particularly useful for developing nations.

Consistent with the classical trade theory framework, a country's ability to produce high-quality products is determined by factor endowments. Schott's (2004) empirical findings give support to this statement. In analyzing the U.S. import unit values between 1972 and 1994, he finds that the capital intensity of the production technique is positively associated with measures of quality. Hence, investments in skills and technology should be positively related to the quality indicators. The Community Innovation Surveys of the European Union (EU) consistently have shown that increasing product quality is one of the main reasons that firms (particularly firms in ECA) innovate. Investments in innovation can enable organizations to improve their internal processes to create higher-quality products and improve their technological absorptive capacity, namely, their ability to identify and absorb existing technologies required to upgrade quality.

In addition, a country's technological level, productivity, and, ultimately, growth are very much determined by its exposure to trade and foreign investments, especially when it does not possess the necessary internal mechanisms to sustain significant domestic research and development (Coe and Helpman 1995; Hall and Jones 1999; Keller 2004). Imports of foreign technologies can unleash competitive forces and spillovers in national markets that support product upgrading by domestic producers. When analyzing the impact of trade- and FDI-related spillovers on aggregated productivity of 47 transition countries from the ECA, Krammer (2010) finds positive and significant effects for both these channels; moreover, in the case of FDI, the effects seem to be larger and more important for ECA countries than for Western European nations. Despite the lack of studies on the effects of spillovers on quality upgrading, the two usually go hand in hand (Fabrizio, Igan, and Mody 2007). Thus, the two main channels of technology diffusion identified by the literature (inward FDI and import openness) should bear positive effects on product quality in the ECA countries as suggested by various case studies (box 1.2).

BOX 1.2

Positive Spillovers of Foreign Direct Investment in Product Quality

A leading Italian manufacturer of cotton and Lycra underwear established in 1972 had annual sales of around €50 million in Europe in 2007. The firm relocated part of its production to Albania in 1995. Its office in Albania is now in charge of ensuring quality of production and organizing logistics for consignment and delivery. The firm now outsources production to seven Albanian companies (with an estimated total of 800 employees in 2008) that produce and pack about 60,000 to 70,000 pairs of underwear per day. Over the years, the firm not only has transferred machinery, training, and expertise on processes to these companies, but also has allowed them to pursue orders with other clients they find. Of the firm's current 80 employees in Albania, 7 are part of a specialized quality control team, and the rest are engaged in logistics associated with handling orders and inputs—every day, one truck arrives with raw materials and semifinished articles and leaves with finished products.

Source: World Bank case studies.

Trade also has positive effects on quality when trade partners demand and use higher-quality practices. The adoption of higher-quality standards—as measured by international management systems standards such as International Organization for Standardization (ISO) 9001 or ISO 14001—is greatly influenced by trade partners (Corbett 2003; Neumayer and Perkins 2004; Albuquerque, Bronnenberg, and Corbett 2007). Thus, the more countries export to high-income regions and countries such as the EU, Japan, and the United States, the more incentives they have to produce goods associated with high-quality standards.

Despite these positive associations of trade and quality upgrading, a country's transition from low- to high-quality exports remains an important area for research. These results must be met with caution because this relationship is complex. For example, Amiti and Khandelwal (2009) adapt the model developed by Aghion and others (2009) that reveals a nonlinear relationship between competition and innovation to show that openness to trade is beneficial for quality upgrading only for products closer to the world's technological frontier. These results suggest that for

ECA countries, lowering trade barriers for all products may lead to slower quality upgrading because firms will face more pressure from international competitors.

The Role of Standards in Supporting Quality Upgrading through Market and Technological Information

Standards have proved effective in promoting the adoption of desirable product characteristics (reliability, durability, and so forth). They are also credited with fostering the diffusion of technological best practices. When knowledge is exchanged in private transactions, it does not generate spillovers to third parties. Because standards are public, they create a pool of technical information that can be freely accessed by the at-large business community and transferred across corporate and national borders.[5]

Another important—though often unintended—benefit of standards is the promotion of innovation. Because information embodied in standards is nonproprietary, it is accessible to scientists and engineers who generate new ideas and technologies. Indeed, the EU's Community Innovation Survey indicates that most innovative firms use standards as a source of information on innovation. A survey of U.K. companies found that more than 60 percent of process and product innovators were inspired by implemented standards—twice the rate of companies that reported their innovations were inspired by universities or research laboratories (DTI 2005).

Adoption of standards enables the private sector to cut transaction costs and increase its competitiveness. The recently developed global standard ISO 18185 on freight containers will enable the 12 countries that pioneered it to avoid unnecessary delays during customs inspections, reducing their times and costs for trading across borders. This new standard dictates a protocol for electronic recognition of the seal number affixed on freight and for electronic checking of the seal conditions. This approach is expected to dramatically expedite customs clearance for cargo in ports and enhance competitiveness for small and medium enterprises. Such enterprises should see their supply chain and security planning

---

5. Public knowledge can result in significant savings for an entire economy, as the British Standards Institution (BSI)—the national standards body of the United Kingdom—attested in the pioneering case of railways, which had tremendous economic relevance in its time: "On 26 April 1901, the first meeting of the Engineering Standards Committee took place. As a result, the variety of sizes of structural steel sections was reduced from 175 to 113... . When applied to tramway rails the number of gauges was reduced from 75 to 5. This brought estimated savings in steel production costs of 1 million pounds sterling over a year. Steel merchants' costs were reduced due to fewer varieties. This made steel cheaper for the users to everyone benefited" (Guasch and others 2007).

needs brought up to the standards of multinational corporations (Guasch and others 2007).

Standardization can lead to lower transaction costs in the economy as a whole, as well as to savings for individual businesses. In a 2000 survey by the Deutsches Institut für Normung (German Institute for Standardization) of firms in Austria, Germany, and Switzerland, 39 percent saw improved opportunities for cooperation, and 36 percent benefited from a greater choice of suppliers.[6] Empirical studies using enterprise surveys of investment climate factors have found that adopting standards have a significant effect on several measures of productivity (Escribano and Guasch 2005a, 2005b).

At the macro level, the introduction of quality and manufacturing standards, together with related testing and certification activities, contributed significantly to productivity and economic growth in advanced economies. The most comprehensive analysis carried out to date, with data from the U.K. standards catalog, concludes that standards accounted for about 13 percent of labor productivity growth and one-quarter of total factor productivity during the postwar period of 1948–2002 (DTI 2005). Another macroeconomic analysis of standards performed for the German economy between 1960 and 1996 showed that standards were at least as important to technical innovation as were patents and second only to capital accumulation in their contribution to growth (Jungmittag, Blind, and Grup 1999).

Although considerable evidence supports a link between standards and growth, standards do not always produce positive outcomes. A standard can hinder innovation if its scope is too narrow or too wide or if its introduction is not well timed. Excessive standardization—that is, the premature introduction of a standard or an overly restrictive standard—can limit product development and block innovation. Theoretical models explain why incentives to innovate can be blunted by standards (David and Greenstein 1990). The legacy of central planning in ECA countries was both too many standards and excessively restrictive standards, which created barriers to entry for products and producers. Many standards in ECA countries are also old, locking producers into using obsolete technologies.

The problems caused by insufficient standardization—that is, the late introduction of a standard or one with vague and inadequate objectives—are a result of legacy and possibly inefficient products and technologies. Insufficient standardization shuts off the diffusion of innovations and raises interoperability concerns that reduce efficiency and increase the costs of goods and services. In many cases, standard setting has trailed

---

6. Deutsches Institut für Normung is the German national organization for standardization and is Germany's ISO member body.

behind innovation, leaving the market to choose between products without considering the benefits that could result from coordinating a single standard, particularly in a context of uncertainty about product quality. Standard setting should be a participatory process and, if possible, one that is led by companies and consumers—an approach that reduces the stifling effects of standards and focuses on the benefits of coordination.

Standards as an Entry Point into Global Value Chains

The nature of participation in the global economy has changed dramatically over the past two decades. Selling to the global market has become increasingly complex. Rarely do producers turn raw materials into final products and sell those to customers directly. Rather, research and development, design, production, marketing, and sales involve a chain of interfirm contractual relationships that has been called a global value chain (Humphrey and Schmitz 2000). In parts of the chain, standards are increasingly used to reduce transaction cost, create interchangeable and modular parts, and ensure that the lead buyer has control over the quality of goods produced throughout its entire supply chain.

Comparative advantages have motivated manufacturers to subcontract subcomponents of their products worldwide rather than to produce them in-house. Interoperability standards foster manufacturing decentralization: the ability to explore and benefit from access to competitive technologies and low labor costs elsewhere. Decentralization extends the reach of quality standards through a vast network of independent suppliers to a much larger extent than vertical production. And the minimum quality frontier is rising. The model developed by Sutton (2007) predicts the existence of a lower bound for quality worldwide, regardless of the low labor costs firms face in their domestic market. Moreover, this lower limit keeps shifting upward in the presence of free trade, and changes in the levels of goods' quality aggregated at the country level have important welfare implications, especially for developing countries.

The global value chain concept has been used to describe and analyze modern organization of economic activities that can link a firm in one corner of the world to markets in another through outsourced or subcontracted firm relationships. For example, a small enterprise in Penang, Malaysia, has a contract with a multinational corporation to assemble printed circuit boards using parts and instructions provided by the corporation. The final assembled printed circuit board is provided to the corporation, which supplies it to one of the world's largest brand-name computer firms for use in its computers and printers. Although the small supplier in Penang has sold into the global market, it has not done so directly but through a series of firm relationships within a global value chain. Firms and producers worldwide are increasingly engaging in such production arrangements as opposed to arm's-length transactions and direct sales to markets. Although no accurate data are available on the amount of subcontracted or outsourced manufacturing occurring globally today, data on intermediate goods trade that can capture part of the trade in parts and in components and inputs point to a rise in the global fragmentation of production. Imported intermediate goods grew from 12 percent of global manufacturing output in 1986–90 to 18 percent in 1996–2000 (UNIDO 2009).

Key actors in a given global value chain are the lead buyers that have shed much of their production processes onto suppliers to focus on their core competencies of research and development, design, marketing, and brand development. Importantly, lead firms undertake some form of "chain governance." They make the key decisions over how production is organized and, more important, *who* participates and *how*, that is, the conditions of participation such as the number of and delivery times of outputs, price, quality, and other specifications. Lead buyers commonly enforce these conditions, particularly on product quality and production processes, through standards. They request that not only their first-tier suppliers meet standards, but also their second-tier suppliers and lower tiers of suppliers in an effort to drive compliance throughout their supply chains (Humphrey and Schmitz 2000; Kaplinsky 2000).

Within global value chains, there are generally four paths to upgrading, which can also be a sequential strategy for firms (Humphrey and Schmitz 2000; Kaplinsky 2005):

- *Process upgrading* involves increasing production efficiency through improved organization of production systems or the use of superior technology.

- *Product upgrading* involves shifting into new or more sophisticated product lines that increase unit values.

- *Functional (or intrasectoral) upgrading* involves adding or moving into new, superior functions—such as coordinating outsourcing, logistics, and quality; design; and marketing—or abandoning lower-value-added functions to focus on higher-value-added activities.

- *Chain (or intersectoral) upgrading* involves moving into a new global value chain, such as moving from the manufacturing of radios into computers, especially if the other forms of upgrading have proven unsuccessful.

Indeed, how firms enter or participate in a global value chain is increasingly tied to compliance with a variety of standards, both private-voluntary and mandatory-regulatory. Standards cover both product and production processes. Product standards can require the use of certain types of technology or the testing of products to ensure they are safe for consumers. Process standards can involve quality management systems or meeting of certain environmental and labor conditions. In recent years, there has been a shift from product standards to process standards. Compliance with process standards can signal to lead buyers the capability and production processes of suppliers down the value chain. The following examples show how entry into global markets and international competitiveness increasingly relies on standards.

- *Auto component suppliers in Brazil (process upgrading).* As part of a significant restructuring and consolidation phase of the automobile industry in Brazil during the 1990s, quality management standards became widely and rapidly implemented by lead assembly firms and global first-tier suppliers of high-value-added components (part of a nationwide diffusion of quality standards in the 1990s in which the annual growth rate of registered ISO certificates was over 100 percent). This change was filtered down to local small and medium second-tier suppliers that produced light components for first-tier firms. Process upgrading through quality standards certification (for example, international standards such as ISO 9001 or ISO 9002 and national and sectoral standards such as QS 9000 of the Quality System Requirements) became an entry ticket for participating in the automobile global value chain. Compliance with these standards became one of the criteria used by first-tier firms for selecting suppliers. Those component suppliers that remained uncertified produced for the low-end replacement market where price competitiveness mattered more than quality (Quadros 2004).

- *Surgical instrument suppliers in Pakistan (process upgrading).* Upgrading became the case for the international medical instrument industry when, in the mid-1990s, the U.S. Food and Drug Administration required medical appliances to meet the U.S. Good Manufacturing Practices (GMP) quality standard. This requirement had implications for small, labor-intensive, export-oriented producers of surgical instruments in Sialkot, Pakistan, that traded directly with large buyers in the United States, which was their primary export market. With assistance from the government, these suppliers became certified with the standard in a few years. Later, those surgical instrument suppliers who were in compliance with the GMP found it easier to comply with the ISO 9000 standard that was imposed as a requirement by European buyers (their second-largest market). And complying with ISO 9000 standards also led to process upgrading. Producers found that ISO

9000 improved their internal production systems and ability to plan production, and importantly, it reduced their average reject rates by more than 50 percent. The majority of medium and large firms found the standard improved their competitiveness. For small firms, the standard was necessary (though not sufficient) for market entry (Nadvi 2004).

- *Turnkey suppliers in the global electronics industry (functional upgrading).* Brand-name American firms within the global electronics industry began outsourcing much of their manufacturing activities to highly competent suppliers during the 1990s. The subcontracted suppliers, who originally specialized in electronics manufacturing, have since taken on higher-value-added production processes and services such as design, logistics, and repair, further improving their capabilities. As a result, they have attracted more outsourced activities from industry leaders and become very large multinational corporations in their own right. This path to upgrading, which began with the handover of manufacturing activities by brand-name firms to suppliers, was made possible through the transformation of design specifications into codified information and knowledge (for example, computerized product design) and production processes into standards (for example, circuit board assembly). In addition, the ISO, International Electrotechnical Commission (IEC), and RosettaNet have helped the industry by developing classifications and specifications of components and processes as well as other supply chain management and business processes, which are used as the basis for firm-to-firm communication. The use of information technology to exchange information has resulted in a rich flow of knowledge and more formal links between brand-name firms and suppliers. Today, brand-name firms are highly dependent on suppliers (Sturgeon 2002).

In addition to transmitting information on quality and technical specifications, standards can show compliance with social and environmental criteria for both product and production processes. Because consumption, particularly in developed countries, is increasingly tied to social and environmental concerns, standards on health and safety, ethics, fair trade, labor practices, and environmental sustainability have become increasingly important for firms. Indeed, civil society organizations have targeted firms, particularly brand names, for corporate social responsibility and accountability over their direct and indirect effects throughout their supply chains. In response, firms have welcomed the use of private, self-regulating standards and begun implementing them throughout their global value chains to convey their responsible practices to customers and critics (Utting 2005).

Social and environmental standards focus more on production and process methods rather than the product itself. They are developed either by international organizations, governments, industry associations, individual firms, or civil society organizations or by a multistakeholder consortium of actors (such as civil society organizations, firms, and sometimes governments) (Ponte and Gibbon 2005). Although initial reactions by producers are based on the high cost of implementing such standards, they can provide opportunities for moving up the value chain.

- *Clothing factories and labor standards in Cambodia.* The Cambodian apparel industry entered the global industry only in the 1990s. The industry rapidly supplied to buyers that sold its products for the U.S. market. After a surge in imports, the U.S. government began negotiations for a bilateral textile trade agreement in 1998 to place quotas on Cambodian products. During the negotiations, factory workers in Cambodia called for improved conditions and found solidarity with American labor groups. The latter lobbied the U.S. government to tie annual increases in export quotas to voluntary factory compliance with International Labour Organization labor codes and standards and national labor laws in Cambodia. With the help of the International Labour Organization, clothing factories in Cambodia are annually inspected for compliance. Many factories have come into compliance as a result of multiple incentives that include international buyers who were sensitive to the reputation of their suppliers' labor conditions, peer pressure from other factories, and, of course, increased market access to the United States. During the duration of the agreement, overall export quotas for Cambodia rose from 9 percent in 2002 to 18 percent in 2004. Recognizing the market demand for their certified products, the Cambodian government and factory owners decided to continue the program even after the end of the textile agreement in 2005. Today, the program receives various sources of funding, including international buyers. Thirty-two brand-name firms—including Gap Inc. (one of the largest buyers), Adidas, Nike, Levi Strauss, Walt Disney, and H&M—have continued to source from Cambodia, buying about 60 percent of its factories' outputs (Polaski 2006).[7]

- *Specialty, sustainable coffee trade.* Increasing consumer concerns over environmental and social criteria for coffee farms and farmers have resulted in the development of sustainability standards for fair trade, organic, and shade-grown coffees by civil society organizations. A fair trade certification is given only to small farmers who meet standards on democracy, participation, transparency, environmental protection,

---

7. See Better Factories Cambodia Web site, http://www.betterfactories.org.

and labor conditions. Thus, most fair trade coffee farmers also comply with organic standards, shade-grown standards, or both. Fair trade coffee is sold in the U.S. and European markets by certified fair trade wholesalers, importers, roasters, and retailers. Organizations that verify and certify fair trade coffee producers and other social and environmental organizations also promote and market the products to brand-name coffee companies, such as Folgers, Starbucks, and Nestle; to supermarkets, such as Tesco and Costco; and to customers (Ponte 2002). Today, gaining access to the upscale, specialty coffee market (which is growing in comparison to overall coffee sales) can require the voluntary fair trade certification (Raynolds 2009). The fair trade principle is based on paying farmers fairly or at a premium for their product to sustain their livelihoods. Farmers under the fair trade label can receive a floor price of US$1.25 per pound for Arabica coffee, an organic premium of US$0.20 per pound, and a social premium of US$0.10 per pound for development initiatives (Raynolds 2009), while the world market price for other coffee hovers around US$0.70 per pound (*Financial Times* 2010).

Standards have been used by lead firms and buyers in global value chains to bring about improved competitiveness to products and production processes. Although standards compliance has resulted in upgrading opportunities for suppliers in some cases, others have found they can contribute to less successful positions in the global market. A noticeable trend has appeared in many sectors, such as apparel and commodities: suppliers are able to upgrade factors related to only processes and not products (for example, through improved research and design). Improvements and innovation in product design (functional upgrading) are activities often jealously guarded by lead firms. Indeed, compliance with standards can be costly, particularly for small and medium firms engaged in low-value, labor-intensive activities, where competitiveness is often still based on prices and production costs. This challenge is compounded by the rising number of standards, which can place a costly and, at times, contradictory burden on suppliers.

For example, small farms that supplied fresh vegetables to U.K. supermarkets have mostly been replaced by large farms that can afford to comply with food safety standards and other storage and transportation requirements that led to their functional upgrading within the global value chain (Gibbon 2001). Similar experiences have been had by small suppliers in other sectors that have been squeezed out of global value chains by lead firms consolidating their supplier base. Finally, with China and India as rising powerhouses of production, the projected domination of South-South trade and consumption may produce a different priority for standards compliance in global value chains. Kaplinsky and Farooki (2010) predict that producers exporting to consumers in low-income countries will face fewer drivers for standards. Compounded by limited regulatory capacity to implement standards, social and environmental conditions, and weak nongovernmental organizations, the value of and demand for standards may be reduced for producers in low-income countries in the future.

The Ability to Comply with Measurement Standards as a Critical yet Invisible Role in Boosting Industrial and Technological Competitiveness

Measurement unit standards (kilograms, meters, volts, and so forth) and the ability to accurately meet them play a significant role in almost every manufacturing enterprise. Measurement errors can lead to either the acceptance of bad products or the rejection of good ones, both of which are undesirable outcomes. All fields need reliable and accurate measurements to mitigate these problems. Solid industrial measurement systems can support quality (photograph 1.1) and help keep costs down while reducing waste (box 1.3). A sound internal metrology system is also a requirement for firms wishing to adhere to international quality standards (box 1.4).

Correct measurements through the use of sound metrology ensure that manufactured parts are interchangeable, that is, that the subcomponents of products manufactured by independent outsourced companies

PHOTOGRAPH 1.1

Measurements are used to ensure the quality of the beer from this Armenian factory.

Source: Contributed by Karl-Christian Goethner.

BOX 1.3

Measurement as a Key Component of Modern Quality Control Methods

In general, any machined workpiece will have some errors in size, that is, its actual dimensions will be different from its nominal dimensions. However, these errors should be within certain given limits, set by tolerances, to obtain the required quality. Traditional quality control methods in manufacturing plants involve statistical sampling procedures, which guarantee that a certain expected fraction defect rate will be generated during the manufacturing process. Not all quality defects are detected with this method. Sometimes, defects can permeate the entire production line and cause errors.

One strategy for achieving improved product quality, high productivity, and reduced lead times is to incorporate the quality control process into the machining of the workpiece. This can be achieved by in-process measurement, which inspects parts while they are on the machine tool. Automated inspection methods are the solution to the increasing demand by customers for near perfection in the quality of manufactured parts and for decreased costs of quality control. These metrology-based inspection methods control the accuracy of the parts during the machining process and provide feedback for corrections, enabling the systematic identification and detection of quality errors early on.

fit together in a manufacturer's assembly line. Metrology also allows for interoperability for different parts of finished products. For example, the complex anatomy of automobiles depends on 15,000 parts fitting together (Brunnermeier and Martin 1999).

Measurement standards also promote industrial competitiveness by increasing the efficiency of trade, both within and across borders (photograph 1.2). Studies in Australia, Canada, and the United States have found the total value of trade transactions involving measurements to be between 32 and 60 percent of gross domestic product (GDP) (Birch 2003). A study in Western Europe found that a metering error of 1 percent in the gas industry equaled about 4 billion cubic meters a year, which could lead to losses of €800 million. And metering errors can easily reach 4 to 6 percent. Estimating the returns from investing in metrology for an entire economy is a very complex task, but one analysis showed that investing €1 in metrology raised GDP by €3 (Kunzmann and others 2005).

Technological advances in human health, safety, and environmental protection depend on pushing the frontier of technology, much of which is linked to increasing the quality and scope of measurements. For example, the ability to treat cancer through radiotherapy requires reliable measurements. Conservative estimates show that improvements in dosimetry—the measurement of the absorbed dose of ionizing radiation into matter and tissue—could cure more than 2,000 cancer patients in Germany each year (EURAMET 2008). The role played by measurement and testing in health is reflected by the €13 billion spent on these activities each year in European health services (Birch 2003; CIPM 2003). In terms of environmental protection, it would be impossible to deploy clean energy technologies such as wind power without proper measurements of wind speeds, electrical power, and wind turbine noise and vibration.

BOX 1.4

A Critical Role for Calibration in the Former Yugoslav Republic of Macedonia's Major Pharmaceutical Company

Alkaloid is the former Yugoslav Republic of Macedonia's knowledge-economy success story. With more than 1,000 employees and 12 subsidiaries in the Balkan countries, Switzerland, the Russian Federation, and the United States, it manufactures drugs, cosmetics, and chemical products and processes botanical raw material. Pharmaceuticals account for 78 percent of its business and include drugs for human use, pharmaceutical raw materials, and veterinary drugs. It markets its products in the former Yugoslav republics, the EU, the Commonwealth of Independent States, and, as of recently, Jordan. In 2009, Alkaloid completed its Institute for Development and Quality Control, an investment of approximately €9 million. The institute is responsible for quality control of the pharmaceuticals and development of new products. Both the building and the equipment are designed according to the international GMP requirements for the production of drugs.

At the heart of Alkaloid's success is its focus on quality, supported by reliable metrology processes. The company's operations are certified for both ISO 9001 quality management systems and ISO 14001 environmental management systems by an internationally recognized Austrian certification body and comply with GMP certification. Alkaloid's pharmaceutical manufacturing facilities undergo regular inspections by foreign pharmaceutical authorities and global buyers. Precise and timely calibration according to the international and manufacturer's standards is necessary for a precise quality control of the product, product consistency, and market security and for compliance with Alkaloid's GMP and ISO 9001 certification.

Alkaloid performs two types of calibration of its metrology equipment—internal and external calibration. Internal calibration is performed at Alkaloid for instruments controlling pressure and moisture, using etalons (reference) calibration instruments, by the Service and Maintenance Department of Alkaloid. The reference measurement standards are calibrated externally each year at the national metrology institute, the Bureau of Metrology. The fees of the Bureau of Metrology are much lower than those in the neighboring countries. Currently, the Bureau of Metrology cannot respond to all of the calibration needs of the research and development metrology equipment at Alkaloid, but it is in the process of procuring new equipment to cover some of these needs, as well as those of other pharmaceutical companies. External calibrations are performed not only at the Bureau of Metrology (for scales and weights), but also through a local company (for temperature) and by representatives of equipment manufacturers who visit Alkaloid periodically, because most of the metrology equipment is sensitive to shipping. Only one piece of equipment, a particle calculating instrument, is shipped to Germany. The shipment cost is over €6,600, and the process takes one to two months. The manufacturer sends a replacement instrument so that the process of production is not disrupted during the calibration period. Total annual calibration costs range from €50,000 to €80,000, half of which are external calibrations.

PHOTOGRAPH 1.2
To compete globally, this Georgian pharmaceutical company must rely on state-of-the-art measurement equipment.

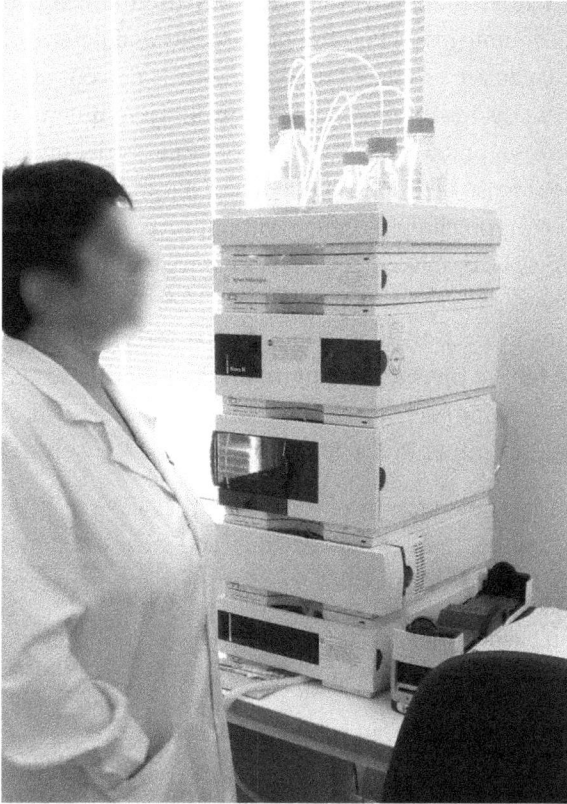

Source: Contributed by Karl-Christian Goethner.

Standards for Potentially Dangerous Products and Consumer Protection

Leaving product choice entirely to consumers when uncertainty exists about a product's quality, or when information about quality is asymmetric between producers and users, can have serious, harmful effects. Notorious examples in recent times include the safety issues raised by imported Chinese toys, pet food, and pharmaceuticals. The safety hazards created by these low-quality products were invisible to consumers and could be identified only with proper testing. The result was a mass recall of unsafe products that hurt China's trade and led its government and private sector to step up enforcement of quality standards.[8] This example

8. See Wayne M. Morrison, "Health and Safety Concerns over U.S. Imports of Chinese Products: An Overview." CRS Report for Congress, Washington, DC (2007). http://assets.opencrs.com/rpts/RS22713_20070828.pdf.

illustrates an important point: attempting to widen cost advantages by sacrificing quality can create risks for consumers.

Here, again measurement standards play a major role. Complying with measurement standards can help decrease the economic costs of accidents. Economic losses because of accidents and defects of industrial products in Japan are estimated to be as high as 4 percent of GDP. One of the major reasons for these accidents is insufficient quality data on the fatigue, corrosion and abrasion, and creep of industrial materials (BIPM 2008). It would also be impossible to assess air pollution as the effect of carbon emissions on climate change without precise measurements. This illustrates how policy makers rely on laboratory testing as a basis for their policy decisions.

Consumer protection regulations and enforcement agencies have come to the fore as mechanisms to inform and protect users. Consumer protection is gaining increasing importance in the EU and other countries. The EU Consumer Policy Strategy of 2007–13 sets three goals:

- Empowering consumers by ensuring that they have real choices, accurate information, market transparency, and the confidence that comes from effective protection and solid rights.

- Enhancing consumer welfare regarding the price, choice, quality, diversity, affordability, and safety of products.

- Protecting consumers from serious risks and threats.

In addition, regulators rely on accurate measurements to protect the health and welfare of consumers, protect the environment, and assess compliance with regulatory and legal requirements. Making the right decision about which technical aspects to specify in technical regulations and when to introduce a technical regulation is not easy, especially in the 21st-century environment of accelerating product life cycles and financial volatility. Technical organizations and policy makers increasingly believe that technical regulations should not be imposed on the private sector unless absolutely necessary from a consumer and public health safety and security perspective. Increasingly, governments base technical regulations on standards, developed together with industry, consumers, and nonprofit organizations to ensure that they consider issues such as trade, technology, the environment, and consumer well-being.

Reduction of Trade Barriers with International Harmonization of Standards and Technical Regulations

Standards can facilitate trade because they "stipulate what can or cannot be exchanged and define the procedures that must be followed for exchange to take place" (Brenton 2004, 1). Complying with standards requirements is crucial in determining market access to foreign markets. Shared standards among exporters and importers can have a positive and significant effect on bilateral trade. A survey conducted by Deutsches Institut für Normung of firms in Austria, Germany, and Switzerland showed that 46 percent were able to save money because they did not need to adapt their products for export markets (DIN 2000). A study by Wilson and Otsuki (2004) covering firms in 17 developing countries highlighted the additional costs of using different standards. Additional compliance costs to meet technical regulations in export markets amounted to 1 to 10 percent of investment costs. Costs included investments in additional facilities, equipment, product redesign, and contracting of additional workers. Another study estimated that a 10 percent increase in shared standards could enhance bilateral trade by as much as 3 percent (Moenius 2004). Thus, it follows that the most efficient way to arrive at shared standards would likely be to base national and regional standards on international standards.

Conformance to international standards is generally considered to promote trade, because many countries use these standards (Swann, Temple, and Shurmer 1996; Moenius 2004; Blind and Jungmittag 2005). Empirical studies based on international trade models find that harmonized (or "shared") standards promote trade, while there is mixed evidence on the role of country-specific (or "idiosyncratic") standards. In a time-series study of intraindustry trade between the United Kingdom and Germany, Swann, Temple, and Shurmer (1996) found that both country-specific and harmonized standards have a positive effect on exports and imports. Moreover, the study finds that adoption of 100 additional U.K. standards raises the United Kingdom's export-to-import trade ratio by about 14 percent. In a similar analysis of trade between Germany and the United Kingdom, as well as in a study of total German foreign trade, Blind and Jungmittag (2005) find that specifically harmonized standards enhance trade. International standards adopted by Germany have a significant positive effect on German exports, while German standards have a negative effect. These results support the hypotheses that idiosyncratic national standards create a competitive disadvantage for exporters and, conversely, that international standards create a competitive advantage for producers, particularly exporters.

From a trade perspective, the global fragmentation of standards, technical regulations, and conformity assessments and the propensity of some authorities to protect their local industry could become stumbling blocks (Guasch and others 2007). Typical examples include the following:

• Differing standards and testing requirements among countries subject products to several levels or types of testing.

- Products are denied access to markets because testing procedures or results are not recognized.

- Mandatory product certification imposes additional costs on exporters in cases where product standards and certification procedures differ by country or where foreign certification marks are not recognized.

- Regulatory authorities require retesting in their own laboratories and do not accept results from accredited third-party laboratories.

- Technical regulations are in place that serve objectives that are not legitimate according to the Agreement on Technical Barriers to Trade standards.[9]

The power of civil society in high-income countries (such as those in the EU), coupled with the clout of pressure groups and the availability of highly sensitive testing regimens, leads to much more stringent regulation to better protect society from a variety of small or even perceived threats. The requirements in those economies can be much tighter than those recommended by international organizations such as the World Health Organization. Low- and middle-income economies with less developed conformity infrastructure often cannot comply with these requirements, leading to considerable losses in sales for their industries. Many differences also exist in mandatory standards and the way they are administered between developing economies, resulting in major barriers to trade.

The World Trade Organization recognizes that technical regulations and standards are important and could be necessary for a range of reasons, from environmental protection, safety, and national security to consumer protection. Thus, they can help trade. However, the need to comply with a high number of different foreign technical regulations and standards could involve significant costs for producers and exporters and, hence, become a barrier to trade. If the standards are set arbitrarily, they could also be used as an excuse for protectionism. The Agreement on Technical Barriers to Trade tries to ensure that regulations, standards, testing, and certification procedures are genuinely useful and do not create unnecessary obstacles to trade.

Thus, international harmonization of standards and of technical regulations can be key drivers of trade, opening new markets for domestic firms, lowering the prices of imports, and increasing consumer choice—particularly for higher-added-value products and services. But their success in spurring trade is also dependent on their contents.

---

9. Legitimate objectives are national security requirements; the prevention of deceptive practices; protection of human health or safety, animal or plant life or health, or the environment; and so forth.

Annex: Important Global Standards

Standards and quality systems need to evolve with manufacturing and retail practices and help firms to meet society's changing demands, to face new challenges to competitiveness, and to adapt to new technological paradigms. Adopting just-in-time production methods, lessening the environmental impact of productive activities, making sure pharmaceuticals are safe before they leave the pipeline, and increasing the speed and security of information and communication technology–based communications are all examples of areas where standards play an important facilitating role, increasing the market relevance of firms and creating confidence and trust between economic agents. This chapter annex describes the implications of new standards that are rapidly changing the way firms operate, including the adoption of quality management standards and environmental management standards and of information and communication technology standards.

Quality Management Systems and the Role of the ISO 9001 Standards

During the 20th century, there was a gradual evolution from traditional inspections of systems and products to a more comprehensive approach to quality management—that is, the steps taken by an organization to fulfill customer's requirements and regulatory requirements while enhancing customer satisfaction and achieving continual improvement of its performance. Mechanisms are established to research and understand customer needs and expectations and to act on results. Special emphasis is placed on the consistent use of documented, standardized procedures to guide processes in the organization. Manufacturing and retail processes subject to such constraints are more likely to enhance product uniformity and, as a result, positively affect productivity and customer satisfaction.

Because the quality of goods and services is the result of many interrelated processes, all these activities need to be coordinated through a quality management system (QMS). In today's competitive marketplace, QMSs provide a platform for firms to consistently meet the requirements of their global customers as well as to anticipate future needs. The implementation of a QMS system relies on a framework of standards dependent on the organizations' needs, industry objectives, and so forth. For example, International Organization for Standardization (ISO) 9001:2000 sets out guidelines for the implementation of QMS and is used commonly by manufacturing, services, and various other industries.

ISO 9001 standards set out requirements for the implementation of a QMS. These standards are the most widely known and fastest growing international quality standards. They were developed by ISO in 1987 and have been implemented in more than one million organizations in 170 countries as of 2008. It is important to note that ISO 9001 standards do not specify the product quality of a management system; they are *process standards* that describe the organizational procedures that an organization should follow to ensure the consistent quality of its products and services. These standards do not dictate how requirements should be met in any particular organization, leaving scope and flexibility for implementation in different business sectors and business cultures. The implementation of an ISO 9001 standard involves one or more of the following stages: (a) the organization itself audits its ISO 9001–based quality system; (b) the organization may invite clients to audit the quality system; or (c) the organization can engage an independent quality system certification body to obtain an ISO 9001 certificate of conformity.

ISO 9001 standards or certification to ISO standards can bring benefits due to both internal and external factors to the organization, and these factors often become the rationale for firms to invest in QMSs. Benefits due to *internal* factors include lower costs and shorter cycle time, higher quality processes, greater customer focus, and greater management involvement in improving quality performance and control over employee performance. Benefits due to *external* factors include greater consumer confidence that products will meet their requirements or regulations, greater consumer satisfaction, and a better image of the organization. The case study of a Cambodian nongovernmental organization (NGO) presented in box 1A.1 shows that firms are not the only organizations can that can benefit from these standards.

Many empirical studies have tried to estimate the *efficiency improvements* and *financial implications* of adoption of ISO 9001 standards and of the certification process itself, with mixed results. Guasch and others (2007) provide an overview of this literature, and key findings are highlighted here. Several studies found a positive association between certification and organizational performance. A cross-sectional analysis of 649 mostly large firms in China, India, Mexico, and the United States by Rao, Ragu-Nathan, and Solis (1997) found that certified firms had higher levels of implementation of quality management practices and higher-quality products or processes. In a survey of 288 Spanish companies, Casadesús and Giménez (2000) found that firms gained from certification through a number of internal benefits related to implementation of a quality system.

These cross-sectional studies do not necessarily imply causality. Sharma (2005) was able to infer causality through a study of 70 firms in Singapore over a six-year period, finding that certification was associated with improvements in (a) operating efficiency, based on profit margins, and growth of sales; and (b) overall financial performance, based on earnings per share. The effects of certification were greater on profit margin than on growth of sales, suggesting that an improvement in overall performance was largely due to improvements in internal business processes.

Yet other studies found limited or no effect of certification on efficiency. In a cross-sectional analysis of 858 manufacturing firms in Australia and New Zealand, Terziovski, Samson, and Dow (1997) showed that ISO 9001 certification was a poor predictor of organizational performance and quality. They argue that many companies pursue certifica-

BOX 1A.1

Implementation of ISO 9001 in a Cambodian Nongovernmental Organization

The Cambodia Trust (CT) is an NGO in Cambodia that specializes in providing artificial limbs and braces to land mine victims, polio sufferers, and people with disabilities. It is one of the few organizations in Cambodia with ISO 9001 certification and one of the very few NGOs in the world to have achieved this.

CT had several reasons for implementing ISO 9001 but identified its primary objectives as (a) building of capacity of local staff to manage the organization and to be involved in the decision-making process; (b) greater accountability to external stakeholders, both donors and patients; (c) improved understanding of customer needs and better service to patients; and (d) improvement in donor confidence and funding.

Implementing ISO 9001 has brought significant benefits to the NGO. In some areas of manufacturing, waste has dropped to 5 percent of the pre-ISO 9001 levels. ISO certification has increased chances of the organization receiving funding. For example, a visiting delegation from Japan committed additional funding to CT because the NGO had achieved ISO 9001 certification. CT has plans to expand its operations and plans to open clinics in Sri Lanka and Timor Leste. Having ISO 9001 certification will streamline the opening of new centers as well as provide a benchmark for quality for these new operations.

The customer focus of ISO 9001 helped CT overcome another challenge faced by NGOs. Because recipients generally do not pay for an NGO's services, they can be slow to criticize the level of service or to offer constructive feedback. In addition, staff members did not feel the need to receive reviews from customers. The ISO 9001 emphasis on customer satisfaction helped staff members refocus on how best to serve beneficiaries. Regular surveys with patients revealed issues that were not brought to the forefront before. ISO 9001 has also streamlined the process of accessing patient records and reduced the time patients are kept waiting while staff members look for their files.

Implementation of ISO 9001 at CT and the organization's effect as a result of this certification demonstrates that ISO 9001 can be effective for a nonprofit organization. Importantly, it provides a mechanism for NGOs to be accountable to two significant stakeholders: clients and donors.

Source: ISO 2007.

tion to satisfy customer requirements but revert to traditional practices immediately after certification, thus nullifying any potential beneficial effect of certification. Quazi, Wing Hong, and Tuck Meng (2002) administered the questionnaire of Rao, Ragu-Nathan, and Solis (1997) to 93 Singaporean firms and found no relationship between certification and quality management practices and quality results.

From a manager's perspective, whether certification leads to improved financial performance is essential. The empirical study of 146 large firms in Singapore by Chow-Chua, Goh, and Wan (2003) showed that certification had indeed led to better overall financial performance. In their study of U.S. manufacturing facilities, Terlaak and King (2005) found that production volumes grew faster following certification, even after controlling for operational performance and inventory. Recent work based on firm-level surveys of investment climate factors in developing economies found that ISO 9001 certification had a significant effect on several measures of productivity. Average productivity gains were estimated to be between 2.4 percent and 17.6 percent for three Central American economies, less than 1 percent for four South East Asian economies, and 4.35 percent in China (Escribano and Guasch 2005a, 2005b).

Recent Developments in Environmental Standards

Environmental degradation in the past decades has increased consumer awareness of the causes and impact of environmental problems and the importance of environmental account-ability. Environmental standards can provide a framework for environmentally sustainable economic development and boost competitiveness for firms while fulfilling a niche consumer need.

ISO 14000 environmental management standards help organizations to minimize their operations' negative effect on the environment and to comply with environmental laws and regulations. ISO 14000, introduced in 1991, is often viewed as an environmental variation

---

BOX 1A.2

Environmental Gain from ISO 14001 for a Manufacturer in the Former Yugoslav Republic of Macedonia

Alkaloid is a leading pharmaceutical, cosmetic, chemical, and food manufacturer in the former Yugoslav Republic of Macedonia with subsidiaries in Albania, Bosnia and Herzegovina, Bulgaria, Croatia, and the Russian Federation. In recent years, environmental considerations have become important at the company, and following the example set by many European companies, the firm decided to adopt an EMS with objectives that included providing safer working conditions and eliminating hazards.

To implement the EMS, Alkaloid first analyzed the environmental status of the organization and identified numerous environmental impacts, such as dust, noise, and waste material generated by the manufacturing process; exhaust gas emissions from the steam boilers; and wastewater levels from washing equipment. These environmental aspects and associated legal requirements were taken into consideration for the objectives of the ISO 14001–based EMS.

In March 2000, Alkaloid's Botanicals Profit Centre achieved ISO 14001 certification and, as a result of the implementation of the EMS, was able to achieve reductions in dust, noise levels, and waste paper. Precertification results were compared with those of the year of certification through measuring stations. The company and the environment also benefited from other improvements such as a reduction in electrical power and water consumption.

Source: Nocev and Dimitrovska 2002.

of the ISO 9001 quality standard, comprising a set of generic environmental management system (EMS) requirements.[10] Like ISO 9001, it is voluntary in nature and pertains to processes rather than end products. The standards are applicable to any organization, regardless of size, type, or location. Even firms that do not produce environmentally hazardous by-products can make use of ISO 14000 because it provides guidelines on more efficient use of resources such as water, energy, or paper.

For many firms, these standards increase awareness of the environment and the way their practices might be environmentally and financially detrimental. The adoption of environmental standards leads to greater awareness of environmental issues—for the firm and their clients and community. EMS standards are helping to reinforce the message that the environment is a business issue and needs to be managed effectively (box 1A.2). A systematic approach to managing environmental issues can help to ensure that environmental incidents and liability are reduced and can also reduce penalties from not meeting environmental legislation. Using standards to systematically identify and manage environmental risk could be seen as a commitment to good environmental management and a sign of due diligence.

Food Safety Standards

In today's world, food reaches consumers increasingly through international supply chains. A weak link in this chain can result in unsafe food that poses dangers to human life. Besides hazards to consumers, food safety or the lack of it could cost food chain suppliers considerably. Because health hazards can enter the food chain at any stage, adequate control and communication throughout are essential. Health hazards from food can arise from the raw materials used, from food handling, storage, processing, transport, and sales. Common food hazards include microbial contaminations (for example, salmonella) and contamination from cadmium and lead.[11] To counteract this threat in a globalized context, countries have set up agencies, such as the European Food Authority established in 2000, to provide independent scientific advice and communication on risks in the food chain.

---

10. This description benefited from the International Trade Centre, UNCTAD (United Nations Conference on Trade and Development)/WTO (World Trade Organization), "Introduction to ISO 14000: Environmental Management Systems—ISO 14000," Bulletin 78, October 2007, http://www.intracen.org/tdc/Export%20Quality%20Bulletins/EQM78eng.pdf. We refer the reader to this document for details. See also chapter 2, titled "ISO 14000 and Sustainable Development," of *Global Climate and Sustainable Development* (Dass 2004, 40–75).

11. The 2008 Chinese milk scandal is an example of a food safety incident that involved milk and infant formula and other food materials and components that had been adulterated with melamine. The chemical appeared to have been added to milk to provide a seemingly higher protein content. With China's wide range of export markets, the contamination affected countries on all continents and created a very negative impression about food products of Chinese origin.

One effective mechanism to achieve the desired level of food safety and accountability is by implementing food management standards. The United Nation's Codex Alimentarius[12] Commission recommends an approach known as Hazard Analysis and Critical Control Points (HACCP), which was conceived in the 1960s to ensure that food was safe for astronauts to consume on NASA (National Aeronautics and Space Administration) flights. HACCP evolved into a systematic preventive approach to food and pharmaceutical safety that addresses physical, chemical, and biological hazards at all stages of the food chain, as a means of prevention rather than finished product inspection. The system can be used from primary production and preparation processes, including packaging and distribution, to final consumption and so forth. Though the use of HACCP is voluntary in most countries, an increasing number of countries have made HACCP, or part of it, obligatory.[13] The system focuses on verifiable control of the process.

At the same time, food quality encompasses much more than food safety. Several other variables determine the expectations of consumers and, hence, the quality of food. The ISO 22000 family of standards published in 2005 is designed to allow all types of organizations within the food chain to implement a food safety management system to ensure overall quality of food management. Developed within ISO by experts from the food industry, together with representatives of specialized international organizations and the Codex Alimentarius Commission, ISO 22000 combines the principles of HACCP and specifies requirements for a food safety management system in the food chain. Systems that conform to ISO 22000 can be certified, which answers the growing demand in the food sector for certifications from suppliers.

Information Security Standards

Information is an all-pervasive asset that drives operations and processes across business areas. Firms have to make sure they manage their information effectively to get the most value from it. Yet the benefits of information and communication technology can reach full potential only if the applications and supporting infrastructure are interoperable and secure. The use of standards is critical to achieving optimal interoperability and security. For information security risks, standards must be managed to ensure that information is not denied, lost, leaked, stolen, destroyed, or corrupted, whether by accident, interference, system failure, or processing error.

---

12. The Codex Alimentarius (Latin for "food code" or "food book") is a collection of internationally recognized standards, codes of practice, guidelines, and other recommendations relating to food, food production, and food safety. The Codex Alimentarius Commission was established in 1963 by the Food and Agriculture Organization of the United Nations and the World Health Organization. The Codex Alimentarius is recognized by the World Trade Organization as an international reference point for the resolution of disputes concerning food safety and consumer protection.

13. For example, the U.S. Food and Drug Administration and the U.S. Department of Agriculture use mandatory juice, seafood, meat, and poultry HACCP programs as an effective approach to food safety and protection of public health.

Neglecting these risks can lead to serious financial consequences, loss of intellectual property rights and of market share, poor productivity and performance ratings, ineffective operations, inability to comply with laws and regulations, or loss of image and reputation.

To support organizations in their efforts to design and deploy a management system for information security, the ISO and the International Electrotechnical Commission recently published standard ISO/IEC 27001:2005, *Information technology—Security techniques—Information security management systems—Requirements*. This standard provides best practice recommendations on information security management, risks, and controls within the context of an overall information security management system, similar in design to the management systems mentioned earlier concerning quality assurance (ISO 9000 series) and environmental protection (ISO 14000 series).

As with other ISO standards, certification is not a mandatory requirement of ISO/IEC 27001:2005. It is a decision of the organization whether or not to take the certification route. However, over 2,000 organizations from over 50 countries have been certified, and the growth in this area is increasing rapidly.

References

Aghion, P., R. Blundell, R. Griffith, P. Howitt, and S. Prantl. 2009. "The Effects of Entry on Incumbent Innovation and Productivity." *The Review of Economics and Statistics* 91 (1): 20–32.

Aiginger, K. 2000. "Europe's Position in Quality Competition." Background Report for "The European Competitiveness Report 2000." Enterprise DG Working Paper (September 2000), European Commission, Brussels.

Albuquerque, P., B. Bronnenberg, and C. J. Corbett. 2007. "A Spatiotemporal Analysis of the Global Diffusion of ISO 9000 and ISO 14000 Certification." *Management Science* 53 (3): 451–68.

Amiti, M., and A. Khandelwal. 2009. "Import Competition and Quality Upgrading." NBER Working Paper 15503, National Bureau of Economic Research, Cambridge, MA.

Baldwin, R. E., and T. Ito. 2008. "Quality Competition versus Price Competition Goods: An Empirical Classification." NBER Working Paper 14305, National Bureau of Economic Research, Cambridge, MA. http://www.nber.org.libproxy.mit.edu/papers/w14305.

BIPM (International Bureau of Weights and Measures). 2008. "Evolving Need for Metrology in Material Property Measurements." Report of the International Committee for Weights and Measures ad hoc Working Group on Materials Metrology, Sévres Cedex, France.

Birch, J. 2003. "Benefits of Legal Metrology for the Economy and Society." Study for the International Committee of Legal Metrology, Paris.

Blind, K., and A. Jungmittag. 2005. "Trade and the Impact of Innovations and Standards: The Case of Germany and the UK." *Applied Economics* 37 (12): 1385–98.

Brenton, P. 2004. "Standards, Conformity Assessment, and Trade: Modernization for Market Access." Moldova Trade Integration Study, World Bank, Washington, DC.

Brunnermeier, S. B., and S. A. Martin. 1999. "Interoperability Cost Analysis of the U.S. Automotive Supply Chain." RTI Project 7007-03, Research Triangle Institute, Research Triangle Park, NC.

Cabral, L. M. B. 2000. *Introduction to Industrial Organization.* Cambridge, MA: MIT Press.

Casadesús, M., and G. Giménez. 2000. "The Benefits of the Implementation of the ISO 9000 Standard: Empirical Research in 288 Spanish Companies." *The TQM Magazine* 12 (6): 432–41.

Chioveanu, I. 2010. "Price and Quality Competition." MPRA Paper 21647, University Library of Munich, Germany.

Chow-Chua, C., M. Goh, T. B. Wan. 2003. "Does ISO 9000 Certification Improve Business Performance?" *International Journal of Quality and Reliability Management* 20 (8): 936–53.

CIPM (International Committee for Weights and Measures). 2003. "Evolving Needs for Metrology in Trade, Industry, and Society and the Role of the BIPM." Report of the International Committee for Weights and Measures, CIPM, Paris.

Coe, D. T., and E. Helpman. 1995. "International R&D spillovers." *European Economic Review* 39 (5): 859–87.

Corbett, C. J. 2003. "Global Diffusion of ISO 9000 Certification through Supply Chain." Working Paper, UCLA Anderson School of Management, Los Angeles, CA.

Dass, S., ed. 2004. *Global Climate and Sustainable Development.* Adarsh Nagar, India: Isha Books.

David, A., and S. Greenstein. 1990. "The Economics of Compatibility Standards: An Introduction to Recent Research." *Economics of Innovation and New Technology* 1 (1/2): 3–41.

DIN (Deutsches Institut für Normung). 2000. *Economic Benefits of Standardization: Summary of Results.* Berlin: Beuth Verlag GmbH.

DTI (Department of Trade and Industry). 2005. "The Empirical Economics of Standards." DTI Economics Paper 12, U.K. Department of Trade and Industry, London.

Escribano, A., and J. L. Guasch. 2005a. "Assessing the Impact of the Investment Climate on Productivity Using Firm-Level Data. Methodology and the Cases of Guatemala, Honduras, and Nicaragua." Policy Research Working Paper 3621, World Bank, Washington, DC.

———. 2005b. "Investment Climate Assessment on Productivity and Wages: Analysis Based on Firm-Level Data from Selected South East Asian Countries." Unpublished.

EURAMET (European Association of National Metrology Institutes). 2008. "European Metrology for Europe's Future." Braunschweig, Germany. http://www.euramet.org/fileadmin/docs/Publications/Euramet.pdf.

Fabrizio, S., D. Igan, and A. Mody. 2007. "The Dynamics of Product Quality and International Competitiveness." IMF Working Paper 07/97, International Monetary Fund, Washington, DC.

Financial Times. 2010. "Markets Data." http://markets.ft.com/markets/commodities.asp (accessed June 7, 2010).

Fontagné, L., G. Gaulier, and S. Zignago. 2008. "Specialization across Varieties and North-South Competition." *Economic Policy* 23 (53): 51–91. http://ssrn.com/paper=1077993.

Gibbon, P. 2001. "Upgrading Primary Production: A Global Commodity Chain Approach." *World Development* 29 (2): 345–63.

Grossman, G. M., and E. Helpman. 1991. "Trade, Knowledge Spillovers, and Growth." *European Economic Review* 35 (2): 517–26.

Guasch, J. L., J.-L. Racine, I. Sánchez, and M. Diop. 2007. *Quality Systems and Standards for a Competitive Edge.* Washington, DC: World Bank.

Hall, R. E., and C. I. Jones. 1999. "Why Do Some Countries Produce So Much More Output Per Worker Than Others?" *The Quarterly Journal of Economics* 114 (1): 83–116.

Hallak, J. C. 2006. "Product Quality and the Direction of Trade."*Journal of International Economics* 68 (1): 238–65.

Hausmann, R., J. Hwang, and D. Rodrik. 2007. "What You Export Matters." *Journal of Economic Growth* 12 (1): 1–25.

Hidalgo, C. A., B. Klinger, A.-L. Barabasi, and R. Hausmann. 2007. "The Product Space Conditions the Development of Nations." *Science* 317 (5837): 482–87.

Hummels, D., and P. J. Klenow. 2005. "The Variety and Quality of a Nation's Exports." *The American Economic Review* 95 (3): 704–23.

Humphrey, J., and H. Schmitz. 2000. "Governance and Upgrading: Linking Industrial Cluster and Global Value Chain Research." IDS Working Paper 120, Institute of Development Studies, University of Sussex, Brighton, U.K.

Hwang, J. 2006. "Introduction of New Goods, Convergence, and Growth." Unpublished, Harvard University, Cambridge, MA.

ISO (International Organization for Standardization). 2007. *ISO Management Systems Magazine Database.* CD-ROM. Geneva: ISO.

Jungmittag, A., K. Blind, and H. Grup. 1999. "Innovation, Standardization, and the Long-Term Production Function: A Cointegration Analysis for Germany 1960–1996." *Zeitschrift für Wirtschafts –u. Sozialwissenschaften* 119 (2): 205–22.

Kaplinsky, R. 2000. "Spreading the Gains from Globalisation: What Can Be Learned from Value Chain Analysis?" IDS Working Paper 110, Institute of Development Studies, University of Sussex, Brighton, U.K.

———. 2005. *Globalization, Poverty, and Inequality.* Cambridge, U.K.: Polity Press.

Kaplinsky, R., and M. Farooki. 2010. "What Are the Implications for Global Value Chains When the Market Shifts from the North to the South?" Policy Research Working Paper 5205, Poverty Reduction and Economic Management Network, International Trade Department, World Bank, Washington, DC.

Kaplinsky, R., and J. Readman. 2001. "Integrating SMEs in Global Value Chains, Towards Partnership for Development." United Nations Industrial Development Organization, Vienna.

Keller, W. 2004. "International Technology Diffusion." *Journal of Economic Literature* 42 (3): 752–82.

Krammer, S. M. S. 2010. "International R&D Spillovers in Emerging Markets: The Impact of Trade and Foreign Direct Investment."*The Journal of International Trade and Economic Development* (May 4).

Kremer, M. 1993. "The O-Ring Theory of Economic Development." *The Quarterly Journal of Economics* 108 (3): 551–75.

Krishna, P., and W. Maloney. 2010. "The Dynamics of Trade Quality: Some Stylized Fact – Abstract." World Bank, Washington, DC.

Kunzmann, H., T. Pfeifer, R. Schmitt, H. Schwenke, and A. Weckenmann. 2005. "Productive Metrology—Adding Value to Manufacture." *CIRP Annals—Manufacturing Technology* 54 (2): 155–68.

Leamer, E. E. 2007. "A Flat World, a Level Playing Field, a Small World After All, or None of the Above?" *Journal of Economic Literature* 45 (1): 83–126.

Lederman, D., and W. Maloney. 2010. "Does What You Export Matter? In Search of Empirical Guidance for Industrial Policies." Paper presented at the Conference on Growth, Competitiveness, and the Role of Government Policies, World Bank, Washington, DC.

Manova, K., and Z. Zhang. 2009. "Quality Heterogeneity across Firms and Export Destinations." NBER Working Paper 15342, National Bureau of Economic Research, Cambridge, MA.

Moenius, J. 2004. "Information versus Product Adaptation: The Role of Standards in Trade." Working Paper, Kellogg School of Management, Northwestern University, Evanston, IL.

Morrison, W. 2007. "Health and Safety Concerns over U.S. Imports of Chinese Products: An Overview." CRS Report for Congress, Washington, DC. http://assets.opencrs.com/rpts/RS22713_20070828.pdf.

Nadvi, K. 2004. "The Effect of Global Standards on Local Producers: A Pakistani Case Study." In *Local Enterprises in the Global Economy: Issues of Governance and Upgrading*, ed. H. Schmitz, 297–325. Cheltenham, U.K: Edward Elgar.

Neumayer, E., and R. Perkins. 2004. "Uneven Geographies of Organizational Practice: Explaining the Cross-National Transfer and Adoption of ISO 9000." Industrial Organization Series 0403006, EconWPA. http://ideas. repec.org/p/wpa/wuwpio/0403006.html.

Nocev, S., and L. Dimitrovska. 2002. "Experiences within Application of an Environmental Management System." *Journal of Environmental Protection and Ecology* 3 (2): 400–06.

Pietrobelli, C., and R. Rabellotti, eds. 2006. *Upgrading to Compete: Global Value Chains, Clusters, and SMEs in Latin America.* Washington, DC: Inter-American Development Bank.

Polaski, S. 2006. "Combining Global and Local Forces: The Case of Labor Rights in Cambodia." *World Development* 34 (5): 919–32.

Ponte, S. 2002. "Standards, Trade, and Equity: Lessons from the Specialty Coffee Industry." CDR Working Paper 02.13, Working Paper Subseries on Globalisation and Economic Restructuring in Africa, Centre for Development Research, Copenhagen.

Ponte, S., and P. Gibbon. 2005. "Quality Standards, Conventions, and the Governance of Global Value Chains." *Economy and Society* 34 (1): 1–31.

Quadros, R. 2004. "Global Quality Standards and Technological Upgrading in the Brazilian Auto-Components Industry." In *Local Enterprises in the Global Economy: Issues of Governance and Upgrading*, ed. H. Schmitz, 265–96. Cheltenham, U.K.: Edward Elgar.

Quazi, H. A., C. Wing Hong, and C. Tuck Meng. 2002. "Impact of ISO 9000 Certification on Quality Management Practices: A Comparative Study." *Total Quality Management* 13 (1): 53–67.

Rao, S. S., T. S. Ragu-Nathan, L. E. Solis. 1997. "Does ISO 9000 Have an Effect on Quality Management Practices? An International Empirical Study." *Total Quality Management* 8 (6): 335–46.

Raynolds, L. T. 2009. "Mainstreaming Fair Trade Coffee: From Partnership to Traceability." *World Development* 37 (6): 1083–93.

Rodrik, D. 2006. "What's So Special about China's Exports?" NBER Working Paper 11947, National Bureau of Economic Research, Cambridge, MA.

Schott, P. K. 2004. "Across-Product versus Within-Product Specialisation in International Trade." *The Quarterly Journal of Economics* 119 (2): 647–78.

———. 2008. "The Relative Sophistication of Chinese Exports." *Economic Policy* 23 (53): 5-49.

Sharma, D. S. 2005. "The Association between ISO 9000 Certification and Financial Performance." *The International Journal of Accounting* 40 (2): 151–72.

Sturgeon, T. J. 2002. "Modular Production Networks: A New American Model of Industrial Organization." *Industrial and Corporate Change* 11 (3): 451–96.

Sutton, J. 2007. "Quality, Trade, and the Moving Window: The Globalisation Process." *The Economic Journal* 117 (524): F469–F498.

Swann, G. M. P. 2000. "The Economics of Standardization." Final Report for Standards and Technical Regulations Directorate, U.K. Department of Trade and Industry, Manchester Business School, Manchester, U.K.

Swann, P., P. Temple, and M. Shurmer. 1996. "Standards and Trade Performance: The UK Experience." *The Economic Journal* 106 (438): 1297–313.

Terlaak, A., and A. A. King. 2005. "The Effect of Certification with the ISO 9000 Quality Management Standard: A Signaling Approach." *Journal of Economic Behavior and Organization* 60 (4): 579–602.

Terziovski, M., D. Samson, and W. Dow. 1997. "The Business Value of Quality Management Systems Certification—Evidence from Australia and New Zealand." *Journal of Operations Management* 15 (1): 1–18.

UNIDO (United Nations Industrial Development Organization). 2009. *Industrial Development Report—Breaking In and Moving Up: New Industrial Challenges for the Bottom Billion and the Middle-Income Countries.* Vienna: UNIDO.

Utting, P. 2005. "Corporate Responsibility and the Movement of Business." *Development in Practice* 15 (3/4): 375–88.

Verhoogen, E. A. 2008. "Trade, Quality Upgrading, and Wage Inequality in the Mexican Manufacturing Sector." *The Quarterly Journal of Economics* 123 (2): 489–530.

Wilson, J. S., and T. Otsuki. 2004. "Standards and Technical Regulations and Firms in Developing Countries: New Evidence from a World Bank Technical Barriers to Trade Survey (preliminary draft)." World Bank, Washington, DC.

CHAPTER 2

Eastern Europe and Central Asia's Position in Quality Competition: Not Quite There Yet

"These bricks and stones, too, which had thus been sent upon so long a voyage, were said to have been of so bad a quality, that it was necessary to rebuild, from the foundation, the walls which had been repaired with them."

—Adam Smith, *An Inquiry into the Nature and Causes of the Wealth of Nations* (1776 [1904])

> **The new European Union (EU) member states from Eastern Europe and Central Asia (ECA) are catching up rapidly to high-income economies on various measures of export quality.**

> **Most of the Balkan countries and member states of the Commonwealth of Independent States (CIS) significantly lag the new EU member states on quality.**

> **Quality indicators suggest that CIS countries have opportunities to upgrade quality by diversifying into sectors that compete on quality, and EU and Balkan countries have opportunities to upgrade quality by diffusing quality practices within the economy.**

Measuring Quality

This chapter is focused on answering the following questions:

- What is the quality position of the individual ECA countries' products?

- Are ECA countries restructuring toward industries in which quality plays an important role?

- Is there evidence of an intraindustry quality-upgrading process?

Quality can be defined as "one or several additional characteristics of a good, which is valued by buyers" (Aiginger 2000, 46). Each such characteristic increases consumers' willingness to pay for goods. However, quality is something difficult to measure in practice. In general, a higher price paid by an importer in a given market should reflect a product's higher quality—that is, if prices are lower in other countries and trade is open. Hence, the unit value of a product, as defined by its sales value divided by its quantity unit (in weight), can be taken as a first, albeit imperfect, indicator of its quality. Other factors can lead to higher prices, such as specific shortages in inputs or rigid elasticities, but the literature generally recognizes the dominant effect of quality on differences in export and import unit values (as discussed later in this chapter).

This chapter investigates how countries in Eastern Europe and Central Asia (ECA) compete on product quality. It presents new indicators to benchmark the quality of their exports and identifies patterns of national quality upgrading. The indicators are based on the premise that high export prices to the EU trading bloc are a reflection of superior product quality. Three sets of indicators are developed. The first set consists of unit values of exports, in absolute terms, relative to imports and to world exports. The second set describes the export structure of ECA countries in terms of their concentration in industries that compete on quality and industries that compete on costs. The third set extracts quality specialization from patterns of intraindustry trade. A combined analysis of the various indicators is used to produce a classification of countries according to their quality strategies—namely, whether they specialize in high-quality products or high-quality industries. Finally, a ranking of ECA countries based on how they compete on quality is constructed from six of these indicators.

Although ECA countries in general tend to export poorer-quality products than do high-income comparator countries in the EU, this chapter finds that they present a fairly heterogeneous group of countries. The new European Union (EU) member states are catching up rapidly on the various quality indicators. Not only do they export higher-quality products than do other countries in ECA, but also they are improving quality and engaging in sectors in which the potential to upgrade quality is high.

The picture is more mixed in the Balkans and Turkey, but the region generally lags the new member states, except for a few high performers such as Turkey. The countries of the Commonwealth of Independent States (CIS) significantly lag. Not only do they mostly export lower-quality products than the rest of ECA, but also they lack any uniform improvement of product quality over time, and most of the CIS countries do not export in sectors that provide many opportunities to upgrade quality. The quality gap between the CIS and the EU countries is widening over time.

The new quality indicators presented in this chapter have their limitations, but taken together with a broader set of indicators, they can provide insight on the effectiveness of the policies and institutions that affect export quality and contribute to national dialogues on export competitiveness. Measuring quality in ECA matters because the few existing proxies for quality collected from opinion surveys, imperfect as they are, show that most ECA countries lag not only high-income countries, but also global middle-income competitors such as China and the world average (figure 2.1). The new indicators can be used to provide rationale for policy reform and to identify needs for capacity building. Importantly, they can complement or replace other traditional measures of quality previously used to inform policy such as International Organization for Standardization (ISO) 9001 certification rates (box 2.1) or subjective measures of quality, such as those of the *Global Competitiveness Report 2009–2010* (World Economic Forum 2009).

This analysis benchmarks the "quality competitiveness" of ECA countries and their quality upgrading strategies through a set of indicators derived from trade unit values (table 2.1). Each of these indicators suffers from its own shortcomings, but if they are used together, and combined

FIGURE 2.1

The Lag in Quality by Most ECA Countries in Opinion Surveys, 2008–09

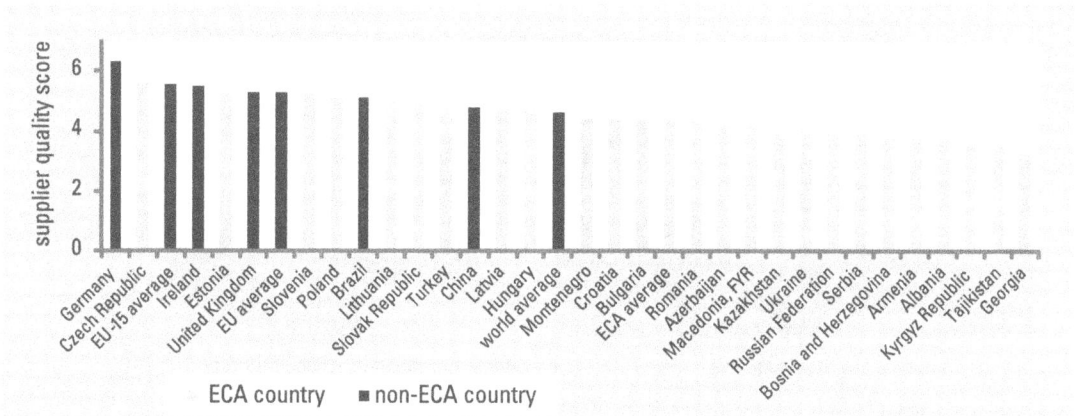

ECA country   ■ non-ECA country

Source: World Economic Forum 2009.
Note: Scores are based on responses to the following question: "How would you assess the quality of local suppliers in your country?" Score ratings are as follows: 1 = very poor; 7 = very good, with 2008–09 weighted average.

with contextual information on trade structure, they provide a starting point for benchmarking how ECA countries compete on quality in global markets. The analysis of ECA countries has been divided into the following sections.

Unit Values

This section provides an initial analysis of ECA's position in quality competition using the unit values as an indicator of quality. The latest findings

---

BOX 2.1

ISO 9001 as an Indicator of Quality Competitiveness

International development organizations and policy makers typically use statistics on ISO 9001 quality management certificates as indicators of how countries compete on quality. This methodology is the result not only of a lack of availability of alternative indicators for quality, but also of a flawed understanding of the implication of the ISO 9001 standard and quality. Whereas ISO 9001 certification supports the continuous *improvement* of quality within the firm, certification to ISO 9001 does not imply that a firm is producing high-quality outputs. As an illustration, a comparison of the number of ISO 9001 certificates standardized by the gross domestic product would suggest that Bulgaria performs almost 10 times better than Germany in terms of quality. ISO 9001 certification data are binary and set a minimum threshold of quality management practices, but the data do not differentiate between the outputs of two ISO 9001–certified plants. Although both a Mercedes-Benz plant producing the latest SL-Class vehicle (below, left) and a Zastava Automobili plant producing budget vehicles (the Yugo[a] — below, right) could be certified to ISO 9001, an appreciable difference exists in the quality of both of these outputs, as measured by the price that consumers are willing to pay—approximately US$100,000 for the former and a fraction of that for the latter. Thus, ISO 9001 certification provides an incomplete picture of product quality.

PHOTOGRAPH 2.1   PHOTOGRAPH 2.2

Mercedes-Benz   **Yugo**

Source: Contributed by Stara Blazkova.   *Source:* Contributed by Rudolf Stricker.

Source: ISO 2008.
a. The last Yugo left the lines of the Zastava Automobili factory in Kragujevac, Serbia, on November 11, 2008.

TABLE 2.1

The Quality Indicator Framework

Method	Objective	Analytical framework	Indicators
Unit values	Determine the quality of exports by comparing prices of goods traded between countries.	Unit values are calculated as sales value over quantity unit (weight).	**Relative unit value of exports to imports:** mean, weighted mean, and median of the ratio of export unit values to import unit values by industry (RUV2) **Relative unit value of national exports to world exports:** mean, weighted mean, and median of the ratio of export unit values to world export unit values by industry (RUV3)
Quality-sensitive industries	Determine the concentration of countries' exports in industry in which quality opens opportunities for trade.	Each industry is classified into one of three Revealed Quality Elasticity (RQE) categories: low, medium, and high. The RQE reflects the effect of an increase in quality of exports in that particular industry on the trade surplus. Industries with high RQE compete on quality, whereas industries with low RQE compete on price.	**Share of exports in high-, medium-, and low-RQE industries** **Trade balance in high-, medium-, and low-RQE industries**
Intraindustry trade	Determine to what degree countries specialize on quality (versus price) within each industry.	The Grubel-Lloyd (GL) index is used to measure the degree of intraindustry trade in total trade.	**Horizontal GL index:** component of the GL index applied to industries in which goods of similar quality are traded **Vertical high-quality GL index:** component of the GL index applied to industries in which export unit values are greater than import unit values **Vertical low-quality GL index:** component of the GL index applied to industries in which export unit values are lower than import unit values

Source: Authors.

in the economic literature that justify the use of export unit values as proxies for quality and their relationship to various performance measures are presented. A quantitative analysis of the export unit values for ECA countries, their evolution over time, and their quality premium are then provided.

Unit Values as Measures of Quality

Unit values form the basis of the indicators used to measure quality in this analysis. They are defined as nominal sales divided by quantity, and export unit values are therefore defined as export values (sales) divided by an export quantity measured in kilograms. In many instances, higher prices for a given product from different suppliers reflect higher quality, and therefore, unit values can be interpreted as an indicator of the consumer's evaluation of product quality. In models of imperfect competition, increases in unit values in heterogeneous markets signal quality improvements, together with growing product differentiation. Therefore, under a broad set of circumstances, unit values can be used to measure the degree of quality of a product (Greenaway, Hine, and Milner 1994). The increasing availability of both price and quantity data for international trade flows has consecrated the use of unit values as proxies for quality at both the firm or plant level (Kugler and Verhoogen 2009; Iacovone and Javorcik 2010) and the country level (Koyota 2008; Schott 2008). However, despite its popularity as a common proxy for quality, the concept of unit value is built on some strong assumptions and should be used with caution (box 2.2).

Prior Empirical Work on ECA Countries

The quality-upgrading process in ECA countries, especially in the countries of Central and Eastern Europe (CEE), has captured the attention of a number of empirical studies. Employing a similar methodology to that developed by Aiginger (1997), Dulleck and others (2003) investigate three dimensions of quality upgrading between 1995 and 2000 in 10 CEE countries, namely, structural shifts to exports of higher-quality industries, higher quality of export goods within an industry, and increasing quality of exports within segments. They obtain substantial results revealing a quality-upgrading process in the Czech Republic, Hungary, Poland, the Slovak Republic, and Slovenia, and their evidence clearly rejects any kind of quality trap in this subgroup of countries. According to their study, the same cannot be argued for Bulgaria and Romania, because these countries show some evidence of specializing in low-quality segments (Dulleck and others 2003).

Kandogan (2004) analyzes the manufacturing exports of 22 ECA countries to 28 market economies between 1992 and 1998 to test whether their increasing share in world trade was due to product upgrading and, if so, to what extent this was a consequence of restructuring of production technologies. Kandogan (2004) observes that, in the early transition

BOX 2.2
Important Caveats on Drawing Conclusions on Quality from Unit Values

There are several important limitations to the unit value approach that warrant using unit values cautiously and paying critical attention to other factors that may influence their relationship with product quality.

First, unit values require a very fine level of disaggregation (6-digit level or higher) to ensure that one is indeed comparing "apples with apples."

Second, in some cases, high unit values for similar product categories could reflect circumstances other than high quality. For example, a high unit value can indicate high costs in a specific location or high market power in specific markets. The absolute levels of unit values can reflect differences in the processing stages of production (with downstream industries typically exhibiting a higher sales value per material unit than upstream industries). The geographic distance between trading partners may influence trade structure. Because of transportation costs, distance will play a bigger role for relatively heavier products (like cement), which generally depict lower unit values. In addition, because of the way that export values are measured,[a] larger distances generally imply larger biases in the export unit values, in addition to having a potential influence on trade structure. Prices can also reflect tariff duties, exchange rate differentials, and nonquantifiable idiosyncratic consumer preferences. All these elements pose significant challenges to extracting robust information on product quality by relying solely on computed unit values.

In some industries, factors other than skills or technology intensity result in high intrinsic unit values of a specific industry compared with other industries. The most prominent examples are the textiles, apparel, and precious metal industries. In the former two industries, high unit values are mainly the result of the low weight of the products, and in the latter case, high unit values (or prices) are the result of limited supply and, specifically, valued characteristics (see Aiginger 2000). Another example is the price of natural resources, such as oil, which usually is set in international markets. As a result, increases in natural resources' unit values may reflect socioeconomic world trends rather than quality.

The recent work of Khandelwal (2010) uses data on exports to the United States and proposes a new and more sophisticated framework to analyze product quality by using information on both prices and product market shares to capture consumer preferences.

Source: Aiginger 2000.
a. Measurement includes cost, insurance, and freight (named destination port) (c.i.f.) using mirror statistics.

stage, countries engage in price competition, exporting low-quality products at low prices (decreasing unit values). As a result of the restructuring process, the quality of products improves and the aggregate unit values increase. Put differently, Kandogan (2004) obtains the stylized effect that, along the transition period, aggregate unit values follow a U-shaped pattern. He finds that, in the CEE's exports, the quality of at least 40 percent of the analyzed products improved in 1999 compared with the previous year, whereas the Baltic States (Estonia, Latvia, and Lithuania) and Belarus, the Russian Federation, and Ukraine performed slightly worse.

This situation stood in sharp contrast to poor quality improvements in the rest of the CIS countries. In Armenia, Azerbaijan, Georgia, Kazakhstan, the Kyrgyz Republic, Moldova, Tajikistan, Turkmenistan, and Uzbekistan, quality improved in only 15 percent or less of the analyzed products.

Fabrizio, Igan, and Mody (2007) investigate the reasons behind the increase in world market shares of eight CEE countries (the Czech Republic, Estonia, Hungary, Latvia, Lithuania, Poland, the Slovak Republic, and Slovenia) between 1994 and 2004. They argue that trade liberalization created opportunities to expand trade and that deep economic reforms (such as privatization and restructuring) allowed a process of quality and technology upgrading in these transition countries. Their results suggest that product upgrading is an important cause of such gains in world market shares and that, even when quality and technology improve together, quality improvement is the major determinant in gaining market shares. Table 2.2 shows a summary of prior empirical work.

The Quality of ECA Exports Based on Unit Value Indicators

Export unit values show that new EU member states lead on product quality, whereas most CIS countries are falling behind. Unit values on the aggregate country level reflect two effects. On the one hand, high unit values may reflect the *structure* effect, which occurs when a country has a high share of industries that, in turn, have higher unit values. These structure effects have been decreased in this analysis by removing textiles and footwear, as discussed later. Conversely, the unit value is influenced by *price* effects, which are also at stake. For each industry, higher unit values will depict the buyers' willingness to pay more, which is a proxy for quality.

Figure 2.2 shows a certain positive relationship between a country's quality of exports—represented in this case by its export unit value—and its per capita gross domestic product (GDP). This relationship is consistent

TABLE 2.2

Summary of Prior Empirical Findings

Reference	Quality upgrading	Quality downgrading or stagnation
Dulleck and others (2003)	**The Czech Republic, Hungary, Poland, the Slovak Republic, and Slovenia** (increased specialization in high-quality segments from 1995 to 2000)	**Baltic States, Bulgaria, and Romania** (increased specialization in low-quality segments from 1995 to 2000)
Kandogan (2004)	**CEE** (improvement in at least 40 percent of products from 1998 to 1999)	**The Caucasus, Central Asia, and Moldova** (improvement in less than 15 percent of products from 1998 to 1999)

Sources: Dulleck and others 2003, Kandogan 2004.

FIGURE 2.2

Unit Values and GDP Per Capita (Excluding Textiles, Apparel, and Leather), 2005

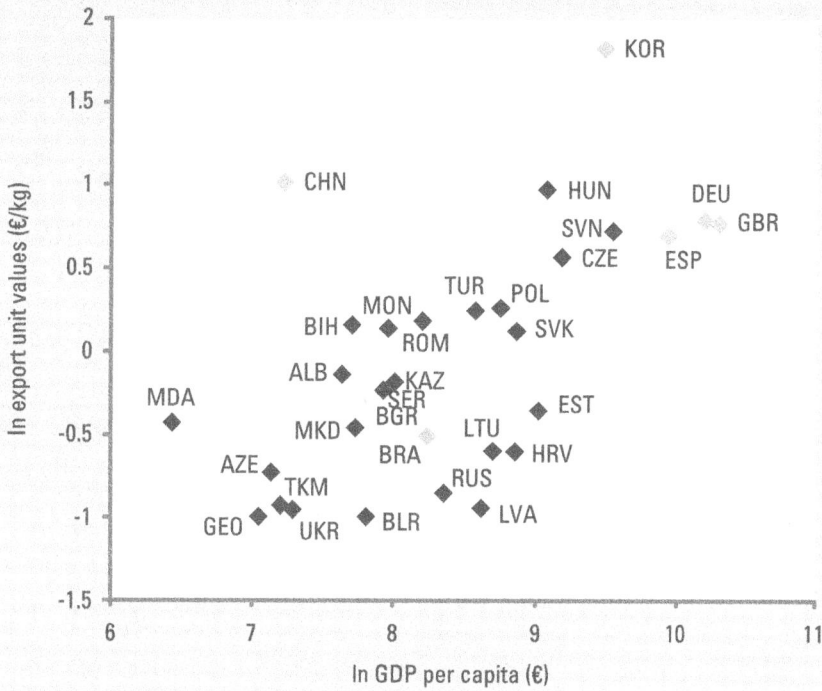

Sources: Authors' calculations based on Eurostat, wiiw Database.
Note: Excludes NACE (Nomenclature Statistique des Activités Économiques dans la Communauté Européenne, or Statistical Classification of Economic Activities in the European Community) 17, 18, and 19. kg = kilogram. Comparator countries outside of ECA are shown in yellow.

with Hummels and Klenow (2005), who assert that high-income countries produce high-quality products. Most CIS countries are concentrated in the low-export-unit-value and low-income quadrant of figure 2.2. At the opposite extreme, Germany, the United Kingdom, and Spain, followed by the Republic of Korea and the CEE5 (Slovenia, the Slovak Republic, the Czech Republic, Poland, and Hungary), show higher export unit values and income levels. For example, China depicts high export unit values for its income level.

Figure 2.3 displays the weighted means of both relative unit values (RUV2 and RUV3). Both of the indicators of countries positioned in the top right quadrant are greater than unity, meaning that their export unit values are greater than their import unit values and also greater than world export unit values. Only the United Kingdom is in that top right quadrant, but Germany, Hungary, and Spain are close. The lowest ECA performers on both indicators are CIS countries.

Figure 2.3 displays changes in the two indicators over the 1999–2005 period. To provide a level of redundancy, the figure shows only quality

FIGURE 2.3

Export Unit Values Relative to National Imports and to World Exports (Excluding Textiles, Apparel, and Leather), 2005

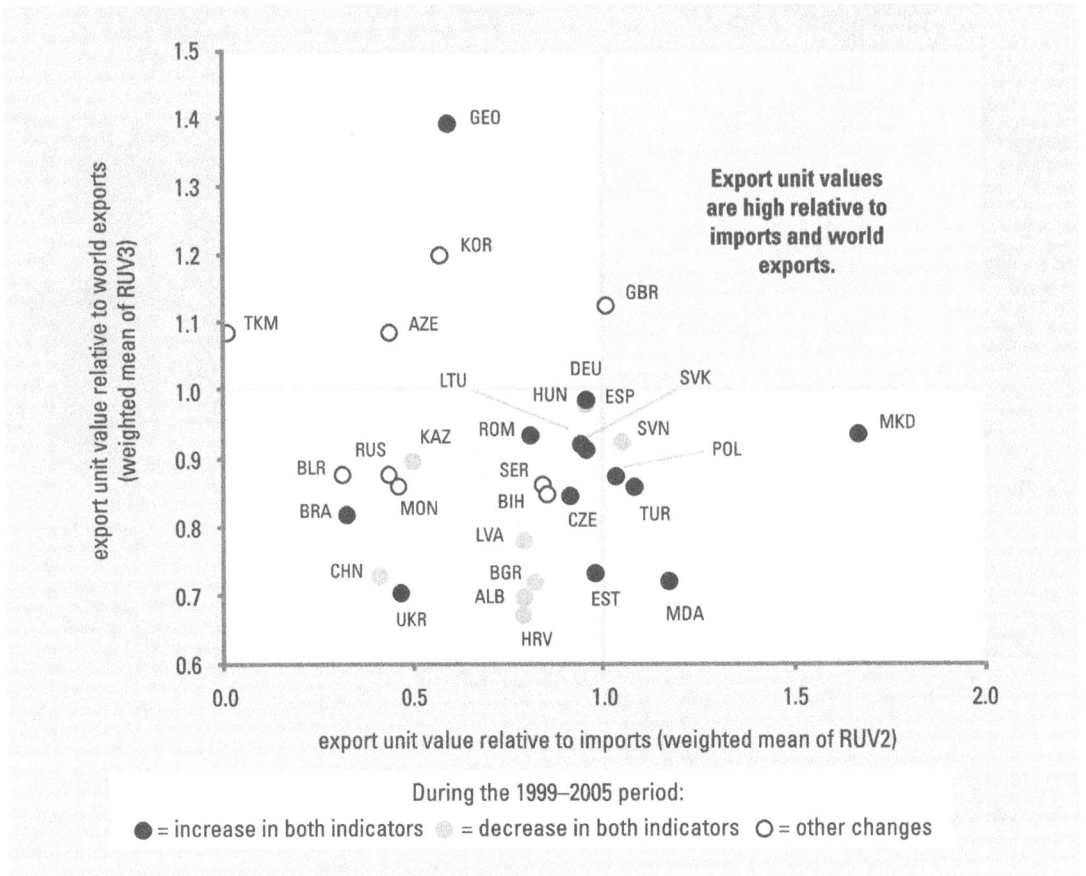

Sources: Authors' calculations based on Eurostat, wiiw Database.
Note: Excludes NACE (Nomenclature Statistique des Activités Économiques dans la Communauté Européenne, or Statistical Classification of Economic Activities in the European Community) 17, 18, and 19. Changes in indicators are not proportional to the bubble size. Data for 1999 are not available for Serbia and Montenegro. Icons indicate country groups.

upgrading or downgrading that occurs in both indicators. The figure shows a mixed bag of quality upgrading and downgrading. With the exception of Georgia and Moldova, no CIS country has improved its quality position through intraindustry upgrading, as measured by a simultaneous increase in RUV2 and RUV3. Moreover, the quality position of Kazakhstan has further deteriorated between 1999 and 2005. Apart from Bulgaria, Latvia, and Slovenia, all new EU member states actually have increased their quality positions, thus widening the quality gap between the new states and the CIS countries. The former Yugoslav Republic of Macedonia is the best performer of the Balkan countries, while Albania, Bosnia and Herzegovina, and Croatia weakened or maintained their 1999 positions.

Another way to identify the diffusion of quality in different industries is by examining the number of industries for which export unit values are greater than import unit values. Figure 2.4 displays each country in the sample according to the number of industries competing on price (export unit values are smaller than import unit values) and the number of industries competing on quality (export unit values are greater than import unit values). The total number of industries displayed for each country varies on the basis of data availability. Figure 2.4 shows that in all ECA countries, more industry sectors compete on price rather than on quality. Only in Germany and the United Kingdom, the two comparator countries, do more sectors compete on quality. Within ECA, new EU member states tend to have both a high number of industries represented in the data, thus strengthening data reliability, and a large absolute number of sectors competing on quality. This high number points to opportunities to upgrade quality by expanding the exports in these sectors or by diffusing quality practices from those sectors to lagging sectors of the economy. In Russia, Turkey, and Ukraine, a large number of industries

FIGURE 2.4

Number of Industry Sectors in Which Countries Compete on Price and Quality, 2005

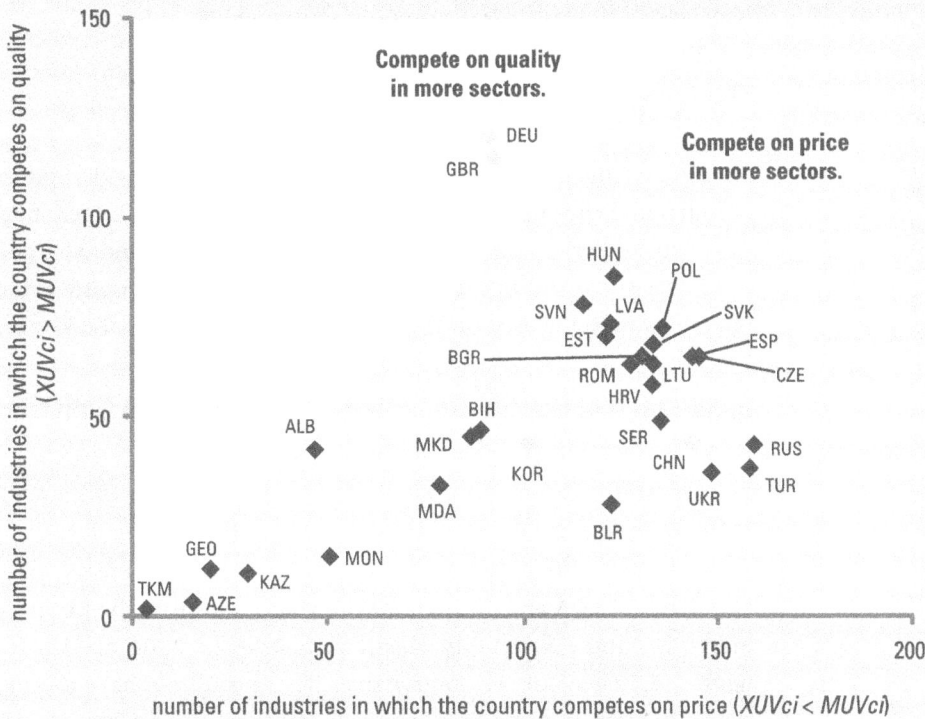

Source: Authors' calculations based on Eurostat Database.
Note: $XUVci$ = export unit value for country *"c"* in industry *"i"*; $MUVci$ = import unit value for country *"c"* in industry *"i"*.
Comparator countries outside of ECA are shown in yellow.

are represented, but a much larger share of industries is competing on price than on quality. Russia and Turkey partially compensate for this low diffusion of quality among industries by having some outstanding industries, for which export unit values are much higher than import unit values or world export unit values. Ukraine does not have any apparent industries that hold the promise of quality leadership in its economy.

Quality-Sensitive Industries

An academic debate is ongoing regarding which types of goods are intrinsically better than others for growth. One strategy countries can use to improve their position in quality competition is to switch from industries that are dominated mainly by price competition to industries in which quality competition plays an important role, that is, the high Revealed Quality Elasticity (RQE) industries.

However, this approach ignores the overall dynamics of industries and countries, characterized by technological change and leapfrogging, that may change the mapping of various industries into price versus quality segments. Despite this circumstance, understanding the structure of a country's production and exports through the lens of quality competition may bear useful policy lessons in the short and medium term.

The Revealed Quality Elasticity

As discussed in chapter 1 of this book, Aiginger (2000) divides industries of individual countries into segments, depending on whether they are dominated by price competition or quality competition and whether the country is successful in the prevailing type of competition. He creates a taxonomy of RQE based on three groups: high, medium, and low RQE.

Importance of Quality-Sensitive Industries in ECA Countries

The most important patterns of interindustry upgrading and downgrading involve CIS countries.

The shares of ECA and comparator countries' exports to the EU in high-, medium-, and low-quality elastic industries in 2006 are shown in figure 2.5. In general, we observe that the CIS countries have low export shares in industries in which quality is found to play an important role. The exceptions are Armenia, Azerbaijan, and Moldova, whose export shares to the EU in high-RQE industries are more than 20 percent. These

FIGURE 2.5

Share of Exports in High-, Medium-, and Low-RQE Industries, 2006

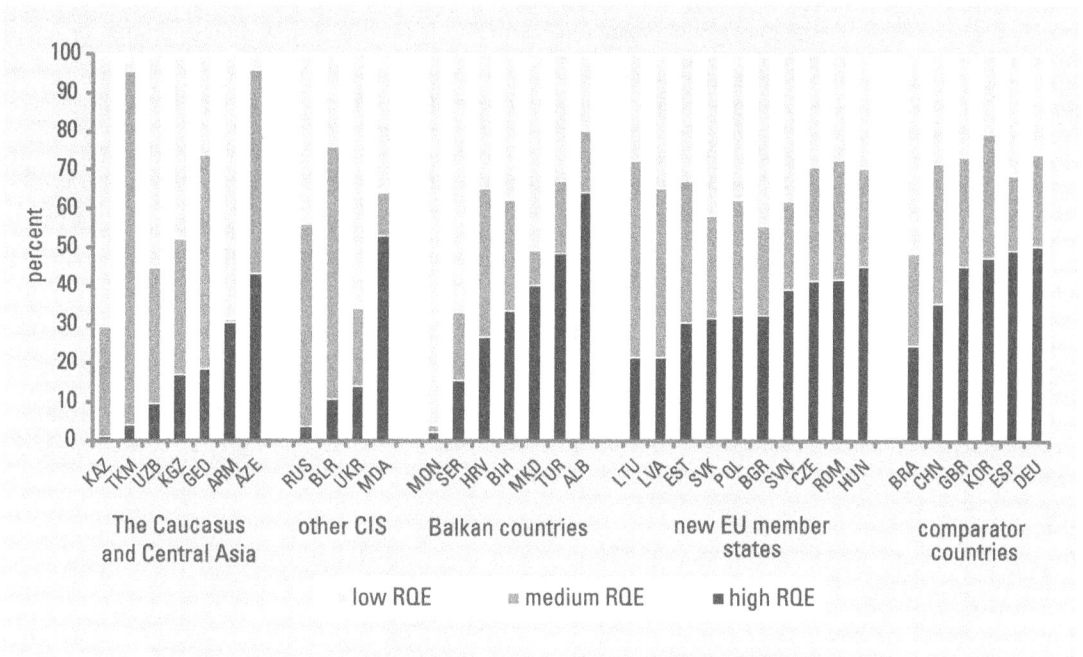

Source: Authors' calculations based on Eurostat Database.

larger shares in high-RQE industries reflect the large diamond-cutting exporting industry in Armenia, jewelry manufacturing exports in Azerbaijan, and apparel manufacturing exports in Moldova.

As shown in figure 2.5, Montenegro and Serbia show large export shares in low-RQE industries. This is mainly because most of Montenegro and Serbia's exports to the EU are ores and minerals (such as aluminum, copper, and iron), and in these industries, prices define the competitive edge and products are rather homogeneous. However, in contrast to Montenegro and Serbia, other Balkan countries exhibit higher shares of exports in high-RQE industries. In the case of Albania and FYR Macedonia, these high shares come mainly from the footwear and apparel industries. Although these are not knowledge-based or high-technology industries, they are classified as high-RQE industries because product quality differentiation plays a key role in exports. Turkey also has a large apparel-exporting industry, but has secured an international position as a producer of motor vehicles and a manufacturer of parts and accessories for motor vehicles.

As expected, high-income countries such as Germany, Korea, Spain, and the United Kingdom have high shares—around 50 percent—in high-RQE industries. The Czech Republic, Hungary, Romania, and Slovenia have shares around 40 percent in industries dominated by quality competition. In the case of the CEE5, the composition of exports resembles that of the four high-income comparator countries. This similarity could reflect their participation in international value-added chains, because Western Europe has partly reallocated production to Central and Eastern European countries (cf. Kaminski 2001; Kaminski and Ng 2001). For instance, motor vehicles and related accessories, telecommunications, and furniture are some of the key exporting industries in the CEE5. Bulgaria and Romania keep exporting large shares of apparel and footwear to the EU—industries characterized by a high RQE. As in several CIS countries, oil is an important component of the Baltic countries' exports to the EU. As a result, Estonia, Latvia, and Lithuania show large shares in medium-RQE industries. Figure 2.6 provides another representation of the data in figure 2.5 by plotting shares of exports in quality-dominated (high-RQE) industries against shares of exports in price-dominated (low-

FIGURE 2.6

Export Shares of Eastern European and Central Asian Countries in Industries That Compete on Quality and on Price, 2006

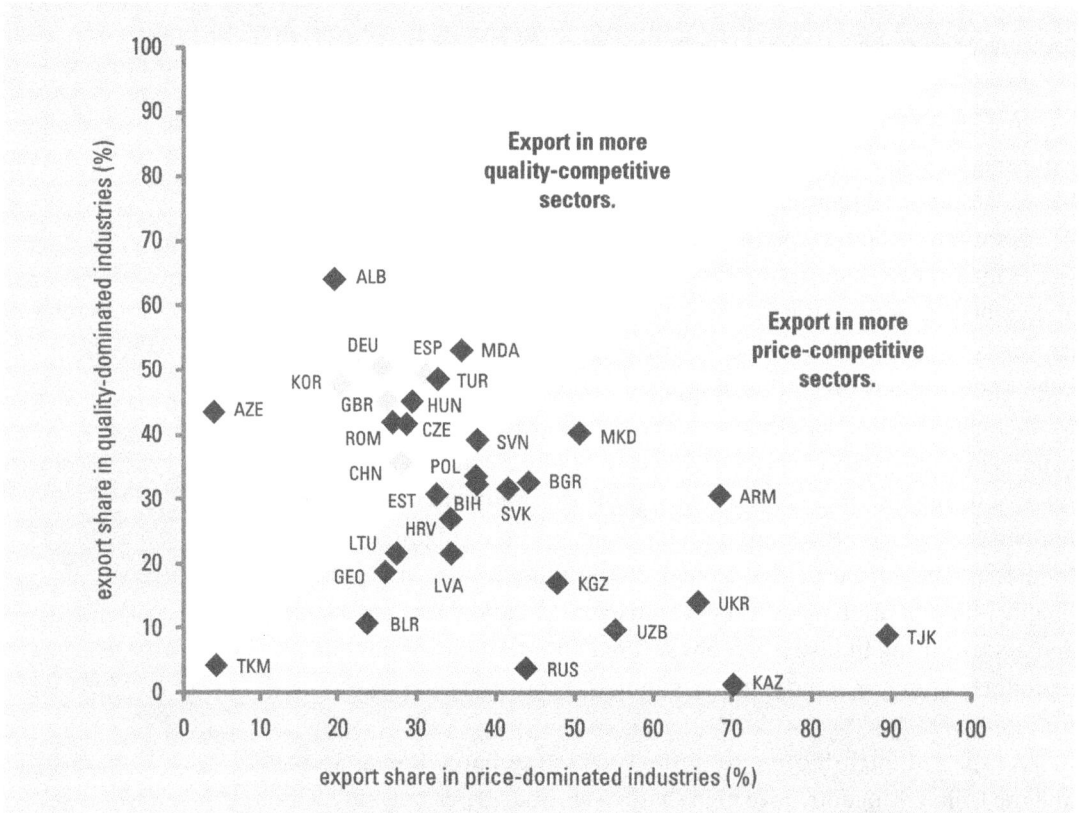

Source: Authors' calculations based on Eurostat Database.
Note: Comparator countries outside of ECA are shown in yellow.

RQE) industries. Countries in the upper triangle export more in sectors in which quality defines the competitive edge. These industries have the most potential for intrasectoral quality upgrading—that is, firms can increase exports by upgrading to higher-quality segments within the same sector. All comparator countries are in this category. Most ECA countries are in the bottom triangle, where their export sectors are dominated by price competition. A disproportionately high share of exports from CIS countries is in price-competitive industries. This category does not include fuels, which are classified as medium-RQE sectors and, thus, are not shown in the figure. China's position in the top triangle differentiates it from CIS countries that compete poorly on quality. Although both CIS countries and China have low relative unit values and compete on price in most of their export sectors (see figure 2.3 and figure 2.4), China exports in quality-dominated sectors and, therefore, has more opportunities to upgrade quality.

The greatest patterns of interindustry upgrading and downgrading can be found among CIS countries.

Structural changes in exports between 1999 and 2006 expose differences across country groups, namely, between the relatively poorer CIS countries and the generally better-off new EU member states and comparator countries. Figure 2.7 reveals individual patterns of interindustry downgrading and upgrading at the country level between 1999 and 2006. The figure shows that movement across RQE groups is largest among CIS countries, but also is noticeable in the Balkan countries. Armenia, FYR Macedonia, Tajikistan, and Ukraine (the yellow arrows in the figure) show unambiguous patterns of quality downgrading, with increases in the export shares of price-dominated sectors accompanied by decreases in export shares of quality-dominated sectors. Azerbaijan, Georgia, the Kyrgyz Republic, and Uzbekistan show patterns of quality upgrading (the dark grey arrows in the figure). For most of this second group, this upgrading is mostly achieved by replacing shares of low-RQE industries with shares of medium-RQE industries rather than with high-RQE industries.

The evidence presented in this section reveals that some ECA countries are well positioned to engage in intraindustry upgrading, namely, the new EU member states, the Balkan countries, and Turkey, with relatively large shares of their exports in industry sectors dominated by quality competition. CIS countries are restructuring away from quality-dominated sectors or are making modest gains toward quality-dominated sectors, but these two patterns are not promising. After the collapse of their manufacturing sector (caused by the disintegration of the Soviet

Union; see Freinkman, Polyakov, and Revenco 2004), the CIS countries have not been able to revitalize their manufacturing apparatus. Instead, they have concentrated their exports on a narrow set of commodities that are easy to sell on international markets.

FIGURE 2.7

Quality Upgrading and Downgrading Trajectories, 1999–2006

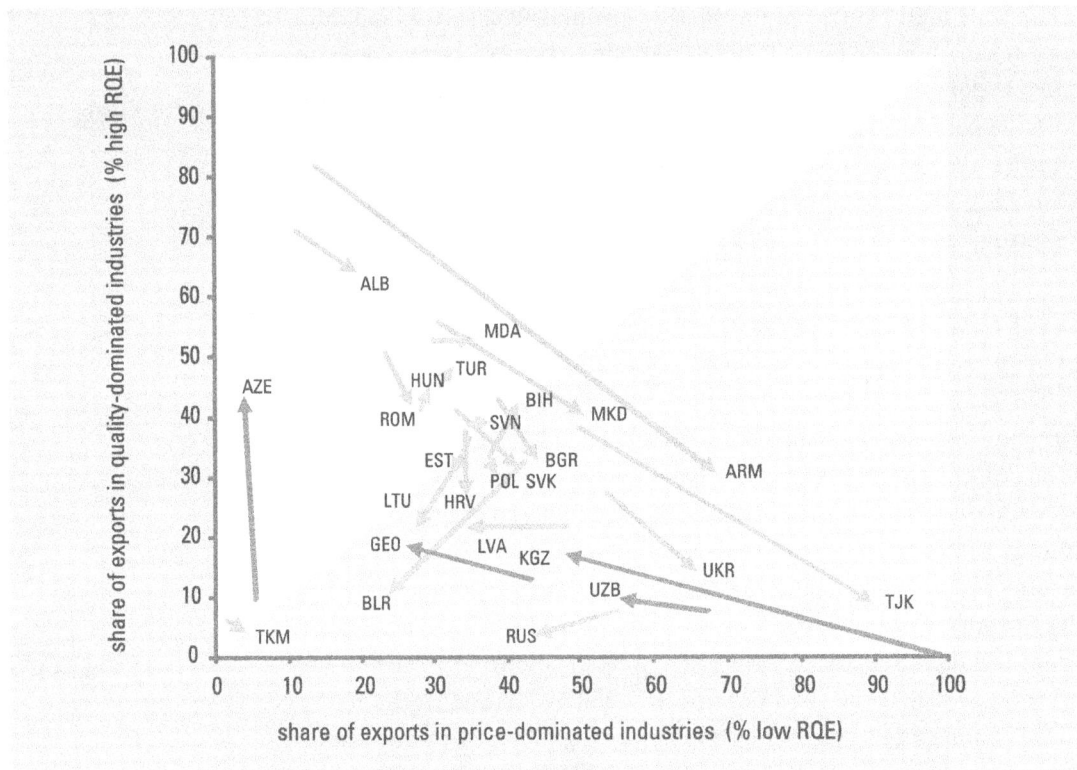

Source: Authors' calculations based on Eurostat Database.
Note: Arrow tails represent 1999 values, and arrow heads represent 2006 values. Yellow arrows represent unambiguous cases of intraindustry quality downgrading, and dark grey arrows represent unambiguous cases of intraindustry quality upgrading.

Quality Position as Revealed by Intraindustry Trade

Intraindustry trade, or two-way trade, refers to the exchange (exports and imports) of goods within the same product category. Krugman (1980) explains this pattern of trade specialization by the theory of increasing returns. Because trade increases market size, countries can specialize in producing a narrower range of products—achieving higher productivity and lower costs—and at the same time increase the variety of products available to their consumers through imports (Krugman and

Obstfeld 2003). Trade costs are also viewed as an important determinant of such trade flows (Bergstrand and Egger 2006). Besides these "usual suspects" of the international trade literature, evidence shows that comparative advantage, defined in a broader perspective than factor endowments or technological differences, bears an effect on intraindustry trade (Siggel 2009).

Intraindustry trade with higher-income countries has implications for product quality because these flows have both a horizontal and a vertical component, as shown in Fontagné, Freudenberg, and Gaulier (2006). Their study disentangles all international flows in these two components, covering nearly 5,000 products and using information on unit values as proxies for quality. Besides documenting the fact that most intraindustry trade occurs between Organisation for Economic Co-operation and Development nations, their analysis emphasizes the increasing role of intraindustry trade in transition economies from Eastern Europe, which are the focus of this work. Moreover, according to Freinkman, Polyakov, and Revenco (2004), intraindustry trade often signals a noticeable spillover effect of foreign direct investment on the local industry, including the adoption of international standards and product quality improvements. This idea is also supported by Faruq's (2006) findings relating foreign direct investment inflows to positive effects on quality.

Horizontal and Vertical Trade

To gain more insight on the quality of intraindustry trade, one can divide it into horizontal and vertical trade and then subdivide vertical trade again into two parts, depending on whether a country is specialized in the higher- or lower-quality segment of vertically differentiated product markets. The objective of this analysis is to assess the position of the ECA countries in these different types of intraindustry trade, with a special focus on the development of high- and low-quality vertical trade. An increase of high-quality vertical trade will indicate intraindustry quality upgrading. High and persistent proportions of low-quality vertical trade will provide evidence of quality gaps.

The Grubel-Lloyd index measures the amount of intraindustry trade between countries or country groups (Grubel and Lloyd 1975). The Grubel-Lloyd index equals 100 if all trade is intraindustry, which is the case when the export and import structures of a country or country group are identical, and zero if all trade is interindustry. One disadvantage of the Grubel-Lloyd index is that it is sensitive to the industry or country aggregation level. According to the literature, however, the four-digit NACE (Nomenclature Statistique des Activités Économiques dans la Communauté Européenne, or Statistical Classification of Economic Activities in the European Community) industry level should be sufficiently disaggregated for intraindustry trade calculations. Appendix B summarizes the Grubel-Lloyd methodology employed to compute the index and disentangle horizontal and vertical intraindustry trade as well as low- and high-quality vertical intraindustry trade.

Less Competition by the Balkan Countries and Turkey on Intraindustry Trade than by the New EU Member States

Intraindustry trade can be two-way trade in goods of similar quality (horizontal) or of different quality content (vertical). In their model of horizontal differentiation, Helpman and Krugman (1985) explain that the more dissimilar two countries' demand and per capita incomes are, the less important horizontal intraindustry trade will be. This situation is because the greater the difference in countries' incomes, the greater the difference in the quality of their products. EU countries generally have higher income levels and, therefore, generally should export higher shares of high-quality products than the Balkan countries, Turkey, and CIS countries.

FIGURE 2.8

Component Shares of the Weighted Grubel-Lloyd Index (Excluding Textiles, Apparel, and Footwear), 2005

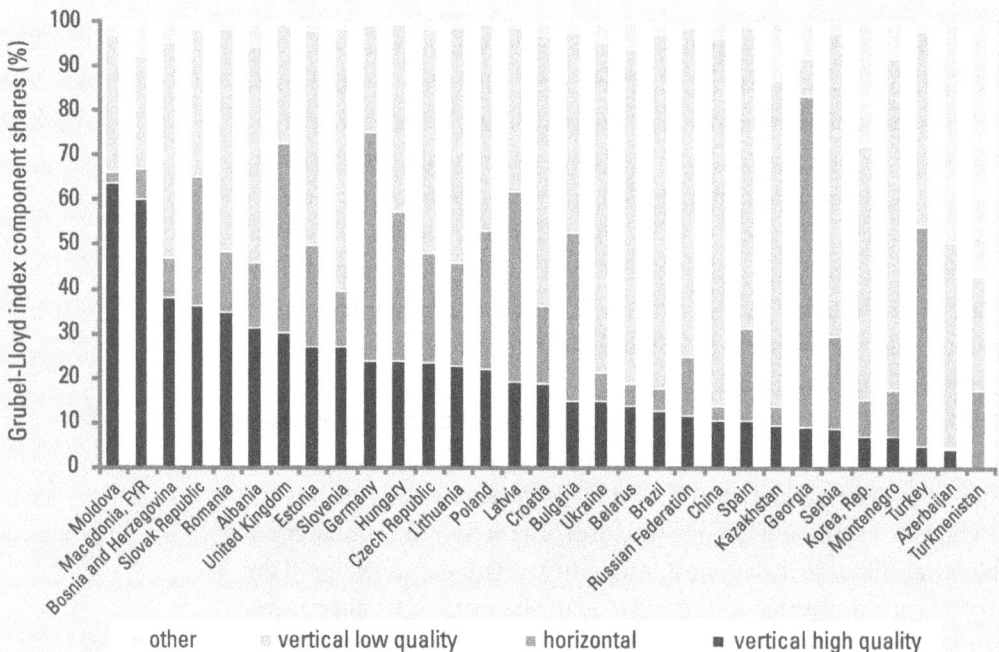

Source: Authors' calculations based on Eurostat Database.

Figure 2.8 breaks down the different components of the Grubel-Lloyd index. As expected, the figure shows that the two highest-income countries, Germany and the United Kingdom, have the highest combined vertical high-quality and horizontal Grubel-Lloyd components, thus indicating they compete on quality in intraindustry trade with the EU. Generally, new EU member states fall not far behind those two countries and are split roughly in half in terms of whether they compete more on quality or price in intraindustry trade. Hungary, Poland, and the Slovak Republic are the top performers among ECA countries.

The Balkan countries are not far behind new EU member states in intraindustry trade quality. Most CIS countries clearly compete on price in the little intraindustry trade they have with the EU. Two exceptions are Georgia and Moldova.[1] The high shares of vertical high-quality trade in Moldova are mainly the result of aircraft and spacecraft products.[2] Although Georgia and Moldova have a high ratio of vertical high-quality and horizontal trade to low-quality trade, intraindustry trade accounts for a much smaller share of total trade than for the new EU member states.

The small share of horizontal intraindustry trade in a number of CIS countries suggests the coexistence of two opposite modes of competition—one dominant mode focusing clearly on vertical low-quality trade and another on vertical high-quality trade—with no continuum between the two. This is the case of Belarus, Kazakhstan, Russia, and Ukraine. This bipolar behavior could be due to a number of elite firms operating at world standards but with limited quality spillovers to the rest of the economy. By contrast, a number of new EU member states have relatively higher shares of both vertical high-quality and horizontal intraindustry trade.

---

1. For disentanglement of intraindustry trade into horizontal and vertical trade, a country's import and export unit values are required on each product category. Azerbaijan, Georgia, and Turkmenistan are some of the few cases in which a significant amount of unit values are missing; thus, in some product categories, the type of intraindustry trade could not be identified. This resulted in a significant residual position. Hence, intraindustry trade figures for Azerbaijan, Georgia, and Turkmenistan should be interpreted with caution. Georgia's high shares in horizontal trade are mostly due to two-way trade in fuels. Calculating intraindustry trade, excluding the coke and refined petrol industry, reveals that horizontal trade barely accounts for 10 percent of Georgia's total intraindustry trade.

2. Between 1999 and 2002, Moldovan exports in the aircraft and spacecraft industry represented a share of less than 1 percent, whereas between 2003 and 2005, they accounted for more than 13 percent of total manufacturing exports. Finally, in 2006, they dropped back to less than 1 percent. These figures could be unreliable.

Quality Strategies

CIS countries compete mostly on price and in price-dominated industries, whereas new EU member states compete on quality in quality-dominated industries. Quality upgrading can be achieved by (a) moving away from price-competitive industries and toward quality-competitive industries (interindustry upgrading), or (b) increasing the share of high-quality exports among trade of differentiated products (intraindustry upgrading). A possible indicator for a country's interindustry upgrading position is the difference between the share of exports in quality-dominated sectors and the share of exports in price-dominated sectors (net RQE). A possible indicator for a country's intraindustry upgrading position is the vertical high-quality Grubel-Lloyd indicator (Aiginger 2000). In this subsection, the interindustry and intraindustry quality positions are compared across countries.

As can be seen in figure 2.9, Germany and the United Kingdom are among the leading countries in product quality competition according to net RQE as well as high-quality vertical intraindustry trade. Conversely, Kazakhstan, Montenegro, and Serbia have large export shares in industries dominated by price competition and low shares of high-quality vertical intraindustry trade in total trade. Although a positive and statistically significant relation exists between both quality strategies, some countries take rather different positions in these two quality indicators. For instance, FYR Macedonia and the Slovak Republic have high shares of high-quality vertical intraindustry trade,[3] with small negative net RQE values. However, Korea's net RQE indicators are relatively large in comparison to its position in high-quality vertical intraindustry trade. One possible reason for this is that Asian Tigers like Korea initially implemented policies that encouraged their exports while restricting imports (Tichy 2008). Conversely, they also focused on industrial and technology policy.

Figure 2.9 reveals a pattern between regions. Compared with other ECA countries, new EU member states generally have slightly negative or slightly positive net RQEs and high shares of vertical high-quality intraindustry trade. That is, they export in a relatively larger share of industries that are dominated by quality, and a relatively high share of their exports is in high-quality market segments. Balkan countries are more evenly distributed between those that export in industries dominated by price and quality and those that export lesser-quality products than are the new member states. With the exception of Moldova, CIS countries export mostly in industries that compete on price, and they export few products in high-quality segments.

---

3. This might result from production in multinational industries.

FIGURE 2.9
Quality Positions, 2005

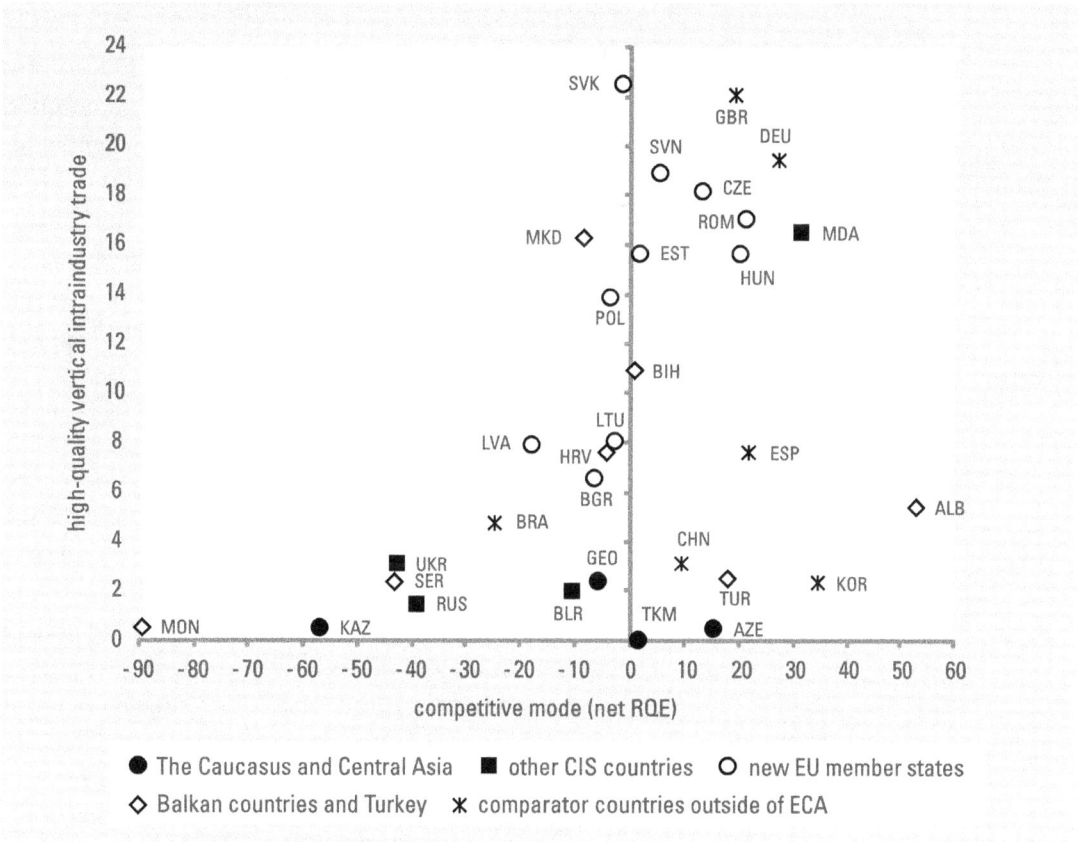

Source: Authors' calculations based on Eurostat Database.
Note: Intraindustry trade excludes NACE (Nomenclature Statistique des Activités Économiques dans la Communauté Européenne, or Statistical Classification of Economic Activities in the European Community) 17, 18, and 19. Net RQE = share of exports in quality elastic industries minus the share of exports in price elastic industries.

Quality Rankings in ECA

This section presents a system to monitor the product quality position of ECA countries based on a set of six quality indicators presented in the study:

- XUV, the export unit value

- RUV2, the weighted mean of the export unit values relative to import unit values

- RUV3, the weighted mean of the export unit values relative to average world export unit values

- High RQE, the share of exports in quality-dominated (high RQE) industries

- HGL, the horizontal component of the Grubel-Lloyd index for intra-industry trade

- VHGL, the vertical high-quality component of the Grubel-Lloyd index for intraindustry trade

Each indicator provides only a narrow aspect of quality in ECA countries, such as outputs, structure, diffusion across industries, and potential for upgrading, and each must be analyzed with the other indicators to depict a complete picture.[4] Table 2.3 summarizes the above indicators with a value related to the region's average for many ECA countries for which the complete data was available. Countries displayed in bold have above-average potential to upgrade quality as measured by the *high-RQE* indicator.

Table 2.3 shows that the Czech Republic, Hungary, Poland, and the Slovak Republic outperform their peers. All of their quality indicators depicted large above-average levels in 2005. Latvia and Lithuania are the worst-quality performers within the new EU member states, because the majority of their quality indicators performed below the region's average. The Balkan countries do not perform as well as the new member states with the exception of Bosnia and Herzegovina. Although Croatia has a higher per capita GDP than the rest of the Balkan countries, it scores at the bottom of that group together with Serbia. CIS countries are positioned at the lower end of the ECA quality spectrum. In fact, six CIS countries do not have a single indicator above the region's average. Only

---

4. For a similar approach, see Aiginger (2000).

TABLE 2.3
Country Quality Rankings: Number of Above-Average Indicators, 2005

Country	Number of quality indicators[a] above ECA average
Czech Republic, Hungary, Poland, Slovak Republic	6
Bosnia and Herzegovina, Slovenia, Turkey	5
Estonia; Macedonia, FYR; Romania	4
Bulgaria, Moldova	3
Albania, Latvia, Montenegro	2
Georgia, Croatia, Lithuania, Serbia	1
Azerbaijan, Belarus, Kazakhstan, Russian Federation, Turkmenistan, Ukraine	0

Source: Authors' calculations.
Note: Countries in bold have greater potential to upgrade quality than the sample average.
a. The six indicators are XUV, RUV2, RUV3, High RQE, HGL, and VHGL. All indicators exclude NACE (Nomenclature Statistique des Activités Économiques dans la Communauté Européenne, or Statistical Classification of Economic Activities in the European Community) 17, 18, and 19, except for High RQE. See appendix B.

Moldova distinguishes itself from the rest of the CIS group with three above-average indicators. The figures for Moldova need to be interpreted with caution, however, because these values may result from measurement inconsistencies. The Moldovan indicators show above-average levels of skill-intensive, technology-driven, and knowledge-based services that stem mainly from a large export share in the aircraft and spacecraft industry (16 percent) in 2005.[5]

What is striking in table 2.3 is a certain virtuous circle of quality upgrading. Countries in the top half of the rankings (shown in bold) are exporting in more quality-dominated industries than the sample average (that is, their *high* RQE is greater than average). In other words, countries that already are performing well on quality also have the most opportunities for intraindustry upgrading because they are exporting in the right type of industry. Conversely, countries in the bottom of the rankings have few opportunities for upgrading in the industries within which they already are exporting. In other words, they will be embedded in cycles of low quality unless they engage in interindustry upgrading by diversifying their economies.

Conclusion

The indicators analyzed throughout this chapter provide robust evidence for differences across countries and groups analyzed—independently of the set of indicators used. The new EU member states—in particular, the CEE5 countries—rank high in all quality indicators. Their exports have a significant quality content, shown by export unit values near or even above import unit values, in addition to having engaged in an interindustry and intraindustry quality-upgrading process. The new EU member states are converging toward the sophistication of exports of the old EU member states, which stands in stark contrast to the CIS countries. The Balkan countries and Turkey hold an intermediate quality position. Among other factors, a possible explanation for these cross-country disparities in the quality of their exported products to the EU is their differences in terms of incentives for adopting international quality standards. For instance, the new EU member states now have full responsibility to harmonize their standards to those of the EU (and, therefore, will enjoy subsequently larger investments from multinational firms).

---

5. As mentioned, the aircraft and spacecraft export share time-series is irregular. Between 1999 and 2002, Moldovan exports in this industry did not represent even 1 percent, while between 2003 and 2005, these exports accounted for more than 13 percent of total manufacturing exports. Finally, in 2006, they dropped back to less than 1 percent. These inconsistent results need to be interpreted with a high degree of caution.

Turkey's long and ongoing accession negotiations with the EU have also pushed it to undertake reforms and adopt compatible standards, thus making it more open and competitive. As an important EU trade partner, Turkey has enrolled in projects such as Support to the Quality Infrastructure in Turkey during 2002 and 2007, whose central goal was the elimination of technical barriers to trade between the two economic entities. In contrast, the speed of reform and standards adoption in several Balkan countries has been quite slow. One hopes that the EU Stabilization and Association Process in the western Balkan countries will result in similar positive spillovers, thus improving these countries' national quality infrastructure. The results show that the CIS countries systematically rank lowest in the set of quality indicators. As a first step toward improving the quality of their products, CIS countries could reform their national quality infrastructure and harmonize their standards.

References

Aiginger, K. 1997. "The Use of Unit Values to Discriminate between Price and Quality Competition." *Cambridge Journal of Economics* 21 (5): 571–92.

———. 2000. "Europe's Position in Quality Competition." Background Report for "The European Competitiveness Report 2000." Enterprise DG Working Paper (September 2000), European Commission, Brussels.

Bergstrand, J. H., and P. Egger. 2006. "Trade Costs and Intra-Industry Trade." *Review of World Economics (Weltwirtschaftliches Archiv)* 142 (3): 433–58.

Dulleck, U., N. Foster, R. Stehrer, and J. Wörz. 2003. "Dimensions of Quality Upgrading: Evidence for CEEC's." Working Paper 0314, Department of Economics, University of Vienna.

Fabrizio, S., D. Igan, and A. Mody. 2007. "The Dynamics of Product Quality and International Competitiveness." IMF Working Paper 07/97, International Monetary Fund, Washington, DC.

Faruq, H. 2006. "New Evidence on Product Quality and Trade." Working Paper 2006-019, Center for Applied Economics and Policy Research, Indiana University, Bloomington.

Fontagné, L., M. Freudenberg, and G. Gaulier. 2006. "A Systematic Decomposition of World Trade into Horizontal and Vertical IIT." *Review of World Economics (Weltwirtschaftliches Archiv)* 142 (3): 459–75.

Freinkman, L., E. Polyakov, and C. Revenco. 2004. "Trade Performance and Regional Integration of the CIS Countries." Working Paper 38, World Bank, Washington, DC.

Greenaway, D., R. Hine, and C. Milner. 1994. "Country-Specific Factors and the Pattern of Horizontal and Vertical Intra-Industry Trade in the UK." *Review of World Economics (Weltwirtschaftliches Archiv)* 130 (1): 77–100.

Grubel, H., and P. J. Lloyd. 1975. *Intra-Industry Trade.* London: Macmillan.

Helpman, E., and P. Krugman. 1985. *Market Structure and Foreign Trade: Increasing Returns, Imperfect Competition, and the International Economy.* Cambridge, MA: MIT Press.

Hummels, D., and P. J. Klenow. 2005. "The Variety and Quality of a Nation's Exports." *The American Economic Review* 95 (3): 704–23.

Iacovone, L., and B. S. Javorcik. 2010. "Multi-Product Exporters: Product Churning, Uncertainty, and Export Discoveries." *The Economic Journal* 120 (544): 481–99.

International Organization for Standardization (ISO). 2008. *The ISO Survey of Certifications 2007.* Geneva: ISO.

Kaminski, B. 2001. "How Accession to the European Union Has Affected External Trade and Foreign Direct Investment in Central European Economies." Policy Research Working Paper 2578, World Bank, Washington, DC.

Kaminski, B., and F. Ng. 2001. "Trade and Production Fragmentation: Central European Economies in EU Networks of Production and Marketing." Policy Research Working Paper 2611, World Bank, Washington, DC.

Kandogan, Y. 2004. "How Much Restructuring Did the Transition Countries Experience? Evidence from Quality of Their Exports." Working Paper 637, William Davidson Institute, University of Michigan, Ann Arbor.

Khandelwal, A. 2010. "The Long and Short (of) Quality Ladders." *Review of Economic Studies* 77 (4): 1450–76.

Koyota, K. 2008. "Are U.S. Exports Different from China's Exports? Evidence from Japan's Imports." Research Seminar in International Economics Working Paper 576, University of Michigan, Ann Arbor. http://ideas.repec.org/p/mie/wpaper/576.html.

Krugman, P. 1980. "Scale Economies, Product Differentiation, and the Pattern of Trade." *The American Economic Review* 70 (5): 950–59.

Krugman, P., and M. Obstfeld. 2003. *International Economics: Theory and Policy,* 6th ed. Boston: Addison-Wesley Publishing.

Kugler, M., and E. Verhoogen. 2009. "Plants and Imported Inputs: New Facts and an Interpretation." *American Economic Review* 99 (2): 501–7.

Schott, P. K. 2008. "The Relative Sophistication of Chinese Exports." *Economic Policy* 23 (53): 5–49.

Siggel, E. 2009. "Is Intra-industry Trade Driven by Comparative Advantage?" Paper prepared for the 2009 congress of the Canadian Society of Economics.

Tichy, G. 2008. "Wie mobil sind Ideen?" *WiPol Blaetter* 0308, Version 03, August.

World Economic Forum. 2009. *Global Competitiveness Report 2009–2010.* Geneva: World Economic Forum.

CHAPTER 3

The National Quality Infrastructure: Basic Framework and Role of the Government

"There is nothing more difficult to plan, more doubtful of success, nor more dangerous to manage, than the creation of a new system. For the initiator has the enmity of all who would profit by the preservation of the old institutions and merely lukewarm defenders in those who would gain by the new ones."

—Niccolo Machiavelli, *The Prince* (1515)

▹ **Most European Union (EU) and other Organisation for Economic Co-operation and Development (OECD) countries have harmonized their approaches to and basic building blocks for national quality infrastructure to reflect best practices of transparency, openness, consensus, impartiality, technical credibility, and the voluntary nature of standards. International organizations help countries harmonize their national quality infrastructure.**

▹ **Market imperfections in the provision of standardization and conformity assessment services, as well as externalities associated with quality upgrading, justify the government's role in the national quality infrastructure.**

Structure of the National Quality Infrastructure in
Market Economies

Structure

Describing products and services at the technical level and proving that they comply with those descriptions require high-level instruments, including those for standards, inspection, testing, certification, metrology, and accreditation. A variety of organizations provide such services and are included in the general framework: a national quality infrastructure (NQI).

This book defines an NQI as the public or private institutional framework required to establish and implement standardization, conformity assessment services (inspection, testing, and certification), metrology, and accreditation. These services are needed to prove that products and services meet defined requirements, as demanded by authorities (technical regulation) or the marketplace (contractually or inferred).

In many countries, conformity assessment services are increasingly being provided by private industry rather than governments, while governments retain responsibility for maintaining the fundamental factors—standards, metrology, and accreditation. The arrangement of an NQI is typically as much an issue of government policy as of market-related service provision. Table 3.1 summarizes NQI institutions and the services they provide in most countries.

These domains of the quality infrastructure are interrelated, and in most cases, the output of more than one quality infrastructure institution is required to give confidence to purchasers, users, or authorities that a product, process, or service meets expectations and requirements. Figure 3.1 illustrates the interrelationships of the various elements of an NQI.

Evolution

NQIs in many countries have followed common development paths. Governments have initially taken a leading role in establishing NQI organizations to provide the necessary technical support infrastructure for the development of the economy and industry. In most countries, when an industry has attained critical mass, NQI organizations—especially those providing conformity assessment services—migrate from government organizations providing subsidized services to commercial organizations providing services at market prices. In large, highly industrialized economies such as the United States, most NQI institutions operate in the private for-profit or nonprofit sectors.

TABLE 3.1
National Quality Infrastructure Services and Associated Institutions

Service		Description	Institutions involved
Standards		Publication of a formal document (standard), generally developed by consensus, containing the requirements that a product, process, or service should comply with. Standards are essentially voluntary, and producers can choose whether to use them. But once standards are contained in contracts or referenced in technical regulations, compliance with them becomes a legal obligation.	• National standards body • Sectoral standards development organizations • Industry standards organizations Most national standards bodies are public or nonprofit entities. Standards development organizations are mostly private but do not exist in many countries.
Conformity assessment	**Inspection**	The examination of a product design, product, process, or installation and the determination of its conformity with specific requirements or, based on professional judgment, with general requirements. Inspection is often conducted on consignments—for example, import inspection—to ensure that the entire consignment is equivalent to the product sample tested.	• Import inspection agencies • General inspection agencies These can be public or private entities.
	Testing	The determination of a product's characteristics against the requirements of the standard. Testing can vary from a nondestructive evaluation (for example, x-ray, ultrasound, pressure testing, electrical, and so forth, where the product is still fit for use) to a total destructive analysis (for example, chemical, mechanical, physical, microbiological, and so forth, where the product is no longer fit for use), or any combination thereof.	• Test laboratories • Pathology laboratories • Environmental laboratories These can be public or private laboratories.
	Certification	The formal substantiation by a certification body after an evaluation, testing, inspection, or assessment that a product, service, organization, or individual meets the requirements of a standard	• Product certification organizations • System certification organizations These can be public or private organizations.
Metrology		The science of measurement. Metrology can be subdivided into • *Scientific metrology:* the development and organization of the highest level of measurement standards • *Legal metrology:* the assurance of correctness of measurements where these have an influence on the transparency of trade, law enforcement, health, and safety • *Industrial metrology:* the satisfactory functioning of measurement instruments used in industry, production, and testing national metrology institute (NMI)	• Calibration laboratories • Legal metrology department (LMD) The NMIs are mostly public organizations, as are, by definition, the LMDs. Calibration laboratories may be public or private.
Accreditation		The activity of providing independent attestation as to the competency of an organization or individual to offer specified conformity assessment services (for example, testing, inspection, or certification)	• National accreditation body (NAB) This is usually a public or nonprofit organization.

Source: Authors' elaboration.

FIGURE 3.1

The National Quality Infrastructure

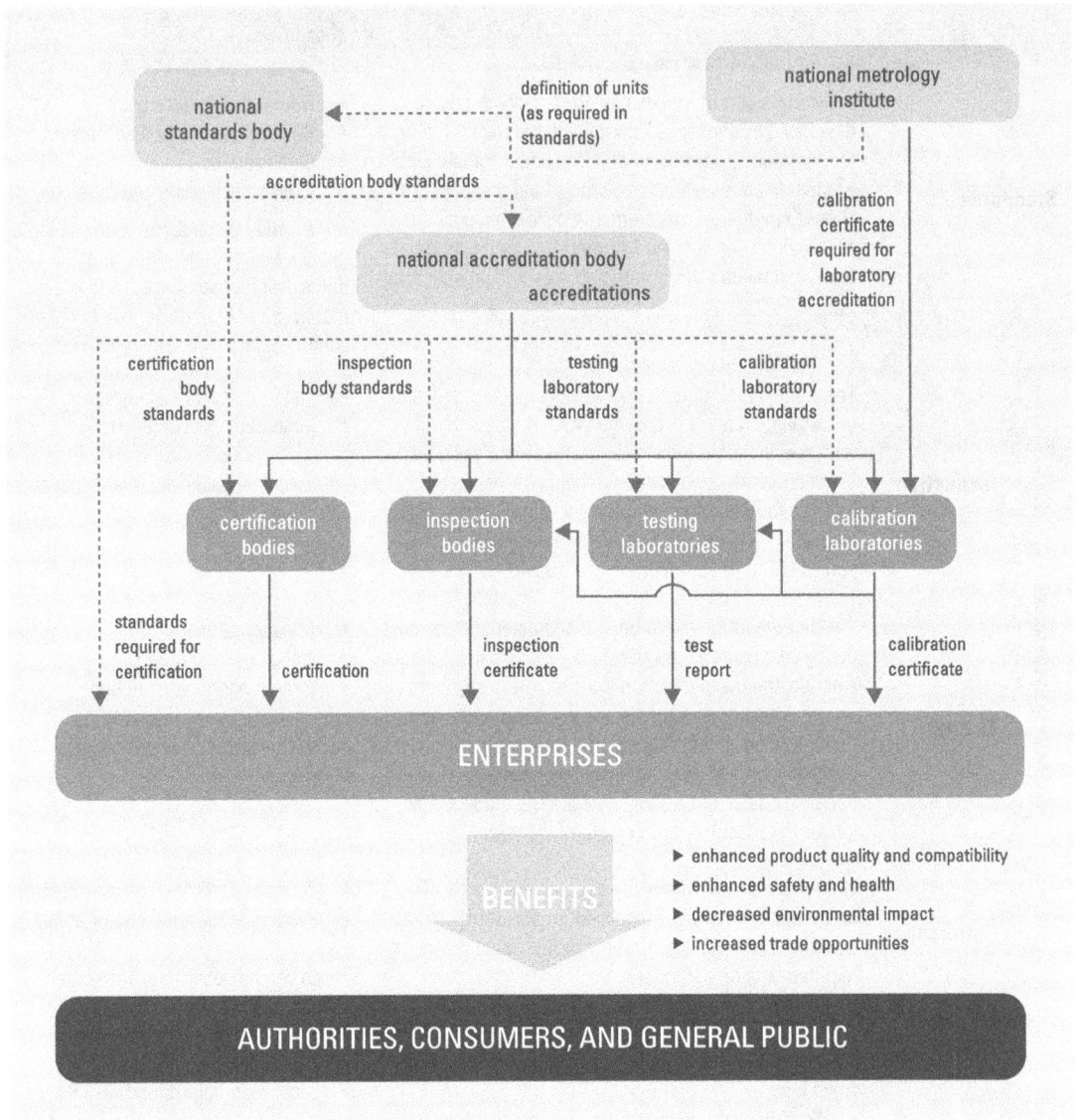

Source: Guasch and others 2007.

Standards

The next step for most countries is to establish national standards bodies. These bodies are responsible for developing and publishing national standards. They are the link to international standards organizations such as the International Organization for Standardization (ISO) and the International Electrotechnical Commission (IEC). Standards bodies are established typically by governments, but also by industry if the country is already at an advanced industrialized stage. In most developing economies, the national standards bodies (NSBs) are government or quasi-government organizations. Although a few NSBs in high-income economies obtain a large proportion of their operating funds from the sales of standards, this is not the case in middle- and low-income economies that have a weak industrial base. However, even in high-income economies, this source of revenue is coming under pressure because of the ease with which standards can be obtained on the Internet. Governments in developing economies have little choice but to remain the main source of funding for their NSBs in the foreseeable future.

Conformity assessment

The NSB also often leverages its knowledge on standards by providing testing and certification services. In fact, this is what the world's first NSB, British Standards Institution (BSI) in the United Kingdom, did by offering its Kitemark two years after being established in 1901. BSI still offers certification and testing services, as do other NSBs in high-income economies, but in each case, there is a clear administrative separation between the two activities.

In some countries, conformity assessment services are heavily subsidized by governments to support industrial development. When industry has developed to the point where it can and should pay market prices for the services, government conformity assessment services are typically run on a purely commercial basis and private industry is given scope to establish itself and develop. In the Organisation for Economic Co-operation and Development (OECD) and European Union (EU) economies, many governments ultimately withdraw from providing conformity assessment services, retaining the responsibility in only very specific and strategically important situations where private industry cannot make the necessary investments.

There are two viewpoints regarding the provision of conformity assessment services by standardization bodies. On the one hand, critics argue that testing and certification should be separated from standards development to ensure that standards bodies stay focused on their primary (but not very lucrative) activity of standards development. On the other hand, the rationale for offering these services through standards bodies in developing countries is that their industry is not at a stage of development where these services can be offered through the market. In developing countries, this latter approach can provide a more effective "one-stop shop" approach and give more visibility to the national standards bodies. This approach also limits the number of directors, other executives, and buildings that need to be funded. Another reason for adopting this approach is that the little technical expertise that is available is better used if standards development and testing are combined. However, problems can arise later when industry has developed and the standards bodies try to retain their monopoly on testing. This situation is where governments have to be very clear—standards bodies should not be given any sort of protection to be the sole providers of conformity assessment services—and market developments should be encouraged.

In EU and OECD countries, NSBs are sometimes involved in certification and testing. However, they are never involved in activities linked to technical regulations or mandatory standards, such as inspection and market surveillance. In these countries, it is believed that giving the NSBs a role in the latter activities would ultimately lead to conflicts of interest, that is, industry would come to see NSBs as regulators and not as organizations established to support business. Therefore, providing such mix of activities should be avoided by governments, and if the mix exists, steps should be taken to separate the regulatory functions from the NSBs.

Metrology

Centuries ago, many governments established weights and measures departments, the precursors to fully fledged legal metrology departments. These weights and measures departments established control systems for measuring the equipment used in trade, protecting consumers from exploitation by unscrupulous merchants. Until national metrology institutes (NMIs) were established, weights and measures departments were usually also responsible for national measurement standards. In all countries, governments retain the final authority over NMIs, national measurement standards, and legal metrology. But national calibration systems can become more commercial as reliable private calibration laboratories are established and provide calibration services that are traceable to the NMIs' measurement standards.

Accreditation

The next phase in the development of an NQI involves establishing a national accreditation body. Figure 3.2 displays a timeline of the United Kingdom's NQI. In the United Kingdom, although some form of NMI probably predates medieval times and although the first NSB was established at the beginning of the past century, a national accreditation system is a relatively new concept that appeared only in 1981. This is because in most industrialized countries, conformity assessment activities increas-

FIGURE 3.2

Evolution of the British National Quality Infrastructure

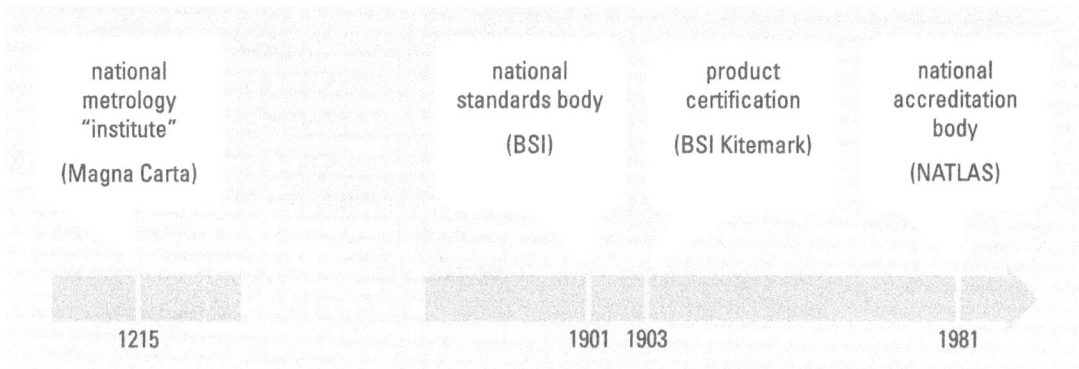

| national metrology "institute" (Magna Carta) | | national standards body (BSI) | product certification (BSI Kitemark) | national accreditation body (NATLAS) |

| 1215 | | 1901 1903 | | 1981 |

Sources: Campion 1985; BSI, http://www.bsigroup.com/en/About-BSI/About-BSI-Group/BSI-History.
Note: NATLAS = National Testing Laboratory Accreditation Scheme.

ingly migrated from the public to the private domain during the course of the past century, and some type of independent verification of their technical competence became necessary.

Accreditation services are provided on a noncompetitive basis worldwide. When a national accreditation body has been established and has been internationally recognized, it typically retains a monopoly over its activities, with a few exceptions where several accreditation bodies are responsible for different areas of accreditation. Because accreditation plays such an important role in determining the technical competency of service providers, including those that act in the regulated domain, governments like to keep oversight of national accreditation bodies. Private accreditation bodies are therefore very much the exception, and many that may have started their operations as nonprofit organizations have been converted into organizations of public law or semigovernment organizations.

Industrial quality services

The final step in the development of an NQI involves establishing a total quality management industry, with consulting and training services. This step is frequently accompanied by the establishment of the appropriate total quality awards, such as the Baldrige Awards in the United States. Unless the NQI has been properly established in the country, and industry is committed to and practices quality, it is debatable whether quality awards are useful as a recognition criterion. Figure 3.3 depicts the typical pattern of development of the NQI in EU and OECD economies.

Integration of the NQI and the Technical Regulation Framework

The integration of the NQI and the technical regulation regime is an issue that occupies political leaders in developing and transition countries. The question is how to organize the many elements of an NQI while considering the financial and labor constraints of a country and promoting quality in the economy. As a further complication, another question is how to lessen the burden of technical regulations on the competitiveness of the productive sector without compromising the safety and health of society and the environment and, at the same time, to ensure that the authorities do not inadvertently lose control over the situation and yet comply with international obligations.

Obviously, no country can afford to establish and maintain two quality infrastructures, one for the regulated domain and one for the non-regulated (voluntary) domain. A typical *best practice* arrangement for developing and transition economies is shown in figure 3.4. It should be stressed, however, that this arrangement does not constitute the only

FIGURE 3.3

Typical Evolution and Funding of the NQI in EU and OECD Economies

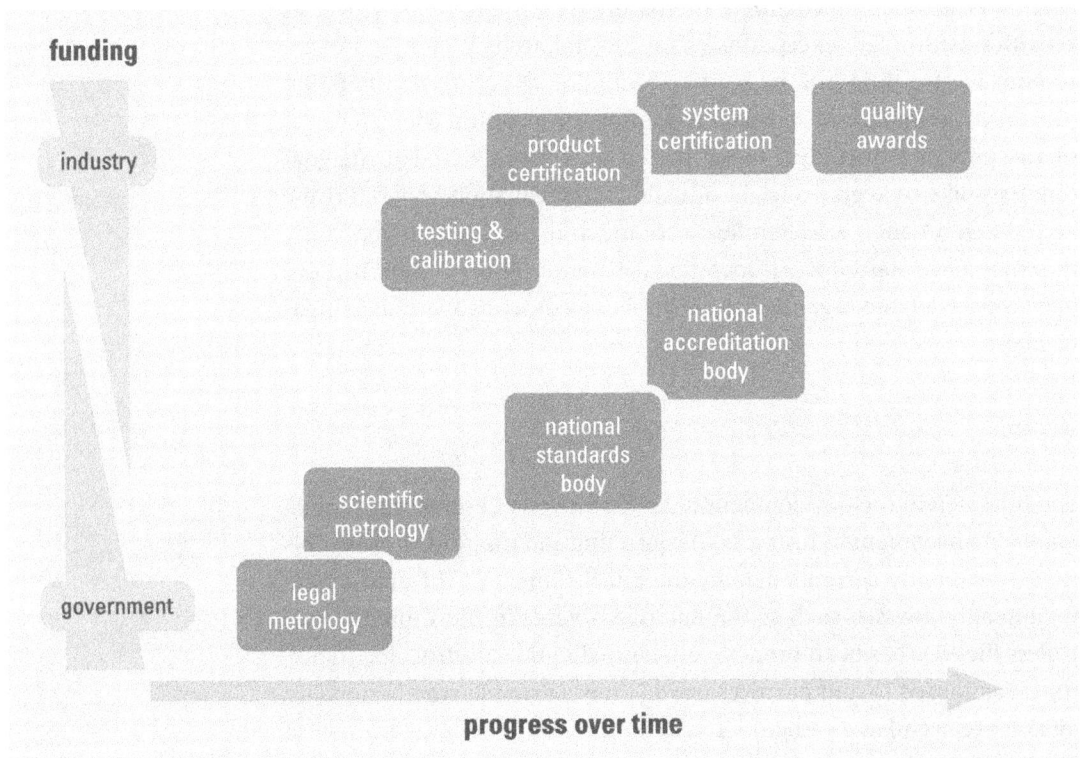

Source: Authors' elaboration.

solution, but it has been shown to be a useful point of departure for a national debate. Similar systems have been implemented in a number of countries that have recently re-engineered their systems, including Brazil, the Czech Republic, Costa Rica, the Kyrgyz Republic, and South Africa. Figure 3.4 shows that the NQI institutions fall under the jurisdiction of a government body responsible for economic competitiveness, such as a ministry of economy or a ministry of industry, rather than the jurisdiction of a regulatory agency. However, intense cooperation occurs between the NQI institutions and the public regulatory bodies. This configuration ensures that the NQI is used as an independent instrument to support technical regulations and not as a revenue-generating body for the state.

International and Regional Coordination

Since the late 19th century, specialized international and, later, regional organizations have been established to help national NQI organizations develop common standards and deliver their services to facilitate trade, coordinate activities, exchange information and knowledge, and conduct peer evaluations to achieve mutual recognition. These organizations now play a major role in establishing the common guidelines and standards currently used in many NQIs, including in developing economies. In the past few decades, there has in fact been a strong trend toward harmonization of the NQIs: in many high-income countries, most official standards are international or regional standards and all major NQI institutions organize their activities, train their staff, and offer services in ways that conform to international standards. Nonetheless, NQIs in all economies still retain some unique idiosyncrasies to better serve their specific national needs.

The international, regional, and national structure of the quality infrastructure is provided in figure 3.5. In brief, there are well-established and influential international organizations in the areas of standardization, metrology, and accreditation. The main international standardization organizations develop standards for industry but also for the management systems of accreditation bodies and for accreditation, and thus, are really relevant to this aspect of the NQI.

The major international quality infrastructure organizations have, over time, developed common rules and guidelines in their respective domains. However, in each domain they have used a different approach to international integration. Harmonization of standards at the international and regional levels has occurred through a consensus-based bottom-up process. In metrology, measurement traceability is more of a top-down approach, where the correct measurement results are not

FIGURE 3.4

Typical Organizational Relationships of the NQI and Technical Regulation System

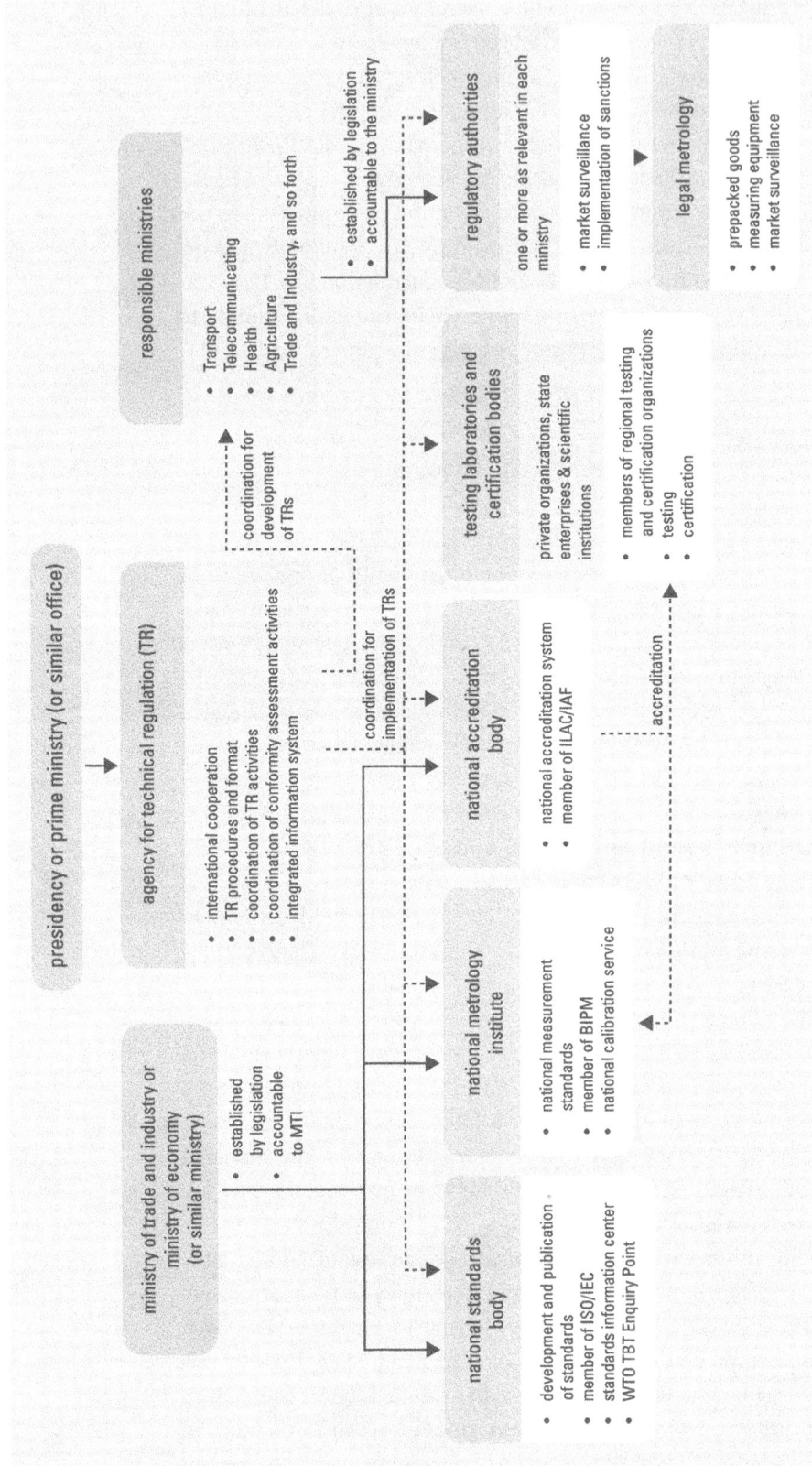

Source: Authors' elaboration.

Note: Dotted lines denote coordination relationships. Continuous lines denote oversight relationships. BIPM = International Bureau of Weights and Measures; IAF = International Accreditation Forum; ILAC = International Laboratory Accreditation Cooperation; MTI = Ministry of Trade and Industry; TBT = technical barrier to trade; WTO = World Trade Organization.

FIGURE 3.5
Structure of International and Regional Quality Infrastructure Organizations

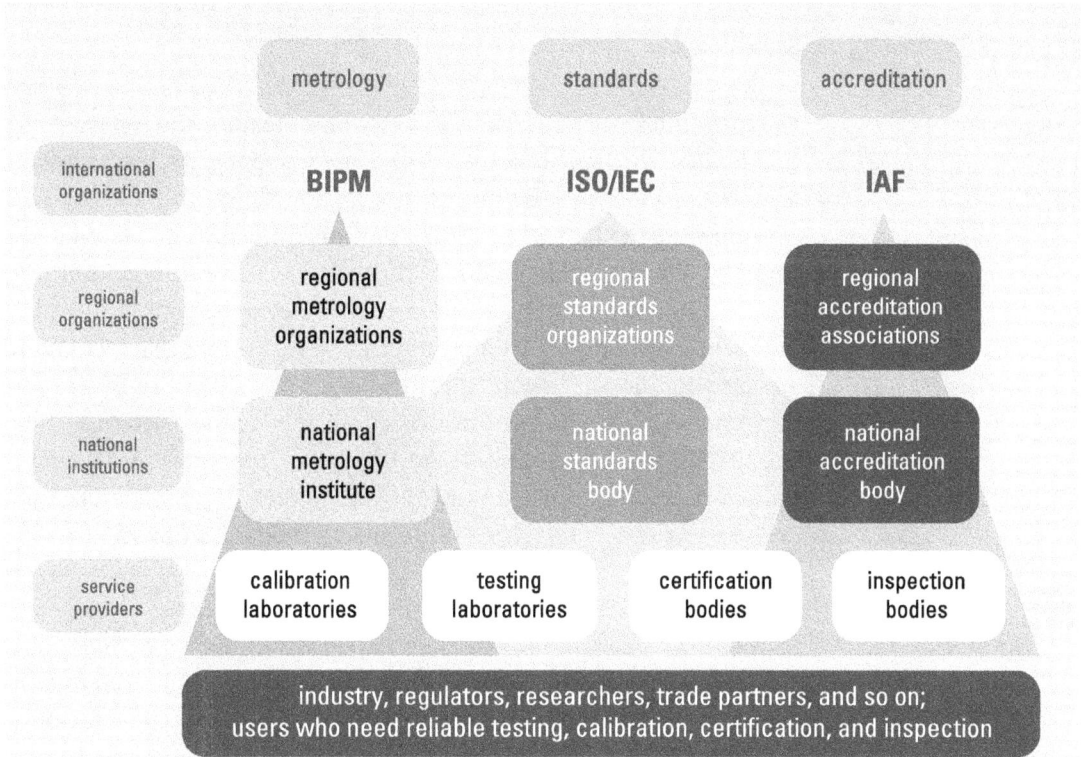

Source: Authors.
Note: BIPM = International Bureau of Weights and Measures; IAF = International Accreditation Forum.

achieved through consensus but strictly through a hierarchy of physical standards and interlaboratory comparisons. However, the results of measurement comparisons are transparent, published, and accessible through the Internet. The international recognition of accreditation bodies is based neither on hierarchy nor on consensus, but rather on the mutual evaluation of equivalence of implementation. In this case, evaluation results are published on the Internet and are accessible to all interested parties worldwide.

The regional organizations mainly use the same criteria, guidelines, or best practices as the international organizations but concentrate on regional harmonization, coordination, and strengthening. When they have demonstrated their competence to the international organizations, they take over some of the functions of the latter at the regional level, including functions such as laboratory intercomparisons or peer evaluations. This is the case with the European metrology and accreditation organizations. In such cases, regional recognition leads to worldwide recognition and does not require another higher-level evaluation.

A brief snapshot of the structure of the international system in standardization, metrology, and accreditation follows.

Standards

The main international organization in this domain is the International Organization for Standardization. There are other international standards organizations, but they do not cover such a broad spectrum as ISO. An exception might be the International Electrotechnical Commission, which works very closely with ISO. Other well-known organizations, such as the Codex Alimentarius Commission, contrast with ISO because they develop recommendations for technical regulations that focus more on harmonization between regulatory bodies.

Some regional standards organizations relevant to Eastern Europe and Central Asia (ECA) include the European Committee for Standardization; the European Committee for Electrotechnical Standardization; and the EuroAsian Interstate Council for Standardization, Metrology, and Certification.

NSBs usually adopt international standards when these are relevant for their economies. In cases of specific interest or strong economic rationale, they develop their own new standards with the intention of later introducing these standards at the regional and international levels so that they can be recognized worldwide as, for example, ISO standards.

Metrology

At the international level, metrology is governed by an intergovernmental treaty—the Metre Convention—signed in 1875. Signatories to the Metre Convention recognize the International Bureau of Weights and Measures (BIPM) as the highest authority in terms of scientific metrology. BIPM provides the basis for a single system of measurement throughout the world under the International System of Units (SI), widely known as the metric system. It acts as the custodian of the highest (most accurate) measurement standards worldwide (mass and time) and coordinates international comparisons of national measurement standards. Since 1999, the BIPM administers an International Committee for Weights and Measures Mutual Recognition Arrangement (CIPM MRA) for national measurement standards and for calibration and measurement certificates issued by NMIs. Since then, the CIPM MRA has been signed by the representatives of 74 institutes and covers another 123 institutes designated by the signatory bodies.

The regional metrology organizations have harmonized their activities with the BIPM system. The two recognized regional metrology organizations of relevance to ECA are the European Association of National Metrology Institutes and the Euro-Asian Cooperation of National Metrological Institutions.

Accreditation

The two principal international organizations involved in accreditation are the International Accreditation Forum (IAF) for certification and inspection bodies and the International Laboratory Accreditation Cooperation (ILAC) for laboratories. Both use the same criteria (ISO standards) as guidelines for the operation of a national accreditation body for their member countries (ISO 2004). In OECD and EU economies, national accreditation bodies (NABs) perform accreditations in compliance with harmonized ISO standards and guidelines. ILAC and IAF use peer evaluation to judge the technical competence of the accreditation bodies and provide them with a mutual recognition arrangement (ILAC MRA) or, in the case of IAF, a multilateral recognition arrangement (IAF MLA). Both arrangements (MRA and MLA) are equivalent concerning procedures and recognition.

Regional accreditation organizations aim to harmonize, interpret, and implement accreditation standards and guidelines. When the regional organizations have developed a firm structure in line with ILAC or IAF and have demonstrated their own technical capability through active and recognized membership, their MRAs become recognized by the international bodies. The main recognized regional organizations of relevance to ECA are European co-operation for Accreditation, Pacific Accreditation Cooperation, and Asia Pacific Laboratory Accreditation Cooperation.

Rationale for Public Intervention

A National Quality Infrastructure Cannot Exist without Government Support

As mentioned earlier, there are no countries where a functioning quality infrastructure has developed without government support. Even in a large, high-income economy with strong business associations and a thriving demand for quality services, such as the United States, the government provides extensive financial resources for metrology. And in the vast majority of countries, accreditation to international standards is not profitable. In some cases, standardization bodies are self-financed, but this income is usually derived from activities other than standardization, such as certification. In most countries, metrology, accreditation, and standardization institutions are government owned. When these institutions operate as foundations or nonprofit entities, governments provide support through official legal recognition of their monopoly areas. Although conformity assessment services are typically provided by private entities, the success of their market depends on public support for metrology, accreditation, and standardization.

This section first presents a rationale for, at minimum, *horizontal* government support for quality upgrading in the economy. It then examines the rationale for government intervention in each of the areas of the NQI: standards, conformity assessment, metrology, and accreditation. In brief, three sets of justifications can be grouped as follows:

- Externalities are involved in quality upgrading, and certain functions of the quality infrastructure can be considered public goods.

- The government itself requires the quality infrastructure for its own regulatory functions.

- The NQI is an important element of trade policy.

Government Can Foster Economic Competitiveness by Supporting Quality Upgrading

The arguments presented in chapter 1 of this book on the role of export quality in economic development do not pretend to resolve whether the government should promote measures to produce particular high-quality goods or particular goods with high potential for quality upgrading. However, the various arguments in favor or against, taken together, do seem to justify at least broad measures of public support for quality upgrading.

First, although chapter 1 establishes that diversification is desirable for growth, diversification, more often than not, involves quality upgrading in some sectors. Diversification can be seen as a public good because it decreases macroeconomic stability, but no single private sector actor has incentives to diversify into sectors that may be less profitable in the short run than the dominant economic sector. Diversification involves producing completely new types of goods for which firms may not yet have developed the capacity to meet minimum quality standards. Chapter 1 also shows that the rise of buyer-driven global value chains has increased the importance of standards in global trade, even for goods that compete on price. And meeting those standards often requires elements like certification bodies, testing laboratories, and calibration laboratories. Increasing diversification may also mean entering new sectors that compete on quality, which warrants further government support for quality upgrading.

Second, chapter 1 also discusses how externalities were involved in conducting quality-intensive tasks. Despite whether the assumption is that the government or the market is best suited to discover these tasks, both cases warrant, at minimum, horizontal government support measures that make quality upgrading possible in the face of market externalities. Many manufacturing tasks with high learning externalities rely on accurate and precise measurements. Such measurements, in turn, rely on national measurement standards and a functioning metrology system.

Finally, chapter 1 also points out that many factors play a positive role in quality upgrading that only the government is equipped to do, because each can be considered a public good. These include providing education, investing in supportive technological infrastructure, lowering barriers to foreign direct investment and trade, and improving the regulatory framework.

Small and Medium Enterprises Face Financial, Knowledge, and Expertise Barriers When Upgrading Their Products, Processes, or Services

Another justification for measures that support quality involves the difficulties faced by small and medium enterprises (SMEs) in quality upgrading in the face of innumerable market and system failures. In most ECA countries, SMEs make up the bulk of companies. SMEs also provide employment for most of the economically active population. But SMEs also tend to lag on technology and quality with respect to large firms.

Quality upgrading can be expensive (box 3.1). It can involve acquiring new equipment, calibrating the equipment, hiring consultants to implement quality systems, purchasing standards, training staff members, or even hiring new specialized staff members. Thus, lack of financing can be a barrier to SMEs, and for a number of well-known reasons, SMEs find it more difficult to access bank loans than do large firms. In addition, it is difficult to obtain financing for investment in something intangible, such as a quality management system. Strong coordination failures in some countries imply that SMEs will be unlikely to pool resources to seek knowledge or technology or to build the testing laboratories that will enable them to upgrade their quality together.

Limited expertise is another major gap. Quality upgrading is not something that can be learned solely by reading a standard. It involves tacit knowledge acquired through learning by doing. It also involves technical skills related to measurement, for example. Limited knowledge is also a gap. SMEs often have a difficult time diagnosing their needs. They may be unaware of the benefits of upgrading some of their internal processes or of opportunities to tap into new markets with products that

Quality Upgrading: An Expensive Endeavor

An Albanian company produces pasteurized milk with a six-month shelf life. The firm currently has 40 full-time employees. The owner faced important losses in the first five years (about €500,000 per year) that were the result of inheriting inadequate technology. After completely changing its machinery in 2005 with an investment of €1.5 million and adding continuous process improvements, the company is currently operating at a profit and had sales of 10 tons per day in 2007, with total annual sales doubling since 2005. But improving quality to reach EU quality standards will require even more investments. The company employed an international specialist in the milk sector to recommend changes to the entire process line, which, after just six months, led to a decrease in the rate of defective products from 20 percent to 1 percent (Tetra Pak average is 2 percent) and a fall in costs of 7 percent. The consultant is now helping the company ensure that its products reach EU quality standards through very specific improvements in its processes and workforce practices (assigning specific tasks to each worker) and supervising a €150,000 investment in a more advanced testing laboratory.

Source: World Bank case studies.

meet certain international standards. Information and a dearth of complementary private sources of knowledge in the economy may simply prevent SMEs from knowing what to upgrade or how to upgrade their quality.

Public financial support, technical support, and awareness-raising and procurement programs can be used to support quality improvements and compliance with standards and technical regulations in the target markets of SMEs. These types of programs are found in a wide range of countries, from high-income economies such as the United States and Singapore to middle-income countries such as Turkey and Croatia to low-income countries such as Kenya.

Market Imperfections Justify a Government Role in the Development and Diffusion of Standards to Support Industrial Competitiveness

Chapter 1 reviews the many economic benefits of standards. Standards can be used to lower transaction costs in the economy as a whole and gain economies of scale. They also diffuse information on technology and markets.

Leaving standardization to markets alone can result in suboptimal outcomes related to the public good nature of standards. For example, it can lead to the underprovision of standards—particularly in developing countries that lack a strong tradition of industry associations. It can also lead to the overprovision of standards, and excess market standards can have negative economic effects.

The government's role in addressing the underprovision of standards rests on the public good characteristics of formal voluntary standards. Formal voluntary standards are nonrivalrous because anyone can benefit from them without diminishing their utility to others. They are nonexcludable because, once created, anyone can use them. Hence, as with other public goods, the free market is unlikely to create the optimal amount of standards. In some cases, multiple market standards simply reflect consumer preferences, but in others, coordination failures occur in adoption of a unified standard. Individual economic actors will be unwilling to take a leadership role in creating formal, nonproprietary voluntary standards unless they dominate the market. And industry consortia are often subject to free-rider problems in which some participants seek to benefit from a standard while minimizing their contributions to creating and maintaining it.

Thus, the government can act as a catalyst for standardization by supporting the establishment, through legal or financial means, of standardization bodies. A single national standardization body, rather than multiple sector-based institutions, can also create administrative efficiency and facilitate coordination among stakeholders.

Governments can also help address the overprovision of standards. In some cases, market forces lead to the wrong kinds of standards, such as the technical content of a standard that imposes too many constraints on innovation. Producers may have difficulties adapting new technologies to existing standards. Standards can also undermine competition if only one or a few companies can internalize their benefits or control their content, as when the contents of a standard cover technological areas for which only a limited number of firms have property rights, exclusive knowledge, or exclusive resources to use. NSBs can help revise or replace obsolete, proprietary, or suboptimal standards. They can also ensure that the standardization process benefits all of society by including small firms, consumer groups, and nonprofit organizations.

Metrology Is a Public Good That Requires Government Investments

In most countries, governments provide support for national scientific and legal metrology infrastructure. Some countries support industrial metrology as well. Support for metrology can be in the form of legal recognition of the NMI's official role in an economy, diplomatic support by signing international treaties such as the Metre Convention, and financial support for fixed and operational costs of maintaining internationally recognized metrological facilities. High-income economies often spend up to 0.01 percent of their gross domestic product on NMIs (CIPM 2003; Quinn and Kovalevsky 2005). In the United States, NMIs received about US$500 million in support from the government in the past few years.[1] NMIs also fund part of their activities through the fees they charge for calibration, consulting, and research and development (R&D) services. However, in high-income countries where the NMIs focus on science rather than on industrial development, fees for services account for a minority of the NMI budgets.

NMIs provide public goods that should be supported by the state because they essentially help to solve market failures associated with R&D, such as spillovers, coordination failures, and systemic failures. Market failures leading to private sector underinvestment in R&D and knowledge diffusion are well-known and have been the basis of public funding policies for decades (Nelson 1959; Arrow 1962). An NMI is essentially an R&D institute that specializes in developing measurement standards and instruments (in the case of high-income countries) or in reverse engineering them and diffusing the knowledge of their accuracy through traceability in the economy (in the case of developing countries). There is little appropriability in metrology, because of the difficulty in patenting or copyrighting the use of a measurement unit in the economy.

Moreover, the science behind metrology and the management of metrological facilities require significant economies of scale, scope, and learning that cannot be performed individually by each economic actor. Although business associations sometimes do pool resources to form a critical mass and invest in common technological infrastructure, this is not always guaranteed; businesses and their shareholders usually want quick returns on investments, in contrast to governments, which can invest in infrastructure with an extended timeframe.

Accreditation Can Be Seen as a Public Good Because It Allows for Creation of a Reliable Market of Conformity Assessment and Calibration Bodies, Which in Turn Allow Firms to Compete on Quality

So how, why, and to what extent should governments support a national accreditation system? Governments can support accreditation in a number of ways. They can enact legislation to officially recognize the NAB and define its responsibilities. They can provide financing to the NAB. Some governments even define the structure, activities, and governance of the

1. See the National Institute of Standards and Technology (NIST) budget on the NIST Web site, http://www.nist.gov/index.html.

NAB through legislation, but this practice can reduce the political independence of the NAB. In recent decades, in very few countries NABs have evolved on their own through market forces. Most have received some form of support from their governments.

An important reason that countries support accreditation is the high fixed and learning costs of setting up an accreditation system. Most national markets are too small to make accreditation an attractive investment opportunity for the private sector. And a critical mass of accreditations is required to raise awareness of accreditation and to decrease the average cost of accreditation, but fixed costs are high. Thus, without an initial large pool of clients, a national accreditation system cannot take off on its own. In many countries, governments commit to subsidize the setup phases of the accreditation system, but NABs are expected to become self-financing in the medium to long term. However, with the exception of countries that have large markets, such as the United States, accreditation is not usually financially self-sufficient and depends on government subsidies (UNIDO 2003). An estimate of revenues and expenses of accreditation bodies in Europe shows that the critical mass of accredited bodies needed to achieve cost recovery is between 100 and 250 clients (figure 3.6). Using the number of ISO 9001 certificates as a proxy for

FIGURE 3.6

Calculation of Estimated Costs and Revenues in European Accreditation Bodies

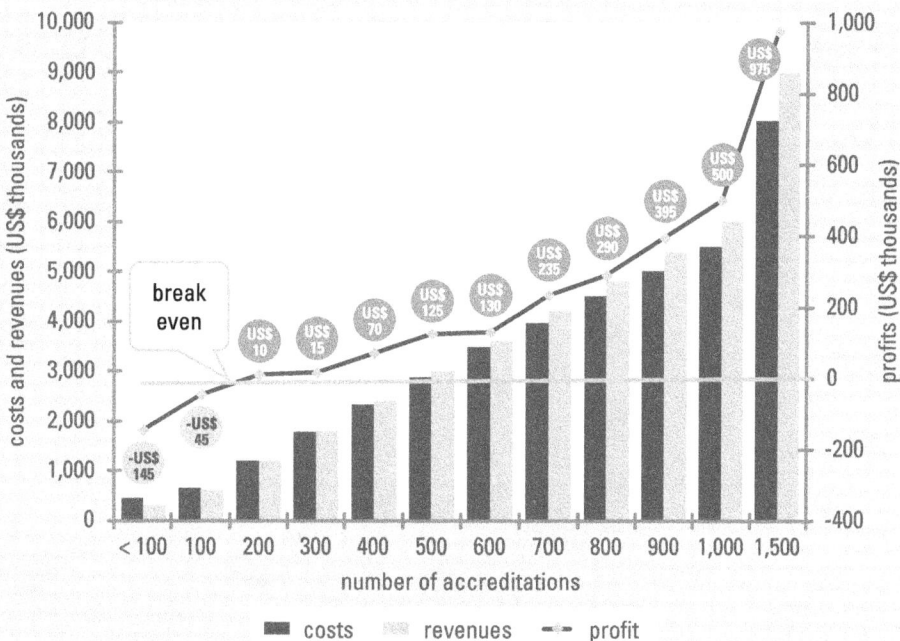

Source: Authors' calculations.

the demand for conformity assessment services in the market, figure 3.7 shows a roughly linear relationship between number of accreditations and demand in European countries. The figure suggests that a critical mass of 100 to 250 accreditations requires roughly 1,600 to 4,000 ISO 9001 certificates in a country. Many ECA countries currently find themselves behind both measures of this threshold because of their small market size or their weak industrial base.

Hence, investing in accreditation needs to be justified by an adequate current or future demand for accreditation from certification bodies and testing and calibration laboratories, or at least a demand for conformity assessment services from domestic firms and organizations. Given the high costs of setting up an accreditation system, some developing countries have decided to provide accreditation services by engaging in agreements with foreign accreditation bodies. This practice must start with the recognition of the other country's accreditation system.

FIGURE 3.7

Relationship between Number of Accreditations and ISO 9001 Certificates in Europe, 2005

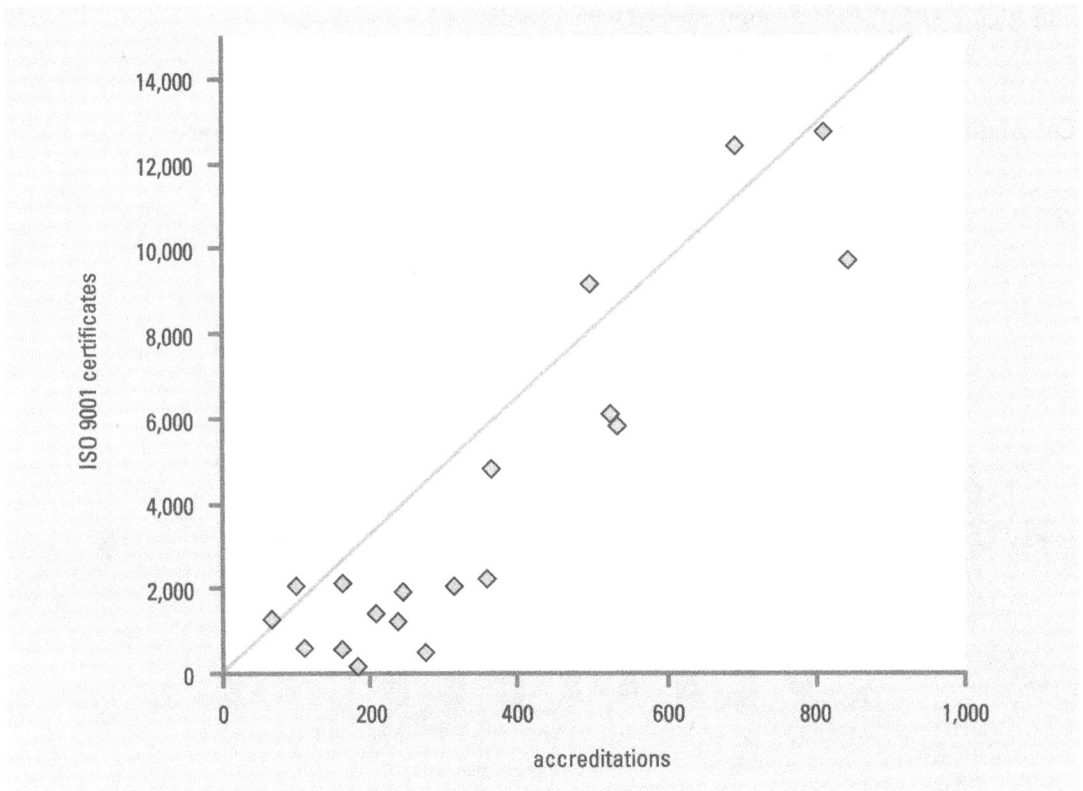

Sources: ISO 2007; European co-operation for Accreditation.

Government Investments in the National Quality Infrastructure Can Also Be Justified by Its Use in Enforcing Government Regulations

The notion that two separate systems are required—one for the authorities and one for the marketplace—can lead to unnecessary duplication and inefficiency, and the trend has been for countries to opt for a single NQI. Civil servants are poorly equipped to develop standards of their own, so technical regulations often refer to standards developed by the NSB to protect the public from potentially dangerous products or to help safeguard the environment. Governments have a vested interest in supporting standardization bodies because they can rely on these bodies to develop standards for public use.

The development and enforcement of legislation and regulations based on metrology require some form of scientific basis that is provided by NMIs. NMIs help enforce legislation and regulations by supporting the legal metrology functions of the state. They are the custodians of reference standards and define the units that will be referred to in the legislation. Moreover, to be credible, measurements made by public legal metrology organizations should be traceable to NMIs.

The rationale for government support of legal metrology organizations is more straightforward. Legal metrology has a public role in reducing disputes, reducing the need for duplicating measurements, and protecting trading partners who do not have the capacity to perform their own measurements. Legal metrology functions are not only always funded by states, but also always carried out by states. This is because regulations are established by public authorities, and national legal metrology institutions have a role in their formulation and enforcement. Furthermore, legal metrology organizations cannot be self-supporting because they conduct supervision and consultancy tasks for which they cannot charge money (Marbán and Pellecer 2003).

Accreditation is also a public good from the standpoint of public safety, health, and the environment, because governments can require conformity assessment organizations wishing to provide services in such regulated areas to become accredited. Official state recognition of a *single* NAB is useful in both mandatory and voluntary markets. In the mandatory market, it creates a better investment climate by reducing the risk of having multiple accreditation bodies require accreditation from the same business and avoids confusing the market on the meaning of accreditation. Germany differs from most other countries in that it has more than 20 accreditation bodies. But in recognition of the disadvantages of such a complex structure and in anticipation of EU requirements for a single NAB, Germany is in the process of consolidating its accreditation system.

A Country's Openness to Trade Depends in Part on the Harmonization of the National Quality Infrastructure

Government intervention is also required to support the NQI's role in decreasing technical barriers to trade. Governments need to ensure that standards are not used as trade barriers for the short-term gains of some— and to the long-term detriment of society. They can also facilitate trade by all economic actors by ensuring that national infrastructure institutions operate on internationally harmonized principles and achieve mutual recognition. Moreover, international agreements such as the CIPM MRA require a single national authority in the area of scientific metrology. Only a government can designate such an authority. Most countries would be unwilling to let the fate of their openness to trade be decided by privately governed NMIs.

An internationally recognized accreditation system is a public good from an economic integration perspective. It not only allows for the protection of exports against unfair discrimination, but also is required for countries wishing to join the EU. In addition, the World Trade Organization Agreement on Technical Barriers to Trade stipulates that verified compliance—for example, through accreditation—with relevant guides or recommendations issued by international standardizing bodies shall be taken into account as an indication of adequate technical competence.[2]

The EU's *acquis communautaire* stipulates that a country's accreditation and metrology systems must be recognized internationally and its standardization system comply with European Committee for Standardization requirements. Hence, EU member or aspiring member states usually support their NABs to ensure this condition is fulfilled, because it has geopolitical implications. And finally, a number of EU New Approach and Old Approach Directives are related to metrology. They must be adopted for countries to fulfill the "Free Movement of Goods" clause of the *acquis communautaire* along with the adoption of European standards.

---

2. See Article 6 of the World Trade Organization Agreement on Technical Barriers to Trade, http://www.wto.org/english/res_e/booksp_e/analytic_index_e/tbt_01_e.htm.

References

Arrow, K. 1962. "Economic Welfare and the Allocation of Resources for Invention." In *The Rate and Direction of Inventive Activity: Economic and Social Factors*, ed. H. Groves, 609–29. Princeton: Princeton University Press.

Campion, P. J. 1985. "Laboratory Accreditation in the UK." *Measurement* 3 (3): 121–24.

CIPM (International Committee for Weights and Measures). 2003. "Evolving Needs for Metrology in Trade, Industry, and Society and the Role of the BIPM." Report of the International Committee for Weights and Measures, CIPM, Paris.

Guasch, J. L., J.-L. Racine, I. Sánchez, and M. Diop. 2007. *Quality Systems and Standards for a Competitive Edge.* Washington, DC: World Bank.

ISO (International Organization for Standardization). 2004. *ISO/IEC 17011: Conformity Assessment—General Requirements for Accreditation Bodies Accrediting Conformity Assessment Bodies.* Geneva: ISO.

———. 2007. *Survey of Certifications 2006.* Geneva: ISO.

Marbán, R., and J. Pellecer. 2003. *Legal Metrology.* Washington, DC: Organization of American States.

Nelson, R. 1959. "The Simple Economics of Basic Scientific Research." In *The Economics of Technological Change*, ed. N. Rosenberg. Harmondsworth, UK: Penguin Books.

Quinn, T. J., and J. Kovalevsky. 2005. "The Development of Modern Metrology and Its Role Today." *Philosophical Transactions of the Royal Society* 363 (1834): 2307–27.

UNIDO (United Nations Industrial Development Organization). 2003. "Laboratory Accreditation in Developing Economies: Tested Once—Accepted Everywhere." Working Paper 2, Trade Capacity Building Series, UNIDO, Vienna.

CHAPTER 4

The Building Blocks of the National
Quality Infrastructure

> **International and regional standards are replacing na-
> tional ones in a growing number of countries. These
> shared standards help diffuse technology and market
> information and facilitate trade between countries.**

> **Conformity assessment services such as certification,
> testing, and inspection help determine whether prod-
> ucts, processes, and services meet predetermined
> characteristics. They create transparency in the mar-
> ket and, thus, promote quality.**

> **Metrology ensures that measurements are reliable
> throughout an economy. It allows industry to control
> product quality and protects consumers from unscru-
> pulous producers.**

> **Accreditation can provide credibility to certification,
> testing, inspection, and calibration bodies so that their
> services are recognized and respected domestically
> and globally.**

What Are Standards, and How Are They Used?

Standards have been around for a very long time. They first emerged
about 3,500 years ago as weights and measures for trade, taxes, and con-

struction. The second type was in the form of written documents and was an outcome of the Industrial Revolution, when the efficacy of mechanized manufacturing depended on codifying the characteristics of products and processes. This section focuses on the second type of standards.

The International Organization for Standardization (ISO) defines a standard as a "document established by consensus and approved by a recognized body that provides, for common and repeated use, rules, guidelines or characteristics for activities or their results, aimed at the achievement of the optimum degree of order in a given context" (ISO and IEC 2004d). The World Trade Organization (WTO) Agreement on Technical Barriers to Trade (TBT Agreement) also defines a standard, but highlights other aspects important to the agreement—that is, the notion that standards are voluntary, with the definition limited to products.[1] The discussion here is based on the broader ISO definition, though the fact that standards should be voluntary is also kept in mind.

This book uses the term "technical regulations" to define mandatory technical requirements set by policy-making bodies. The term "standards" is used exclusively in the context of voluntary compliance in many countries outside of Eastern Europe and Central Asia (ECA). However, in ECA countries—particularly Commonwealth of Independent States (CIS) countries—all standards were mandatory under central planning—a practice that has carried over to current systems. The term "mandatory standard" is reserved for standards that are declared mandatory by the national standards body, a practice that does not exist in European Union (EU) and Organisation for Economic Co-operation and Development (OECD) countries.

Voluntary Standards

Standards originate from a wide range of organizations.

Standards can be developed and published by many public and private bodies, whether international, regional, or national. Increasingly, standards are developed by industry. International standards play a growing role in the global economy, forming the basis for an increasingly large

---

1. A standard is a "document approved by a recognized body, that provides, for common and repeated use, rules, guidelines or characteristics of products or related processes or production methods, with which compliance is not mandatory. It may also include or deal exclusively with terminology, symbols, packaging, marking or labeling requirements as they apply to a product, process or production method." WTO TBT Agreement 1995, Annex 1, http://www.wto.org/english/docs_e/legal_e/17-tbt_e.htm.

share of national standards. The three organizations responsible for developing most international standards are the ISO, International Electrotechnical Commission (IEC), and International Telecommunication Union (ITU).

In addition to standards developed by government-backed standardization organizations, a vast number of standards have also been developed through market forces. Market, or de facto, standards are the result of industry self-regulation. Market standards fall into three categories: unsponsored standards, sponsored standards, and industry consortia standards. Unsponsored standards do not involve any proprietary rights or identifiable author. They are the result of a succession of uncoordinated design and purchasing decisions leading to collective innovation. One example is the computer keyboard. The QWERTY English-language keyboard layout was not established through a collective decision between manufacturers and consumers. It occurred through a bandwagon effect of successive decisions by independent agents.

Sponsored standards involve proprietary rights, in which owners set technical specifications and extract rents from their use. Technical specifications for the portable document format (pdf) by Adobe Acrobat® are an example. Their market dominance makes them a market standard, but only the Adobe Acrobat® software can be used to read files in this format.

Finally, a growing number of standards have been developed by industry consortia, notably in information and communication technology. In 1996, a group of seven leading information and communication technology giants, including Compaq, DEC, IBM, Intel, Microsoft, NEC, and Nortel, introduced the universal serial bus (USB), a standard for computer peripheral devices such as keyboards and disk drives. The rest is history. Today, virtually all desktop and laptop computers, even those developed by rival companies, include USB ports. Many of these industry consortia have no official government mandates to develop standards.

The role of industry consortia in developing standards is expected to grow, because national standards bodies have increasing difficulty keeping up with technological changes. In EU and other OECD economies, national standards bodies agree on standards based on consensus, so developing standards may take much longer than in industry organizations. In some cases, the latter can be more exclusive in their memberships, which leads to less dissent on standardization options. But even industry consortia can be multinational, such as those that developed standards for cellular phones. Many industry-based standards, particularly those from the United States and Canada and from EU countries, have become important in international trade because of the influence of the specific industry consortia.

International and regional organizations provide clear guidelines on standardization.

International guidelines for national standards bodies, established over many years by the international standardization organizations, were codified in ISO and IEC directives (ISO and IEC 2004c, 2008). This process was subsequently included as a Code of Good Practice in the WTO TBT Agreement,[2] which is open to acceptance by any standardizing body, whether national, subnational, or regional: WTO members shall ensure that their central government standardizing bodies accept and comply with the code and shall take reasonable measures to ensure that local government and nongovernment standardizing bodies within their territories, as well as regional standardizing bodies of which they are members, accept and comply with the code. The European Committee for Standardization (CEN) and the European Committee for Electrotechnical Standardization (CENELEC), the regional standards organizations, require that their EU and European Free Trade Association (EFTA) members and their EU-neighboring affiliate members comply with international best practices. Because CEN membership is a condition for EU accession, adoption of international best practices by standards bodies is often driven by aspirations for EU membership.

Generally, the WTO Code of Good Practice requires that the development of a standard be a consultative process that takes into account the views of all relevant stakeholders—public, private, and civil society. Interested parties shall be offered an opportunity to submit comments on draft standards, and the standardizing body shall take into account, in the further processing of the standards, the comments received during the period for commenting.

The standardization process generally starts with the recognition that a standard is required to bring about order—that is, variety control, usability, compatibility, interchangeability, health, safety, environmental protection, product protection, mutual understanding, economic performance, trade, or any combination of these elements. A standards body commits the required resources and then brings together all stakeholders in a technical committee to develop a draft standard. Members of the technical committee are not paid in EU and OECD economies. This condition is part of the process of building consensus and is often the most difficult to manage, especially when competing business interests are at stake. Given this range of views, consensus is not meant to imply unanimity, but rather general agreement—characterized by (a) the absence of sustained opposition to substantial issues by any important party and (b) a process that reconciles conflicting views (ISO and IEC 2004d).

---

2. See WTO TBT Agreement 1995, Annex 3, http://www.wto.org/english/docs_e/legal_e/17-tbt_e.htm.

Once a technical committee has developed a draft standard, it is circulated to the public for general comment. This is a requirement of the WTO TBT Agreement's Code of Good Practice.[3] After public comments have been collated, they are considered by the committee and the draft is finalized. The final draft is presented to the governing organs of the standards body for final approval as a standard. The approved standard is then released for publication and made available in either hard copy or electronic format.

Only a small number of strong, industrial economies are *standards makers*, because developing standards tends to be costly and requires extensive technical knowledge. Most countries, particularly low- and middle-income economies, are *standards takers*. This term means that in these economies the technical committee process usually involves conducting research on which standards are available on a particular subject, either at the international level or from more advanced countries, and deciding which to adopt. Factors that affect the decision-making process include requirements of major trade partners; regional trade bloc preferences; and the availability of international standards such as ISO, IEC, and CODEX STAN.

However, international standardization has become so ubiquitous that the trend is to adopt international standards wherever possible. This policy is not without its challenges for low- and middle-income economies, where industry is seldom at the technological level of that of more industrial countries. But failure to adopt international standards can limit an economy's industry from competing in world markets. Economically important regional standards, such as European Standards, are adopted less frequently because they are often based on international standards, so it is deemed better to go to the original source. In addition, copyright issues with European Standards cannot be resolved as easily as in the case of international standards.

Standardization at the international and regional levels

The standards development process at the international and regional levels is very similar to the national level process. Many of the practices are the same; the only difference is that instead of national stakeholders being involved in the standards development process, countries are represented at the international level and consensus must be built among competing national interests. This is also the main reason that interna-

3. The WTO TBT Agreement, Annex 3, requires the draft national standard to be circulated for a period of not less than 60 days, unless it is fully equivalent to a recognized international standard, in which case the public comment period may fall away.

tional standards normally take longer to develop than national standards or industry standards.

International Standards

In the case of ISO and IEC, the major responsibility for the technical committees (that is, chairperson, secretariat, technical support, and so forth) is devolved to the country member that agrees to host the facilities for undertaking this work. The technical committees of ISO and IEC consist of delegations from countries that have indicated interest in participating in the development of the specific international standard. The member states decide how the delegations are selected, but most try to have a proper mix between standards body personnel and industry experts. These organizations adopt decentralized systems for conducting technical work in different locations away from headquarters because of both the volume of work and the financial resource constraints. ISO, IEC, and the Central Asian Cooperation (CAC) are responsible for over 85 percent of the trade-related standards developed every year (International Trade Centre 2004).

The decentralized system adopted by ISO, IEC, and CAC suffers from one serious limitation. The host country where the technical work is conducted is in a privileged position to show leadership in specialist committees; this gives it prestige and, especially, influence. As a result, major industrial countries keep vying with each other to host the secretariat of international technical committees. However, developing economies can and should participate in the international standards–making process but usually lack the financial and technical resources to participate meaningfully, let alone host such committees. Therefore, the influence they can exert on the process of international standards development is quite minimal. This situation is often to the detriment of the domestic industries in developing economies, and it is one of the major issues with which the international standards community grapples. ISO, IEC, and ITU, in particular, have established mechanisms and special funds to support developing country members in participating more meaningfully in international standardization.

Together with international standards, regional standards represent a growing share of the standard stock of many countries, particularly of EU countries. A number of regional organizations are active in the ECA region. In Europe, CEN, CENELEC, and the European Telecommunications Standardization Institute develop regional voluntary standards. In CIS countries, this role is performed by the EuroAsian Interstate Council for Standardization, Metrology, and Certification (EASC). CEN, CENELEC, and EASC have developed a significant number of standards, rivaling the stock of standards developed by ISO and IEC (figure 4.1).

FIGURE 4.1

Large Stock of International and Regional Standards in Eastern Europe and Central Asia

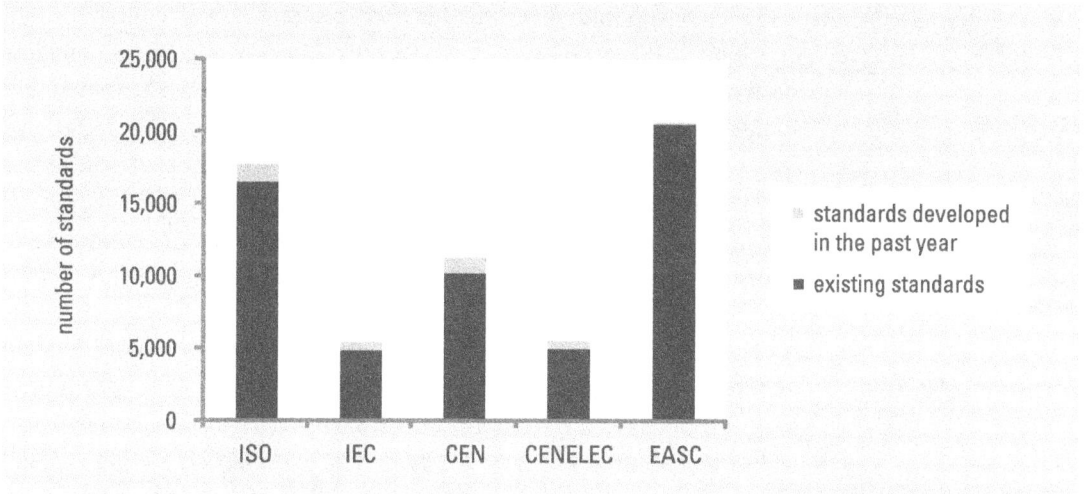

Sources: ISO, http://www.iso.org; IEC, http://www.iec.ch; CEN, http://www.cen.eu; CENELEC, http://www.cenelec.eu; EASC, http://www.easc.org.by.
Note: Data are as of December 31, 2008, for ISO, CENELEC, and EASC; as of December 31, 2007, for CEN; and as of June 26, 2009, for IEC.

EU Standards

The EU and EFTA have established three standardization bodies—CEN, CENELEC, and European Telecommunications Standardization Institute—to coordinate their voluntary standardization work. These bodies produce European Standards. EU member states are obliged to adopt European Standards and withdraw conflicting national standards. In fact, adopting 85 percent of EU standards is a condition for EU accession. The standardization process in the EU regional standards bodies is based on consensus and is similar to that followed by their international counterparts. The actual work is conducted in technical committees that are representative of the national standards bodies.

The scope of the EU regional bodies and that of the international bodies—ISO, IEC, and ITU—are very similar. Formal agreements exist between these EU and international bodies to harmonize their work as much as possible. As a result, many ISO and IEC standards have been adopted by CEN and CENELEC as EU standards. About 30 percent of European Standards are identical to ISO standards (CEN 2004). About 70 percent of CENELEC's standards are identical to IEC standards.[4] The influence of this cooperation on international standardization has not gone unnoticed by the region's other trading blocs.

4. For more information on CENELEC's standards, visit http://www.cenelec.eu.

CIS Standards

EASC is the CIS intergovernmental body responsible for standardization, metrology, and certification. It is a legacy of the Soviet Union's standardization system, and it develops the GOST standard (Gosudarstvennyy standart, or state standard)—not to be confused with the Russian Federation's national standards, known as GOST-R. An important difference between the European standardization bodies and EASC is that while the latter has developed more than 20,000 GOST standards, CIS countries are under no obligation to adopt them. Hence, GOST standards are used to varying degrees across CIS countries.

EASC also remains somewhat internationally isolated, with far fewer members than its European counterparts. Although trade opportunities with the EU have attracted a number of countries from outside the EU and EFTA to CEN and CENELEC as affiliate members, little international demand exists for adopting GOST standards outside the CIS (figure 4.2). As a result, some EASC members have started either to join the European regional bodies as affiliate members (Armenia, Moldova, and Ukraine) or to leave EASC altogether (Georgia in 2009). Moreover, only a few GOST standards are aligned with international standards: 22 percent are harmonized with ISO and IEC standards, while more than 40 percent of CEN and CENELEC standards are aligned with ISO and IEC standards.

Finally, there are reasons to believe that GOST standards are not keeping pace with the international technology frontier and that many may be obsolete. The standards development process at EASC is slow. Only 79 new GOST standards were published in 2008, representing 0.4 percent of the GOST standards stock, compared to about 9.0 percent of standards by European regional bodies. During the Soviet period, however, an estimated 15,000 standards, or three-quarters of GOST standards, were published. By contrast, the average age of an ISO standard is approximately 2.5 years.[5]

Technical Regulations

The WTO TBT Agreement defines a technical regulation as a "document which lays down product characteristics or their related processes and production methods, including the applicable administrative provisions, with which compliance is mandatory. It may also include or deal exclusively with terminology, symbols, packaging, marking or labeling requirements as they apply to a product, process or production method" (WTO TBT Agreement 1995, Annex 1, http://www.wto.org/english/docs_e/

---

5. Interview with ISO representative.

FIGURE 4.2
Memberships of International and Regional Standards Bodies

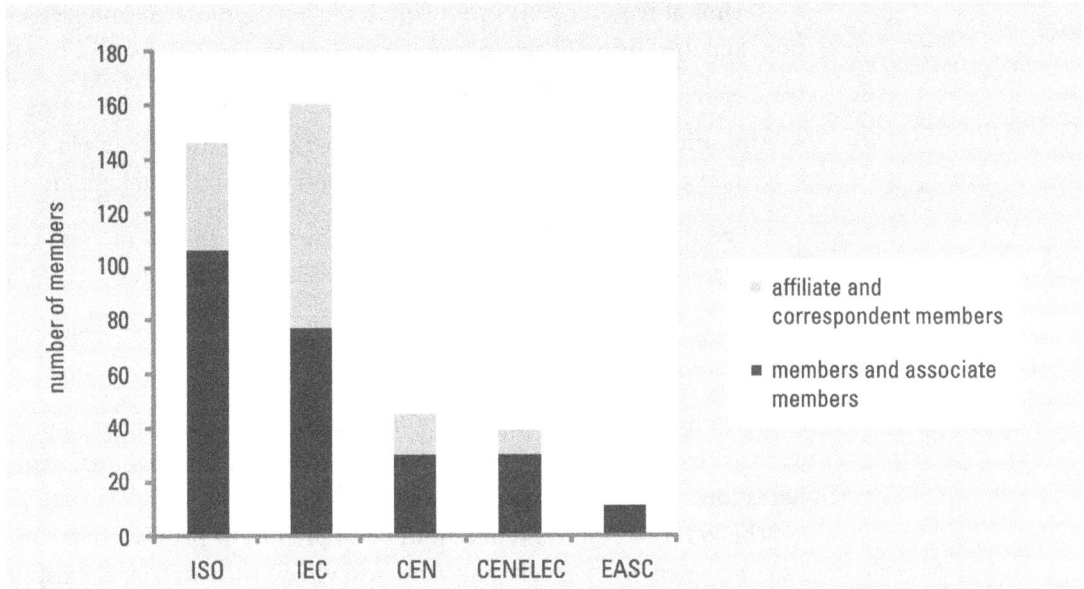

Sources: ISO, http://www.iso.org; IEC, http://www.iec.ch; CEN, http://www.cen.eu; CENELEC, http://www.cenelec.eu; EASC, http://www.easc.org.by.
Note: Data are as of December 31, 2008, for ISO, CENELEC, and EASC; as of December 31, 2007, for CEN; and as of June 26, 2009, for IEC.

legal_e/17-tbt_e.htm). Again, a technical regulation is mandatory, while a standard is voluntary.

Technical regulations have been around for centuries as governments have sought to control the quality of products to protect citizens from harmful market practices and failures. The WTO TBT Agreement lists five basic reasons for which technical regulations can be legitimately implemented:

- National security requirements

- Prevention of deceptive practices

- Protection of human health or safety

- Protection of animal or plant life or health

- Protection of the environment[6]

---

6. See Article 2.2 of the WTO TBT Agreement, http://www.wto.org/english/docs_e/legal_e/17-tbt_e.htm. The Preamble of the TBT Agreement also recognizes that "no country should be prevented from taking measures necessary to ensure the quality of its exports."

An overview of the types of technical regulations that typically fall within the ambit of the WTO TBT Agreement is provided in table 4.1.

Technical requirements can theoretically be incorporated into legislation, and this course of action is preferred by many legislators. But this is not considered an efficient option for three reasons:

- Ministries or their agencies seldom have the infrastructure in place to ensure an appropriate level of consultation with all the stakeholders.

- When the text of a standard has been included in legislation, it is very difficult to update the text as rapidly as technology changes.

- The WTO TBT Agreement notification obligations are often forgotten.

Referencing standards is generally considered to be the better approach to designing technical regulations. The technical requirements can be dealt with by referencing the national, regional, or international standards (depending on the legal system of the country).

The WTO TBT Agreement requires that product or process characteristics be based on international standards, where such standards exist or their completion is imminent, except where such standards would be ineffective or inappropriate.

TABLE 4.1

Examples of Sectors and Products Subject to Technical Regulation

Sectors	Products
Household appliances (electrical safety)	Television sets, VCRs, DVD players
Electrical distribution	Components used in the wiring of premises, switches, wiring, lightbulbs, earth leakage protectors, plugs, and sockets
Building and construction	Building materials
Telecommunications	Telephones
Vehicles and vehicle components	Tires (new and retreaded)
Trade based on measurement	Trade measuring equipment (such as fuel pumps, scales, and volume measures)
Industrial equipment	Pressurized equipment (such as pressure vessels and pipes)
Food and feed[a]	Fresh produce from animal origin

Source: Authors.
a. These products are normally also subject to sanitary and phytosanitary requirements.

The building block approach

No definitive model for technical regulations has yet been agreed on at the international level, nor is one likely to be decided on in the near future. However, technical regulations are generally developed through the building block approach depicted in figure 4.3. The actual methods by which these building blocks are implemented and linked at the regional or national levels depend on the legal systems, the available institutional frameworks, customs and practices, and many other factors. As a result, the effectiveness of a technical regulation depends on the proper placement and functioning of these building blocks.

Administrative procedures consist of conformity assessment requirements, regulatory authority activities, and sanctions. Conformity assessment provides the regulatory authority with information to guide decisions on the integrity of products in the marketplace. The regulatory authority administers technical regulations at the national level and institutes sanctions, should they be required. Sanctions are required when suppliers or products fail to meet the requirements of the technical regulations. It is considered good practice to conduct an impact assessment to evaluate the effect of the envisaged technical regulations on trade, as well

FIGURE 4.3

Building Blocks of a Technical Regulation Framework

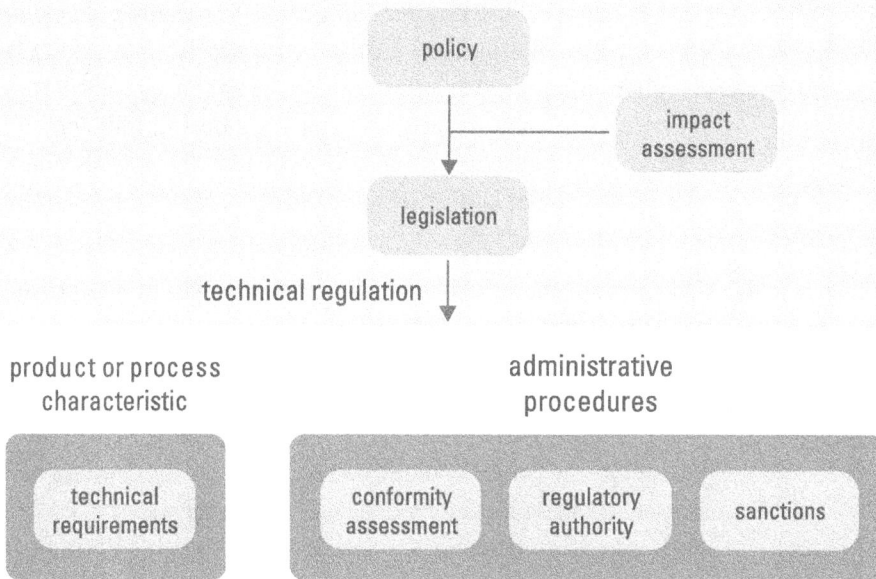

Source: Authors.

as a cost-benefit analysis to determine whether the required result can be achieved through less onerous means.

Due to the wide range of products and services that are regulated, many economies decentralize their regulatory activities. Instead of one super regulatory agency, every ministry retains responsibility for affecting the development and implementation of technical regulations within its own sphere of accountability. Thus, technical regulations are developed and implemented by many ministries and their agencies in each country, often in a fragmented manner as officials develop differing customs and practices over many years. However, some developing and smaller economies often limit the number of agencies or establish a single regulatory agency (for example, the Czech Republic).

Around the world, ministries and agencies often do not comply with the requirements of the WTO TBT Agreement regarding technical regulations. These entities commonly ignore rules such as technical regulations being based on international standards, local and imported products being accorded the same treatment, regulations not being made more trade restrictive than necessary, and the WTO being notified before implementation of regulations.

The diversity of approaches to technical regulations and the fragmentation and overlap among ministries is bad news for businesses. It is also a major impediment to free trade. Many longstanding WTO members recognize this situation and are streamlining their approaches. OECD members in particular have committed to implementing better regulatory frameworks. Countries applying for WTO membership are finding that having a cohesive system of technical regulation development and implementation is likely to facilitate their accession into the WTO. Nonmembers of the WTO are also likely to see enhanced trade if they streamline their regulatory regimes, because opaque and fragmented technical regulation systems subject to the whims of the officials administering them do not benefit anyone.

Distinction between technical regulations and sanitary and phytosanitary measures

One of the major sources of confusion in the area of regulation relates to the relationship between technical barriers to trade and sanitary and phytosanitary measures as identified in the WTO agreements. Whether a particular regulation adopted by a country—for the protection of the life of its human and animal population or its plants—is a *technical regulation* or a *sanitary or phytosanitary measure* depends on the objectives for which it was adopted. Generally, sanitary or phytosanitary measures[7] have the following objectives:

- Protection of animal or plant life or health from risks arising from the entry, establishment, or spread of pests, diseases, disease-carrying organisms, or disease-causing organisms

- Protection of human or animal life or health from risks arising from additives, contaminants, toxins, or disease-causing organisms in foods, beverages, or feedstuffs

- Protection of human life or health from risks arising from diseases carried by animals, plants, or products thereof or from the entry, establishment, or spread of pests

- Prevention or limitation of damage caused by the entry, establishment, or spread of pests

International and Regional Integration in Standardization

Rapid advances in technology and immense growth in the trade of manufactured goods between countries have created unprecedented demand for international and regional standards. But the right of sovereign nations to frame their own rules and regulations can be made compatible with the universal desire to eliminate trade barriers.

Strategies for Harmonizing Standards

Countries can use three closely linked strategies to harmonize their standards:

- *Adopting international standards*, preferably those used by existing and potential trade partners, together with standards with high knowledge content such as ISO 9001

- *Influencing international standardization activities*, to ensure that the international standards eventually adopted by their trade partners will also meet domestic needs

- *Working with trade partners to develop regional standards*, which are appropriate for the region's needs

7. For more information, see World Trade Organization, "Understanding the WTO Agreement on Sanitary and Phytosanitary Measures," http://www.wto .org/english/tratop_e/sps_e/spsund_e.htm.

Adopting international standards

Adopting international standards is the most straightforward method of harmonizing standards from an institutional perspective, because it does not require building consensus with other countries but can be done unilaterally. It occurs when a technical committee at a national standards body decides to adopt an international standard, instead of designing a national one from the ground up. It is also relatively cost free, when the fixed cost of membership in an international organization has been paid.

However, greater costs may be incurred when the standard has been adopted. Small and medium enterprises (SMEs) in developing countries are not at the same level of development as firms in high-income countries. They find it difficult, if not impossible, to implement international standards because the necessary technological level of understanding is absent or the industry has not yet developed to the same technological level because of lack of infrastructure or investments. Thus, many developing countries are pushing for a dual system of national standards—one for local manufacturing and another for exports. But the question remains: When does a country change over to the international standard? When standards deal with health and safety or with environmental protection, trickier questions arise: Why should the populations of less developed economies make do with standards of safety lower than those of industrial countries?

These are real challenges, and solutions need to be found to help the low- and middle-income countries bridge the gap. Some national standards bodies (such as the South African Bureau of Standards) have debated the notion of "bridging standards." These bridging standards would help SMEs better understand international standards by providing missing information. Unfortunately, no such standards have been developed. In some cases, international standards are well understood, but developing local industries to levels where they could meet international standards would require heavy investments—in processes, plants, and the like—that are unlikely to be forthcoming soon.

Influencing international standardization activities

Countries can ensure that their voices are heard in international standardization activities by participating in the technical committee work of organizations such as ISO, IEC, and ITU. In this way, a country can influence the type of standards to be adopted by its trading partners, rather than adopting international standards that are being used internationally but are not appropriate in its national context. This situation is of particular importance to developing countries that need to protect their interests in view of their industrialization objectives and the interests of their main industries, presenting a country-specific position in relation to the technical content of the international standards being developed (box 4.1). Participation by actual attendance at technical committee meetings is essential for arguing the country's case in person.

Another reason to participate in international technical committee work is that delegates to international technical committees are sensitized to the developments of future standards and can report back to their industries, helping them to plan appropriately for any impending changes. It is not good enough just to adopt international standards when they have been developed and published. International technical committee work can be used as an early warning system for changes and developments in products, systems, and service standards that could influence local industries in the near future; what is discussed at ISO technical committees today are next year's standards. Local industries could have an advantage if they are forewarned and plan their strategies accordingly.

Working to develop regional standards

In recent decades, coordination strategies have been developed at the regional levels as trading blocs endeavor to facilitate intraregional trade as much as possible. As shown in map 4.1, most countries in the world

---

BOX 4.1

Participation in International Standardization Committees Is Crucial: Medical Rubber Gloves Industry in Malaysia

The issue: Doctors in the United States and parts of Europe reported that some patients had died from allergic reactions to rubber gloves. At the same time, complaints of allergic reactions to rubber gloves by medical staff were increasing. These issues were highlighted during discussions at international standards committees. Calls were being made to allow alternative materials in the production of medical gloves and even to restrict the use of natural rubber. Malaysia is a major producer of rubber medical gloves, with several factories and thousands of workers employed. If the changes to the international standards were to go into effect, the local industry would be devastated.

The strategy: Research quickly indicated that proteins in the latex rubber were producing these allergic reactions. Although rubber gloves are made to Malaysian standards, the standards did not provide for these aspects of the gloves. Malaysian industry was made aware of the problem and quickly initiated programs to solve the problem of allergic reactions to natural rubber gloves by reducing the proteins during processing. It was able to respond in a timely manner, thereby saving the industry on the basis of advance information.

Source: International Trade Centre 2005.

MAP 4.1

Membership of Most Countries in Regional Standardization Organizations, 2011

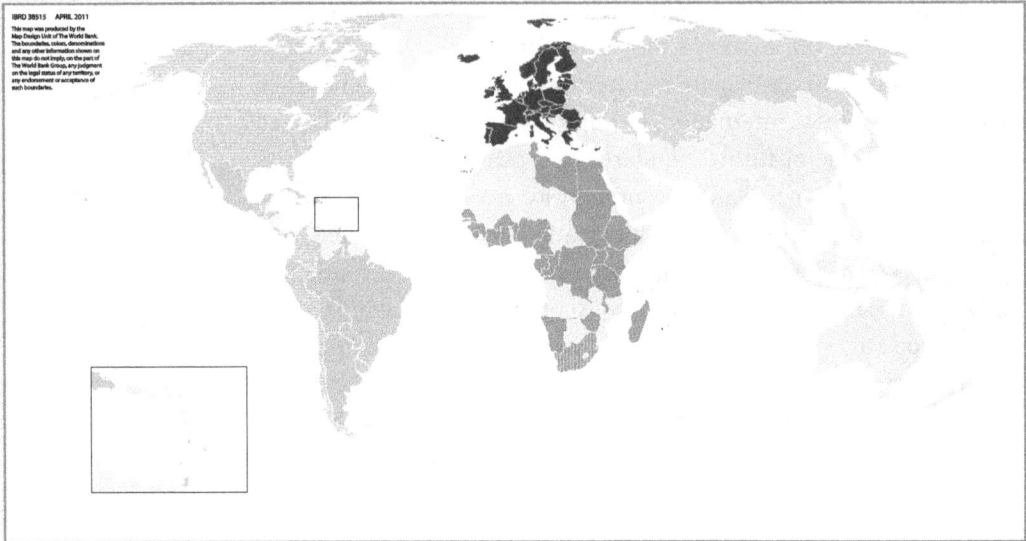

    EASC (EuroAsian Interstate Council for Standardization, Metrology, and Certification)

    PASC (Pacific Area Standards Congress)

    CEN (European Committee for Standardization)

    ARSO (African Organization for Standardization)

    COPANT (Pan American Standards Commission)

    member states of both COPANT and PASC

    member states of both ARSO and PASC

Source: Authors based on information from EASC, http://www.easc.org.eu; PASC, http://www.pascnet.org; CEN, http://www.cen.eu; ARSO, http://.www.arso-oran.org; COPANT, http://www.copant.org.

are now full or partial members of regional standardization organizations. Of direct relevance to ECA countries that are potential members of the EU or that trade heavily with the EU, is the European approach to harmonization of standards. Another approach is the CIS model. The East African Community (EAC) offers another model for cooperation among developing countries.

There could be several reasons for limiting the international harmonization or "upgrading" of regional standards. First, this limitation enables regional standards to follow the pace of industrial modernization in the region. Hence, firms are not faced with adopting standards that require a level of technological sophistication that they cannot meet. Second, a gradual harmonization process ensures that all EASC member countries are able to adopt any new standard. This coordinated upgrading ensures that all regional trading partners are able to use the regional standards in synchrony, with no laggard country that is a weak link and reduces adoption incentives for other trading partners. This gradual harmonization strategy, based on voluntary adoption by member states, needs to be weighed against the more aggressive standards upgrading strategies that not only favor intraregional trade, but also trade outside the region. The aggressive adoption of international standards can also be used as a strategy to drive technological change in developing countries. This is the strategy adopted by the EAC.

One of the major issues with low- and middle-income economies is that international standards may be far too high or advanced for their industries to implement (box 4.2). This observation has two sides. First, international standards are developed by the large standards makers, that is, industrial nations. Their industry is at an advanced level of technological development, and the international standards obviously reflect this reality. During the development of an international standard, a certain level of technological prowess is therefore considered a given, and the standard itself does not contain any references in this regard.

BOX 4.2

Do Developing Countries Really Need International Standards? The "Sugar Standard" in the EAC

In the EAC, the development and approval of a harmonized standard, based on the international standard for refined sugar, has been a challenge. Sugar is produced from sugar cane by extracting the juice from the cane in sugar mills through milling and diffusion. This juice is purified by filtration and other methods, the excess water is evaporated, and the sugar is crystallized from the remaining syrup. The sugar that is obtained from this process is very slightly brown or tan but quite safe for human consumption; it is also known as raw sugar. The raw sugar is thereafter refined in a sugar refinery using various clarification processes to produce its white color. In Uganda, there are no refineries and the sugar provided to the population for decades by Ugandan sugar mills has always been slightly tan in color. Now, with the development of a harmonized sugar standard for the EAC, Kenya and Tanzania are pushing for refined, white sugar to become the only standard, basically banning the very light brown, unrefined sugar. This approach would seriously undermine the viability of the Ugandan sugar industry, unless major capital investments are made to build a sugar refinery. This debate, regarding a regional versus an international standard, has not yet been resolved in the EAC. (In advanced economies, brown sugar is sometimes refined sugar that has been artificially colored to give it a brown or yellowish color.)

Coordination of Technical Regulations

The WTO TBT Agreement: The basic framework for international coordination

The WTO TBT Agreement ensures that standards and technical regulations and conformity assessment systems developed and implemented by WTO member states do not result in unnecessary barriers to trade. The agreement includes the following main principles and provisions:

- *The avoidance of unnecessary obstacles to trade:* the TBT Agreement takes into account the existence of legitimate divergences of taste, income, and geographical and other factors between countries and accords a high degree of flexibility in the preparation, adoption, and application of national technical regulations. However, this flexibility is limited by the requirement that the technical regulation is not prepared, adopted, or applied with a view to, or with the effect of, creating unnecessary obstacles to trade, that is, when (a) it is more restrictive than necessary to achieve a given policy objective or (b) when it does not fulfill a legitimate objective.

- *Nondiscrimination and national treatment:* the TBT Agreement includes the General Agreement on Tariffs and Trade's most-favored nation and national treatment obligations. In respect of their technical regulations, the agreement provides that products imported from any other member shall be accorded treatment no less favorable than that accorded to like products of national origin and to like products originating in any other country.

- *Harmonization:* the TBT Agreement encourages member states to use existing international standards for their national regulations, or for parts of them, unless the use would be ineffective or inappropriate to fulfill a given policy objective. It also encourages the members' participation, within the limits of their resources, in the work of international bodies for the preparation of standards and guides or recommendations for conformity assessment procedures.

- *Equivalence:* the TBT Agreement introduces a complementary approach to harmonization, known as equivalence, whereby members shall give positive consideration to accepting as equivalent technical regulations of other members, even if these regulations differ from their own, provided they are satisfied that these regulations adequately fulfill the objectives of their own regulations.

- *Mutual recognition:* the TBT Agreement strongly encourages WTO members to enter into negotiations with other members for the mutual acceptance of conformity assessment results. It also points out that compliance by conformity assessment bodies with relevant guides or recommendations issued by international standardizing bodies can be regarded as an indication of adequate technical competence.

- *Transparency:* the TBT Agreement requires members to provide notice (a) whenever a relevant international standard or guide or recommendation does not exist, or the technical content of a proposed or adopted technical regulation or regulation is not in accordance with the technical content of relevant international standards or guides of recommendations; and (b) if the technical regulation or conformity assessment procedure may have a significant effect on trade with other members. Bilateral or plurilateral agreements on issues related to technical regulations, standards, or conformity assessment procedures that may have a significant effect on trade shall also be notified. As a complement to the notification requirements, each member must set up a national enquiry point.[8]

Regional harmonization in technical regulations

Various attempts have been made to harmonize technical regulations at the regional level. However, experience suggests that harmonization of technical regulations is not as easily achieved as in the case of standards. This difference has to do with the voluntary nature of standards, whereas technical regulations are by definition mandatory. Coupled with this is the consensus tradition among standards makers, which spans decades. For the authorities responsible for technical regulation, *consensus* is new territory—they are used to a top-down approach. The EU tried very hard to harmonize technical regulations from 1958 to the mid-1980s—denoted the *Old Approach* to technical harmonization and standards—and largely failed.

European Union

The EU was able to progress only when the *New Approach* was agreed to in the late 1980s and finally implemented in 1992. Under the New Approach, legislative harmonization, encompassed in the EU directives,

---

8. For more information, see the World Trade Organization, "Technical Information on Technical Barriers to Trade," http://www.wto.org/english/tratop_e/tbt_e/tbt_info_e.htm.

is limited to essential requirements that products placed on the market must meet if they are to benefit from free movement within the EU. The technical requirements of products meeting the essential requirements set out in the directives are laid down in the European *harmonized standards* developed by the regional standardization bodies CEN, CENELEC, and European Telecommunications Standardization Institute. Products manufactured in compliance with the harmonized standards, which are voluntary, benefit from a presumption of conformity with the corresponding essential requirements and, thus, can circulate freely across borders in Europe. The harmonized standards are prepared in accordance with general guidelines agreed between the European Commission and the European standards organizations and follow a mandate issued by the European Commission after consultations with the member states.

The experience of the EU does not mean that harmonization of technical regulations is impossible. The need to harmonize technical regulations remains paramount if an efficient intraregional trading regime is being pursued. Other economic regions, realizing that fragmented approaches in technical regulation are not conducive for trade, are also attempting to harmonize their technical regulation development and implementation approaches. The EU's New Approach has largely been effective, but it has come at a tremendous cost and must be supported by very sophisticated quality infrastructure. Whether this approach will be possible or necessary in developing economies or economies in transition is not all that clear yet.

Eurasian Economic Community

The Eurasian Economic Community (EurAsEC) comprises Belarus, Kazakhstan, the Kyrgyz Republic, Russia, Tajikistan, and Uzbekistan. The EurAsEC Intergovernmental Council approved four agreements dealing with technical regulations in 2005 and 2006. These four agreements include the basics of technical regulation in the member states, a list of general technical regulations to be developed, a model framework for such technical regulations, and an agreement on the application of a single marking demonstrating conformity to technical regulations in the EurAsEC.[9]

The members agreed that technical regulations should be adopted for the purpose of harmonizing EurAsEC legislation in the area of technical regulation, for protection of human life and health, for environmental protection, for prevention of deceptive practices, and for the elimination of unnecessary restrictions to regional trade. A list of 28 general technical regulations was agreed upon.

---

9. For more information, see World Trade Organization, "Notification to the WTO," Document G/TBT/10.7/N/KG, http://www.wto.org.

Conformity Assessment Bodies

Conformity assessment shows whether specified requirements relating to a product, process, system, person, or body have been fulfilled. It adds credibility to claims that these requirements are fulfilled, giving users greater confidence in such claims. Standards are often used as the specified requirements because they represent a broad consensus of what is wanted in a given situation. Inspection, testing, and certification, and are the three types of conformity assessment.[10] Table 4.2 provides a snapshot of their main features.

TABLE 4.2

A Comparison of Inspection, Testing, and Certification

	Inspection	Testing	Certification
What does it do?	Examines a product design, product, process, or installation and determines its conformity with specific requirements or, on the basis of professional judgment, with general requirements	Determines one or more characteristics of an object of conformity assessment, according to a procedure	Issues a statement, following a review, that fulfillment of specified requirements for a product, process, system, or person has been demonstrated
How is it done?	Examines one piece or sample typically without specialized equipment (or with very specialized equipment)	Examines one piece or one sample typically with specialized equipment	Assures that, in the future, a producer is able to correctly produce or will correctly produce according to specified requirements; grants certification on the basis of audits, usually supplemented by testing or calibration or inspection

Sources: ISO and IEC 2004a and practical definitions.

Inspection and Testing

Inspection and testing are two essential steps that generally precede any certification but can also be carried out on their own.

10. In some countries, calibration laboratories are also considered conformity assessment bodies, while in other countries they are not. There is an open debate among international organizations for metrology, accreditation, and standardization on whether calibration laboratories should be considered conformity assessment bodies. To make the situation even more unclear, many CIS countries used the term "calibration" for verification processes inherited from the Soviet era that are closer to conformity assessment than what is known as calibration in OECD and EU economies. For the purpose of this book, calibration laboratories will not be considered conformity assessment bodies and will be treated separately in chapter 7 dealing with metrology.

Inspection, as defined by ISO, is the "examination of a product design, product, process or installation, and determination of their conformity with specific requirements or, on the basis of professional judgment, with general requirements" (ISO and IEC 2004a). Inspection makes use of simple equipment and, more often than not, is based on the professional judgment of the inspector. However, the border between inspection and testing is not always that clear. Inspection is frequently used when a consignment must be checked to determine whether it meets specified requirements, without it necessarily having been certified previously (for example, inspection of imported products at the port of entry). In many economies, however, the term "inspection" is also synonymous for market surveillance activities. Care should therefore be exercised when using or reading about inspection as a concept.

Testing is undertaken by laboratories, involving the use of sophisticated test equipment and according to objective and standardized test methodologies by trained laboratory personnel (photograph 4.1). Testing laboratories can play an important role in supporting innovation, because they allow firms to test and refine product prototypes.

The Voluntary Certification Market: A Global Industry

Types of certification

The moment a buyer wishes to establish whether a product or service meets the specified or implied requirements of a standard, three choices present themselves. The buyer can do the following:

- Accept the declaration of the manufacturer or supplier.

- Conduct an assessment of whether the product or service complies.

- Rely on the services of an independent body—that is, a third party—to provide evidence that the specified requirements have been fulfilled (ISO and IEC 2004a).

The first option is seldom accepted at face value, the second option is very expensive, and, hence, certification by third parties is often considered the most viable option.

Third-party certification is a need of individual buyers as well as regulatory authorities, major purchasers, retail organizations, and many others. Their needs are not all the same, and the certification industry—which has become a major business at the global level—has diversified tremendously to provide its customers with the required services. The globalization of markets is also reshaping the certification business, with

Testing of construction material ensures that proper quality and safety requirements are met.

Source: Contributed by Karl-Christian Goethner.

certification bodies investing in subsidiaries around the world. Factors driving this change include the following:

- As they globalize their markets, customers of certification bodies are seeking certification that is accepted in a wider range of markets.

- Multilateral recognition arrangements between countries are making it easier for certificates in one country to be accepted in many others.

- Regulatory authorities are beginning to open their procedures to independent certification bodies.

Types of certification schemes vary from pure product certification on one end of the spectrum, whereby a manufacturer is given a license to affix the certification mark on the product (that is, pure system certification such as ISO 9001), to the other end of the spectrum, where processes are considered instead of products. In between, there is a continuum of various schemes, providing more or less assurance that the product or system or a combination of both comply with specified requirements. Certification consists of many service providers and myriad rapidly evolving certification standards and schemes, making it difficult for developing economies to keep pace.

Product certification

Product certification schemes come in many forms, and a wide variety of approaches can be followed. The least intrusive certification systems are limited to granting certification on a batch of products based on testing, inspecting, and appraising product samples. These systems have severe limitations and carry big risks that nonconforming products will be accepted. They are also very expensive to implement if done properly, because of the underlying statistical sampling that needs to be employed. To obtain a high probability that defective products will be identified, one must use very high sample rates. In most developing economies, the implementation of this type of system, especially in import inspection, leaves much to be desired and provides a false sense of security.

More thorough national product certification schemes also include surveillance through a number of approaches that can be combined, including

• Testing or inspection of samples from the open market

• Testing or inspection of samples from the factory

• Quality system audits combined with random tests or inspections

• Assessment of the production process or service

In a developing economy, these approaches to certification provide the best assurance that products bearing the certification mark will actually comply with the relevant standard on a continuous basis.

System certification

System certification's success story is ISO 9001, the international standard dealing with the generic requirements for a quality management system. This standard is part of a series of standards dealing with quality management and all its aspects. It was first published in 1987 and has since twice been revised, with the 2000 edition being the latest.

There are approximately one million ISO 9001–certified[11] organizations, and it is estimated that more than 750 certification bodies are active all over the world (ISO 2008). This is truly a multibillion dollar business. ISO 9001 certification does not say or guarantee anything about the quality of an organization's products or services and, thus, is not of great concern for consumers. ISO 9001 certification is primarily used by major purchasers who wish to ensure that the companies they are dealing with have proper quality management systems in place and, hence, can be relied on to produce products that consistently comply with their contractual obligations. In addition, ISO 9001 certification is required by a growing number of regulatory authorities as a prerequisite for companies providing products with fairly high risks to the marketplace. It is a require-

11. In some markets, "registration" is used rather than certification (for example, in the United States).

ment for some of the quality assurance modules underpinning the New Approach directives of the EU.

The certification process

International best practices have developed over the years for certification schemes. When a supplier or manufacturer decides to seek certification to fulfill a market requirement or regulatory demand, the appropriate certification body needs to be selected. In deciding which certification body to use, companies need to heed the caveat emptor principle, or buyer beware, at all times and should base their decision on the following specifics:

- Accreditation for the relevant certification service required by an accreditation body that enjoys international recognition

- Proximity—the closer the better

- The reputation, image, and experience in the relevant markets

- Recognition by regulatory authorities in the relevant market if products and services are subject to technical regulations

Thereafter, the process will follow a common routine. The certification body conducts an initial review of the company to establish whether it is ready for an assessment and what the extent of the full assessment will be. In the meantime, products are selected and sent for testing in the relevant laboratories, if product certification is contemplated. A full assessment is then conducted by the certification body on the premises or in the plants of the supplier. Any deficiencies are noted, and the supplier and the certification body agree on a time scale for their rectification.

When all the requirements for certification have been fulfilled—that is, products comply fully with the relevant standard, production controls comply with stated requirements, or quality management systems meet ISO 9001 or similar standards—the certification body recommends certification to its certification board. The certification body will conduct follow-up surveillance visits at given intervals, taking additional products for retesting if relevant, to ensure that all the requirements are continuously being fulfilled. System certification is normally valid for three years, when a full assessment is conducted again. Product certification varies widely; some are valid for only a year, while others are open ended—withdrawn if the products no longer meet requirements or the supplier quits voluntarily.

Conformity Assessment Bodies and Technical Regulations

Conformity assessment bodies providing services for technical regulations need to satisfy three criteria to perform their job well. They need to remain at the forefront of technological development to be able to assess whether the latest products and processes meet technical regulations. They need to be technically competent. They also need to enjoy the trust of the regulatory agency. The required continuous investments to keep pace with technological change are often out of reach of developing country governments. Hence, the trend is for commercial service providers to supply an increasing number of the testing, certification, and inspection procedures required in the regulated domain. However, regulatory agencies need to retain some understanding of the technical competence of the conformity assessment service providers because they have to accept their results.

In view of these often conflicting demands on the conformity assessment system, it is important that the most effective, efficient, and internationally acceptable solution be found for a developing economy. Issues that need to be considered include the following:

- Conformity assessment services should be provided by independent third-party service providers. These suppliers can be in either the private or the public sectors but should be independent from the regulatory agency. Such independence allows the regulatory agency to make use of the most appropriate and technically competent service providers. A regulatory agency that provides these services itself will be tempted to retest everything that has already been tested to keep its laboratories busy and earning money.

- Producers should have a choice of service providers when the market is large enough. In small markets, this may not be feasible.

- Evidence of the technical competency of conformity assessment bodies can be provided by appropriate accreditation for the specific service (for example, inspection, testing, and certification) that they provide. The accreditation body could be of national or regional character, but should ideally be part of an international mutual recognition mechanism and needs to be recognized by the government.

- The conformity assessment service providers should carry legal liability in the countries where they provide conformity assessment services. This is important to the regulatory authorities because they need to have legal recourse should the conformity assessment service providers fail in their duties. Various mechanisms are available to governments to implement this requirement, such as demanding local registered offices of foreign bodies, mutual recognition agreements, and the like. Although a regulatory authority could be entitled to unilaterally accept the conformity assessment results from any service provider, even one outside the country, the risks need to be understood—namely, that the regulatory authority will have no legal recourse against the conformity assessment service provider. This is often the only practical way to deal with the issue in developing or smaller economies where conformity assessment services are not available, especially economies without local manufacturers.

- In the EU, conformity assessment service providers for the New Approach directives are formally designated by the ministry, government departments, or the regulatory authority when they have met the necessary criteria.

Self-declaration of conformity

Self-declaration of conformity is often touted as being the most cost-effective way to provide the required evidence. The EU uses a mix of self-declaration and third-party assessments in its so-called Global Approach to conformity assessment (box 4.3). For many of the products imported into developing economies, this approach could be quite ade-

---

BOX 4.3

The EU's Global Approach to Conformity Assessment

At the EU level, the New Approach directives spell out the technical regulations relevant for product safety in the nonfood area. They regulate product safety requirements and some other aspects by establishing essential requirements and allow for the use of EU standards to fulfill the requirements. As such, the mandatory and voluntary fields of product design are strongly interlinked.

The EU's Global Approach to certification and testing establishes European Community policy on conformity assessment for the New Approach directives. The CE (conformité Européenne, or European comformity) marking on a product symbolizes conformity to all the obligations required by the applicable New Approach directives. In some cases, a CE marking requires a third-party assessment, in which case member states assign so-called Notified Bodies for the conformity assessment (certification, testing, and inspection). Notified Bodies can be governmental or private institutions. But under many circumstances, the use of a third party is not required and firms can affix a CE marking on their products on their own, thereby demonstrating compliance with New Approach directives.

Source: European Commission 2000.

quate, especially if the supply chain generally has a record of compliance over a lengthy period of time. To be effective, a self-declaration of conformity scheme must go hand in hand with a very effective market surveillance mechanism and stringent product liability legislation (WTO 2000).

Sanctions

Finally, sanctions are required in the case where suppliers or products fail to meet the requirements of the technical regulations. Sanctions can range from the administrative type of sanctions (for example, removal of the commodities from the marketplace by the supplier, repair or destruction of noncompliant products, or re-export to the country of origin) to court actions should the supplier fail to heed administrative sanctions.

The Costs of Conformity Assessment

Demonstrating compliance with international standards can be expensive. International standards typically reflect the level of technology of high-income economies. The level of technological development of low- and middle-income economies is inevitably much lower. To upgrade, enterprises must invest in more modern manufacturing and process technology and equipment and in more sophisticated testing equipment. They may be required to invest in more appropriate production facilities and environmental control and handling equipment. Over and above these technological improvements, workers may have to be retrained to use more up-to-date technologies or organizational processes to control quality.

Although the greatest conformity assessment costs for SMEs are often those for upgrading the production and organizational processes to meet the relevant standards, there are also fees for obtaining certification. The actual cost of preparing for certification will vary according to the size and complexity of operations of the company. For a management system certification, the assessment and verification of a medium-size plant takes approximately five days. The candidate for certification needs to cover the day rates and travel fees of the assessors. The total is typically increased by additional fees charged for issuance of certificates (in some cases, up to US$2,000). Certification from internationally recognized certification bodies can be particularly expensive when they do not have a domestic team, because international auditor day rates can be high (US$1,500 per day) and their travel costs from their home countries must be borne by the certification candidate. These expenses can bring total certification fees to well above US$14,000 for a medium-size plant. The certificates issued vary in time of validity and usually must be reverified annually. These renewal audits last typically three days, giving a likely annual cost burden of about US$6,000 to US$8,000. In addition, once every three years the full assessment is repeated. Surveys of total ISO 9001 implementation and certification costs in middle-income countries including Argentina, Brazil, and South Africa showed that averages varied from US$13,000 to US$166,000 for SMEs and up to US$526,000 for large companies (Guasch and others 2007).

Closing the Loop with Market Surveillance

Fundamentals of Market Surveillance

Although market surveillance it not typically included in the notion of national quality infrastructure, it is a critical complementary function that allows public authorities to monitor whether products and services meet basic health, safety, and environmental regulations. Market surveillance is one of the major responsibilities of the regulatory authorities for ensuring that suppliers and products meet the requirements of technical regulations, whether products are imported or locally produced. Market surveillance is particularly important in markets where the responsibility for the testing and certification of products falling within the scope of technical regulation has been placed squarely on the suppliers, that is, the authorities do not test and release products before marketing. This is the case of the EU's New Approach. Market surveillance can be conducted only by a regulatory authority that has been given the required legal powers and that is suitably protected against spurious legal claims by unhappy enterprises. This legal authority is quite necessary because the inspectors conducting market surveillance need to have immense legal powers of entry, search, and confiscation to be effective.

Market surveillance is conducted on products that fall within the scope of technical regulation at the moment of being placed on the market and may include visits to commercial, industrial, and storage premises; work places; and other premises where products are put into service or on the market. In this respect, it differs quite markedly from the mandatory certification practiced by many low-income and transition economies, which is basically a premarket approval system. Market surveillance consists basically of random and spot checks, taking of samples for reexamination or testing, and gathering of necessary information. Market surveillance can be either planned or off schedule, depending on the ongoing nature of the activity, the handling of an immediate threat, or the request of the courts.

Approaches to Market Surveillance

Market surveillance is a major challenge for ECA countries when they change from a premarket approval system, such as mandatory certification, to a more modern, postmarket surveillance system. The two major questions that surface are the following:

- Is one centralized regulatory authority necessary for market surveillance of all products, or should each responsible ministry or agency establish its own?

- How should market surveillance be financed? Should the state's budget provide funds, or should suppliers pay for the "pleasure of being policed"?

The natural tendency would be to establish a regulatory authority in every ministry that is responsible for the implementation of technical regulations. But some countries, such as the Czech Republic, have opted for a single, centralized regulatory authority. Although such a constellation is sensible because it optimizes scarce labor and other resources, it has some negative aspects. The main challenge is that the ministries responsible for the development of technical regulations often are no longer interested because they perceive a loss of power from the removal of their market surveillance activities.

However, if every ministry establishes its own regulatory authorities, this is a very expensive option and low- and middle-income economies frequently lack adequately trained personnel to do it effectively. Hence, some countries follow a middle road, by establishing two or three regulatory authorities. One could be responsible for all foods and feeds, the other for all safety and consumer products, and so forth. In ECA countries, this is currently a very real issue; some countries have established a centralized regulatory authority (such as the Czech Republic), and some are in the process of establishing a regulatory authority in every ministry and agency (such as the Kyrgyz Republic). The challenges to make sure these regulatory authorities work in an effective and efficient way and to provide the required funding remain formidable.

The question of financing market surveillance is complex. Purists would argue that because the government implemented the technical regulations in the first place, it should also be fully responsible for funding the market surveillance. This approach means that all taxpayers share the burden. Others would argue that producers should pay for the market surveillance activities, because they are the ones who need to be checked. Producers, however, pass the costs on to the end consumer, so only a limited part of society pays. In this case, imported and locally produced products should be levied in the same way to avoid falling foul of the

WTO TBT Agreement principles. Funding from the government is always under pressure and can limit effective market surveillance activities. Funding by producers is more secure, but resented by industry. Both systems are in use in various economies, both systems can work well, and both systems frequently are strained. The decision is ultimately more one of philosophy, custom and practice, and legal system interpretation.

Scientific, Industrial, and Legal Metrology

Metrology is the science of measurement and its application. Measurement is a necessary tool in all scientific fields—for example, chemistry, environmental control, geology, medicine, and biology. In most aspects of daily life (and often unnoticed by common citizens), measurements are needed for ensuring quality and efficiency of production in industry, fairness in trade, consumer protection, health and safety of human and animal life, and protection of the environment. Metrology also promotes innovation, thus facilitating market access and trade.

Metrology is present in everyday life and confers reliability and credibility to measurements. Reliable measurements reduce expenses by avoiding duplication of measurements, improve quality assurance by ensuring that products and processes adhere to standards, and help sell market goods and services by transmitting accurate information to buyers. Metrology also helps protect human health and the environment at the national level. A society's ability to determine whether food is edible, water drinkable, pharmaceuticals safe, and factories too polluting depends, to a large extent, on the trust it has in its metrology infrastructure (comprising the public and private laboratories that provide measurements for legal and business purposes). For all these reasons, accurate and consistent measurements are integral to a well-functioning economy. Estimates show that 1 to 6 percent of the gross domestic product (GDP) of industrial countries is related to measurement activities (CIPM 2003, Section 4.2). However, accurate and consistent measurements require specialized metrology skills, well-equipped laboratories, and regional and international cooperation.

Metrology can be subdivided into scientific, industrial, and legal metrology. Depending on the size and structure of an economy, different institutional arrangements are possible for each of these categories. Some countries clearly separate different metrology functions into different organizations. In other countries, single institutions play multiple roles—realizing, maintaining, and disseminating measurements throughout the economy, while also providing further commercial and legal metrology services. In mature industrial economies, the public or private national metrology institutes (NMIs) are responsible for scientific metrology, and commercial calibration laboratories are responsible for industrial metrology. However, NMIs can also play a role in high-end industrial measurements. Public legal metrology organizations oversee the regulatory field (table 4.3).

Calibration is the process through which the high-level measurement standards of NMIs are diffused throughout economies. Calibration involves determining the relationship between an instrument's input and the magnitude of its output. It establishes the accuracy and precision of a measuring instrument by comparing it to a reference standard of known accuracy. Calibration is needed periodically to recover measurement reliability and compensate for instrument offset. It serves industrial producers, testing laboratories, inspection bodies, research laboratories, universities, and other end users. Many conformity assessment bodies require that equipment and measurement reference systems be calibrated, or be *traceable* to widely accepted metrological references provided by calibration laboratories, before being issued product or system certificates.

A measurement is *traceable* to a reference standard when its value can be related through an unbroken chain of comparisons with known uncertainties to that standard. Measurement comparisons are most often obtained by calibration. The arrows in figure 4.4 denote the traceability of length measurement (a) from the instruments used by manufacturers,

FIGURE 4.4

Traceability of Industrial Measurements to Reference Standards at the National Metrology Institute

Source: Authors.

TABLE 4.3

Metrology Fields and Responsible Bodies

Fields	Responsible bodies
Scientific metrology refers to the realization and dissemination of units of measurement, the maintenance of measurement standards, and the promotion of their acceptance and equivalence. It concerns the establishment of measurement units, development of measurement methods, and the traceability of these measurements to users in society.	***National metrology*** institutes establish national measurement unit systems, develop and maintain national measurement standards, and disseminate measurement units in the economy. They are typically empowered by governments to be the final authority in the domain of metrology. NMIs are the designated custodians of countries' ***reference standards***. Reference standards are measurement standards of the highest metrological quality, made in or derived from a given location or organization.[a] ***Measurement standards***, or etalons, are material measures, measuring instruments, reference material, or measuring systems intended to define, realize, conserve, or reproduce a unit or one of more values of a quantity, to serve as a reference (photograph 4.2) (Marbán and Pellecer 2002). NMIs are equipped with a wide range of equipment and expertise to provide precise measurements and calibrations of a large variety of instruments. NMIs often conduct research and development activities in areas related to metrology to develop new systems and deepen their technological capabilities.
Industrial metrology concerns the application of measurement science to manufacturing and other processes, ensuring the suitability of measurement instruments and the calibration and quality control of measurements. Metrological services to final industrial users, such as manufacturers or product designers, are denoted as the ***secondary calibration market*** (in contrast to the market for metrological services from the NMI to commercial calibration laboratories, which is denoted as the ***primary calibration market***).	***Commercial calibration laboratories*** provide measurements to ensure quality and efficiency of production in industry. They are involved in the secondary calibration market. Calibration laboratories can be hosted by NMIs and legal metrology organizations, but in industrial economies, most of these laboratories are operated by the private sector. They can be internal, serving only the needs of a particular firm, or provide services on a commercial basis.
Legal metrology comprises all activities for which legal requirements are prescribed on measurement, units of measurement, measuring instruments, and methods of measurement. These activities are performed by or on behalf of governmental authorities to ensure an appropriate level of credibility of measurement results in the national regulatory environment (OIML 2004).	***Legal metrology organizations*** ensure, in a regulatory or contractual manner, the appropriate trust and quality of all measurements (official controls, trade, safety, and the environment). Legal metrology organizations mainly conduct verification activities that determine whether commercial measurements are within acceptable tolerance, as defined in the relevant technical regulations. They also conduct "type" approval, which involves the approval of new measuring instruments before they are introduced in the market. In most countries, legal metrology is decentralized and a large number of responsibilities, including verification and inspection, are delegated to states or municipalities. Violations of legal controls can result in fines.

Source: Authors.

a. Reference standards can be classified as *primary standards* (these have the highest metrological quality) or *secondary standards* (the value for these is assigned by comparison with a primary standard of the same quantity). NMIs in countries with sophisticated industries that need precise measurements (for example, nanotechnology and pharmaceuticals), and with large government budgets for metrology, usually benefit from having a number of primary standards. NMIs in other countries mostly have secondary standards, which are traceable to primary standards in more industrialized countries.

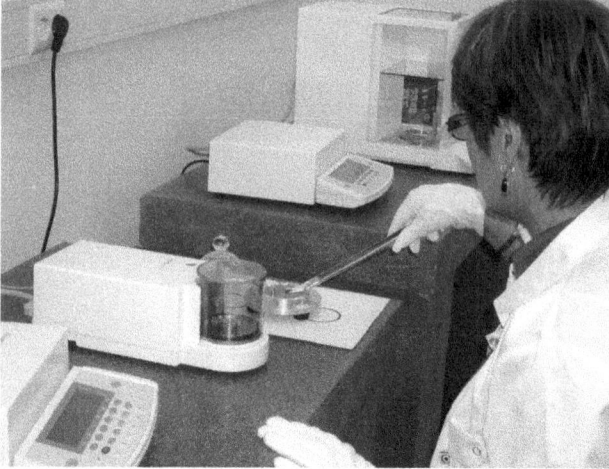

PHOTOGRAPH 4.2
A metrologist handles the national reference standard for mass in Georgia's national metrology institute.

Source: Contributed by Karl-Christian Goethner.

research institutes, and universities to design new products, (b) to the commercial calibration laboratories that periodically calibrate these instruments with their gauge blocks and other equipment, and (c) to the NMI, which uses a laser interferometer as a reference standard for length.

Countries often have a single NMI, but when there are several NMIs, each is responsible for distinct measurement areas. This strategy occurs when a central NMI is not able to establish metrological activities in all the fields of interest to an economy. The government or the central NMI then designates other public or private institutes to maintain national measurement standards and related calibration facilities for one or more quantities and measurement ranges.

Accreditation and metrology are interdependent. When public or private calibration laboratories are accredited under the international quality system standard ISO/IEC 17025 (ISO and IEC 2005), they provide the market and governments with a level of confidence in their technical competence and the knowledge that their measurements are traceable to proper reference standards of known uncertainty. When they have been accredited by internationally recognized bodies, they can demonstrate their ability to consistently produce valid results that are recognized among trade partners and by regulators across borders.

Legal metrology is an essential component of regulation. Buying a can of food, taking a metered taxi, filling up at the gas station, and paying the electricity bill all involve trusting the sellers' measurements as the basis for paying a known amount. There is no way consumers can verify the reliability of each measurement, so this responsibility is given to public authorities. Governments can protect their citizens against unintended or fraudulent losses by imposing controls on the use of measurements for the purpose of transactions. This decreases disputes and transaction costs, thus increasing the efficiency of the market. Legal metrology also helps regulate areas related to human health, safety, and the environment. It supports regulations involving specific measurements that are aimed at the public interest, such as determining the permissible amounts of contaminants in water and monitoring automobile emissions. Finally, legal metrology reduces legal and fiscal arbitrariness and provides for a more predictable business environment. It leads to fairer law enforcement (for example, in the area of road safety) and helps governments collect revenue through excise and taxes based on measurements.

Most countries have specific legislations with respect to measurements. No universal law in metrology equally suits all countries and all purposes. Metrology must fulfill specific needs in different countries based on the constitutions; domestic interests; and government regulatory functions, responsibilities, and practices. A law on legal metrology precisely defines the functions of state metrological control, supervision, inspection, and market surveillance. It also clearly addresses the measurement functions and obligations of the government that may or may not be delegated under strict governmental control to third-party bodies.

International Cooperation in Metrology and Trade

An internationally harmonized metrology system ensures that each and every measurement that affects quality or consumer protection issues is interpreted in the same way anywhere in the world, that is, what equals one kilogram in Bulgaria is the same amount in Uzbekistan. International harmonization works only while the users have trust into the system and all players in each level follow the same best practices, maintain independence and transparency, and compare their measurements frequently with their peers.

International trade involves enormous amounts of money, and small measurement errors—be it for oil exports from Kazakhstan, hydroelectric power exports from the Kyrgyz Republic, or fruit juice from Moldova—can represent significant costs. Moreover, in an era of global value chains, compatibility and interchangeability of parts sourced from different countries for common systems require harmonized national metrology systems. Finally, exported products need to demonstrate that they satisfy the technical regulations of their client countries, and thus, a common understanding of the equivalence of measurements made in different countries is needed.

International and regional cooperation in metrology has four roles:

- Ensuring that measurements made in one country are accepted everywhere without the need to replicate them in each country

- Rationalizing metrology resources to reduce duplications of investments in each country

- Exchanging scientific information on metrology

- Supporting knowledge transfer and capacity building

Methods of Organization

The Metre Convention, signed in Paris in 1875, was the first intergovernmental treaty on metrology. It now has 80 signatories or associates, including all the major industrial countries. The Metre Convention recognizes the authority of the International Bureau of Weights and Measures (BIPM) in matters of scientific metrology. The BIPM's mandate is to provide the basis for a single system of measurement throughout the world, traceable to the International System of Units (SI).[12] NMIs represent countries at the BIPM and in regional metrology organizations, including the European Association of National Metrology Institutes (with 37 members and associates in Europe) and the Euro-Asian Cooperation of National Metrological Institutions (with members drawing from 17 former or existing central-planning economies). Although signatories of the Metre Convention agree to adopt a common set of units, the treaty does not imply that they recognize the equivalence of each other's measurements.

Mutual Recognition Arrangements (MRAs), however, provide a framework for the formal recognition of national measurement standards and calibration capabilities. A decade ago, a number of signatories of the Metre Convention came together to create the International Committee for Weights and Measures Mutual Recognition Arrangement (CIPM MRA) under the authority of the BIPM. Through measurement comparisons, the CIPM MRA establishes the degree of equivalence of national measurement standards maintained by NMIs, and thereby guarantees the international acceptance of measurement results that are traceable to the NMI by the other MRA signatories. It also provides governments and other parties a secure technical foundation for wider agreements related to trade and regulatory affairs. Hence, it allows measurements and test results that are traceable to the NMI in one signatory country to be recognized abroad (box 4.4). This procedure decreases the costs of redundant measurements, which pose technical barriers to trade. There are currently 72 signatory and associate countries to the CIPM MRA that together make up the vast majority of the world's trade.

But merely signing the CIPM MRA is not sufficient. To establish their international comparability, signatory NMIs must continuously benchmark their measurements against those of other NMIs. They do this by

12. See the International Bureau of Weights and Measures Web site, http://www.bipm.org.

Lowering of Korean Firm's Cross-Border Business Costs because of the CIPM MRA

Daewoo Shipbuilding and Marine Engineering (DSME) is one of the largest shipbuilding companies in the world with US$4.7 billion sales in 2005. In 2002, the company received a contract from British Petroleum (BP), the British energy giant, to construct an offshore plant. As construction of the plant got underway, DSME was faced with an issue concerning the calibration of measuring instruments that were to be used in the construction. BP asked that DSME calibrate all 130 instruments used during construction to the National Institute of Standards and Technology (NIST). This request meant a total additional spending of US$1 million on DSME's part. The firm would be required to cover costs to have its instruments calibrated abroad and to purchase substitute equipment while the existing equipment was being calibrated. Further- more, DSME would have to pay US$10 million if the project was not completed by the agreed date. After searching for ways to reduce losses and maintain delivery schedules, DSME found a solution to this problem. It contacted the Korea Research Institute of Standards and Science (KRISS), knowing that KRISS and NIST were signatories of the CIPM MRA. Furthermore, the Korea Laboratory Accreditation Scheme (KOLAS) had accredited KRISS. KOLAS is an internationally recognized accreditation body, being a mem- ber of Asia Pacific Laboratory Accreditation Cooperation and the International Laboratory Accreditation Cooperation Mutual Recognition Arrangement. DSME demonstrated traceability of its reference stan- dards to KRISS and obtained confirmation of the mutual recognition of calibration and measurement ca- pabilities issued by KRISS and NIST (because both these institutes were CIPM MRA signatories). NIST confirmed that while DSME was keeping traceability to KRISS, the instruments could be calibrated by KRISS. BP was informed of this situation and agreed to accept KOLAS accreditations and calibration certificates issued by KRISS. DSME was able to satisfy its client's requirements by ensuring traceability of calibrations to NIST. Furthermore, DSME saved valuable time and a significant amount of resources by having calibrations performed locally by KRISS and met its delivery target date.

Source: International Bureau of Weights and Measures, http://kcdb.bipm.org/NL/06/DSME_case_study.pdf.

participating in interlaboratory comparisons organized by their regional metrology associations. The best NMIs in each region participate in *key comparisons* at the international level. These chains of comparisons estab- lish the international traceability of measurements. For each type of mea- surement with established international traceability, an NMI receives a calibration and measurement capability (CMC) that is recognized inter- nationally through the CIPM MRA. More national CMCs mean more national measurements are recognized abroad.

International Integration of Legal Metrology

International cooperation among legal metrology organizations can reduce technical barriers to trade. The International Organization of Legal Metrology (OIML), with 115 member states or corresponding member states, was created to promote the global harmonization of legal metrology. The organization develops model regulations on an international basis, and members can use these regulations to establish national legislation on measuring instruments. Membership in the OIML helps countries harmonize policies on the trade of products and services whose commercial value is based on measurements and, also, the trade in measuring instruments. Without harmonized means and procedures for verifications and tests, it is difficult to establish whether metrological control is equivalent in different countries. The OIML can also provide governments with technical assistance for the development of metrology policies. The organization recently created a Mutual Acceptance Arrangement whereby signatories accept measuring instruments approvals, test reports, and certificates issued by other participants. This allows a country to develop or use measuring instruments that have been approved in other countries, thereby decreasing technical barriers to trade in an area of importance to technology adoption (that is, import of measuring instruments). It also allows domestic firms to use testing facilities in other countries if adequate facilities are not available in the home country.

Accession to the EU requires harmonization of legal metrology by new member countries. A number of EU New Approach and Old Approach directives are related to metrology. They must be adopted for countries to fulfill the Free Movement of Goods clause of the EU's *acquis communautaire*. Most of the practical activities related to harmonization of legal metrology in Europe take place in the European Cooperation in Legal Metrology, a regional organization. This organization is open to EU and EFTA member countries and to certain EU candidate countries on an ad hoc basis.

The Role of Accreditation

Accreditation is the last level of quality control of the conformity assessment services delivered in both the voluntary and the mandatory spheres. It is the procedure by which an authoritative body gives formal recognition that another body or person is competent to carry out specific tasks.[13] Accreditation reduces risks for governments, businesses, and consumers by ensuring, through regular surveillance, that conformity assessment bodies and calibration laboratories are independent and competent (figure 4.5). It is usually provided for a very specific scope, such as a type of test or a type of certification. Accredited bodies must be free of conflicts of interest or undue influence from interests that may benefit from a certification decision. A 2007 survey of European accreditation showed

13. See the International Accreditation Forum Web site, http://www.iaf.nu/.

FIGURE 4.5
FIGURE 4.5

Accreditation Pyramid

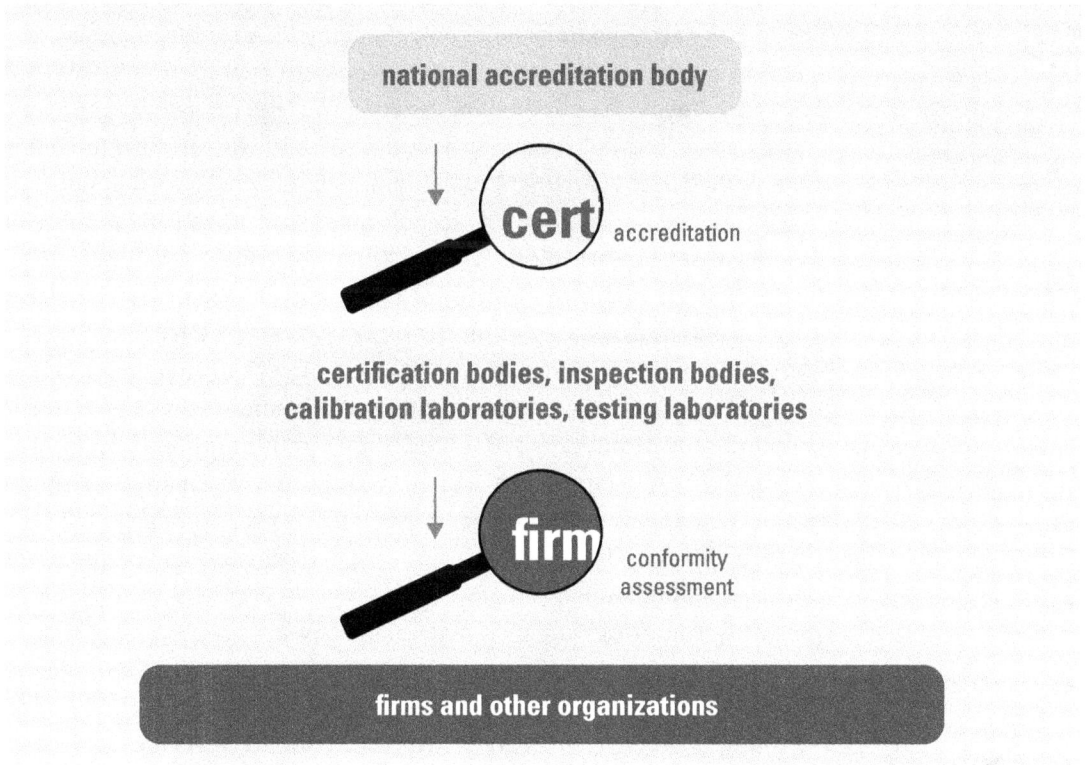

Source: Authors.

that about one-half of accredited bodies are testing laboratories, about one-fifth are inspection bodies, and certification bodies and calibration laboratories account for much smaller shares.[14]

Accreditation is granted on the basis of audits[15] and evaluates management systems, people, and people's skills and knowledge. Audits are performed at regular intervals and can involve observing the conformity assessment body's staff members conducting their own activities (testing, calibration, inspection, or certification) to ensure their competency. Audits can even require measurement and practical tests. An unsuccessful audit can lead to an accreditation certificate being refused, suspended, or withdrawn. Because each accreditation has a narrow technical scope, accreditation bodies must involve technical assessors who are recognized specialists in their fields.

14. See the European co-operation for Accreditation Web site, http://www .european-accreditation.org.
15. An audit is a systematic, independent, documented process for obtaining records, statements of facts, or other relevant information and assessing them objectively to determine the extent to which specified requirements are fulfilled.

The quality of the technical staff of the national accreditation body (NAB) determines the objectivity of the accreditation process. Assessors must go through specialized training programs, which are usually offered by mature accreditation bodies only. In many ECA countries, the accreditation system is relatively new and assessors are sent for training abroad. A comprehensive accreditation system also relies on assessment teams with a wide body of scientific and technical skills who are able to understand the latest testing and calibration technologies in a wide range of fields. Because it is impossible for full-time assessors to be experts in all fields, assessors are often selected from accredited organizations or academic or technical institutions and are engaged on short-term contracts. The assessment team can also engage external technical experts for assistance with accreditation. In 2004, a survey of accreditation bodies in 37 countries[16] by the German Metrology Institute PTB (Physikalisch-Technische Bundesanstalt) found that a minimum staff of 15 was typically required, which can be prohibitive in small developing countries, and that this number grows roughly proportionately with the number of accreditations. Most surveyed accreditation bodies had fewer than 40 staff members.

Most countries with an accreditation body have some type of legislation recognizing the role and, sometimes, the structure and funding of the NAB. In the vast majority of cases, there is a single NAB. This is the preferred practice in every newly established accreditation system. Accreditation bodies have different legal statuses in different countries. They are found with various degrees of government involvement, but the trend has been in favor of public autonomous agencies or nonprofit organizations rather than a ministerial department. This approach is due to a recognized need for greater flexibility and independence; for their ability to comply with internationally accepted standards, guides, and codes of conduct[17] that emphasize the need for impartiality, objectivity, nondiscriminatory policies and practices; and for the avoidance of conflicts of interests. Conflicts of interests can arise when accreditation bodies are involved in other activities or are branches of other organizations involved in other activities. Offering certification, testing, and calibration services is a source of conflict of interest because it puts the accreditation body in competition with potential candidates for accreditation.

In many countries, both public and private stakeholders are involved in the governance and technical functions of the NAB. This practice helps ensure that the NAB is impartial and builds confidence in the organizations. Technical consultative committees of external specialists also

16. There were 15 countries in Western Europe; 7 in Eastern Europe; 10 in Asia; and 5 in North, Central, and South America and Africa.
17. See, for example, ISO and IEC (1993, 2004b), and the IAF Code of Conduct (IAF 2003).

ensure that accreditations are granted on the basis of sound and objective technical decisions.

International and Regional Integration in Accreditation

There are two benefits to having a national accreditation system that is recognized abroad. First, it provides industry, consumers, and the government in the home country the assurance that the NAB is independent and competent and delivers its services in the most timely and cost-effective way. Because international recognition is difficult to achieve, it enhances the NAB's credibility, and the prestige of a national accreditation increases domestic demand for accreditation. Second, it promotes trade by ensuring that the work performed by a country's conformity assessment and calibration laboratories will be accepted in other countries. According to the WTO TBT Agreement, "in this regard, verified compliance, for instance through accreditation, with relevant guides or recommendations issued by international standardizing bodies shall be taken into account as an indication of adequate technical competence" (WTO TBT Agreement 1995, Article 6.1.1, http://www.wto.org/english/docs_e/legal_e/17-tbt_e.htm). Through full international recognition, an ISO 9001 certificate obtained by a certification body accredited by one country's NAB is recognized in another country. This is the concept of "one-stop testing" or "certified once—accepted everywhere," according to which these checks do not have to be repeated in each country. In the EU, for example, the European Commission estimates that the perfect operation of mutual recognition of accreditation could yield trade benefits of as much as 1.8 percent of EU GDP (Commission of European Communities 2001).

A first step toward achieving international recognition is to establish an accreditation system that conforms to international standards[18] and guidelines. These standards and guidelines define both the way in which an NAB operates, to guarantee objectivity, impartiality, and transparency,[19] and the types of procedures used to evaluate individual conformity assessment bodies during the accreditation process. These international standards are developed by ISO and IEC and are adopted by all international and regional accreditation organizations.

---

18. See, for example, ISO/IEC 17025 for calibration and testing laboratories (ISO and IEC 2005).
19. For example, ISO/IEC 17011:2004 specifies general requirements for accreditation bodies assessing and accrediting conformity assessment bodies. It is also used as a requirements document for the peer evaluation process for MRAs between accreditation bodies (ISO and IEC 2004b).

As a second step, NABs can join international and regional accreditation organizations. Membership in those organizations enhances an accreditation body's prospect of gaining international credibility. These organizations also play an important role in facilitating knowledge transfer and provide fora for learning from other experienced accreditation systems. The International Accreditation Forum (IAF) and the International Laboratory Accreditation Cooperation (ILAC) are the two principal organizations involved in the development of accreditation practices and procedures. IAF is concerned with the accreditation of certification bodies and ILAC with the accreditation of laboratories and inspection bodies. Regional accreditation organizations are shown in map 4.2. There is no regional association specific to ECA countries or to the CIS region, but some EU accession countries from ECA are members of the European co-operation for Accreditation (EA) while Russia is a member of the Asia Pacific Laboratory Accreditation Cooperation. Other ECA countries in the Balkans and in the CIS are not associated with any regional organization. For a period of several years, the Central Asian Cooperation on Metrology, Accreditation, and Quality was also recognized as a regional organization by ILAC, but its membership terminated in 2008 when the ILAC General Assembly considered it no longer operational. To become full members of IAF, ILAC, or recognized regional organizations, NABs must demonstrate that they are committed to operate at high international standards. Although membership enhances a NAB's reputation, it falls short of guaranteeing international recognition.

Opening of Doors with a Mutual Recognition Arrangement in Accreditation

The final step to achieving *full* recognition is to join MRAs[20] with other countries. This can be done at the international level through IAF and ILAC, as well as through regional organizations such as the EA in Europe. MRAs are based on a process of peer evaluation processes through which members evaluate each others' compliance with the agreed-upon requirements and evaluate the performance of assessment staff. They usually cover specific accreditation types (for example, quality management system certifiers).[21] MRAs eliminate the need for multiple accreditations and multiple assessments. Conformity assessment bodies accredited in one country may operate in a different country on the basis

---

20. MRAs are also referred to as multilateral recognition arrangements (MLA) in the case of the IAF.
21. When MRAs cover accreditation in the areas of product certification, testing, or calibration, they usually cover the entire range of possible subareas (that is, accreditation for all types of products, all types of tests, or all types of calibrations), not a specific subarea only.

MAP 4.2
Regional Accreditation Organizations, 2011

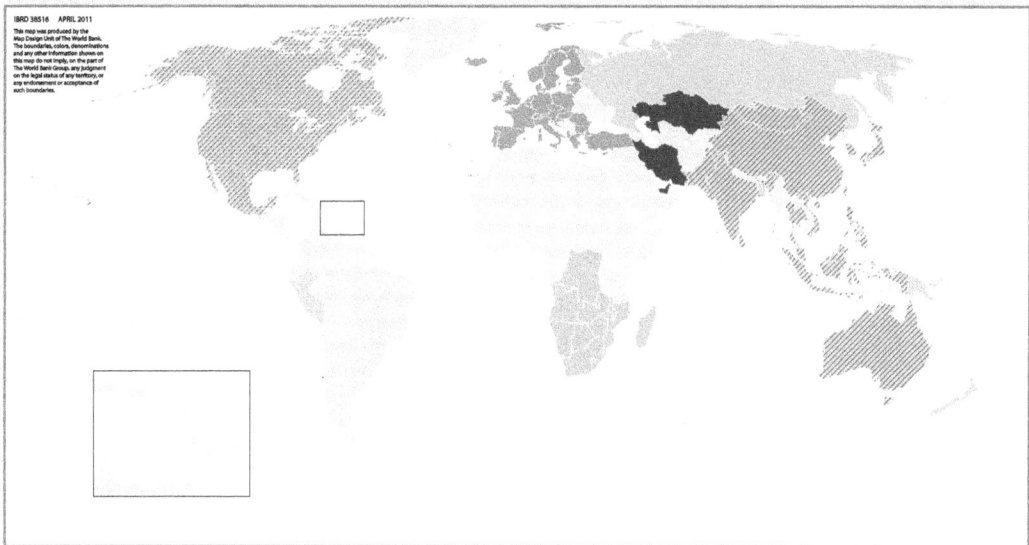

- APLAC (Asia Pacific Laboratory Accreditation Cooperation)
- EA (European co-operation for Accreditation)
- IAAC (InterAmerican Accreditation Cooperation)
- PAC (Pacific Accreditation Cooperation)
- SADCA (Southern African Development Community Accreditation)
- EAAB (East Africa Accreditation Board)
- member states of both SADCA and EAAB
- member states of both APLAC and PAC
- member states of IAAC, PAC, and APLAC
- second-tier members of IAAC (associate or stakeholder members)
- no membership

Source: Authors based on APLAC, http://www.aplac.org/; EA, http://www.european-accreditation.org/content/home/home.htm; IAAC, http://www.iaac.org.mx/; PAC, http://www.apec-pac.org/; SADCA, http://www.sadca.org/; and EAAB, http://www.eac.int/trade/index.php?option=com_content&view=article&id=111&Itemid=96.

of a single accreditation. And organizations owning certificates or test reports from MRA-accredited bodies do not need to have their systems or products or services reevaluated in each country where such products and services are marketed.

MRAs are now widespread among industrial countries. Table 4.4 understates the number of IAF and ILAC signatories because these MRAs recognize the signatories of MRAs of several regional organizations, such as EA. As a result, MRAs now affect an increasing portion of traded prod-

TABLE 4.4

Examples of MRA and Multilateral Recognition Arrangement Memberships, January 1, 2009

MRA and MLA	Number of member countries
IAF Quality Management System MLA	40
ILAC Testing MRA	50
EA Quality Management System MLA	26
EA Testing MLA	34

Source: EA, http://www.european-accreditation.org/content/home/home.htm; IAF, http://www.iaf.nu; and ILAC, http://www.ilac.org.
Note: MLA = multilateral recognition arrangement.

ucts. The latest available figures from 2001 show that 21 percent of industrial production, or 7 percent of GDP, inside the EU was covered by mutual recognition (Commission of European Communities 2001). A study of 17 developing countries by Wilson and Otsuki (2004) showed that most firms agreed that it would be easier to export to developed countries that have an MRA with a firm's home country.

Accreditation as a Central Role in EU Accession

In an effort to integrate its internal market, the EU has long depended on mutual recognition of conformity assessment systems. In fact, harmonization of the national accreditation system with international norms is a condition for satisfying the EU requirements of free movement of goods. The EA Multilateral Recognition Arrangement (MLA) forms a centerpiece of trade integration. The EU recognizes accreditation by a member of the EA MLA as a means to appoint Notified Bodies—conformity assessment bodies that act in the EU's mandatory sphere. In fact, as of January 1, 2010, accreditation has been formally anchored into the EU's regulatory framework (European Parliament and Council of the European Union 2008). All EU member and candidate countries are required to organize their accreditation systems according to criteria that largely reflect international best practices.

The regulation foresees that each member state shall assign a single accreditation body. However, the regulation also allows member states to decide against the establishment of an accreditation body if this is not economically reasonable. In this situation, countries should rely on the accreditation bodies of other member states. The accreditation body does not necessarily have to be a public organization, but it must be operated on a nonprofit basis, shall not offer any activities or services that conformity assessment bodies provide, and shall not provide consultancy services. Furthermore, "each member state shall ensure that its national accreditation body has the appropriate financial and personnel resources for the proper performance of its tasks," including international and European cooperation (European Parliament and Council of the European Union 2008). This can be a challenge for small ECA countries. The regulation requires the independence, objectivity, impartiality, and competence of the accreditation body and membership in the EA.

The regulation imposes requirements for cross-border accreditation. It prohibits competition among accreditation bodies. Cross-border accreditation is allowed only in cases when a member state has not established an accreditation body, when the national accreditation body does not perform the services required by the conformity assessment body, and when the national accreditation body has not undergone successful peer evaluation and lacks international recognition. This situation means that once recognized abroad, ECA member and candidate countries' national accreditation bodies become de facto monopolies in their domestic markets. The challenge will be for their government to ensure they remain effective.

The following chapters describe the different elements of the national quality infrastructure (NQI) in more detail, namely, standardization, conformity assessment, metrology, and accreditation. Each chapter includes an analysis of the NQI in ECA countries, based on both a survey of NQI institutions (conducted over the 2006–09 period) and case studies.

References

CEN (European Committee for Standardization). 2004. "Compass: European Standardization in a Nutshell." 2nd ed. CEN, Brussels.

CIPM (International Committee for Weights and Measures). 2003. "Evolving Needs for Metrology in Trade, Industry, and Society and the Role of the BIPM." Report of the International Committee for Weights and Measures, CIPM, Paris.

Commission of European Communities. 2001. "Statistical and Technical Annex to the 'Report on the Functioning of Community Product and Capital Markets.'" http://ec.europa.eu/internal_market/economic-reports/docs/cardiffstat_en.pdf.

European Commission. 2000. *Guide to the Implementation of Directives Based on the New Approach and the Global Approach.* Brussels: European Commission.

European Parliament and Council of the European Union. 2008. "Regulation EC 765/2008: Setting out the requirements for accreditation and market surveillance relating to the marketing of products." *Official Journal of the European Union*, August 13.

Guasch, J. L., J.-L. Racine, I. Sánchez, and M. Diop. 2007. *Quality Systems and Standards for a Competitive Edge.* Washington, DC: World Bank.

IAF (International Accreditation Forum). 2003. "Code of Conduct for Accreditation Body Members of the IAF." Policy Document IAF PL 1:2003, IAF, Cherrybrook, Australia.

International Trade Centre. 2004. *Influencing and Meeting International Standards: Challenges for Developing Countries.* Geneva: International Trade Centre.

———. 2005. *A Strategic Approach to the Quality Assurance Challenge.* Geneva: International Trade Centre.

ISO (International Organization for Standardization). 2008. *ISO Survey of Certifications 2007.* Geneva: ISO.

ISO (International Organization for Standardization) and IEC (International Electrotechnical Commission). 1993. *ISO/IEC Guide 58:1993: Calibration and Testing Laboratory Accreditation Systems—General Requirements for Operation and Recognition.* Geneva: ISO.

———. 2004a. ISO/IEC 17000:2004: *Conformity assessment—Vocabulary and general principles.* Geneva: ISO.

———. 2004b. *ISO/IEC 17011:2004: Conformity assessment—General requirements for accreditation bodies accrediting conformity assessment bodies.* Geneva: ISO.

———. 2004c. *ISO/IEC Directives —Part 2: Rules for the Structure and Drafting of International Standards.* 5th ed. Geneva: ISO and IEC.

————. 2004d. *ISO/IEC Guide 2:2004: Standardization and Related Activities—General Vocabulary.* Geneva: ISO and IEC.

————. 2005. *ISO/IEC 17025:2005 (E): General requirements for the competence of testing and calibration laboratories.* Geneva: ISO and IEC.

————. 2008. *ISO/IEC Directives —Part 1: Procedures for the Technical Work.* 6th ed. Geneva: ISO and IEC.

ITC (International Trade Centre). 2005. *Innovations in Export Strategy: A Strategic Approach to the Quality Assurance Challenge.* Geneva: ITC.

Marbán, R., and J. Pellecer. 2002. *Metrology for Non-metrologists.* Washington, DC: Organization of American States.

OIML (International Organization of Legal Metrology). 2004. OIML D 1 "Elements for a Law on Metrology." International Document OIML D 1 Edition 2004 (E), International Organization of Legal Metrology, Paris.

Wilson, J. S., and T. Otsuki. 2004. "Standards and Technical Regulations and Firms in Developing Countries: New Evidence from a World Bank Technical Barriers to Trade Survey." World Bank, Washington, DC.

WTO (World Trade Organization). 2000. "Second Triennial Review of the TBT Agreement." World Trade Organization, Geneva.

CHAPTER 5

Standards and Technical Regulations in Eastern Europe and Central Asia: A Double-Edged Sword

"Mandatory certification and standardization are among the major barriers to innovation and development in Ukraine. They make introducing a new product next to impossible."

—President Viktor Yushchenko, Ukraine, 2008[1]

▷ **Although European Union (EU) members of Eastern Europe and Central Asia (ECA) have replaced domestic standards with regional and international standards, many Balkan and Commonwealth of Independent States (CIS) countries still rely on national or regional standards dating from the Soviet era.**

▷ **Standards in many ECA countries remain mostly mandatory and are imposed by the state—posing serious barriers to entrepreneurship and innovation. By contrast, EU and Organisation for Economic Co-operation and Development (OECD) countries have independent national standards bodies that develop voluntary standards based on stakeholder consensus.**

---

1. Third Presidential Forum, "State and Business Are Partners," Kyiv, Ukraine, July 10, 2008.

> ▶ **ECA countries contribute very little to international standardization. As a result, international standards do not always reflect their needs and they tend to be late adopters of the latest standards.**
>
> ▶ **ECA countries can make their firms more competitive by abolishing mandatory standards, streamlining technical regulations, and harmonizing standards with those of regional and international trade partners.**

Standards and Technical Regulations in ECA

Many institutions, processes, and roles are involved in the development of international and national standards and technical regulations.

Institutions

Before transition, the national quality infrastructure was organized as a top-down structure purely in the mandatory domain.

The international national quality infrastructure (NQI) scheme described in chapter 4 of this book was not implemented in the former Soviet Union and in Eastern Europe under central planning. Although similar components were used to control quality under central planning, the approach differed in two crucial aspects:

- Whereas the NQI scheme based on International Organization for Standardization (ISO) guidelines and standards is centered around a purely *voluntary* system (although this system can be used by regulatory bodies), the Soviet standards system, governed by the *Gosstandart*, and most systems in Eastern Europe were *mandatory* in each and every aspect.

- The Gosstandart system and most other systems under central planning covered all quality infrastructure components under one roof; it was a top-down approach with almost no feedback, and improvements arose through competition or comparisons or from regular evaluation of technical competence of the various service providers in the NQI (figure 5.1). Concerns about possible conflicts of interest or lack

FIGURE 5.1
Monolithic NQI under Central Planning

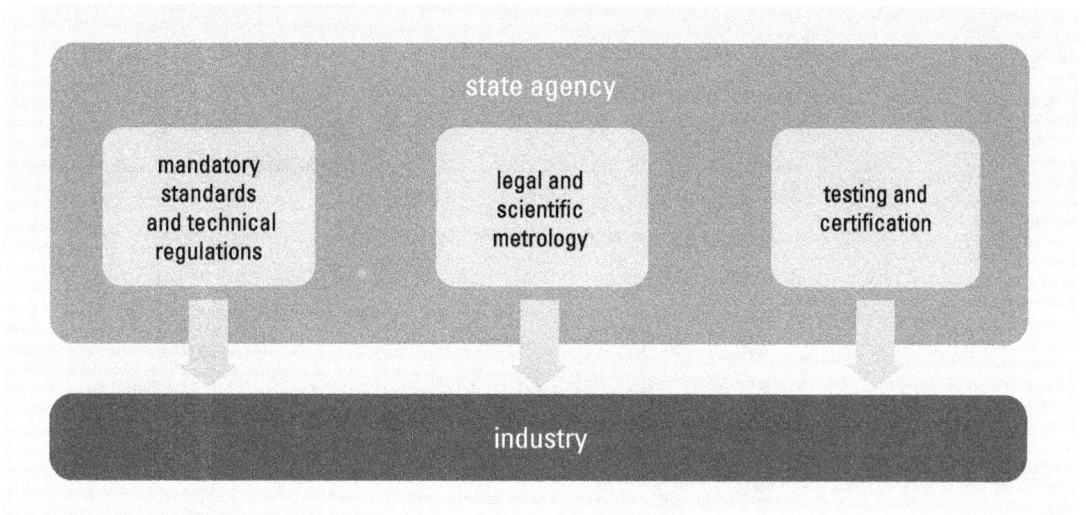

state agency

| mandatory standards and technical regulations | legal and scientific metrology | testing and certification |

industry

Source: Authors.

of transparency in the system were not considered because everything was state run and state controlled.

The central components of the Soviet system were the mandatory GOST standard (Gosudarstvennyy standart, or state standard), equivalent to a technical regulation. GOST standards were generally more prescriptive than international standards; there were tens of thousands of them; and their scope extended far beyond that of technical regulations in Western economies to, namely, safety, health, and environmental protection and to technical product prescriptions and quality parameters. The certification process could sometimes require testing and verification of measurement equipment. Accreditation or evaluation of technical competence was not considered because each step and procedure in the system implementation was regulated and controlled. The Gosstandart system covered the entire territory of the Soviet Union and exerted significant influence through the economic zone of socialist economies, the Council for Mutual Economic Assistance.

Before the 1990s, the Turkish NQI model clearly differed from that of other ECA economies because it was not under central planning. It had a mix of voluntary and mandatory standards and also used a number of international standards. Nonetheless, the system was very centralized and had some features in common with other ECA economies—the national standards body (NSB) operated in a somewhat top-down process and participated in both the development and the enforcement of technical regulations.

Almost two decades into transition, ECA countries have reformed their NQIs to varying degrees.

Although in the early days of the Soviet Union's industrialization the Gosstandart system might have produced acceptable quality results, it was evident that in the later decades the system was too rigid to keep up with the fast-changing needs of the market and with the increasingly stringent industrial requirements of accurate testing and measurement. For these same reasons, the Gosstandart was no longer able to provide optimal food, agricultural, and health safety for the population (World Bank 2007).

After the breakup of the Soviet Union, the Gosstandart system lost much of its international influence. One reason was that a number of transition economies reoriented themselves toward the European Union (EU). GOST standards and conformity assessment methods became unattractive to these countries because they were not recognized in market economies and were incompatible with World Trade Organization (WTO) requirements and the even more stringent EU requirements.

Several countries of Eastern Europe and Central Asia (ECA) abolished their old standardization agencies and reestablished their national standards bodies (NSBs) with new functions and responsibilities. In EU countries, the administration of technical regulations was removed from NSBs, metrology was separated from standardization and was established under independent institutes, and the markets for testing and certification were liberalized. A number of countries even separated conformity assessment activities from standardization, motivated by EU accession. This was the case in the Czech Republic, Estonia, and Poland, as well as a number of Balkan countries that aspired to eventual trade integration with the EU. The EU has also accepted countries where conformity assessment and standardization were separated through internal administrative mechanisms but continue to be part of a single organization, as is the case of some of the older EU member states.[2]

Restructuring of the NQI is severely lagging in most CIS countries.

In spite of its shortcomings, the legacy of the Gosstandart system is strong in a number of Commonwealth of Independent States (CIS) countries for

---

2. In the United Kingdom, the British Standards Institution operates well-regarded and very successful testing and certification subsidiaries, and the NSB in Germany, Deutsches Insitut für Normung, is one of the three majority shareholders in one of the largest system certification bodies in Europe, DQS Holding GmbH.

a variety of reasons. Most important, trading in CIS countries is still dominated by intraregional trade, particularly with the Russian Federation, which continues to use a derivative of the Gosstandart system. Institutional inertia and the financial and political cost of reform also naturally played a role in impeding reform.

Although each CIS country now maintains its own independent NQI, the Gosstandart system was inherited by a new regional body, the EuroAsian Interstate Council for Standardization, Metrology, and Certification (EASC). EASC concentrates on developing normative documents that NSBs in the CIS can choose to adopt. But EASC goes further and still defines much of the NQI policy and the mutual recognition criteria for CIS countries. The EASC technical commissions for metrology, accreditation, conformity acceptance, and harmonization of technical regulation are, to some extent, taking on the role of specialized technical regional organizations without being officially recognized by the relevant international organizations. In fact, by virtue of their EASC membership, CIS countries recognize each others' product, testing, and verification (calibration) certificates. However, in contrast to the international system, this recognition is done without independent evaluation of the technical capabilities of the entities issuing certificates. Hence, the incentives for transitioning to an international NQI model can be weak. For a country that trades mostly with the CIS, abandoning the EASC model would mean losing markets without a guarantee of finding new ones to the East or to the West of the CIS.

As a result, a number of CIS countries retain monolithic top-down NQI systems where most functions—standards, technical regulations, metrology, certification, testing, and accreditation—are under the responsibility of a single agency (box 5.1). Nonetheless, the growing importance of China in world trade may change this situation. As seen in table 5.1, China has mostly separated functions within the NQI.

Industry and consumer groups still have limited influence in ECA's national standards bodies.

In reforming countries, the separation of NQI functions from NSBs has been accompanied by changes in the legal status, autonomy, and governance structure of NSBs. Many NSBs are now independent institutions that have converged toward the market-economy model of increased institutional autonomy, as opposed to being just departments or directorates in ministries or being nonprofit organizations of public law. As a result, all EU-based NSBs and several others from the ECA region now benefit from as much institutional autonomy as best-practice institutes in market economies (figure 5.2). Institutional autonomy limits political

In Ukraine, a Single National Institution Performs a Combination of Functions That Can Lead to Conflicts of Interest

The State Committee for Technical Regulations and Consumer Protection (*Derzhstandart*) is responsible for the development and approval of standards, product certification, inspections of producers, and market surveillance and protection of consumer rights. This combination of responsibilities can lead to significant conflicts of interest.

As an example, although Derzhstandart prepares the technical regulations and the rules for certification, only certification bodies operating within its own network of conformity assessment bodies, UkrCEPRO (Ukrainian Certification of Products), are allowed to offer services in the domain of mandatory certification. Although UkrCEPRO does include a number of private certifiers, the latter need to be authorized by Derzhstandart in addition to being accredited by the Ukrainian National Accreditation Agency; the vast majority of certificates are issued by Derzhstandart's own certification centers, with private sector certifiers composing only a minor share. Hence, the entire process is completely controlled by Derzhstandart. Both this overlapping of commercial and regulatory functions and the discretionary powers of Derzhstandart to control the certification market create considerable conflicts of interest.

Many of Derzhstandart's functions also overlap to some extent with those of other government authorities, including the Sanitary and Epidemiological Service and the State Committee for Veterinary Medicine. This overlap creates confusion and conflicting requirements and reduces the effectiveness of supervision. Moreover, with two state agencies overseeing the same products, the state wastes scarce budget resources and businesses are subjected to excessive burdens.

Source: IFC 2008.

influence in standards development, staffing, or international cooperation. NSBs in Armenia, Uzbekistan, and Tajikistan are under tighter control of the states. This is particularly true of Tajikistan, where the NSB cannot select its own workforce without state approval. Nonetheless, it is important to consider that autonomy is not an end by itself and may not be desirable if the NSB does not operate in an open and transparent manner.

Some of this openness and transparency can be affected by governance structure. In most EU or OECD economies, NSBs are not operated in a top-down fashion by public servants but have governance structures that include stakeholders from industry and consumer groups as well. A general assembly of public and private sector members often exerts influence by electing all or part of the executive bodies or electing NSB presidents. As table 5.2 shows, although this is the case in the EU and comparator countries, it is not yet the case in all Balkan and CIS countries. Table 5.2 also highlights the fact that the executive councils of NSBs in ECA countries tend to be more influenced by the state than those in comparator countries. However, on the positive side, a number of CIS

TABLE 5.1
National Standards Bodies and the Scope of Their Activities, 2007

	Country	Abbreviation	Standards	Metrology	Conformity assessment	Accreditation	Technical regulations
EU countries	Bulgaria	BDS	✓				
	Czech Republic	CNI	✓				
	Estonia	EVS	✓				
	Hungary	MSZT	✓		✓		
	Latvia	LVS	✓				
	Lithuania	LST	✓		✓		
	Poland	PKN	✓				
	Romania	ASRO	✓		✓		
	Slovak Republic	SUTN	✓				
	Slovenia	SIST	✓		✓		
Balkan countries and Turkey	Albania	DPS	✓				✓
	Bosnia and Herzegovina	BAS	✓				
	Croatia	HZN	✓				
	Macedonia, FYR	ISRM	✓				
	Montenegro	ISME	✓				
	Serbia	ISS	✓		✓		
	Turkey	TSE	✓		✓		
CIS countries and Georgia	Armenia	SARM	✗		✗		✗
	Azerbaijan	AZSTAND	✗	✗	✗	✗	✗
	Belarus	BELST	✗	✗	✗	✗	✗
	Georgia	GESTM	✓	✓			
	Kazakhstan	KAZMEMST	✗	✗	✗		✗
	Kyrgyz Republic	KYRGYZST	✓	✓	✓		
	Moldova	MOLDST	✗	✗	✗		✗
	Russian Federation	GOST R	✗	✗	✗	✗	✗
	Tajikistan	TJKSTN	✗	✗	✗	✗	
	Turkmenistan	MSST	✗	✗	✗	✗	✗
	Ukraine	DSSU	✗	✗	✗		✗
	Uzbekistan	UZSTANDARD	✗	✗	✗	✗	✗
Comparator countries	China	SAC	✓				✓
	Germany	DIN	✓				
	Korea, Rep.	CSK	✓	✓	✓		
	Spain	AENOR	✓		✓		
	United Kingdom	BSI	✓		✓		

Sources: ISO 2007 and Web sites of the national standards bodies.
Note: The cross check mark (✗) denotes a conflict of interest.

FIGURE 5.2

Limited Institutional Autonomy of Several ECA Standards Bodies, 2007–09

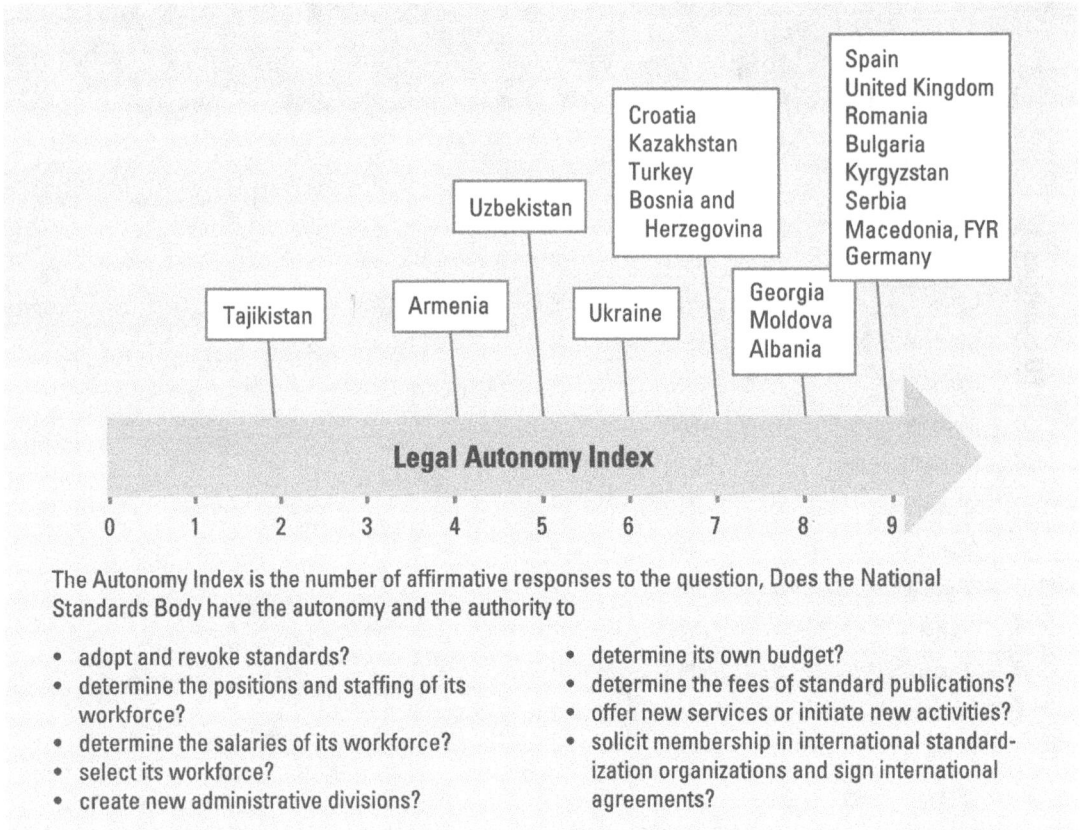

| | | | |
| Spain |
| United Kingdom |
| Romania |
| Bulgaria |
| Kyrgyzstan |
| Serbia |
| Macedonia, FYR |
| Germany |

Croatia
Kazakhstan
Turkey
Bosnia and
Herzegovina

Uzbekistan

Tajikistan

Armenia

Ukraine

Georgia
Moldova
Albania

Legal Autonomy Index

0   1   2   3   4   5   6   7   8   9

The Autonomy Index is the number of affirmative responses to the question, Does the National Standards Body have the autonomy and the authority to

- adopt and revoke standards?
- determine the positions and staffing of its workforce?
- determine the salaries of its workforce?
- select its workforce?
- create new administrative divisions?

- determine its own budget?
- determine the fees of standard publications?
- offer new services or initiate new activities?
- solicit membership in international standard-ization organizations and sign international agreements?

Source: Authors based on World Bank survey of national quality infrastructure institutions.

and Balkan countries now have consultative councils with private sector representation, although these tend to have only a weak influence on governance.

NSBs in ECA have diverse sources of funding, but some rely heavily on public transfers.

The most successful NSBs, such as Deutsches Institut für Normung in Germany, are able to cover most of their costs through standardization-related activities, namely sales of standards and membership fees (figure 5.3). However, this is more an exception than the norm, and in most countries, governments supplement NSBs' budgets with annual subsidies. Standards sales are, in any case, a diminishing business; as standards become more internationalized, it does not really matter who sells the standards, and industries need to obtain only one copy instead of one from each country they wish to trade with. ISO 9001 is the same whether

TABLE 5.2

Governance of the National Standards Bodies, 2007–09

	Country	General assembly of public and private members	Share of executive council designated by the state (%)	Executive director appointed by the state	Consultative council including private sector
EU countries	Bulgaria	Yes	20	No	Yes
	Hungary	Yes	33	No	No
	Romania	Yes	5	No	Yes
Balkan countries and Turkey	Albania	No	No executive council	Yes	Yes
	Bosnia and Herzegovina	No	No executive council	Yes	Yes
	Croatia	No	30	Yes	Yes
	Macedonia, FYR	Yes	30	No	No
	Serbia	Yes	43	Yes	Yes
	Turkey	Yes	55	No	No
CIS countries and Georgia	Armenia	No	No executive council	Yes	Yes
	Georgia	No	No executive council	Yes	Yes
	Kyrgyz Republic	No	100	Yes	No
	Moldova	No	100	Yes	Yes
	Tajikistan	No	100	Yes	No
	Ukraine	No	No executive council	Yes	Yes
	Uzbekistan	No	No executive council	Yes	No
Comparator countries	Germany	Yes	23	Yes	Yes
	Spain	Yes	0	No	No
	United Kingdom	Yes	0	No	Yes

Source: World Bank survey of national quality infrastructure institutions.
Note: Data in bold orange type indicate combinations that lead to a strong influence of the state over governance.

bought in Germany, the United Kingdom, Australia, or directly from ISO in Switzerland. Another important source of revenue in some economies is conformity assessment services, where NSBs compete with other providers in a competitive market (for example, in Spain). A few NSBs in ECA derive income from such services (for example, in Hungary, Romania, and Turkey).

Figure 5.3 highlights the mix of funding in NSBs in ECA and the fact that in many of the smaller countries, NSBs are heavily dependent on government funding. In CIS countries, such as Armenia, a significant share of funding is derived from conformity assessment services in regulated areas where the NSB often has a quasi-monopoly (see box 5.1 on Ukraine). In such cases, there is significant pressure on NSBs to retain their technical regulations development and mandatory certification activities because little additional sources of funding can be obtained from the government.

The Process for Developing Standards and Technical Regulations

The standards development process is less open in Central Asia than in the rest of ECA.

As noted, although not perfect, the development of standards in EU and Organisation for Economic Co-operation and Development (OECD) economies involves wide stakeholder participation. Under central planning, in most ECA countries the standardization process was a closed process involving technical committees appointed by the states. No public review of standards was made by either producers or consumers concerning their suitability to their needs. Although many ECA countries no longer follow this model, the development of standards is still a tightly state-controlled process in a few CIS countries. One proxy for the open-

FIGURE 5.3

Sources of Funding for National Standards Bodies, 2007–09

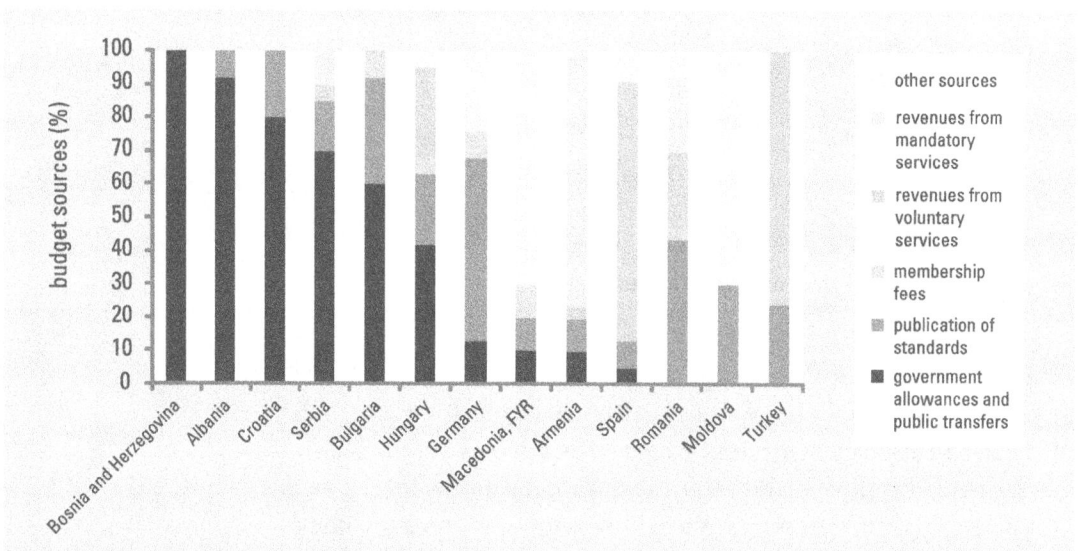

Source: World Bank survey of national quality infrastructure institutions.

ness and transparency of the standards development process is the WTO's Code of Good Practice. All standardization bodies from ECA's WTO members have notified their acceptance of the Code of Good Practice. However, the basis of these notifications is difficult to verify. For example, some NSBs indicated in the World Bank survey that they did not allow for the time period of public review of draft standards mandated in the code. In CIS countries outside the WTO, particularly in some Central Asian countries, there is limited opportunity for public review to influence the national standards. In Kazakhstan, for example, although a public review process exists, technical committees are appointed by the state from among the public research and technical institutes. In Uzbekistan, there is no public review process.

The process for developing technical regulations is not guided by WTO principles in most ECA countries outside the EU.

Assessments of ECA countries have highlighted a number of weaknesses in national technical regulation customs and practices. Some common findings from these assessments indicate the following:

- In most economies, technical regulations are developed and implemented by many ministries, authorities, or agencies.

- Authorities have developed their own unique ways of doing so over time. These customs and practices may or may not comply with WTO Agreement on Technical Barriers to Trade (TBT Agreement) requirements.

- Invariably, overlaps and duplication have developed.

- Regulatory authorities, having grown accustomed to a position of absolute power in the past, do not easily shift toward a more consultative approach.

- The use of voluntary standards as the basis for technical regulation is not the norm.

Even ECA countries that are WTO members do not always adhere to sound principles. Why this is the case is not always clear. One contributing factor may be that many older WTO members have not been challenged to prove that their technical regulation systems comply with WTO rules, as countries currently seeking accession must do. Hence, old, inefficient, and noncompliant systems are still in place. But these weaknesses create barriers to trade.

In most CIS countries, national standards bodies are developing mandatory standards, contrary to international good practices.

In many ECA countries, authorities have found it useful to develop and implement the concept of mandatory standards. These are, in essence, technical regulations that are developed by NSBs. Although from a practical perspective scarce technical resources are used optimally, the system eventually leads to conflicts of interest and is not in the best interests of a modern market-related trading system in the long term. The problems with such a system can be one or more of the following:

- The NSB shifts its focus to developing standards that it knows are destined to be declared mandatory and neglects standards that are needed by industry for its development.

- Standards are declared mandatory even for products that do not fall within the legitimate objectives defined by the WTO TBT Agreement— usually to protect local industry.

- The system operates on the premise that products need to be certified before they are placed on the market, ensuring that only products complying with the mandatory standards reach the market. Hence, little or no market surveillance is in place to determine market failures.

- The NSB unnecessarily retests imported products or products that have been certified by other organizations before releasing them to the market, ensuring that its own laboratories are kept busy and earn revenue.

- Perceptually, and sometimes even legally, the responsibility for the integrity of products is shifted from the suppliers to the authorities, and the suppliers take no responsibility if anything goes wrong.

Compulsory registration of standards or of technical specifications is still necessary in several CIS countries.

A practice unique to CIS countries is the registration of standards developed by enterprises at NSBs (table 5.3). In a number of countries, enterprises are required to develop and register new standards or technical specifications to market products for which no national standards exist. This practice takes time and money away from the entrepreneurs and stifles technological change by discouraging imports of new consumer products and equipment, as well as local innovation. According to a recent International Finance Corporation study, 17 percent of Ukrainian

TABLE 5.3
Mandatory Registration of Industry Standards by Several CIS Countries, 2007–09

	Country	Registration by the national standards body of standards developed by industrial enterprises	Number of registered standards
EU countries	EU member states		0
Balkan countries and Turkey	Albania		0
	Croatia		0
	Macedonia, FYR		0
	Serbia		0
	Turkey		0
CIS countries and Georgia	Armenia	✓	n.a.
	Georgia	✓	652
	Kazakhstan	✓	n.a.
	Kyrgyz Republic	✓	n.a.
	Moldova		0
	Tajikistan	✓	88
	Ukraine	✓	1,759
	Uzbekistan	✓	953

Source: World Bank survey of national quality infrastructure institutions.
Note: n.a. = not applicable.

small and medium enterprise (SME) manufacturing firms registered or amended technical specifications in 2006, at an average cost of US$8,000 each. That year, SMEs spent US$59 million on technical specifications. (IFC 2008). In market economies, firms are never required to register technical specifications for new products. They can change specifications as they please.

Standardization Activities

In most cases, it is difficult to make any meaningful interpretation of a country's total number of national standards. Whether the total number of national standards should be correlated to the level of industrial activity or the predisposition for technical regulation remains a moot point. The structure of individual standards differs far too much to conduct a meaningful analysis. Some countries prefer a standard to be all-inclusive, whereas other countries subdivide the requirements for a specific product into a number of different standards. A country's legal framework also has an influence on the number of national standards. Some legal systems do not allow reference to standards from outside the country (that is, ISO, International Electrotechnical Commission, or others) in technical regulations; hence, these international standards must be adopted as national standards. In other legal systems, this is not an issue at all. Whereas the absolute number of standards in a country may not provide much insight into the performance and effect of the country's NSB, the nature of the country's standards—their voluntary or mandatory nature, the growth in the number of standards, and the internationalization of the standards—offer significant insight.

ECA is moving toward voluntary standardization, but technical regulations still thrive in several CIS countries.

For the past decade, the trend throughout the world and in ECA has unambiguously been in the direction of voluntary standards. This course has been largely driven by WTO and EU membership requirements, the

BOX 5.2

Employment Generation Led by Reforms in Technical Regulation and Testing in Serbia

IKEA, a Swedish furniture maker and retailer, is seeking to locate some of its new production activities in Serbia in cooperation with a local producer. The firm has already invested €650,000 in plant machinery and is expected to export €4.8 million of furniture over the next three years. This could imply boosting the value of production contracted to Serbian suppliers to between €10 million and €15 million by the end of 2010. A new IKEA department store would also employ about 2,000 people in the local Serbian market.

Although IKEA's investment prospects represent a unique opportunity for Serbia, challenges are ahead. Serbia's legislation stipulates that imported furniture must undergo laboratory tests in the country. Given the country's limited testing laboratory capacity, it could take up to two years to test IKEA's portfolio of 15,000 products. This lag is because the Serbian quality infrastructure still relies largely on technical regulations from the Yugoslav era that require all products to be tested instead of relying on consumer feedback about the quality of goods. Moreover, Serbia has not signed an accreditation mutual recognition arrangement and does not recognize test results from other countries. Serbia is now faced with accelerating its transition to voluntary standards or jeopardizing a major investment.

Source: Executive Newsletter 1781, Belgrade, June 10, 2009. http://www.bizinfo.co.rs.

latter being much more strict. As a result, ECA's new EU member states and those wishing to eventually join the EU have been removing all but the most essential technical regulations. In the Balkan countries, even those with no short-term prospects for EU accession have removed mandatory standards to exploit trade and investment opportunities with the EU (box 5.2). Apart from Albania, all EU and Balkan countries have removed them from the official mandate of their NSBs. A number of CIS countries have also been stronger reformers. Georgia, Moldova, and the Kyrgyz Republic have transitioned from systems based entirely on mandatory standards to those based entirely on voluntary standards in the past decade.

Some ECA countries are taking a more gradual approach to voluntary standardization, including Russia, which retains approximately 40 percent of its standards as mandatory. All or nearly all standards are still mandatory in Azerbaijan, Kazakhstan, Uzbekistan, and Turkmenistan. In countries that are not closely monitored by the EU for accession purposes, it is very difficult to gauge the number, scope, and effect of technical regulations, because they are generally developed by a number of agencies and often with little central coordination. In Tajikistan, for example, four government ministries and two government agencies develop technical regulations (IFC 2006).

A number of studies by the International Finance Corporation on the business environment in CIS countries point to the continued prevalence

Serious Threat to Modernization by Mandatory Standards in Ukraine

In Ukraine, nearly all goods and many services need to comply with mandatory state standards. This requirement poses a serious obstacle to technology adoption and innovation. New equipment cannot be imported and used and new products cannot be put on the market unless they satisfy state standards or firms register technical specifications with the NSB. Existing technical regulations are very prescriptive and complex, much more than is necessary to ensure safety. Instead of focusing on the end result, that is, safety, technical regulations prescribe the precise technical characteristics that technologies need to adopt.

Moreover, many of these technical regulations are outdated and are not compatible with modern technological processes, thereby preventing firms from introducing newer and safer technologies. In Ukraine, mandatory standards include almost 17,000 GOST standards developed before 1992. Almost half of these were developed before 1980. As a result, Ukrainian SMEs spent over US$127 million in 2006 going through procedures associated with technical regulations, including standardization, certification, and inspections.

Source: IFC 2008.

and negative impact of technical regulations. These technical regulations tend to cover a larger number of goods and services and are excessively prescriptive and complex (box 5.3). Among the former Soviet economies, Georgia has adopted a unique approach to rapidly removing business barriers from technical regulations by simultaneously adopting the technical regulations of 36 other countries. This ambitious approach has run into serious implementation difficulties (box 5.4).

As regards the percentage of standards that are considered mandatory in relation to the total body of national standards, some caution is indicated. NSBs are not the only agencies implementing mandatory standards; a vast number of other regulatory agencies operate in most countries, and in the CIS countries, these often still use the GOST standards. Mandatory standards developed by these regulatory agencies are not considered national standards by most CIS countries; hence, they are usually not included in their count of national standards. Figure 5.4 points to the rift between countries transitioning to voluntary standards

BOX 5.4

Difficulty in Keeping Up with International Technical Regulations Regime in Georgia

In Georgia, according to a recent government resolution titled "On Recognition and Application of Technical Regulations of Foreign Countries," the technical regulations of 36 countries are now recognized in Georgia's internal market. These include EU and OECD countries as distant as New Zealand, the Republic of Korea, and Mexico. This recognition means that certification, testing, and inspection of products and services can be carried out in accordance with the technical regulations of any of the countries listed in the resolution, in addition to Georgia's old technical regulations. Firms wishing to use foreign technical regulations bear all costs related to translation into Georgian and to registering of the regulations with the NSB. The firms then notify the relevant inspection agencies that they are operating under foreign technical regulations.

The challenge now facing Georgia is limited technical capacity in the country sectors to apply the conformity assessment methods required by this web of foreign technical regulations (most of which are incompatible with existing old regulations and assessment methods traditionally used in Georgia). As a result, inspections are conducted by the state authorities using the old methods and technical regulations, regardless of discrepancies with their foreign versions. Thus, firms usually fail the inspection process even when they are in conformance with the foreign technical regulations.

Another challenge has been the translation of foreign technical regulations. Translations of technical regulations are complex, and it can be a burden on businesses to provide appropriate translations. Ideally, all recognized foreign technical regulations should be translated into Georgian. However, for a small economy, this would pose a difficulty. Another approach would be for the government to provide translations to businesses on demand.

Source: IFC 2009.

FIGURE 5.4

Voluntary and Mandatory Standards, Various Countries, 2007–09

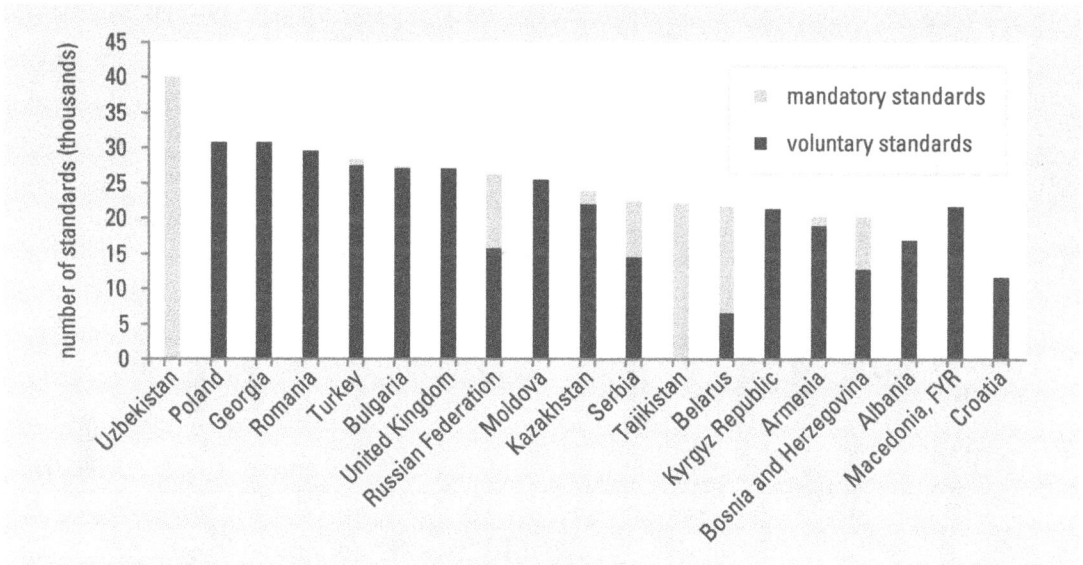

Source: World Bank survey of national quality infrastructure institutions.

and those still following the philosophy of technical regulations. However, it provides only part of the picture because, in countries using voluntary standards, other regulatory agencies may still be developing mandatory standards that are not considered national standards by NSBs.

Growth in standards in EU accession countries, the Balkan countries, and Turkey is fueled mostly by the adoption of international and regional standards.

Figure 5.5 provides an indication of the state of national standards in ECA countries. Some countries have aggressively undertaken the adoption of EU standards in their efforts to meet accession requirements. This is the case for all of ECA's new EU member states. These countries are following the general global trend of regional and international harmonization. In fact, in countries such as the United Kingdom, the vast majority of standards are regional or international. All EU member states and candidates have adopted most EU standards as a requirement of the EU's *acquis communautaire*. Because EU standards are largely harmonized with ISO and International Electrotechnical Commission (IEC) standards, these countries' standards have a wide global reach.

The situation in the Balkan countries and Turkey is still very mixed, indicating the relative movement of the various ECA countries toward

FIGURE 5.5

National Standards by Origin, 2007–09

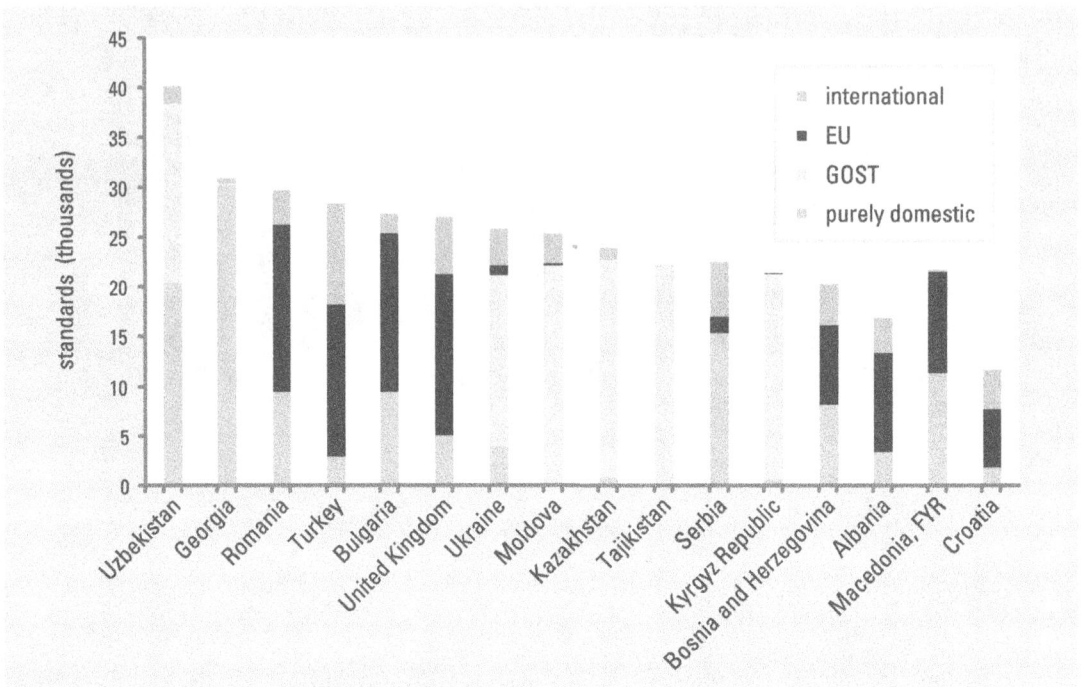

Source: World Bank survey of national quality infrastructure institutions.

integration with the EU system. Most countries seem to be just over half-way toward integration with the EU regarding the adoption of all European Standards as national standards. Turkey has met all EU requirements and is remarkably well integrated at both the regional and the international levels. Albania, Bosnia and Herzegovina, and Croatia have made considerable headway in adopting EU standards, particularly when compared to the situation in 2000. Other countries, such as the former Yugoslav Republic of Macedonia and Serbia, are further behind, not because of lack of political will but largely because of the limited capacities of their NSBs in managing the standards upgrading process.

CIS countries have seen more modest growth in their standards stock because of the dependence of many of these countries on existing GOST standard documents. Countries that have Russia as a major trade partner have retained a large body of GOST standards (that is, Kazakhstan, the Kyrgyz Republic, and Tajikistan). Many of the more than 20,000 GOST standards are still being used extensively, especially in technical regulations, despite their technical obsolescence. The relatively heavy reliance on mandatory standards in Russia (mostly GOST standards) is a disincentive for CIS countries to switch out of the GOST regime, for fear of losing their main trade partner. Although this reliance opens trade opportunities with Russia and other large CIS countries, it can also translate into a loss for local industries trying to compete in markets outside the region.

An issue that is slowly emerging as a limitation on the adoption of international standards is that of language. The most common reason given for the lack of adoption of international standards is the lack of official Russian translations of ISO and IEC standards. Since the demise of the Soviet Union, neither of these two organizations has continued to provide Russian translations. The result is that only a handful of the current ISO and IEC standards are available in Russian. This is a particularly worrisome issue for CIS countries where Russian is widely spoken. They do not always have the finances to have the standards translated. Translations have to be purchased at some cost from Russia. These could be the full adoptions of the ISO and IEC standards, but could also contain deviations appropriate for Russia but not necessarily for other ECA countries. On the one hand, Russia is probably the major trading partner of many ECA countries, so it helps them to harmonize standards with Russia. On the other hand, if Russia's standards (GOST-R) are different from those of the international community, then future international trade may be compromised.

Contributions to International and Regional Standardization

Membership in international and regional standardization organizations allows countries to adopt international and regional standards as part of their national standards and allows them to influence the technical content of those standards. Although virtually all ECA countries could be classified as standards takers rather than standards makers, it is still very useful for smaller countries to participate in international and, especially, regional standardization activities. By participating actively in a few, but important, technical committees, even developing economies and economies in transition can influence the outcome of the standards development process to their own advantage. In addition, the advanced information that national delegations bring back from technical committee meetings about future international standards provides opportunities for local industry to preserve their markets or open up new ones. In many regions, such as the EU, regional standardization activities tend to have greater implications than international standardization activities. More often than not, regional standards are the actual basis of technical regulation harmonization within a region; hence, they are binding on all of the region's members. Active participation to protect national interests is therefore of paramount importance. Providing only written comments to technical committees is not an adequate strategy—countries need to be present to argue their cases.

Most ECA countries have taken steps toward integrating with international and regional standardization bodies.

Table 5.4 shows that all ECA countries are members of two of the three main international standards organizations: the ISO and International Telecommunication Union (ITU). Membership in the third, IEC, remains weak in the CIS, particularly for smaller countries. A positive mark for ECA is also the almost complete membership in the Codex Alimentarius Commission, which is the source of much of the food and feed standards at the international level.

At the regional level, membership details are provided for the European Committee for Standardization (CEN) and European Telecommunications Standardization Institute (ETSI), the two EU standards bodies that mirror ISO and ITU at the international level. The EASC is the regional construct of the CIS countries, with Russia in its center. EU economies are all full members of the regional organizations CEN, the European Committee for Electrotechnical Standardization (CENELEC), and ETSI, as mandated by EU's requirements of free movement of goods. Although countries outside the EU are not allowed to obtain full membership (voting rights) in CEN and CENELEC, a number of countries neighboring the EU have chosen to become Affiliate Members, largely driven by aspirations to join the EU (Croatia and Turkey) or to increase trade ties with Europe through negotiations on free trade agreements (Armenia, Georgia, and Ukraine). Although Russia has no immediate EU membership aspiration, its affiliate membership in CEN suggests a gravitational pull toward standards harmonization with the EU, something that should be watched closely by Russia's main trade partners in the CIS as they devise their standardization strategies. CIS countries are also members of EASC, the intergovernmental organization that replaced the former Council of Gosstandart.

Most ECA countries are standards takers, with limited influence over standards used in global trade.

The decentralized nature of the ISO system allows member organizations to exert an immense influence on the strategies of standardization work by hosting the secretariats of technical committees. An analysis of leadership and participation in ISO technical committees shows that ECA's influence is limited in these committees. Figure 5.6 shows that only Poland (with two committees) and Ukraine (with one committee) retain a little bit of sway. The picture in IEC is not much different. For the time being, ECA countries can be known only as standards takers. It would be an important and strategic move by ECA countries to host the secretariats

TABLE 5.4

Country Memberships in International and Regional Standards Bodies, 2008

	Country	International bodies			Regional bodies			
		IEC	ITU	ISO	CENELEC	CEN	ETSI	EASC
EU countries	Bulgaria	✓	✓	✓	✓	✓	✓	
	Czech Republic	✓	✓	✓	✓	✓	✓	
	Estonia	Assoc.	✓	Corr.	✓	✓	✓	
	Hungary	✓	✓	✓	✓	✓	✓	
	Latvia	Assoc.	✓	Corr.	✓	✓	✓	
	Lithuania	Assoc.	✓	✓	✓	✓	✓	
	Poland	✓	✓	✓	✓	✓	✓	
	Romania	✓	✓	✓	✓	✓	✓	
	Slovak Republic	✓	✓	✓	✓	✓	✓	
	Slovenia	✓	✓	✓	✓	✓	✓	
Balkan countries and Turkey	Albania		✓	Corr.	Aff.	Aff.	✓	
	Bosnia and Herzegovina	Assoc.	✓	✓	Aff.	Aff.	✓	
	Croatia	✓	✓	✓	✓	✓	✓	
	Macedonia, FYR	Assoc.	✓	✓	Aff.	Aff.		
	Montenegro	✓	✓	Corr.	Aff.	Aff.		
	Serbia	✓	✓	✓	Aff.	Aff.	✓	
	Turkey	✓	✓	✓	Aff.	Aff.	✓	
CIS countries and Georgia	Armenia		✓	✓		Aff.		✓
	Azerbaijan		✓	✓		Aff.		✓
	Belarus	✓	✓	✓	Aff.	Aff.		✓
	Georgia		✓	Corr.		Aff.	✓	✓
	Kazakhstan	Assoc.	✓	✓				✓
	Kyrgyz Republic		✓	✓				✓
	Moldova		✓	Corr.		Aff.		✓
	Russian Federation	✓	✓	✓		Aff.	✓	✓
	Tajikistan		✓	Corr.				✓
	Turkmenistan		✓	Corr.				✓
	Ukraine	✓	✓	✓	Aff.	Aff.	✓	✓
	Uzbekistan		✓	✓			✓	✓
Comparator countries	Brazil	✓	✓	✓			✓	
	China	✓	✓	✓			✓	
	Germany	✓	✓	✓	✓	✓	✓	
	Korea, Rep.	✓	✓	✓			✓	
	Spain	✓	✓	✓	✓	✓	✓	
	United Kingdom	✓	✓	✓	✓	✓	✓	

Sources: Web sites of the international and regional bodies.
Note: All ECA countries are members of ISO and ITU. Aff. = Affiliate Member, Assoc. = Associate Member, Corr. = Corresponding Member.

Distribution of ISO Technical Committee Secretariats by Country, 2008

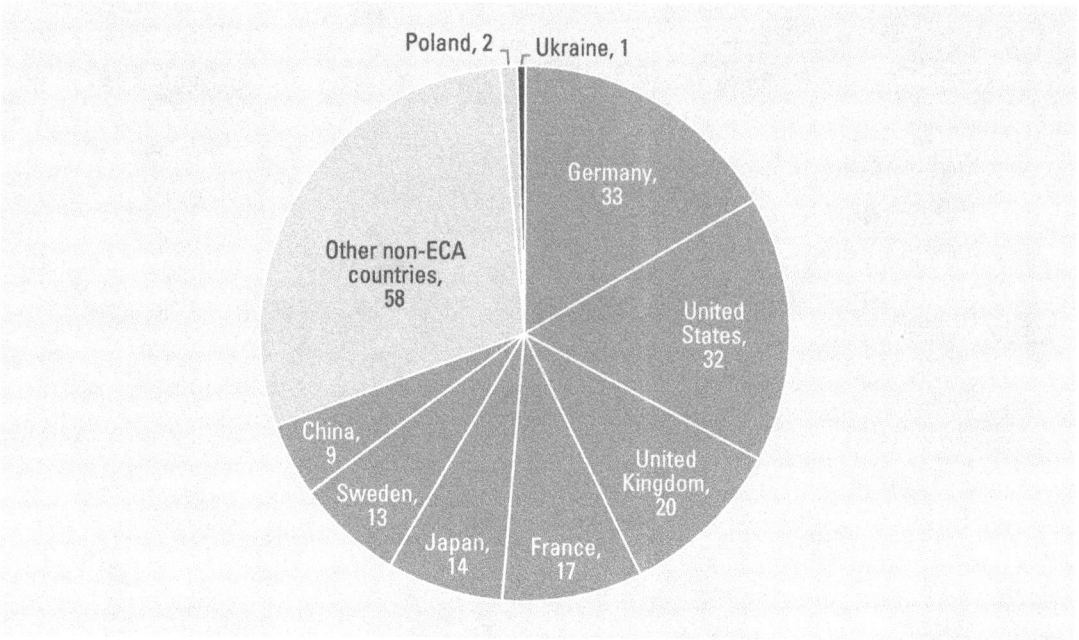

Source: International Organization for Standardization Web site, http://www.iso.org.

of technical committees that really matter for their industries, as, for example, India, Malaysia, and South Africa have done.

Figure 5.7 highlights the dominance of the five traditional standards makers—Germany, France, Japan, the United Kingdom, and the United States. In combination, they are responsible for nearly 60 percent of the technical committees of ISO. China quickly surpassed ECA in its number of technical committees—from three in 2005 to nine (three times more than all of ECA) in 2008. As the world's largest manufacturer, China's growing interest in ISO and IEC is an indication of the increasing influence of these standards in global trade. ECA countries risk being left behind with standards that are unsuited to their economies, unless they participate more actively in the international standardization process. Other low- and middle-income countries have become important players in standards of interest to their economies:

- South Africa, as a major coal export country, hosts ISO/TC 27, *Solid mineral fuels.*

- Malaysia, as a major producer of natural rubber and rubber products, hosts ISO/TC 45, *Rubber and rubber products,* as well as ISO/TC 157, *Mechanical contraceptives.*

- India, with its large leather industry, hosts ISO/TC 120, *Leather.*

This is a clever strategy to follow, because probably none of these countries, with the possible exception of India, has the capacity to host tens of committees. Hosting is an area in which ECA countries, with the exception of Poland, are seriously lacking in strategy and, hence, influence. The two technical committees that are allocated to Poland, ISO/TC 98, *Bases for design of structures*, and ISO/TC 195, *Building construction machinery and equipment*, both deal with building operations, an area in which Poland has expertise.

Some of the larger ECA countries are more active in international standardization, not as leaders but as participants of technical committees. However, mere participation in technical committees does not necessarily show how active countries are in committees. Keeping this in mind, one sees that quite a few ECA countries are at the same level of involvement as the top comparator countries, for example, the Czech Republic, Poland, Russia, and Romania (figure 5.7). Hungary, Serbia, and the Slovak Republic compare well with Brazil. This is a positive sign. However, a small number of ECA countries remain completely absent from ISO's technical work, including small countries such as Albania and Georgia, but also the more populous Uzbekistan.

The membership data of ISO shows that some ECA countries are, on paper at least, actively involved in the technical work of ISO. Unfortunately, quite a few are not making use of the opportunities that ISO membership provides. Others are members of ISO in name only and do not enjoy any of the real benefits that are the reason for becoming mem-

ISO Technical Committee Representation by Country, 2008

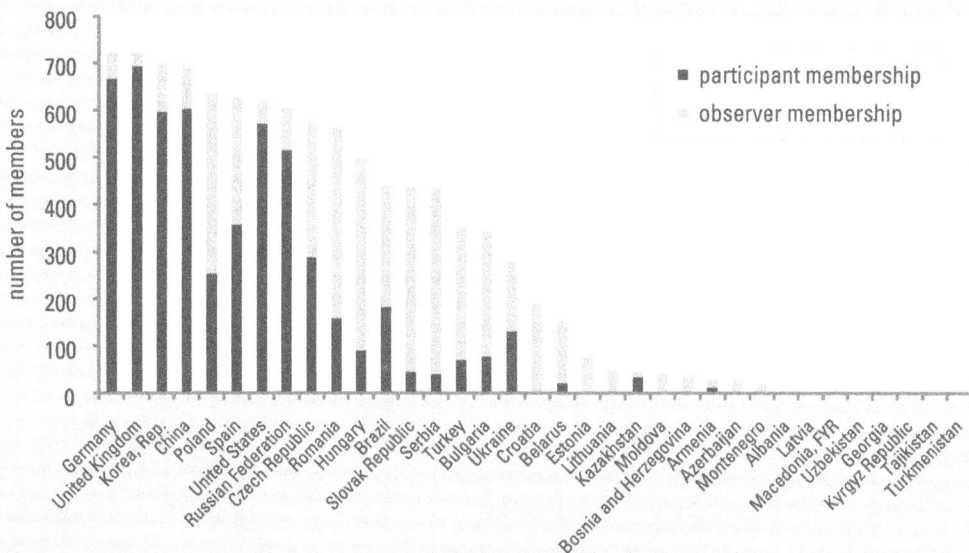

Source: International Organization for Standardization Web site, http://www.iso.org.

bers. Relative to the comparator countries, which are all very active in the technical work of ISO, the ECA region's participation level is mixed. Therefore, policy makers in the region should introduce some appropriate corrective measures very soon.

Improving Standards

Standards can be improved with a focus on national standards bodies, the standards development process, and international and regional integration of standards.

Refocusing the Activities of National Standards Bodies

CIS and Balkan countries can ensure that standardization bodies are not used to hamper competition or protect markets by making standards voluntary.

All ECA countries should move from the obsolete Soviet system based on a mandatory system of standards to a system based on technical regulations. The fact that standards are voluntary needs to be made abundantly clear. Only when standards are declared mandatory under the authority of enabling legislation can compliance be made obligatory for all suppliers. Educating and informing all interested parties about concepts, status, objectives, similarities, and differences between technical regulations and standards is a first step. The national standards body or its governing council or board should not be given the authority to declare standards mandatory. This should be the responsibility of the relevant minister or equally high authority, who can be held accountable at the international level for such decisions, for instance in the WTO.

Many ECA countries will need to strengthen the capacity of ministries and agencies to develop technical regulations. The national standards body should not have any role in the development of technical regulations. However, standards should be used as the basis for all technical regulations by all ministries or agencies that have been given the authority to develop and implement technical regulations, and not only by the ministry responsible for trade. The text of such standards should not be replicated in the relevant regulation, because this would defeat the whole object of making technical regulations more efficient and compliant with international obligations. Officials developing technical regulations as countries transition away from mandatory standards will need to be trained on legal, administrative, and technical issues. They should introduce the practice of regulatory impact assessment and establish interdisciplinary and interministerial working groups for the elaboration and implementation of priority technical regulations.

ECA countries can ensure that standardization bodies are impartial and effective by clearly separating standardization from commercial activities.

There are many countries, such as Korea, Spain, and the United Kingdom, where the national standards body offers commercial services such as certification and testing, but the separation of functional areas in the standards body is typically made explicit by law or in government agreements. In the United Kingdom, the Memorandum of Understanding between the British Standards Institution (the national standards body) and the government requires that management decisions concerning the standardization division not be influenced by other British Standards Institution business activities. The memorandum also subjects any collaboration of the standardization division and other commercial division to competition law. It guarantees the absence of conflicts of interest in the standardization body's functions. This memorandum is typically a core condition for full membership in the European regional standardization organizations CEN and CENELEC. Where institutions are weak, certification functions should be completely eliminated from standardization bodies.

CIS countries should review and gradually abandon the practice of registering technical specifications.

This practice has no economic or social function under a modern technical regulations regime. Firms should be free to use their own unofficial industry standards as they do in technologically advanced economies.

Improving the Standards Development Process

ECA countries, particularly in the CIS, can improve the standardization process to ensure that standards serve society.

Many ECA countries already follow the practices enshrined in ISO/IEC directives and in the WTO TBT Agreement's Code of Good Practice. However, a number of associated policy issues merit attention:

- The technical committee membership should be a reasonable balance between authorities, suppliers, academia, and consumer organizations and should not consist only of delegates of ministries. The national standards body should not limit technical committee membership. Membership should be open, and decisions should be made on the basis of consensus.

- The general practice of payment for technical committee members should be seriously reconsidered, especially in national standards bodies that battle with funding, because it severely curtails technical committee activities. It constrains the number of committee meetings that can be held in the budget period, and it unnecessarily limits the number of committee members. There are no volunteers on technical committees, only representatives looking after the interests of their respective organizations. If nobody is prepared to attend technical committee meetings without payment, then the question can rightfully be asked whether the standard being developed is really needed. The only exception could be consumer associations, because they usually find attendance difficult due to even greater financial constraints.

- The secretariat of the technical committees should remain with the national standards bodies. In this way, the standards development process can be properly managed and compliance with the WTO Code of Good Practice assured. Subcontracting the secretariat of technical committees to other organizations such as academia or regulatory agencies is fine in theory. But anecdotal evidence in most developing countries indicates that the standard development work suffers or grinds to a halt, because such organizations have a different focus and because standards development is rather low in their list of priorities, over and above the fact that their funds are as scarce as those of the standards body. Nevertheless, the chair of technical committees could, and should, go to an organization outside of the national standards body, giving major stakeholders a say in the policy direction of the committees.

All ECA countries should strive to remove obsolete standards from the pretransition era.

Most ECA countries inherited a significant number of standards from the central planning era. Several Balkan countries and most CIS countries still retain thousands of obsolete Yugoslav or Soviet standards. These standards were not developed according to international best practices; they hamper technology upgrading and create barriers to trade. ECA countries should devise strategies to systematically review their national standards to reduce and modernize their standard stocks.

Government funding is necessary to create and run a modern standardization body.

Funds needed for the full development of a standardization system may be up to US$2 million over five years. Funds are needed for expertise transfer, development of technical committees, and sometimes for information technology equipment and related software for a standards depository system. Most operational costs of the standards body must also be covered by government sources, unless the standardization body is engaged in commercial activities. Although membership fees and sales of standards generate some income, it is unlikely that such monies will generate sufficient income in most of ECA's small economies and in economies where demand for voluntary standards is still low because of lack of awareness.

Achieving International and Regional Integration

A first step toward better trade opportunities and knowledge inflows is to prioritize the adoption of international and regional standards over national standards.

ECA countries will be able to choose among a vast pool of harmonized standards by joining international standardization organizations. A first step for ECA countries is to obtain and retain membership in the relevant international standardization organizations, especially ISO, IEC, and Codex Alimentarius Commission. If at all possible, the membership level should be high enough that the national standards body has unlimited access to international standards for adoption at the national level and can participate actively in technical committees. The government must ensure that the appropriate funds for membership fees and technical committee work are available on a long-term basis.

EU candidates, potential candidates, and countries negotiating free trade agreements with the EU have a clear path. EU accession can be achieved only by joining the three European standardization bodies— CEN, CENELEC, and ETSI. Free trade agreements, including those that will be negotiated by Armenia, Georgia, and Ukraine, require lowering technical barriers to trade (TBTs) in at least some economic sectors. Because EU New Approach directives rely on regional standards, this lowering of TBTs implies harmonizing standards with the EU. Non-EU countries can become Affiliate Members, which gives them rights to be involved in the technical committees and adopt EU standards, but no voting rights. Because CEN and CENELEC standards are based largely on ISO and IEC standards, the tradeoff between adopting international and regional standards is not very important for these countries.

CIS countries will need to skillfully maneuver between Russian and international standards, but harmonization strategies must be guided by technical committees, not by government intervention.

ECA countries that have Russia as their major trading partner are to some extent in a bind. On the one hand, they need to align their standards with international standards if they wish to expand their trade to the international level. On the other hand, they must ensure that their industry remains competitive within their major market, namely Russia. This is a fairly unique situation, because most of the major trading blocs that include developing economies and economies in transition in other parts of the world—Association of Southeast Asian Nations, East African Community, Southern African Development Community, Common Market for Eastern and Southern Africa, Southern Cone Common Market, and so forth—tend to underwrite and support the international standardization process and have policies in place for the adoption of international standards at the regional or national level, or both. This is not yet the case of Russia.

The only other trading region that shows some similarities to CIS countries is the region covered by the North American Free Trade Agreement, where the U.S. industry associations and organizations (American Society for Testing and Materials, American Petroleum Institute, Society of Automotive Engineers, American Society of Mechanical Engineers, and so forth) basically determine to a large extent which standards are relevant to the market, and these standards are demonstrably seldom aligned with international standards. However, the purchasing power of the U.S. market is of such a magnitude that suppliers are quite prepared to provide products meeting both standards for that market and international standards for other markets. Electricity supply is a case in point: the United States runs on 110V (volt) 60Hz (hertz), whereas most of the rest of the world runs on 230V 50Hz. Other suppliers, especially those in Mexico that supply only the U.S. market, obviously manufacture products that meet U.S. standards and nothing else. A key difference between the United States and Russia is that exports to the United States are likely to provide many more opportunities for quality upgrading, technology transfer, and higher-value-added markets than exports to Russia.

Two issues are germane in this regard. First, standards that are used in the development and implementation of technical regulation in Russia leave CIS countries little choice but to align their standards accordingly if they have industry supplying Russia in any meaningful way. Where this is not the case, CIS countries will obviously have more freedom in aligning their standards with international standards. Second, standards that are not used as the basis for technical regulation must still be considered carefully. In this case, the requirements of the purchasers will be the defining mode. If the purchasers prefer international standards, then international standards will be adopted. If they do not, then a decision must be made whether Gosstandart will be considered the exception or the norm.

Whether Russia will regain the influence in international standardization that the Soviet Union enjoyed in the years following World War II is debatable because it is being eclipsed as a global manufacturer by countries such as China. If Russia embarks on an aggressive trade policy that supports the development of trade in manufactured goods in the international markets, it will have little choice but to adopt international standards for its industry to gain a foothold in such markets. It may be that the industry will begin by manufacturing products that comply with both Gosstandart and international standards, but the pressure from industry will soon be to internationalize standards as much as possible. Compliance with two sets of standards is fundamentally more complicated and, hence, more expensive than compliance with one set of standards. This situation remains very fluid and will require skillful interpretation from all CIS countries concerned, especially their ministries that are responsible for trade policy.

ECA countries can make regional and international standards more relevant to their needs by participating in standardization activities.

ECA countries contribute very little to international or regional standardization. As a result, international standards do not always reflect their national needs and they remain late adopters of the latest standards. What is often missing is a clear policy on the level of involvement of ECA countries and the funds to be actively involved.

ECA countries should deepen their involvement in CEN, CENELEC, ETSI, or EASC technical committees. The policy should also be clear that important industrialists should be part of the delegation, which is still a major issue in the CIS environment. The appropriate funds should be made available to facilitate this structured and managed involvement. Otherwise, ECA countries will not be able to influence the standards development process and provide advance information on important developments. Involvement in CEN and CENELEC technical committees is of particular importance for EU members and potential member states.

Many of the European standards are Harmonized Standards and effectively support legislation transposed from European directives that these countries must adopt. Failure to participate actively in such regional committees will result in regional standards and harmonized requirements for technical regulation that may not be in the best interest of the country, but which must then be implemented as part of its regional obligations.

The national standards body, in cooperation with the ministry responsible for trade, the industry, and other stakeholders, should develop and follow a policy of active participation in international technical committees, the output of which might be of paramount interest to local industry. They should develop guidelines as to which sectors of industry are important for the development of the country. These sectors should be the priorities of the national standards bodies in becoming involved in regional cooperation, because they cannot cover all the technical committees due to financial and human resources constraints. The national standards body should establish "mirror" committees at the national level so that a national position can be agreed upon that the delegation at the international or regional technical committee can defend. The number of such committees may be very small, even as small as one or two, depending on the main products traded by the country at the international or regional level.

Larger ECA economies such as Poland, Russia, and Turkey have the potential to significantly increase their participation and leadership in international standards bodies. Currently, they are vastly underrepresented in ISO and IEC technical committees.

Sorting Out Technical Regulations

Although harmonizing standards can be part of a strategy to decrease TBTs, this strategy must also consider technical regulations. Developing technical regulations that protect consumers and the environment with minimal negative effects on trade and innovation is a challenging task for every country.

Measures by CIS and Balkan Countries That Ensure Technical Regulations Do Not Impose Technical Barriers to Trade and Constrain Businesses

Most of the measures to reduce technical barriers can be related to the implementation of good regulatory practices. The technical regulation regime should be simplified, rendered more transparent and predictable, thereby enhancing certainty. Market forces should be allowed to operate wherever possible without compromising the safety and health of people and nature. In most cases, this also means that the government should change its strategy from testing and approving products before they are marketed to a postmarketing surveillance approach, placing the responsibility for the integrity of products squarely on the shoulders of suppliers. Such an approach necessitates effective market surveillance and strong product liability legislation that is rigorously enforced. This plan will focus the energy and effort of the authorities on problem cases, rather than unnecessarily harass the bulk of the suppliers that are consistently complying with technical regulations.

Many countries recognized this reality more than a decade ago and have developed a body of guidelines to effect better regulatory practices.[3] A number of low- and middle-income countries are also in the process of reviewing their technical regulation practices, for example, Brazil, Chile, South Africa, and Uganda. ECA countries that are now current or aspiring members of the EU have had to radically transform their technical regulation systems to comply with the EU's *acquis communautaire*. In this process, three phases can be identified—deregulation, regulatory quality improvement, and regulatory management, which are progressively implemented (figure 5.8). Many countries start with a drive to deregulate, that is, getting rid of obsolete regulations. The next logical step would be to improve the performance of the institutions that are involved in technical regulation. A World Bank project is currently assisting the government of the Kyrgyz Republic to strengthen the capacity of the public sector to develop the new technical regulation framework (box 5.5).

In addition, the decision-making mechanism as to when to implement technical regulations is improved by using regulatory impact assessments. But all of these steps are to some extent tinkering with the current, normally fragmented system. It is only when the system is addressed holistically, that is, when regulatory management is considered, that real progress is achieved. These phases are therefore interdependent, and all of them must be considered in reducing technical barriers to trade.

A first step toward strengthening the technical regulations system is an effective national regulatory management system.

A regulatory management system needs to be established at the highest political level and rigorously implemented. Two very important elements

3. For example, see the following OECD documents: "Guiding Principles for Regulatory Quality and Performance," http://www.oecd.org/dataoecd/19/51/37318586.pdf; and "OECD Reference Checklist for Regulatory Decision-Making," http://www.oecd.org/dataoecd/20/10/35220214.pdf.

FIGURE 5.8
Phases of Regulatory Reform

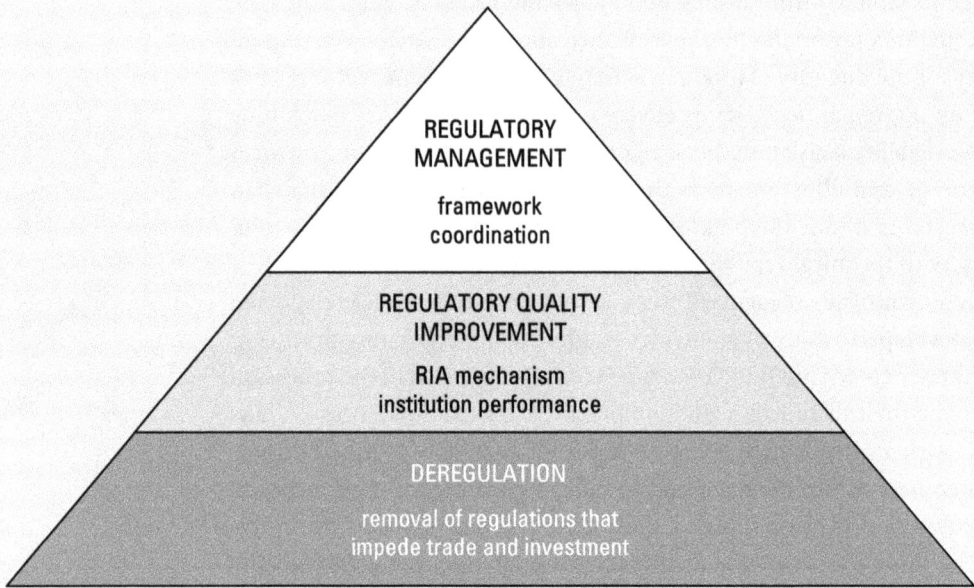

REGULATORY
MANAGEMENT

framework
coordination

REGULATORY QUALITY
IMPROVEMENT

RIA mechanism
institution performance

DEREGULATION

removal of regulations that
impede trade and investment

Source: OECD presentations at the WTO.
Note: RIA = regulatory impact assessment.

of such a regulatory management system are a technical regulation framework and a coordination mechanism.

First, a national technical regulation framework is required so that all the responsible ministries and agencies can follow common principles and procedures in developing and implementing technical regulations.

BOX 5.5
World Bank Support for Technical Regulation in the Kyrgyz Republic

The World Bank's Reducing Technical Barriers for Entrepreneurship and Trade (RTBET) project in the Kyrgyz Republic provides support for upgrading the NQI and for transitioning to an effective technical regulations system. The objective of the technical regulations component is to strengthen the capacity of the public sector to develop the new technical regulation framework based on the Law on the Fundamentals of Technical Regulation in the Kyrgyz Republic. In line with this objective, the technical regulation component provides capacity building, technical assistance, and operational support to the Technical Regulation Authorized Body of the Ministry of Economic Regulation responsible for coordinating the Kyrgyz Republic's technical regulation reform.

A number of recent achievements supported under the RTBET project can be highlighted:

- **Adoption of five sector-specific technical regulations:** In addition to the three technical regulations adopted in mid-2009 on (a) safety of machinery and equipment, (b) environmental safety, and

(c) safety of land transportation vehicles, the Parliament passed two new technical regulations in December 2009 on (d) safety of buildings and (e) safety of building materials, which are now pending presidential signature.

- **Other technical regulations under development:** The Government Technical Regulation Program includes a revised list of 50 technical regulations to be developed and adopted by 2012. To support the government's ambitious program and timetable, the RTBET project is funding local and international experts on an as-needed basis to help guide the work of the Technical Committees tasked with the development of sector-specific regulations. To accelerate the Kyrgyz Republic's transition from the previous Gosstandart system to a modern WTO-compliant risk-based technical regulations system, the government will make more systematic use of existing technical regulations developed and vetted by the EU or the Eurasian Economic Community (EurAsEC). Thus, where possible and applicable, preference will be given going forward to the adoption of existing international technical regulations rather than developing new home-grown drafts. At the same time, the Kyrgyz Republic will continue to actively participate in EurAsEC's Technical Regulation Committee and the development of regional standards where warranted. For example, the Kyrgyz Republic was recently entrusted by the committee to take the lead on developing technical regulations for water and honey on behalf of and for the CIS region. Further acceleration of the Kyrgyz Republic's technical regulation reform may also be expected from the recent amendments to the Law on the Fundamentals of Technical Regulation simplifying the adoption process of technical regulations. Indeed, although umbrella technical regulations will continue to be submitted to Parliament for adoption into laws, secondary technical regulations may be approved by sectoral ministries.

- **Continued progress in the government's deregulatory efforts:** The Ministry of Economic Regulation is leading the government's deregulatory efforts through (a) summary termination of outdated regulations and (b) application of the regulatory impact assessment methodology toward the development of new regulations, such as technical regulations. The government's deregulatory efforts translated into further reductions in the list of products subject to mandatory certification, which was reduced to 684 from 1,600 in January 2010.

- **WTO Enquiry Point on Technical Barriers to Trade:** The Kyrgyz WTO Enquiry Point established with RTBET support in cooperation with the United Nations is fully operational and has submitted 15 notifications to the WTO Secretariat on the progress achieved in the development and adoption of technical regulations in the Kyrgyz Republic. In 2009, the Enquiry Point also channeled enquiries to the Kyrgyz Republic from EU countries and from Canada, India, Pakistan, the United States, and Uruguay.

- **Integrated Information System in support of Technical Regulation Development:** The technical specifications for the Integrated Information System in support of Technical Regulation Development, which were prepared with the support of an information technology specialist with extensive international experience in system development for the public sector in the region, are now finalized. The Integrated Information System will support the technical regulation reform by facilitating documentation flow and cooperation among the various agencies involved in the development of sector-specific technical regulations.

Source: Authors.

This framework must be developed taking into consideration the international and regional agreements and major trading links, as well as the needs of society regarding safety and health and environmental issues. It must be approved by the highest political authority in the country to give it legitimacy because it is a cross-cutting issue. Such an approach has the advantage that suppliers, when familiar with the overall system, can then easily find their way to the appropriate regulatory authorities and the relevant information, that is, transparency is enhanced. It is also one of the more efficient ways to ensure that the country continues to comply with WTO TBT Agreement obligations.

This regulatory framework should deal with issues such as the preferred structure of technical regulations, the use of international norms and standards as a basis for technical regulation, and conformity assessment modalities. It should clearly indicate the responsibilities of the regulatory authorities, guidelines for market surveillance practices, and the imposition of sanctions. The rights of suppliers—appeals—should not be left out either. Normally, the framework would also deal with regulatory quality improvement (see below), principles of transparency, nondiscrimination, and proportionality. During the process of developing a modern technical regulation framework, many of the older and trade-restrictive measures such as mandatory product certification, retesting of all products by regulatory authorities, and so forth, need to be phased out.

Second, a mechanism to coordinate all the activities of the various regulatory authorities must be established. This is necessary to get past the "silo" mentality of most ministries and agencies. Hence, in many countries a form of oversight authority has been established, which has the authority and responsibility to ensure that all regulatory authorities comply with the national technical regulation framework. These oversight institutions have varying mandates, depending on local conditions and the extent of their activities, and are known by many names, such as Office of Regulatory Reform (Australia); Authorized Body for Technical Regulation (the Kyrgyz Republic); Czech Office for Standards, Metrology, and Testing (the Czech Republic); and U.S. Office of Management and Budget (United States). These oversight bodies need to have the relevant legal and perceptual authority to deal with ministries and agencies that are powerful in their own right. Hence, they are usually accountable to the prime minister, president's office, or similar entity.

A second step toward strengthening the technical regulations system is the use of regulatory quality improvement systems.

The social norms reflected in technical regulation are shaped by a mix of domestic and international views. However, although the demand for technical regulation may become similar across countries with widely disparate levels of income, the possibility of satisfying such technical regulation may be exceptionally costly for less wealthy societies and smaller economies. The second implication is that exports to the richer countries become subject to the relentless rise in norms. These two facts present governments in developing and transition countries with a serious dilemma. Should they seek to replicate at home what is being shaped internationally? What costs would such a policy entail? What are the ways to minimize costs or seek international partnerships that can overcome the obstacles? Close scrutiny of opportunities and obstacles is required.

It is possible, with the use of a variety of methodologies, to arrive at fairly good estimates of what damage or improvement to levels of protection is likely to result from new or revised technical regulations. These estimates can be combined with information about the probable costs of various ways of satisfying technical regulations to generate a regulatory impact assessment. Therefore, mechanisms through which technical regulation are developed and implemented are rapidly becoming the subject of serious, systematic enquiry and analysis. This work must combine three basic components: technical knowledge of the issue; economic analysis of all alternative ways of achieving the desired impact; and consensus building, to ensure that all parties believe that the approach chosen represents the most suitable option available.

The second element of regulatory quality improvement involves the improvements at the technical, organizational, and performance levels of the many institutions that are involved in a modern technical regulation regime. These levels include technical regulation development, standards and conformity assessment issues, metrology, and accreditation, all of which are discussed in great detail throughout the book.

Deregulation as a High Priority for Balkan and CIS Countries

Most Balkan and CIS countries have a wide variety of technical regulations on the statute books. Some are decades old, others are recently developed. Many of the older ones are no longer relevant, or are technically outdated, and are sometimes even unknown to the authorities. A concerted effort should therefore be made to embark on a deregulation exercise (box 5.6). This could be coordinated by the regulatory oversight authority (see above). As a first step, all existing technical regulations on the statute books should be identified.

When all the technical regulations have been identified, the responsible ministries should establish a proper review program, for example, all regulations need to be reviewed and then withdrawn (if no longer relevant), revised (if technically outdated), or confirmed (if still necessary

Radical Regulatory Reform—the Mexican Way

Before joining the North American Free Trade Agreement in January 1994, Mexico had to embark on a major regulatory review program to ensure that its technical regulations (which were antiquated and to- tally fragmented) were rendered compatible with those of the United States and Canada as required by the agreement. Any technical regulation not reviewed, reconfirmed, or revised during this period was automatically rendered ineffective and struck off the statute books. By the mid-1990s, Mexico had swept a large number of technical regulations from their statute books, thereby eliminating most of the obsoles- cence from their system. Approximately 180 regulations were so terminated.

Source: O'Brien 2003.

and technically relevant). Such a review program must have a time limit; otherwise, it will drag on forever. A novel idea is to provide for a sunset clause in legislation, which would automatically render all technical reg- ulations null and void after a specified time, such as five years, if they have not been reviewed and reconfirmed or revised.

Risks may be associated with decreasing typical technical barriers to trade, and these need to be mitigated. In many CIS and Balkan econo- mies, mandatory certification is still in force for a vast array of products. A typical example is the Kyrgyz Republic, with a list of 2,000 products. When these technical barriers to trade are decreased—the mandatory certification requirements are removed or the list of products is drastically reduced to include only health and safety issues—the local manufactur- ing industry may face increased foreign competition that it cannot cope with, because they are locked into a type of technology that is tailored to comply with the mandatory standard. Moreover, discriminatory techni- cal regulation, especially if imposed on imported products only, protects the local industry. The local industry therefore has limited exposure to the relentless competition of the international market, and grows com- placent, and investment in new technology suffers. When these technical barriers to trade are removed, the market is flooded with lower-cost prod- ucts, sometimes at better quality than those locally produced. The costs of the required structural adjustment are borne by companies that need to invest in new technologies to remain competitive or risk going out of business and by workers who lose their jobs and run down their savings while looking for new employment opportunities or undergoing retrain- ing (Falwey, Greenway, and Silva 2006). This scenario does not imply that mandatory standards should be kept, but that social and technology upgrading measures must be considered when removing mandatory standards.

References

Falwey, R., D. Greenway, and J. Silva. 2006. "Trade, Human Capital, and Labour Market Adjustment." Globalizations and Labour Market Research Paper Series 2006/03, University of Nottingham, United Kingdom.

IFC (International Finance Corporation). 2006. "Business Environment in Tajikistan as Seen by Small and Medium Enterprises." Report, IFC, Dushanbe, Tajikistan.

———. 2008. "Technical Regulations in Ukraine: Ensuring Economic Development and Consumer Protection." Policy Paper, IFC, Washington, DC.

———. 2009. "Reform of the System of Inspection of Hazardous Equipment and Construction of Special Category Buildings in Georgia." Policy Paper, IFC, Washington, DC.

ISO (International Organization for Standardization). 2007. *ISO Members 2006.* Geneva: ISO.

O'Brien, P. 2003. "Technical Regulations in a Changing World: Towards a Realistic Approach." Paper prepared for Southern African Development Community and U.S. Agency for International Development. http://www.google.com/url?sa=t&source=web&cd=1&ved=0CBIQFjAA&url=http%3A%2F%2Fwww.acp-eu-trade.org%2Flibrary%2Ffiles%2FOBrien%2520%25E2%2580%2593%252001-03-%2520Technical%2520Regulations%2520in%2520a%2520Changing%2520World%2520%25E2%2580%25A6.pdf&ei=ejuJTMnlMMX7lweH76y-Dw&usg=AFQjCNH6VysN0Ag2EdxTiCnJkP1FklsC4Q.

World Bank. 2007. *Food Safety and Agricultural Health Management in CIS Countries: Completing the Transition.* Washington, DC: World Bank.

CHAPTER 6

Conformity Assessment: Sometimes, But Not Always, a Seal of Quality in Eastern Europe and Central Asia

"Today, most certification centres are largely fictitious offices—they have service contracts with laboratories that either do not exist or whose technological capacities are decades old and have not been renovated since the USSR."

—President Dmitry Medvedev, the Russian Federation, 2010[1]

> **Certification to international standards in Eastern Europe and Central Asia (ECA) is growing, but Central Asia and the Caucasus still lag significantly.**

> **Compulsory product certification is mostly a relic of the past in new European Union (EU) member states and the Balkan countries, but it is thriving in the Commonwealth of Independent States (CIS), where it imposes unnecessary costs on firms and creates opportunities for corruption and rent-seeking.**

---

1. Speech given at the Meeting of Presidential Commission for Modernisation and Technological Development of Russia's Economy, January 10, 2010.

> **ECA countries in the EU and the Balkan countries have restructured their conformity assessment organizations and liberalized their certification and testing markets. Investments by foreign conformity assessment bodies have led to dynamic and competitive markets in most of these countries.**

> **In the CIS, state conformity assessment bodies have yet to be restructured. They often operate as parts of bodies developing mandatory standardization, leading to conflicts of interest. Moreover, modern conformity assessment services that can help firms comply with the requirements of export markets in high-income countries are often missing or are not recognized by trade partners.**

> **Government financial and technical support can help small and medium enterprises (SMEs) upgrade quality but requires carefully designed delivery mechanisms.**

The Market for Conformity Assessment in ECA

Trends in Certification to International Voluntary Standards

An analysis of certification to international standards in Eastern Europe and Central Asia (ECA) can provide a snapshot of whether firms are willing and able to improve their internal processes on a voluntary basis, whether there is appetite for international standards, and whether there is an adequate and reliable supply of certification services. This section focuses on adoption of management system standards, because there is more information on their adoption rates than product standards. Moreover, the implementation of management systems has become an important element of quality assurance in global supply chains, substituting product certification to some extent. As a result, management system standards are the most widespread international standards. The best known standard is the International Organization for Standardization (ISO) 9000 series. It should be mentioned that certification according to ISO 9001 and other management system standards is a condition in many procurement firms and can, therefore, be regarded as quasi-mandatory if an enterprise wants to enter a market. The ISO 9001 standard is implemented by a huge variety of organizations, governmental and private, small and large, covering almost all sectors of economic activity (box 6.1).

ECA's global share of quality management system certificates is growing, but Central Asia and the Caucasus still lag significantly.

Adoption rates of ISO 9001 standards can be used as a proxy for adoption of international standards in an economy. The ISO 9001 standards have become ubiquitous, and certification statistics from accredited bodies are available for all countries. Moreover, unlike sector-specific standards, for which adoption rates are highly dependent on industry structure, ISO 9001 standards are generic process standards that are adopted in a wide range of organizations in the industry and services sectors. Only in the extractive and agricultural sectors is there generally little demand for

BOX 6.1

Benefits from Investing in Certification for Moldovan Agro-Processing Firm

Monicol, founded in 2001, is a small Moldovan enterprise specializing in producing and exporting walnut kernels and dried fruits. It exports its products predominantly to the European Union (EU). In fact, its most important export markets are Germany, Austria, France, and Greece and the Baltic countries. It has recently entered the Russian Federation's market, though with great difficulties.

Monicol has acquired ISO 9001 and HACCP (Hazard Analysis and Critical Control Points) certification from the Swiss certification body SGS with a subsidiary in Moldova. SGS is a major multinational certification body, and its certificates are recognized globally. Implementing the changes required by ISO took over one year, and the overall expenditure associated with obtaining this certificate amounted to US$8,000, or about seven times Moldova's gross domestic product per capita. To maintain its certifications, Monicol incurs additional expenditures on annual audits undertaken by SGS. Since 2005, Monicol's products have also been certified organic according to EU and USDA/NOP (U.S. Department of Agriculture/National Organic Program) regulations by an international certification body. Organic certification has taken the company three years of efforts and has required adjustments in its production process.

Internationally recognized certification has enabled the company to access more sophisticated buyers who can settle their accounts on time. Certification has also allowed it to charge a higher price for its product and has facilitated the export procedure. Recently, Monicol started exporting to Commonwealth of Independent States countries: Belarus, Russia, and Ukraine. These markets have not been asking for proof of certification yet, but there is a sense that the role of certification in these markets is growing. If this is correct, Monicol will be well positioned to compete in these markets.

Source: World Bank Moldova case studies.

ISO 9001 certification. Although ISO 9001 standards are becoming so widespread in some Western European markets that they are losing a bit of their significance, they continue to play an important role in the global supply chains, particularly those involving low- and middle-income economies with no longstanding reputation for quality. The world's manufacturing powerhouse, China, accounts for more than one-fifth of global ISO 9001 certificates (figure 6.1).

ECA is a relative latecomer in the adoption of ISO 9001 certification, which originates in Western Europe, but is catching up with the rest of the world. As a region, ECA accounted for 9 percent of worldwide certificates as compared to only 2 percent in 1997. This increase was not only due to growth in the region's certification rates, but also due to decreases in certification rates in mature markets such as the United Kingdom, where a number of sector-specific standards derived from ISO 9001 have been on the increase.

ECA's growth in certification rates has mainly been fueled by the adoption of the standards in the new European Union (EU) member states in the late 1990s. Growth has picked up in the Russian Federation only since 2004, but the country barely registers more standards than Hungary or the Czech Republic alone. Some of ECA's smaller economies, such as Armenia, Albania, and Georgia, are starting from a very low base, but growth has very recently risen. Certification rates in the rest of the

FIGURE 6.1

Steady Growth in Certification in ECA

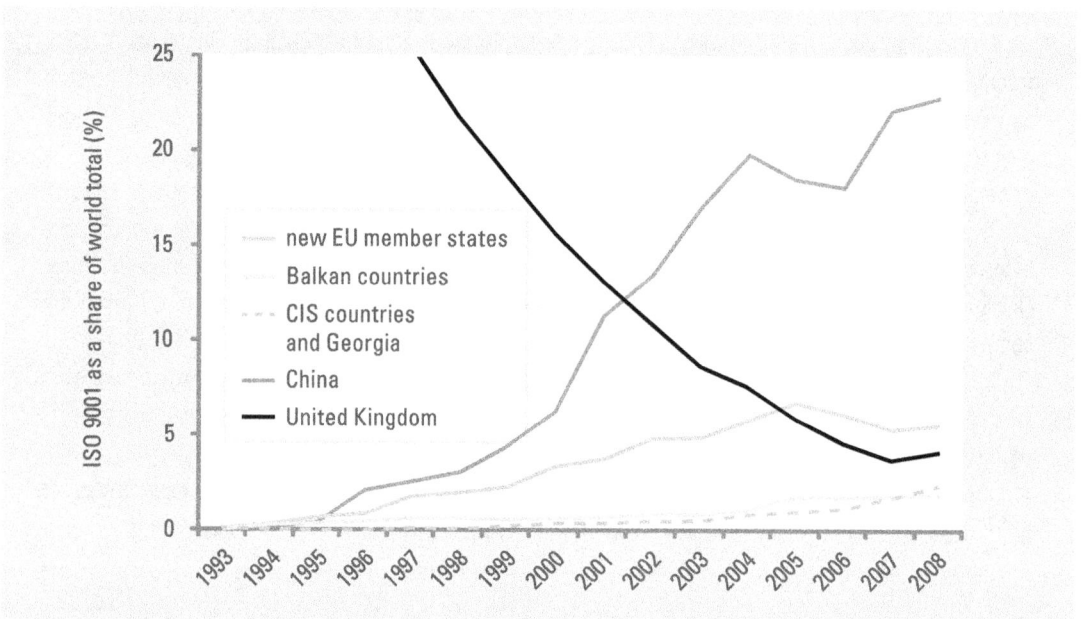

Sources: ISO 2001, 2003, 2005, 2006b, 2008, 2009.
Note: CIS = Commonwealth of Independent States.

Caucasus and Central Asia are dismal. In Tajikistan, only a single internationally recognized certificate was registered as of December 2008, while there were three in the Kyrgyz Republic and six in Turkmenistan. This rate compares poorly to the thousands of standards registered in EU accession countries such as Bulgaria and Romania.

When one considers economic size and structure, the new EU member states outperform China and the United Kingdom by far, but countries in Central Asia and the Caucasus perform poorly. Countries with a larger agricultural sector can be expected to have fewer ISO 9001 certificates because these are not very relevant to farmers and fishermen. Smaller countries can be expected to have fewer certificates by virtue of having fewer establishments and manufacturing facilities—even in a large economy with a consolidated economy, each production facility would need its own certifications. Figure 6.2 presents the number of certificates in ECA countries, when adjusted for value added in industry and services. The figure shows the new EU member states leading the rest of the region as well as the two comparator countries, China and the United Kingdom. In sum, these countries are well integrated into global trade networks that value quality in buyer-supplier relationships. The Balkan countries perform on par with China, implying that low certification rates in that region could be due to the prevalence of the agricultural sector.

FIGURE 6.2

ECA's Certification Rates

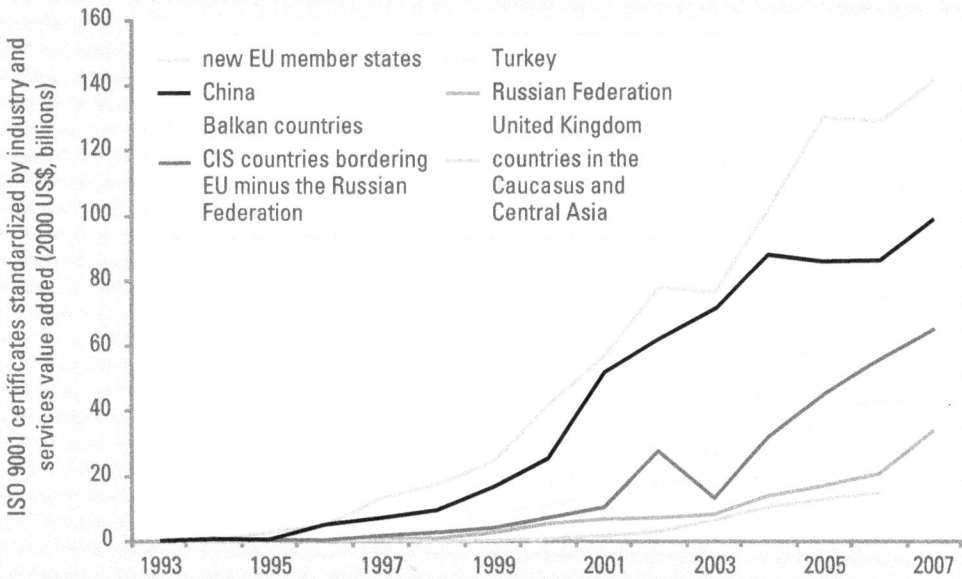

Sources: ISO 2001, 2003, 2005, 2006b, 2008, 2009; World Bank World Development Indicators (WDI) Database.
Note: CIS = Commonwealth of Independent States.

The new EU member states, the Balkan countries, and the Commonwealth of Independent States (CIS) countries neighboring the EU all display high growth rates. Again, countries in Central Asia and the Caucasus
appear cut off from the rest. Their certification rates are much lower than
justified by their economic size and structure.

*New EU member states and Turkey have adopted
sector-specific standards, such as automotive standards,
that allow them to compete in global supply chains.*

Although comprehensive global statistics on sector-specific standards are
not collected, data are now available for the automotive industry. Almost
10 years ago, the world's largest auto suppliers from Europe, North
America, and East Asia agreed on ISO/TS (Technical Specification)16949
as a common quality management standard for producers in automotive
supply chains. Many of the global brands now insist that suppliers be
certified to the standard. Since transition, many European automakers
have located new production facilities in the new EU member states and
in Turkey. A network of locally and foreign-owned suppliers quickly
developed. Figure 6.3 shows that in many of these countries, there are a
competitive number of certified firms relative to the number of domestic
vehicles produced. Figure 6.4 provides complementary data showing
more room for improvement, when one adjusts for the number of certificates for the number of motor vehicle and trailer industry producers.
This implies that a share of auto parts are likely being imported from

FIGURE 6.3

Isolation of Auto Parts Suppliers in CIS Countries from Global Buyers, 2007

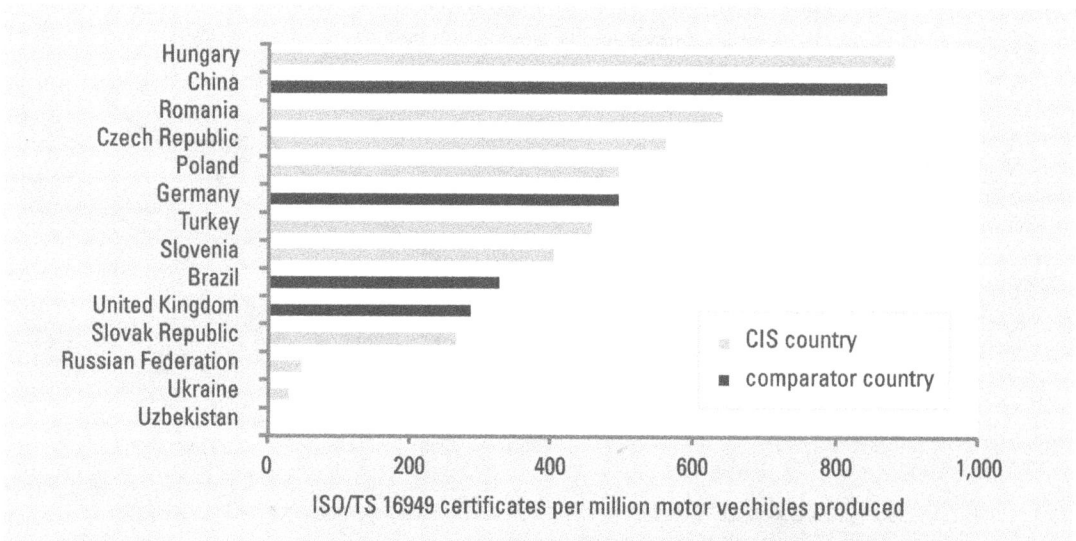

ISO/TS 16949 certificates per million motor vechicles produced

Sources: ISO 2008; International Organization of Motor Vehicle Manufacturers, 2007 Production Statistics Database.

certified producers rather than produced locally. Strikingly, two CIS countries with sizable automotive production sectors—Russia and Ukraine—register very few certificates, pointing to their relative isolation from global supply networks. Uzbekistan is completely isolated with not a single ISO/TS 16949 certification (figure 6.4).

Compulsory Certification

Compulsory product certification is mostly a relic of the past in new EU member states and Balkan countries but is thriving in CIS countries.

ECA's new EU member states have fully aligned their conformity assessment systems with the EU's *Old*, *New*, and *Global Approach* directives and the remaining Old Approach directives while the Balkan candidate countries are well on their way to doing so. In the EU, mandatory third-party certification is required only for a limited set of products associated with safety, health, or environmental hazards.

In contrast, mandatory certification remains prevalent in CIS countries, and in some Central Asian economies little has changed since Soviet times. Certification is not sought by businesses on a voluntary basis to demonstrate the higher quality of their products, processes, and services to their customers. Rather, it is imposed on them by the state. It covers a larger number of goods and services, including products that are not of particularly high risk and do not require certification in Organisation for

FIGURE 6.4

Demand Not Met by Number of Internationally Certified Suppliers in New EU Member States and Turkey, 2007

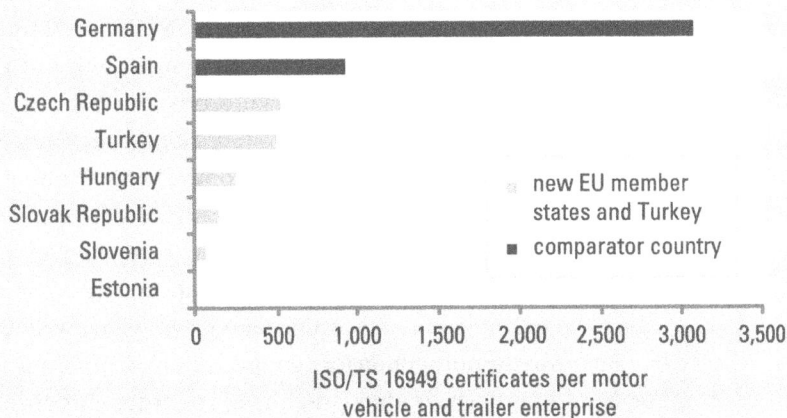

Germany
Spain
Czech Republic
Turkey
Hungary
Slovak Republic
Slovenia
Estonia

0   500   1,000   1,500   2,000   2,500   3,000   3,500

new EU member states and Turkey
comparator country

ISO/TS 16949 certificates per motor vehicle and trailer enterprise

Sources: ISO 2008; Organisation for Economic Co-operation and Development Structural and Demographic Business Statistics Database.

Economic Co-operation and Development (OECD) countries. In Moldova, a special certification is required for all domestically produced wine. Moldovan standards are not recognized in the EU, a fast-growing export market for Moldovan wine. In Ukraine, soft drinks are subject to certification. The official storage time established by the relevant national standard is 15 to 20 months, but the certificate is only valid for 6 months. This timing implies that the company must recertify the soft drink every 6 months.[2]

In many cases, technical regulations developed by different government bodies overlap, so goods are subject to certification and inspection multiple times, by different agencies. This is often the case with food products that can be regulated by the national standards body, the ministry of agriculture, and the ministry of health.

Compulsory certification affects a significant number of businesses. According to the latest International Finance Corporation (IFC) surveys of entrepreneurs, 18 percent of small and medium enterprises (SMEs) were required to certify their goods in Tajikistan. This number reached almost one-quarter of respondents in Uzbekistan, as well as in Ukraine, where it affected on average 84 percent of the revenues of respondents requiring certification. In the EU, only 4 percent of the commodity list requires certification. In Ukraine, one in every four food service businesses is subject to mandatory certification. These businesses include cafes, restaurants, and catering services, most of which are not subject to any certification in the EU (IFC 2005b, 2006).

In CIS countries, product certification is used where process certification or market surveillance would be more effective.

A distinguishing feature of CIS countries is the emphasis placed on product certification versus other types of control mechanisms that pose less of a burden on the economy and can be more effective. Process certification for technical regulations is virtually nonexistent in CIS countries. According to an IFC survey of the enterprises in Uzbekistan requiring certification, 90 percent required product certification (IFC 2005a). This requirement forces manufacturers to complete certification procedures over and over again. In the EU, under the Global Approach to conformity assessment, only one category of products covered under the New Approach directives—specific types of appliances burning gaseous fuels— leaves the examination and certification of individual products by Notified Bodies as the only option for demonstration of conformity assessment. For New Approach products requiring the intervention of a Notified

---

2. See Frishberg and Partners, "Certification of Goods and Services," Kiev. http://www.frishberg.com/articles/Certification%20of%20Goods%20and%20 Services.pdf.

Body, the Notified Body needs to approve and control the quality system for final product inspection and testing (and in some cases, for production) set up by the manufacturer. For some products, the Notified Body supervises the tests carried out by the manufacturer, carries out product checks at random intervals, and carries out surveillance of the manufacturer by means of periodic and unexpected visits (European Commission 2000). None of these practices is equivalent to the type of batch certification present in CIS countries, which is much more involved and time consuming. Focusing on product rather than process certification involves imposing a large list of detailed technical product characteristics to ensure there are no deviations. For food products in Ukraine, this can even take the form of imposing recipes. Product certification can be less effective in the case of food because it does not involve systems to monitor health hazards on a continuous basis or a traceability mechanism on the production side.

Intrusive conformity assessment mechanisms such as certification, testing, and inspection are also used more heavily than market surveillance. For example, in many CIS countries, packaged foods and beverages bear certification marks, while in OECD economies, this is generally not the case. OECD countries emphasize labeling and control of production processes. Market surveillance authorities are then responsible for carrying out periodic checks of products placed in the market. In the EU, self-declaration of conformity by the manufacturer is used for the majority of goods subject to the New Approach directives. For example, products subject to the Low Voltage directives can be affixed with the CE (conformité Européenne, or European comformity) marking by the manufacturer and do not require any intervention by a Notified Body. Even new designs of regulated goods such as toys and personal protection devices do not require the intervention of a third party in conformity assessment, provided they conform to harmonized standards, which are loosely defined.

Compulsory certification creates unnecessary burdens for entrepreneurs and opportunities for corruption in CIS countries.

First, as discussed above, an excessive number of goods and services are subject to mandatory certification. Second, as described in chapter 5 of this book, the technical regulations associated with certification tend to be overly prescriptive and do not consider inputs from the manufacturers. And third, such certification provides opportunities for corruption.

The number and overlap of technical regulations is often confusing to entrepreneurs because no single agency deals with all of them. Entrepreneurs often have difficulty collecting information on mandatory conformity assessment requirements. The process is also lengthy and expensive. In Ukraine, enterprises take 30 days on average to prepare the relevant documents and obtain the certification. For 10 percent of respondents of the IFC survey, the procedure took between three months and one year. Average annual certification costs for Ukrainian SMEs, including labor costs, testing, and official and unofficial payments, amounted to US$2,000, or roughly the country's average income. In Ukraine, the estimated total costs to SMEs going through procedures associated with technical regulations were estimated at over US$127 million in 2006 (IFC 2008).

In a number of CIS countries, it is an open secret among businesses and government ministries that corruption is rampant throughout the state-owned testing, certification, and calibration laboratories covering mandatory product requirements. This anecdotal information can be backed up by the results of IFC surveys of enterprises in various countries showing important rates of unofficial payments. In Uzbekistan, 14 percent of respondents reported giving unofficial payments in exchange for state certification (IFC 2005a). In a recent Ukrainian survey, one-tenth of respondents subject to mandatory standards or registering specifications reported the need to make unofficial payments (IFC 2005b). In Tajikistan, 36 percent of respondents used unofficial means to obtain certificates and 19 percent resorted to unofficial payments to solve certification-related issues (IFC 2006).

The low level of salaries forces staff members to find other sources of income for their means of living. These sources could be a second job or corruptive behavior in which conformity assessment in the mandatory field is involved. In both cases, the activity leads to the issuing of certificates without ever using a testing or calibration facility. As long as the whole system of quality infrastructure is based on these principles and no demand exists for correct results from enterprises, and as long as consumer protection is not developed, there is no interest in the supervising of institutions to control the situation.

The Supply of Conformity Assessment Services in ECA

Certification bodies, inspection bodies, and testing laboratories are dedicated to assessing the conformity of products, services, institutions, or persons to specific requirements. Thus, they are the institutions with the closest contact to producers and service providers. They are the link between standards and industry. As noted in the previous section, conformity assessment bodies can cover both technical regulations and voluntary standards. This section describes the nature of the conformity assessment supplier market in ECA and its capacity to help producers meet global quality requirements.

*In the new EU member states, the Balkan countries, and
Turkey, some state-owned conformity assessment bodies still
exist, but they tend to operate in competitive markets.*

Many have survived transition in one way or another and function under
different organizational forms. They provide testing, inspection, and certification services in the voluntary field as well as in the regulatory field.
Some are Notified Bodies according to the New Approach directives or
are other authorized facilities. They regularly provide services in various
fields of conformity assessment and have a broad scope accredited. Some
of these institutions received support from donor organizations for the
modernization and restructuring of their services.

Restructuring has taken different forms in different countries. As discussed in chapter 5, several of the national standards bodies of the region
still offer certification services, including those in Hungary, Romania, and
Turkey. But in all cases, the standardization and certification functions
have been administratively and financially separated, as required by
membership rules of the regional standards body (European Committee
for Standardization). A similar structure can be found in Western European countries, including France, Spain, and the United Kingdom. The
Polish Centre for Testing and Certification is the successor of the Central
Office for Product Quality, which was established in 1958. In 2003, it was
transformed into a single share company owned by the State Treasury.[3]
In the Czech Republic, seven state-owned institutes involved in testing
and certification decided to pool their resources in 1993 to form a common certification body, Czech Association for Quality Certification.[4] In
Slovenia, in 1992, the Slovenian Institute of Quality and Metrology (SIQ)
was founded as the successor of the state-owned Institute of Quality and
Metrology. In both of its governing bodies, it integrates representatives of
the public agencies, economic and industrial associations, and delegates
of institutions representing SIQ's customers.[5] In Serbia, the Organization
for Quality Systems Certification was founded in 1997 by a joint-stock,
socially owned inspection company, Jugoinspekt Beograd.[6] Other institutions were taken over by foreign enterprises, either multinational conformity assessment bodies or industrial enterprises.

---

3. See the Polish Centre for Testing and Certification Web site, http://www
.pcbc.gov.pl.
4. See the Czech Association for Quality Certification Web site, http://www.cqs
.cz.
5. See the Slovenian Institute of Quality and Metrology Web site, http://www
.siq.si.
6. See the Organization for Quality Systems Certification Web site, http://www
.yuqs.org.

But under whichever shape or form they survive, most of the inheritors of central planning–era conformity assessment bodies have become independent from policy-making bodies and no longer hold monopolies in their domestic markets, although a few exceptions remain (box 6.2). Figure 6.5 shows that with the exception of SRAC (Romanian Society for Quality Assurance) in Romania and SIQ, and in spite of their formerly dominant role in the economy and their largely public ownership, none of these organizations dominates their home markets for certification more than the three comparator companies shown in the figure, namely, those in Austria, Germany, and Spain. Some of these institutions have also become competitive outside of their home markets and provide their services in other countries (figure 6.6).

Foreign direct investment has been a driving force for certification to international standards in the new EU member states, the Balkan countries, and Turkey.

Conformity assessment has become a globally competitive market given the international harmonization of standards and their importance in global supply chains. This situation has given rise to a number of multinational conformity assessment bodies, most operating as private for-profit companies and some as nonprofit organizations and employing thousands of people in dozens of countries. The largest in the world, SGS,

BOX 6.2

A Bulgarian Certification Body's Slow Transition

The government of Bulgaria provides testing and certification services to industry through the Executive Agency for Certification and Testing (EA CT), which holds approximately 4 percent of the market for ISO 9001 certification. It is also the only provider of electromagnetic compatibility testing in Bulgaria. In 2002, EA CT was separated from the national standards body, Bulgarian Institute for Standardization, and created as a transitional structure that would be transformed and registered into commercial law after two years. A sufficient network of private conformity assessment bodies and laboratories was expected to be developed during EA CT's transitional period as a state-owned agency. However, although the private sector market for certification and testing is now dynamic, EA CT remained state owned as of 2007.

The market for certification is now mature in Bulgaria, with more than 20 certification bodies, and it no longer justifies the support of certification services by the state. Nonetheless, when EA CT is privatized, it is not clear that it will be able to maintain its unique electromagnetic compatibility testing facilities in a commercially viable way as a stand-alone entity. The government may need to consider options such as continued subsidies, a merger, or liquidation.

Source: World Bank 2008.

FIGURE 6.5

Domestic State-Owned Certification Bodies, 2008

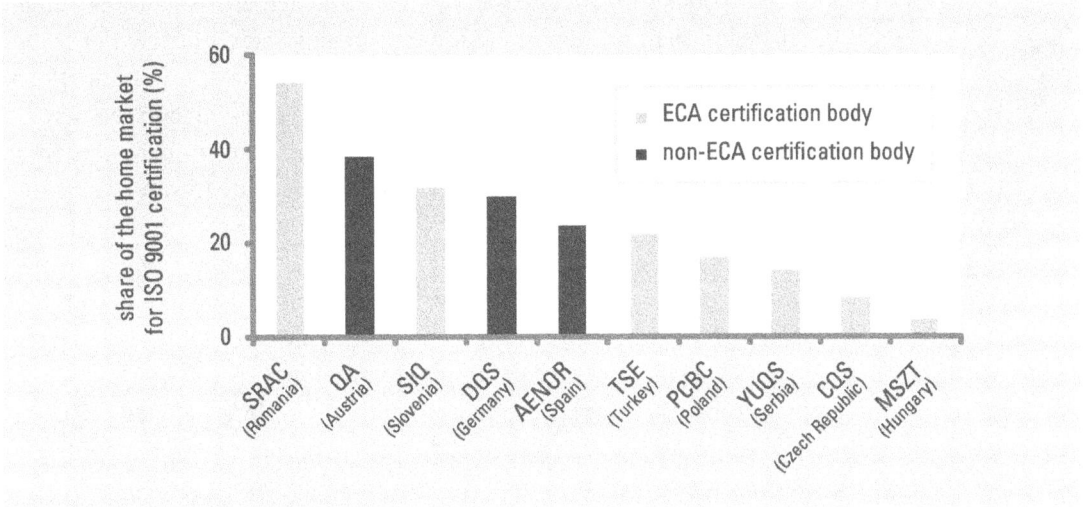

Sources: IQNet Database; ISO 2008.
Note: Shares shown are approximate only.

FIGURE 6.6

Some of ECA's Certification Bodies as Regional Players, 2008

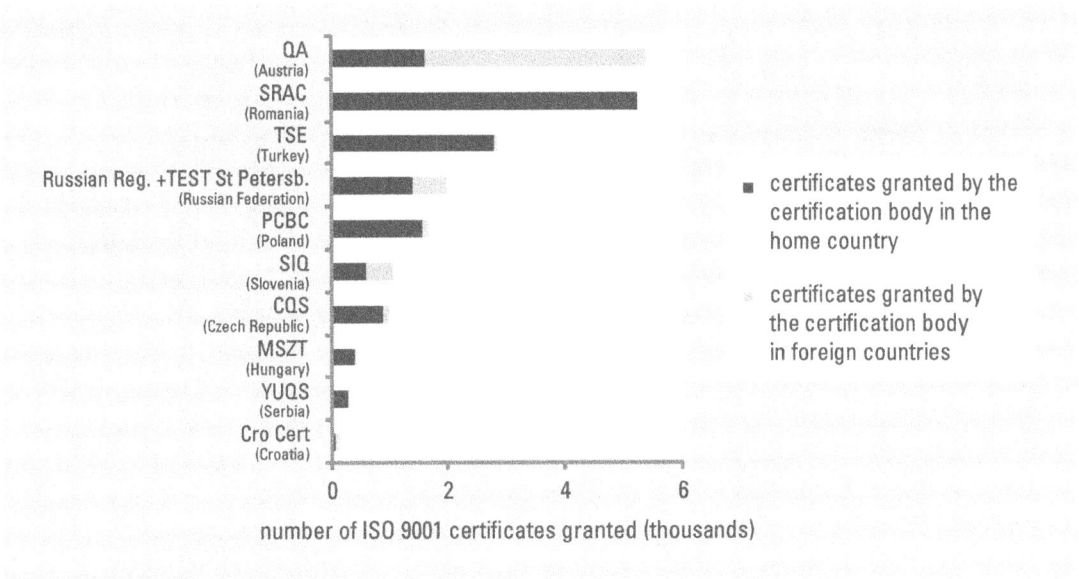

Sources: IQNet Database; ISO 2008.
Note: Russian Reg. = Russian Register, TEST St Petersb. = TEST St. Petersburg.

a Swiss-based company, employs over 56,000 people and operates a network of more than 1,000 offices and laboratories around the world. Other major companies include the TÜV (Technischer Überwachungs-Verein, or Technical Inspection Association), Bureau Veritas, Underwriters Laboratories, and LRQA (Lloyd's Register Quality Assurance). Multinational conformity assessment organizations are well represented in the new EU member states (figure 6.7). Multinationals were able to penetrate these markets early after transition because they benefited from brands that were recognized and trusted globally and that were all accredited by signatories of mutual recognition arrangements in their own countries. They used and still use their home accreditation for activities in countries without recognition. Hence, to some extent the lack of international recognition is circumvented by foreign certification bodies. They also brought with them their long experience working with international standards and up-to-date testing methods. Domestic conformity assessment bodies faced a steep learning curve. In fact, many of these markets are dominated by multinationals. In Bulgaria, they hold three-quarters of the quality management system market (figure 6.8).

FIGURE 6.7

Multinational Conformity Assessment Bodies with Subsidiaries throughout ECA, but Fewer in Central Asia and the Caucasus

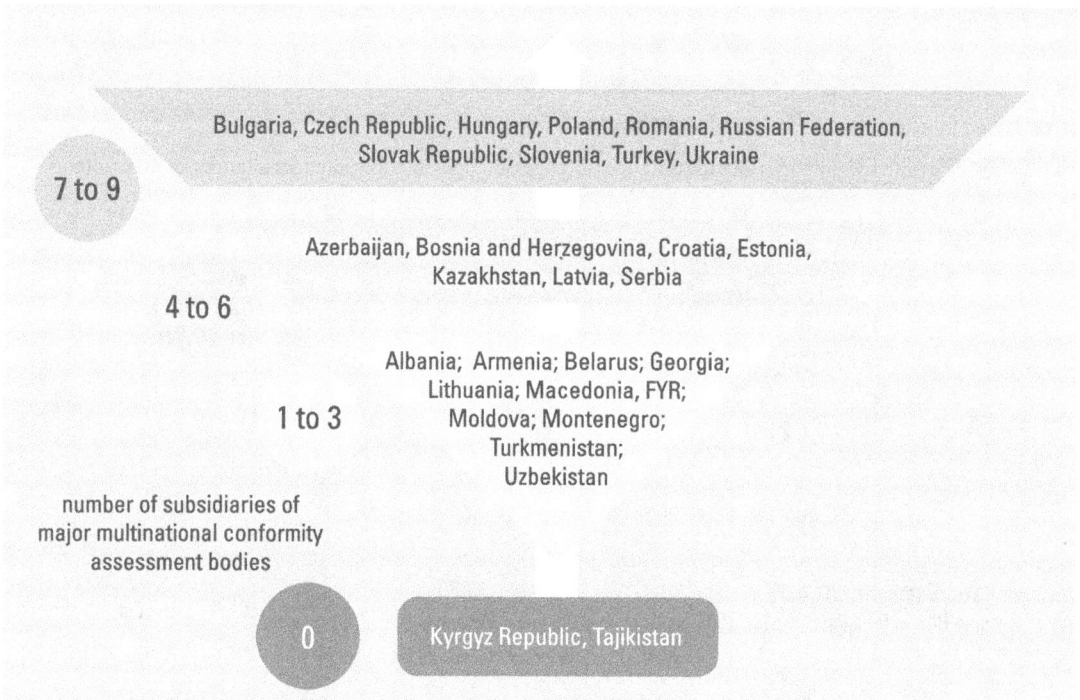

7 to 9   Bulgaria, Czech Republic, Hungary, Poland, Romania, Russian Federation, Slovak Republic, Slovenia, Turkey, Ukraine

4 to 6   Azerbaijan, Bosnia and Herzegovina, Croatia, Estonia, Kazakhstan, Latvia, Serbia

1 to 3   Albania; Armenia; Belarus; Georgia; Lithuania; Macedonia, FYR; Moldova; Montenegro; Turkmenistan; Uzbekistan

number of subsidiaries of major multinational conformity assessment bodies

0   Kyrgyz Republic, Tajikistan

Sources: SGS, Bureau Veritas, LRQA, TÜV Nord, TÜV Rheinland, TÜV Süd, Underwriters Laboratories, Moody International, Det Norske Veritas, and DQS-UL Group Web sites.

FIGURE 6.8

Domination of the Certification Market by Multinational Bodies in Bulgaria

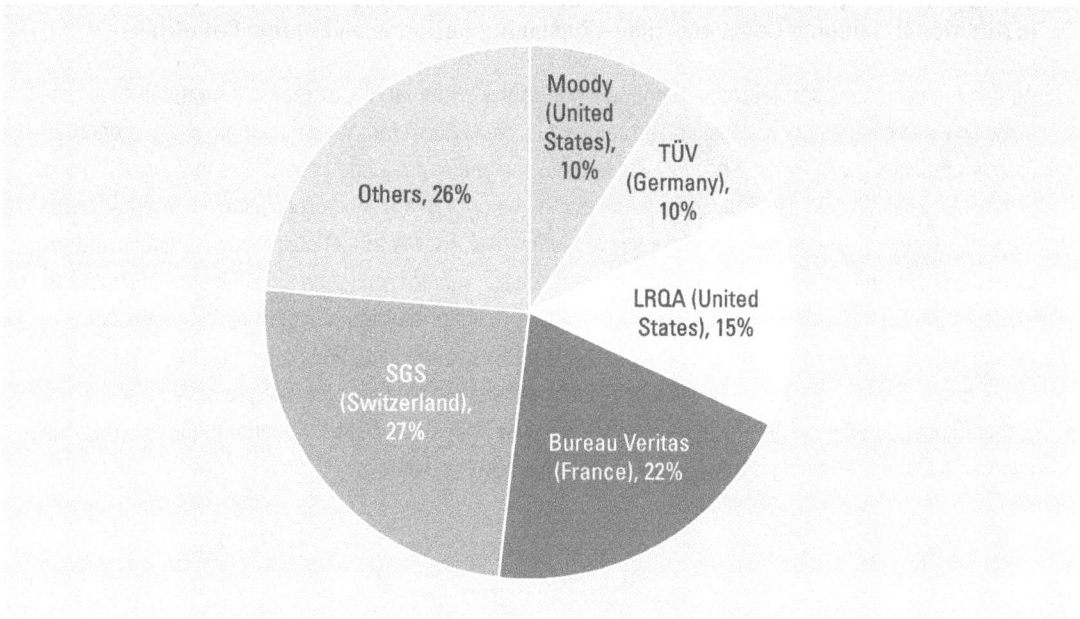

Source: Interviews with certification bodies operating in Bulgaria.
Note: Market shares are for ISO 9001 certification as of July 2007.

Countries with small markets often take advantage of cross-border certification, but sometimes there are limits to this practice.

It must be made clear that not every economy needs a complete set of conformity assessment bodies because of the possibility of cross-border conformity assessment. For example, multinational bodies have invested in the Balkan countries, although less so in small economies such as Albania, the former Yugoslav Republic of Macedonia, and Montenegro. Given the short distances between the countries, they can serve a market from a representation abroad. The Slovenian certification body SIQ has its offices in Slovenia, but derives much of its business from neighboring countries such as Croatia, FYR Macedonia, and even Italy.

In some cases, the lack of a domestic conformity assessment body creates obstacles for entrepreneurs who must incur prohibitive shipping costs, customs duties, and time resources to certify and test their products abroad (box 6.3). Whether this justifies government measures to support domestic testing facilities or not is a question that only a careful market assessment and clear market signals can answer.

BOX 6.3

In Small Balkan Economies, a Weak Certification and Testing Infrastructure Can Result in Additional Shipping Costs and Time-Consuming Reliance on Foreign Countries

An Albanian company specializes in the production of the essential oils extracted from the natural aromatic and medicinal plants of Albania. The company is well known for the excellent biological properties of their products. It was established in 1992 and has five major production operations in various regions of Albania. The company is engaged in cultivation of major herb and spice species as an alternative for the preservation of the aromatic and medicinal biodiversity, for the use of nonproductive lands, and for more job opportunities for the rural community. It received organic certification in 2005 and is licensed to export to the EU and U.S. markets. One of the company's major barriers to export is the weak domestic testing infrastructure. The state laboratory is costly and takes too long, and its results are not accepted by the firm's clients. As a result, the company must send product batches for testing to its Austrian clients without knowing whether they will be rejected because they do not satisfy quality requirements. This imposes additional shipping costs, as well as customs costs and delays.

Source: World Bank case studies.

> *The new EU member states appear to have developed a network of Notified Bodies commensurate with their needs.*

Notified Bodies play a key role in the Global Approach because they act as the EU's officially recognized conformity assessment bodies for products regulated under the 29 New Approach directives. Some of the Notified Bodies cover more than one directive. The number of Notified Bodies in an economy can act as a proxy to the quantity and quality of providers of conformity assessment in the market: the *quantity* because many Notified Bodies also provide services in the voluntary market and the *quality* because Notified Bodies need to demonstrate their technical capabilities for the relevant directives they cover and need to be accredited.

Every new member state and one candidate country, Turkey, has between 10 and 100 Notified Bodies serving their economies. Many are national. Figure 6.9 highlights the fairly linear relationship between the number of Notified Bodies and value added in industry and services in Europe. If anything, ECA countries have more Notified Bodies than would be predicted by the size of their economy, with the exception of Turkey, which has only 13 Notified Bodies compared to 74 in Poland, which has a smaller economy. One reason may be that Turkish Notified Bodies have been recognized by the EU only since 2006, and it takes time for conformity assessment bodies to build the knowledge and skills required to become a Notified Body. But figure 6.9 also suggests that

Turkey's conformity assessment market may not be as developed as that of the new EU member states, when considering its economic size and structure.

In CIS countries, state conformity assessment bodies have yet to be restructured.

Conformity assessment bodies remain closely integrated with technical regulations agencies. This is the case in almost all CIS countries (table 6.1). In most of these countries, state-owned certification and testing bodies retain monopoly power in the mandatory sector and have little pressure to improve their service delivery.

There are political and financial obstacles to the restructuring of the conformity assessment market and the development of a private conformity assessment market. As already discussed, political obstacles arise from the integration of technical regulation and conformity assessment in a single agency with a captive revenue stream. Many of the state-owned organizations offering certification fear losing their sources of revenue if compulsory certification is eliminated, because most do not offer quality-enhancing services that would be sought voluntarily by the pro-

FIGURE 6.9

ECA's New EU Member States Well Served by Notified Bodies

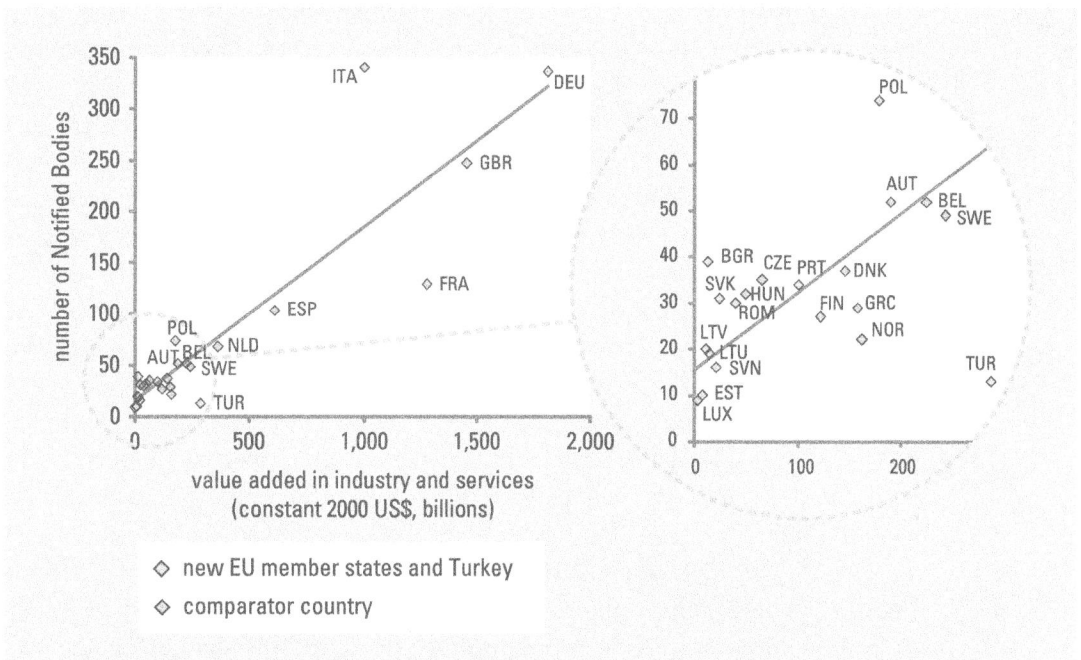

Sources: WDI Database; Nando (New Approach Notified and Designated Organisations) Information System.
Note: Value added data is as of 2006. Number of Notified Bodies is as of November 25, 2009.

TABLE 6.1

Conflicts of Interest for Conformity Assessment Bodies in CIS Countries, 2010

Countries where the technical regulations agency is also involved in conformity assessment	Countries where the two functions are in different institutions
Armenia, Azerbaijan, Belarus, Kazakhstan, Moldova, Russian Federation, Turkmenistan, Ukraine, Uzbekistan	EU, Balkan countries, Georgia, Kyrgyz Republic, Tajikistan, Turkey

Sources: ISO 2006a and Web sites of the national standards bodies.

ductive sector. Financial obstacles arise because in some sectors of the market, entry requires high investments, for example, for testing laboratories. Whereas technical expertise exists in CIS countries, the knowledge about internationally recognized procedures and methodology is still limited.

Multinational certification bodies have had a limited effect on fostering a market for quality in CIS countries, with the exception of Russia and Ukraine.

In the new EU member states, multinational conformity assessment bodies, most of them from Western Europe, played an important role during transition. They brought in both their expertise and their international recognition when neither of these existed in the target market. Moreover, they introduced competition in the market. Subsequently, many of the state-owned or formerly state-owned institutes reacted by upgrading their expertise, offering a new line of international certification and testing schemes and seeking foreign accreditation (when their accreditation systems were not yet recognized), and later by becoming Notified Bodies.

Although one could expect the same reaction to occur throughout the CIS, this has yet to be the case. The multinationals have mainly been attracted to Ukraine and Russia, two of the larger economies of the CIS with important trade relations with the EU. Several have also invested in the natural resource extraction–based economies of Azerbaijan and Kazakhstan, in part drawn by the requirements of oil and gas companies operating there. But the rest of the CIS countries remain fairly untouched by the multinational conformity assessment bodies. None of the 10 major multinational conformity assessment bodies considered in figure 6.7 have offices in Armenia, the Kyrgyz Republic, or Tajikistan. Small markets, little demand for voluntary quality services because of both the predominance of the mandatory sector and the limited orientation toward non-CIS export markets, and unfavorable business environments make it difficult for these countries to attract foreign investors in conformity assessment. Moreover, an important barrier to any foreign investment in testing laboratories is the lack of international traceability offered by the national metrology system. Its measurements are not recognized abroad, so foreign investors would have to return their laboratory equipment to their home markets for periodic calibration.

Limited awareness of quality in the market hampers the transition to voluntary conformity assessment services.

The conformity assessment market will develop only if there are enterprises that require quality. Demand from producers could be driven by consumer requirements in their home markets, export markets requirements, or foreign investment from high-quality markets. So far, demand is insufficient to accelerate the transition of quality infrastructure in Central Asia and in the smaller economies of the CIS. Quality awareness of local consumers and producers is still low and does not lead to respective demands toward quality infrastructure. Foreign investment in manufacturing, a sector that requires quality services, is also limited.

In addition, transition to a private market is challenged by the fact that the terminology of the services (testing and conformity assessment) remains the same while the concepts behind this terminology change considerably. This discrepancy causes confusion for potential customers of the conformity assessment bodies. Given the history of conformity assessment in the region, enterprises consider conformity assessment bodies more as control organs than as partners and are reluctant to use the services for quality assurance of their products. The transition of the conformity assessment market requires a leap from the concept of control to the concept of services that create trust and transparency.

As a result of unreformed state-owned institutions, limited foreign investment, and lack of demand, the certification and testing sector is weak in much of the CIS.

In Russia and Ukraine, two parallel systems coexist: the mandatory conformity assessment market, used for goods and services for the local market, and the voluntary conformity assessment market, used for goods and services for global markets or foreign-invested companies. The remaining CIS countries suffer from a shortage of voluntary conformity assessment bodies. Whereas the economic structure has evolved in these countries, the structure of the state-owned conformity assessment sector often reflects the economic structure of the central-planning era. Their laboratories are ill-equipped to provide the modern certification and testing services required by global markets. Given the weak national accreditation systems and the prohibitive cost of being accredited abroad, most of these organizations do not operate following international guidelines. They survive either through state subsidies or as monopoly service providers for obsolete technical regulations.

Moreover, as will be discussed in chapter 8 of this book, most CIS countries have not signed an accreditation mutual recognition agreement. This means that the certificates and testing reports issued by domestically accredited bodies are not recognized globally. Moreover, few multinational organizations offer internationally recognized services locally in most CIS countries. As a result, countries must bear high costs, waiting time, and uncertainty, while they have their products tested in export markets (box 6.4).

The lack of recognition of foreign certification and test reports creates import barriers in CIS countries.

With the exception of Russia, CIS countries have not signed mutual recognition agreements in accreditation. Moreover, although in some CIS countries legislation exists on the unilateral recognition of foreign certification and test reports, this legislation is not often enforced. As a result, most CIS countries require goods certified and tested abroad to be retested and recertified domestically. This marks up the price of imported equipment and inhibits technology upgrading. In theory, through a political agreement, CIS countries accept each others' certificates. In practice, experience shows that this is often not the case, and imported goods need to be recertified by authorized domestic agencies (box 6.5) (IFC 2006).

The globalization of the certification business is posing new challenges to some ECA countries. On the one hand, in many ECA countries, particularly those in the CIS, mandatory product certification is still widespread. The national standards body enjoys a legalized monopoly in mandatory certification and testing, and it constitutes the bulk of its activities and income. On the other hand, the global certification business has established myriad market-related voluntary certification schemes, serving, for example, the international automobile industry and the major retailers in Europe. These schemes are typically not compatible with the national mandatory certification schemes. Experience shows that developing economies also find them very difficult and costly to implement. This poses obstacles to certification in ECA.

Barriers to Demand for Conformity Assessment in ECA

As discussed above, limited demand for services such as certification, testing, and calibration is an important barrier to the development of conformity assessment in ECA. Limited demand for quality among domestic buyers, technological gaps, lack of finance, and externalities constitute some of the barriers to more widespread certification.

BOX 6.4

Hindrance of Value Chain Integration in the Food-Processing Sector from Lack of Testing Facilities in the Kyrgyz Republic

Thanks to informal networks (friends, family, and diaspora), a small Kyrgyz firm supplies intermediate goods in a European food-processing value chain. The firm buys locally grown beans from small farmers and, after initial processing, supplies a large Dutch food company that sells the final product in the EU. The Dutch company has the beans shipped to the Netherlands for testing and certification, and then ships the tested goods to local traders and distributors across Europe through the Benelux.

The Kyrgyz firm is affected by high transaction costs because of freight charges and delays throughout the distribution network, which diminish its profit margin. Furthermore, the absence of internationally recognized local testing services prevents the Kyrgyz firm from establishing more direct business relationships with potential partners at the distribution end of the value chain, although its beans appear on the shelves of supermarkets around Europe. As depicted in the simple chart below, an internationally recognized Kyrgyz conformity assessment system would enable the firm to eliminate some of the most costly and time-consuming stages (numbers 3 and 4) and increase its margin by being able to obtain testing certificates recognized by end buyers without the need of intermediate parties.

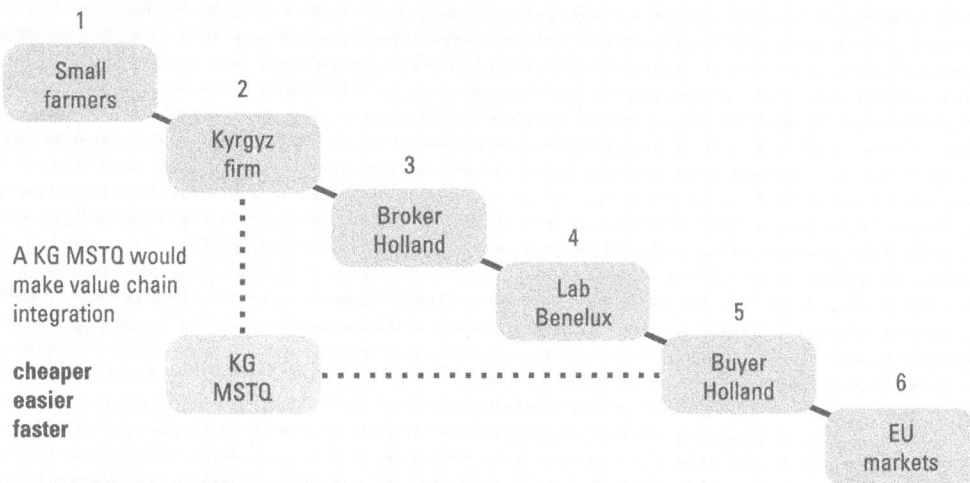

Source: Authors' elaboration.
Note: KG MSTQ = Kyrgyz Republic measurements, standards, testing, and quality.

BOX 6.5
Redundant Certifications Required for Imported Food

PHOTOGRAPH 6.1
Packaging

Source: Authors.

Even products that are circulated within CIS countries often need to be recertified in each importing country. This is the case of the tomato juice package produced by a well-known Ukrainian juice manufacturer. The back of the package, shown on the left, displays certification marks for each country where the product is commercialized. In addition to the "trident" certification mark from the manufacturing country, Ukraine, there are four additional certification marks from Belarus, Moldova, Kazakhstan, and Russia. Information printed on the label shows that each certification refers to a different technical specification (not harmonized). In OECD and EU economies, certification would be recognized across borders due to mutual recognition agreements, and packaged foods and beverages also would not require certification. They are subject to market surveillance and labeling requirements.

Source: Authors.

Awareness issues among domestic buyers have already been mentioned. Consumers who associate standards with state control and not with quality may be unlikely to value certification. In many cases, the greatest incentives for domestic firms to acquire certification come from export markets. However, the drive to export markets can be weak in a number of CIS countries, where trade barriers provide a protected market to domestic firms. Multinational corporations (MNCs) can also provide a push for their suppliers to acquire certification. This has been the case in the Turkish automotive industry.

However, in some cases, even when MNCs operate in the market or when openness to trade exists, the technological gap is too large. In Kazakhstan, few domestic suppliers have the technical expertise and skills to obtain the certification required by the large MNCs operating in the country's oil and gas sector. In spite of domestic policies requiring local content, MNCs are able to procure only low-value inputs from the national market, the rest being imported from abroad. And limited technical capacity often implies that firms face information gaps in choosing which standards or testing process to use for export markets.

The lack of finance for certification and testing can also be a barrier. Meeting new certification and testing standards incur learning-by-doing costs that SMEs can often not absorb. With little capital to use as collateral and with high information asymmetries, SMEs are less likely to receive credit from banks than large enterprises. And because certification does not guarantee a market, the first firm to acquire certification in a specific country bears all the risk in discovering the appropriate market but can then easily be imitated by others (Hausmann and Rodrik 2003).

In the case of high introduction costs, SMEs often decide against certification, because they lack the finances. Obviously, this type of decision will not improve the productivity and competitiveness of the company, but in the short term, it may not jeopardize its existence either. The longer-term prospects, however, are not as rosy because international market forces will eventually extort their toll.

Market Surveillance in ECA

Market Surveillance Functions of the New EU Member States, the Balkan Countries, and Turkey

The new EU member states had no choice but to separate their standards and conformity assessment structures from the technical regulation authorities to join the EU. Market surveillance is mandated by both the New Approach and the Global Approach. Regulatory authorities need to practice market surveillance when a product subject to technical regulations has been placed on the market. This is a major break for the better from the past system of mandatory standards, where premarket approval is the norm. Premarket approval systems are expensive if they are to be effective, that is, the authorities have to maintain and fund vast inspectorates and laboratories. In addition, the suppliers then often consider it the responsibility of the authorities to ensure that products meet regulatory requirements and not themselves, leading to major arguments in assigning accountability if problems arise in the marketplace. In some areas, such as foods and feeds, automotives, and pharmaceuticals, the EU system is a mixture of premarket approval and postmarket surveillance.

One example of transition to market surveillance is the Czech Republic, where a central market surveillance organization (Czech Trade Inspection) was established. This regulatory authority is accountable to the Ministry of Trade and Industry and is responsible for the market surveillance of the New Approach directives. The standards body has no more say in the administration of technical regulations. Balkan countries have also largely reformed their legislation and institutions to shift from mandatory certification to market surveillance.

In the CIS countries, market surveillance is not very developed. One exception is the Kyrgyz Republic, which separated conformity assessment and market surveillance on accession to the World Trade Organization. Prior to the Kyrgyz Republic's accession to the World Trade Organization, the national standards body was responsible for the mandatory premarket testing and certification of products falling within the scope of the approximate 22,000 Gosstandarts. On accession, the regulatory powers of Kyrgyzstandard (now renamed NISM) were taken away, and it was only allowed to provide conformity assessment services on demand. Each ministry had to establish its own regulatory authority, and the focus shifted to market surveillance, rather than premarket approval.

Market Surveillance in the CIS

The situation in most CIS countries is fragile. Countries that are endeavoring to implement proper postmarket surveillance, such as the Kyrgyz Republic, find it very difficult. Market surveillance is completely different from the mandatory standards system and, hence, is not part of common practices and thinking. In addition, many argue that the new system does not really bring any changes for the better; thus, there is a strong undercurrent to return to the mandatory standards system as an easier system to implement. The cost of establishing market surveillance systems is another major issue. Under the mandatory standards, suppliers had to pay for the inspection, testing, and certification, whereas market surveillance in its pure form has to be funded by government as a "public good" activity. This approach places an additional burden on fiscal resources.

The old system of mandatory standards has broken down or has been abolished in name in several CIS countries and in Georgia, but an effective replacement has yet to be established. The result is that markets operate without the necessary controls regarding safety and health. Hence, the safety and health of the people and the environment are being compromised, and the dumping of low-cost products of dubious quality is an enormous problem and a growing political issue.

Supporting the Market for Standards and Conformity Assessment

Adoption of international standards and quality practices in ECA is growing, but some countries still lag significantly. While fully functional and internationally harmonized metrology, accreditation, and standardization bodies constitute a necessary condition for the diffusion of modern standards throughout the economy, it is not a sufficient condition. It is not uncommon that newly upgraded quality infrastructure institutions find themselves with little demand for their services. This usually stems from two gaps: (a) a weak network of conformity assessment service providers and (b) a weak demand for conformity assessment services by industry or lack of quality awareness in society in general. ECA governments can help address these two gaps through targeted policies.

Supporting the Supply of Conformity Assessment Services

Building the supply of conformity assessment services must focus on the many aspects of establishing multiple providers. Countries must thread a fine line between providing state support that addresses genuine market and system failures and distorting the market for conformity assessment.

Policy options for developing a modern network of conformity assessment providers

In CIS countries, the first step to developing a modern network of conformity assessment providers is to remove unnecessary requirements for mandatory certification.

Compulsory product certification is mostly a relic of the past in the new EU member states and the Balkan countries, but is thriving in the CIS, where it imposes unnecessary costs for firms and creates opportunities for corruption and rent-seeking. It not only creates barriers for entrepreneurship, but also stifles the emergence of a voluntary conformity assessment market. Conformity assessment bodies with a guaranteed revenue stream from mandatory services have few incentives to expand and upgrade their services to voluntary international standards. And as long as firms see certification, testing, and calibration as instruments of regulatory enforcement, they are unlikely to seek these services on a voluntary basis. Most SMEs are unable to differentiate between services with real value added (such as calibration) and regulatory activities (such as verification) if both concern the same industrial equipment or are offered by the same service provider. A culture of quality cannot develop in a culture of overwhelming regulatory enforcement.

As a second step, the government can use several complementary approaches to strengthen the supply of services.

In the Balkan and CIS countries, conformity assessment bodies offering a particular type of service are lacking or they offer services that do not meet international norms. Supporting the rapid development of a conformity assessment market is particularly critical when the public sector relies on these bodies to enforce standards related to safety, consumer protection, health, and the environment. There are several complementary options for developing the supply of conformity assessment services:

- Establishing new public or nonprofit conformity assessment service providers

- Privatizing public service providers

- Creating incentives to strengthen existing service providers, such as matching grants and loans for accreditation, training, and capacity building

- Attracting foreign conformity assessment bodies

Each of these options is reviewed in more detail below.

Establishing new conformity assessment service providers

There is a historical case for ECA countries to invest in public or nonprofit conformity assessment bodies, but this must be done as a last option.

Public and nonprofit conformity assessment bodies have a long history of coexistence with private bodies in market economies. Several of today's successful conformity assessment bodies from Western Europe and North America originate from the public or nonprofit sectors. Western European national standards bodies operate public or nonprofit entities, and most compete in their national conformity assessment markets. Some of the world's largest global conformity assessment bodies were established in the 19th century as nonprofit organizations, including Lloyd's Register in the United Kingdom, Underwriters Laboratories in the United States, and Det Norske Veritas in Norway.

ECA governments can address coordination failures and other system failures linked to technology diffusion by supporting the establishment of new certification and inspection bodies and testing and calibration laboratories. In many cases, the market does not provide enough incentives for private actors to establish new services, but these services are required to catalyze industrial development.

Establishing new organizations, or providing direct subsidies to existing public organizations, is the most risky and expensive option. That should be the choice only when it is clear that building up existing private sector organizations through incentives, restructuring or privatizing public organizations to enhance their effectiveness, or attracting foreign service providers are not feasible.

ECA governments should also aim to invest in existing public organizations rather than creating new ones. Testing and calibration laboratories can be established in research and development institutes and universities with existing technical capabilities. This strategy also increases the market orientation of these institutions, which is generally weak in ECA countries. Conformity assessment bodies can also be established through firm consortia, industry associations, and chambers of commerce.

Establishing a nationwide conformity assessment system from the ground up is a long-term and expensive endeavor.

A typical time frame for the establishment of a certification body accredited by an internationally recognized body is two to three years. The learning curve is steep. It requires training staff members and auditors, managing internal processes according to international standards, and going through the accreditation process. During this time, the certification body will not be able to earn much income. After three years, the certification body should become self-sufficient and, later, even make a profit. Typical full costs for establishing a certification body are US$500,000 for two to three scopes, which include international accreditation costs of approximately US$35,000 for the initial assessment and the accreditation fee for the first year. The typical income that can be expected in the first three years of operation will be only US$100,000 to US$200,000. The shortfall will have to be borne by the sponsor—the government or the national standards body.

Specific issues that need to be considered by government in this respect include the following:

- The policy of government should be to establish a conformity assessment service—inspection, testing, and certification—as part of its overall national quality infrastructure strategy. This means the conformity assessment service should be established for the more important of the export products destined for the difficult markets, based on demonstrable needs of industry or other stakeholders.

- As part of the policy, the conformity assessment service must be developed so it can ultimately be accredited by an internationally recognized accreditation body to ensure maximum acceptance of its output by the target markets.

- The conformity assessment service should be managed in accordance with sound business principles; the governing body should be allowed to take full responsibility for fiduciary and strategy decisions within a given policy framework without having to revert to a minister or a ministry for every small decision.

- To avoid distorting the market, such a conformity assessment service provider needs to require payments in accordance with market pricing, and provide equal access to public and private players. This approach means that the conformity assessment service provider should not be required to artificially keep prices below cost, that is, subsidize the service.

The establishment of laboratories would follow similar paths, but additional complications arise, namely, the provision of appropriate laboratory buildings, environmental control, uninterrupted electricity supply, and properly trained technical staff. Laboratory instrumentation is extremely expensive, and appropriate calibration and maintenance systems must be guaranteed. This presupposes a proper metrology infrastructure and national calibration service. Government policy will need to consider these issues—follow a holistic approach. Otherwise, sustainable laboratories will not be established.

Privatizing public conformity assessment bodies

Privatization of conformity assessment bodies can improve their ability to respond to market needs. The risks attached to a conformity assessment service provided by a national institution such as the national standards body are manifold. They include the following:

- Insufficient attention to standardization activities in view of the higher revenue-generating capacity of conformity assessment

- Micromanagement by the authorities in cases where national standards bodies are directly accountable to ministries or a minister

- Lack of managerial freedom to make business-like decisions, especially regarding pricing policies

- Low level of remuneration and, hence, high staff turnover when they have been properly trained

- Lack of customer focus

It is a useful policy for governments to withdraw from the conformity assessment service provision when these services are commercially viable. This can be done by way of a joint public-private partnership or similar arrangement. Another possibility would be to transfer the activities to a nonprofit entity or to a government corporation. The ultimate setup would be to establish the conformity assessment service provider as a private company, possibly with some government shareholding.[7] This approach will depend largely on the prevailing practices and legislative framework of the country. However, the main issue is to ensure that the conformity assessment service provider is detached from the national standards body as a "going concern,"[8] and not as an entity struggling financially. The latter situation will inevitably lead to failure.

Creating incentives for service providers

In CIS countries, governments can stimulate the supply of conformity services by liberalizing the market.

In CIS countries, conformity assessment bodies often need to seek government authorization to operate in a certain area of conformity assessment. In some CIS countries, commercial conformity assessment bodies need to seek accreditation from the same public agency they wish to compete with in the conformity assessment market. As a result, there are few conformity assessment service providers in the market and few competitive pressures to upgrade to services compatible with international standards. CIS governments can encourage entry into the conformity assessment market and upgrading of existing suppliers by liberalizing the market.

In all ECA countries, governments can stimulate supply through financial and technical support.

Governments can create incentives for upgrading by providing financing to conformity assessment bodies in the form of matching grants or loans

---

7. Even if a country would wish to follow the practice of some developed economies where national standards bodies are involved in the certification business, it should be noted that these bodies are totally separated from the main standards activities. For example, in the case of Germany, DIN (Deutsches Institut für Normung) holds 30 percent of the shares in DQS (Germany's largest certification body), but DQS is registered as a private company with its own Board of Directors. In the case of the United Kingdom, BSI (British Standards Institution) Certification is completely separated organizationally and financially from the standardization activities. The same applies in Australia and South Africa.

8. The term "going concern" means that the entity to be commercialized is in a financially sound position. It has developed a market, has an appropriate number of certified companies (new and old) on its books, is accredited, and has registered auditors in its employment or subcontracted. In addition, all its costs are covered by self-earned income, including a surplus that is needed for future developments. It should not be dependent on any government subsidies to balance its books.

for implementation of quality systems, upgrading of equipment, and the accreditation process. Training courses, seminars, and demonstrations can also stimulate upgrading.

Attracting foreign conformity assessment bodies

ECA countries can develop their supply of conformity assessment services by attracting multinational bodies. Multinational conformity assessment bodies have contributed to the diffusion of international standards and quality in EU accession countries—Russia, Ukraine, and Turkey. But they are still largely absent from countries in the Caucasus and Central Asia and some of the smaller Balkan countries.

ECA countries can use several complementary policies to attract multinational bodies. Openness to foreign direct investment and an enabling business environment are a starting point. No matter what the incentives, it will be difficult to attract foreign direct investment with a high regulatory burden, corruption, and an unpredictable macroeconomic environment. Countries can also use their foreign investment promotion agencies to facilitate the entry of multinational bodies. Offering attractive infrastructure such as technoparks or special economic zones can also facilitate entry. Finally, countries must be able to offer a suitable workforce to foreign investors. Training programs in the area of conformity assessment can help.

Supporting the Demand for Quality Upgrading

Governments can provide support for quality upgrading through financial instruments.

There are examples throughout developing and transition countries showing that governments can provide financial support to SMEs to address market failures without distorting the market or falling foul of conflicts of interests. The two main policy instruments used are matching grants and low-interest loans. Tax incentives for certification have also been used quite frequently, but their success has not been demonstrated. Examples of programs include the following:

- A competitive fund reimburses up to 50 to 65 percent of eligible costs incurred for successful testing, certification, and implementation of a quality system. Eligible costs can include the testing fees, consultancy fees for implementing a quality management system, and costs for purchasing the relevant international standards and training of staff in quality management, including international travel to study requirements abroad. Both Croatia and Moldova, for example, offer matching grant programs for quality upgrading (box 6.6).

- Export marketing incentive assistance covers up to 50 percent of product registration in foreign markets, that is, patents, trademarks, and product certification marks.

- A sector partnership fund that supports five or more companies in the development and execution of collaborative projects. These could include improved product or service quality, uniformity, and reliability, thereby enhancing the image of the whole industrial sector.

Comprehensive programs that ensure that firms are committed to quality upgrading and that monitor their progress are likely to be more effective than one-off certification support schemes.

Evidence is mixed on the effect of ISO 9001 certification on measures of quality, productivity, exports, or financial performance. However, empirical evidence suggests that firms are likely to draw more internal benefits

BOX 6.6

Public Support for Quality and Technology Upgrading in Croatia

The Business Innovation Center of Croatia (BICRO) is a publicly funded organization under the Ministry of Science and Technology that aims to support innovation, technology upgrading, and entrepreneurship in the private sector. One of its core programs, the Productivity and Quality Facility (KONCRO), was designed to enhance the competitiveness of SMEs. The program provides 50–50 matching grants to help SMEs pay for technological and management expertise to increase productivity, improve product quality, implement certification schemes (such as ISO 9001), patent products, design products, and minimize environmental externalities.

In addition to helping SMEs, the program also stimulates the market for quality and technology consulting. To qualify for support under KONCRO, firms must use independent quality service providers, or consultants. An employee of a firm cannot act as a service provider for the same firm. The choice of service provider is made by the recipient firm. The KONCRO program staff advises clients about options or possible specialist service providers who have registered with BICRO. Average grant sizes are €6,000.

The Productivity and Quality Facility (PQF) is operated by BICRO. Day-to-day management is the responsibility of a PQF (Program) Unit established as an organizational unit of BICRO. The PQF Unit comprises a small team of locally recruited staff members, including a project director and technical and administrative support. Team members have industrial engineering experience and organizational and language skills and are able to travel throughout Croatia as part of the job.

Source: Authors.

from quality management system certification when it is used for improving organizational performance than when it is used for branding purposes as a response to customer demand (Guasch and others 2007). This view suggests that programs that focus on supporting quality management system certification with no follow-up may have limited effect on actual quality upgrading. Moreover, quality management system standards such as ISO 9001 do not provide all of the skills and expertise to improve all aspects of quality and do not guarantee product quality. Rather, they provide an organizational framework for continuous quality improvement.

Programs that focus on purely financial support also tend to ignore the knowledge gap. SMEs typically apply for technical support cofinancing based on their self-diagnosed quality upgrading needs. Often, SMEs are unaware of their technological and organizational needs to upgrade quality, and even in high-income countries, the market for technical advisory services tailored to SMEs is rather limited. This market is not lucrative for consultants because of the small contract sizes associated with SMEs, as well as their greater adversity to take risks with consultants.

To address these issues, a number of countries have created more comprehensive and open-ended approaches to quality upgrading that do not focus solely on a single aspect such as certification (box 6.7). These programs are completely absent in most of ECA. In the United States and the United Kingdom, manufacturing advisory centers with advisers evaluate an enterprise to help it diagnose its strengths and weaknesses. When this evaluation is completed, the adviser makes recommendations and draws up action plans, and grants are made available for preferred service providers that provide the required technical upgrades.

Other countries have introduced supplier development programs. Their objective is to help a select group of firms improve their capabilities to meet the quality standards and other requirements of large locally established buyers, typically transnational corporations (TNCs). Selected firms are initially evaluated—sometimes with a series of assessments monitoring their receptivity to technical advice over time—and those with the highest potential are selected for intensive technical assistance and training. Partnerships with buyers are facilitated to allow suppliers to gain new business. The firms that complete the program become approved suppliers to TNCs that are involved in shaping the program from the beginning. Supplier Development Programs in the Czech Republic (box 6.8), Hungary, Ireland, and Serbia have allowed those countries to increase the share of local inputs purchased by local subsidiaries of TNCs. The incentive for the TNCs to participate in this program is a combination of cost saving, mainly from logistics, and the reliability and flexibility that comes from using local suppliers.

Governments must use caution in the mechanisms they use to deliver public support to SMEs.

When the market for quality consultants is lacking, or is very weak, the government can subsidize specialized training programs or offer consultancy directly through existing agencies. Such programs are likely to be most effective when the implementing agency has a certain level of institutional autonomy and has the proper incentive structures in place to respond to the needs of the economy. Such agencies should operate as completely separate entities from conformity assessment bodies to avoid conflicts of interest.

BOX 6.7

Multipronged Approach to SME Growth from Integration of Quality in Industrial Programs

Industrial extension was first implemented by a few states in the United States in the 1960s and has been significantly expanded by the federal government since 1989, in reaction to the loss of international competitiveness of U.S. manufacturing in the 1980s. Currently, 59 nationwide Manufacturing Extension Centers (MECs) and 440 satellite locations of the federal Manufacturing Extension Partnership (MEP), with a total staff of nearly 1,600 specialists in business and manufacturing, provide direct assistance to SME customers throughout the United States. These centers provide small and medium-size manufacturers with an array of services that focus on growth, productivity, quality, and efficiency, primarily by helping clients adopt more advanced, existing, and proven technology, processes, and techniques.

Assistance is provided in the areas of quality, manufacturing and business systems, engineering services, human resources and organizational development, and information technology. Assistance is offered through a combination of initial visits, engagements, assessments, technical assistance projects, and applications for grants. MECs offer training services, but also conduct outreach activities such as coordinating group projects and organizing workshops, seminars, and demonstrations. Technical assistance is provided on request. Questions by firms range from broad issues concerning the general management to detailed questions concerning manufacturing productivity. Experienced field agents can provide individual firms with advice and practical assistance for general problems. Field agents often follow their initial assessment with referrals to outside field experts through their extensive networks of private consultants, economic development organizations, community colleges, and universities.

MEP has completed nearly 392,000 customer engagements since the program's inception, including technical assistance projects, training programs, networking events, and long-term strategic support. In 2008 alone, 31,961 manufacturers were served, and the total federal budget was US$89 million, slightly lower than the previous two years (over US$100 million). According to a survey conducted by MEP of 5,981 clients with projects completed in FY2007, MEP assistance resulted in increased or retained sales of US$10.50 billion, cost savings of US$1.44 billion, and new client investment of US$2.19 billion. Moreover, rough estimates of employment effect show that 17,316 jobs were created and 39,763 jobs were retained.

Source: World Bank 2009.

The Czech Experience with Supplier Development Programs

Through a program of supplier development, the Czech Ministry of Economy created a methodology for improving the supply chain position of Czech firms dealing with TNCs operating in the Czech Republic. Although the automotive and electronics industries were well represented in the Czech Republic, they purchased only very-low-value items, small plastic parts, fastenings, and so forth. Through supplier development, Czech suppliers were brought to international standards of production in a short time. The program also arranged meetings between suppliers and buyers. As a result of the program, 17 of the 20 companies involved achieved sales of US$46 million directly attributable to participation in the program. The pilot was followed by a larger program in different sectors, and supplier development is now a standard part of economic development in the Czech Republic. It is worth noting that the Czech Ministry of Economy believes, after considerable research, that supplier development plays a large role in the attraction and retention of inward investment. The Czech Republic is now one of the top five countries in the world for foreign direct investment attraction.

Source: John Varney, personal communication.

Organizations selected to run quality upgrading programs should be selected to create conditions and incentives for good performance. Typically, selecting a ministry department as an implementation agency is not constructive. The ministry should not be tempted to design policies that increase its administrative size. An independent public or nonprofit agency should manage the program. In the United States and the United Kingdom, central government agencies manage and finance the manufacturing support programs, but their implementation is contracted out to local organizations such as business organizations, universities, regional agencies, and even private consulting firms.

In addition, mechanisms for financial support can make an important difference. The agency providing financial support for SME testing, certification, and calibration should not be a public conformity assessment body. Financial support to the SMEs should not be channeled through the conformity assessment service provider in the form of subsidies or artificially low pricing. This practice distorts the market. The most useful practice is to provide a payback to SME companies from a business support agency on presentation of achieved results—positive test reports, certificates, or assessment of quality upgrading progress by an independent third party. Financial and technical support should have a ceiling. This limit could be, for example, US$50,000 per company over a three-year period in ECA, with additional assistance granted on the basis of past progress. In addition, companies that wish to qualify for such assistance should comply with certain prerequisites, such as minimum size and staff qualifications. A useful mechanism to enhance the sustainability is to offer further financial support after two or three years.

Finally, in all cases, periodic monitoring and evaluation of progress and of the effect of the policies and programs is essential. This approach allows the agency to identify good practices and changing needs in the market and to revise the programs accordingly.

Enhancing quality awareness through campaigns and awards can stimulate demand for quality upgrading.

An important barrier to quality adoption by industry and consumers in ECA is the lack of quality awareness. For many decades, quality was defined by the state in ECA, not by industry or consumer preferences. This is still largely the case in a number of CIS countries with an abundance of technical regulations and mandatory standards. Moreover, the national quality infrastructure served as an enforcement agency rather than a service provider. The transition from a mandatory to voluntary system creates uncertainty and apprehension in industry of the role of that national quality infrastructure. Moreover, SMEs in ECA countries that export smaller amounts to high-income economies such as the EU have little understanding of the quality and standardization needs of those markets.

As a result, SMEs in ECA often perceive compliance with standards, certification, testing, and calibration as additional burdens, not as sources of competitive advantages. Certification to ISO 9001 is often conducted without following the spirit of the standard and, in a number of countries with weak accreditation systems, through low-cost and often unethical certification bodies that "sell" their certificates without proper audits. This attitude limits demand for internationally recognized conformity assessment services and inhibits investments in training and equipment for quality upgrading.

Quality campaigns, implemented through, for example, a national quality council or through industry associations, can help raise awareness of quality among both industry and consumers. They can help sensitize industry to the role of the NQI in the economy and to the importance of quality over price to consumers.

In high-income economies, quality awards such as the Baldrige Award in the United States or the European Excellence Award recognize companies whose quality practices have progressed far beyond the certification requirements for their management systems, such as ISO 9001 and ISO 14000. These awards have been fostered mainly by business and industry associations. This practice presupposes that the industry has reached a quality level that supports the award criteria, which are obviously very high. ECA countries can usefully link up with the European system and need not develop their own regional approach.

Even though quality or excellence awards in high-income economies are largely initiated and managed by industry itself, albeit under the patronage of a very senior political level (the U.S. president in the case of the Baldrige Award), governments in developing economies often consider these to be a useful vehicle to raise quality awareness in industry. This may be so, but then the government must ensure that the quality award system is properly constituted, carefully managed in accordance with international best practices criteria, and appropriately funded. When a national scheme is fully functioning, linking it to an overarching regional system would be a very useful strategy to gain even more exposure.

In the EU, the European Foundation for Quality Management (EFQM)[9] is the umbrella organization managing the European Excellence Award. Over and above managing the awards, EFQM also provides a tremendous amount of information and training on excellence models and practices. It operates through national partner organizations. Within the ECA countries, such partner organizations exist only in Hungary, Poland, Russia, Slovenia, and Ukraine. There is therefore much scope for the bulk of ECA countries to establish national quality or excellence fora and link up with the greater European movement. It is very important that such quality or excellence fora are representative of both the authorities and the industry, especially the "captains of industry"—industrialists with large power bases.

The public sector can take an active role in quality upgrading—leading by example and promoting procurement policies.

Finally, the public sector should practice what it preaches to support the diffusion of quality in the economy. Ministries and government agencies should adopt good quality practices, starting, where relevant, with registration to ISO 9001. Resources should be made available to such agencies for such purposes. Similarly, governments, as buyers of goods and services, should demand that their suppliers comply with the relevant quality standards. Such procurement programs should be phased in gradually so as to allow existing suppliers to upgrade their quality practices and qualify.

---

9. See the EFQM Web site, http://www.efqm.org.

A number of factors lie behind ECA's export quality performance.

Trade barriers in most CIS countries limit competitive pressures for technological upgrading on domestic producers and increase export costs. And consumers in low- and middle-income countries tend to be less demanding on quality than those in high-income countries, meaning that producers are more inclined to compete on cost than on quality in internal markets. In ECA countries outside of the EU, the intensity of competition is also limited and markets are captured by large domestic firms with few incentives to improve product quality or to meet international standards. Foreign direct investment, a source of expertise, technology, and demand for quality upgrading, is limited from many non-EU ECA countries. When it does exist, it is focused on natural resource extraction, a sector with fewer opportunities for knowledge spillovers and local procurement than manufacturing. In natural resource–rich countries, investors are also more attracted to extractive industries than to sectors that compete on quality. Macroeconomic conditions in certain ECA countries linked to inflation and exchange rates can also reduce incentives for investing in quality. In ECA countries where the business environment is better and trade barriers are low, such as in and around the EU, deficiencies in skills, limited investments in research and development (R&D), and lack of links between knowledge institutions and firms reduces the capacity to upgrade both product and process quality through technology absorption.

One explanation is that most R&D in ECA countries occurs in the government and academic sectors and that these sectors have limited links to the productive sector. Hence, the link is expected to be weaker than in Western European or North American economies, where the majority of R&D is performed in the private sectors and where the transfer of knowledge and technology is greater across government, industry, and academia.

References

European Commission. (2000). *Guide to the Implementation of Directives Based on the New Approach and the Global Approach.* Luxembourg: European Communities.

Guasch, J. L., J.-L. Racine, I. Sánchez, and M. Diop. 2007. *Quality Systems and Standards for a Competitive Edge.* Washington, DC: World Bank.

Hausmann, R., and D. Rodrik. 2003. "Economic Development as Self-discovery." *Journal of Development Economics* 72 (2): 603–33.

IFC (International Finance Corporation). 2005a. *Business Environment in Uzbekistan as Seen by Small and Medium Enterprises.* Washington, DC: IFC.

———. 2005b. *Business Environment in Ukraine 2005.* Washington, DC: IFC.

———. 2006. *Business Environment in Tajikistan as Seen by Small and Medium Enterprises, 2006.* Washington, DC: IFC.

———. 2008. *Technical Regulations in Ukraine: Ensuring Economic Development and Consumer Protection.* Washington, DC: IFC.

ISO (International Organization for Standardization). 2001. *ISO Survey of ISO 9001:2000 and ISO 14001 Certificates — Tenth Cycle.* Geneva: ISO.

———. 2003. *ISO Survey of ISO 9001:2000 and ISO 14001 Certificates — 2003.* Geneva: ISO.

———. 2005. *ISO Survey of Certifications 2004.* Geneva: ISO.

———. 2006a. *ISO Members 2005.* Geneva: ISO.

———. 2006b. *ISO Survey of Certifications 2005.* Geneva: ISO.

———. 2008. *ISO Survey of Certifications 2007.* Geneva: ISO.

———. 2009. *ISO Survey of Certifications 2008.* Geneva: ISO.

World Bank. 2008. *Bulgaria: Investment Climate Assessment.* Washington, DC: World Bank.

———. 2009. "Turkey Innovation Report." Unpublished. World Bank, Washington, DC.

CHAPTER 7

Metrology: Making Sure
Everything Fits

*"There shall be but one measure for wine throughout our realm,
and one measure for ale, and one measure for corn, namely 'the
London quarter'; and one width for cloths whether dyed, russet
or halberget, namely two ells within the selvedges. Let it be the
same with weights as with measures."*

—Magna Carta, 1215 A.D.

▷ In many Commonwealth of Independent States (CIS)
economies, the concepts of measurement traceability
and uncertainty are not widespread; there is no way of
knowing whether a measurement taken by one economic actor is equivalent to that taken by another, with
obvious negative effects for product quality.

▷ In countries in Central Asia and the Caucasus, measurement errors for much equipment are dictated by
the state, and national metrology institutes operate
mainly as regulatory control agencies. In other Eastern
Europe and Central Asia (ECA) countries, measurement
errors are mainly determined by end users, and metrology institutes help them meet their needs by providing
reliable calibration services.

> **While ECA's new European Union (EU) member states and its larger economies are well integrated with the international metrology system, countries in the Balkans, Central Asia, and the Caucasus remain isolated. Their measurements, and all of the tests and certifications that depend on them, are not recognized abroad—posing obvious barriers to trade.**

> **Equipment and infrastructure in ECA's metrology systems are in desperate need of upgrading, but such efforts will be useless unless accompanied by upgrading of human resources and quality systems and achievement of international traceability. An incremental approach, one laboratory at a time, avoids repetition of mistakes.**

> **Small ECA economies can minimize the cost of their national metrology systems by relying as much as possible on the services of internationally recognized metrology institutes in neighboring countries.**

Metrology in ECA

Metrology Under Central Planning

The state dictated measurement errors for all equipment in the top-down metrology process under central planning.

The metrology and calibration infrastructure in Eastern Europe and Central Asia (ECA) has a unique history and is still in a transition phase in many countries. For an understanding of the challenges faced by metrology systems today, it is worth examining its structure prior to 1991.

The *Gosstandart* system was entirely mandatory and based on the verification system *Povjerka,* the Russian term for "control." Voluntary calibration did not exist in the Soviet system, and in fact, it was not even necessary because all measurements were mandatory, state defined, and state controlled.

Nevertheless, there was a metrological hierarchy in the system that was linked to the International System of Units (SI) through the Soviet Union Primary Etalons,[1] largely maintained in laboratories in then Leningrad and Moscow (Russia) and Kharkov (Ukraine). Outside of Russia and Ukraine, the other Soviet Republics had branches of the Gosstandart agency with their own working etalons (measurement standards) that could be traced back to the Soviet Union Primary Etalons.

With the establishment of the economic zone for socialist countries in 1949—the Council for Mutual Economic Assistance (COMECON) led by the Soviet Union—the Gosstandart system became important for trading partners in Eastern Europe. A system of COMECON Primary Etalons was developed, which represented the highest metrological level for all COMECON members.

Not using measurement traceability and uncertainty concepts widely in the economy affected product quality negatively.

The metrology system used under central planning was significantly different from those used in the West, with the exception of legal metrology. Rigid and predetermined measurement uncertainties were imposed uniformly on all users of certain measurement equipment. In contrast, in the West, measurement uncertainties were selected by the users according to their specific quality requirements, quality management systems, and technical competence. However, there were exceptions—such as scientific institutes, research and development institutes, and the military—that could define their own measurement requirements or even develop their own procedures.

Povjerka is somewhat similar to the metrological verification of measuring devices that are covered in the Western world under legal metrology for consumer protection purposes (for items such as weighing scales in markets, gasoline or water pumps, and electricity or gas meters in households). One distinguishing feature of Povjerka was that it allowed for only a "yes" or "no" answer, depending on whether the metrology equipment satisfied the permissible error or not. This system was unlike the Western concept of calibration, which provided measurement uncertainty and traceability. Routine internal checks of measuring devices were often conducted, but their rigor fell far short of that set by international industrial calibration guidelines.

---

1. The term "etalons" is sometimes used in ECA to denote national measurement reference standards.

The Institutional Framework for Metrology in ECA

The EU and Balkan countries' Harmonized Systems with the European Model during the transition: CIS countries followed the old model that was rife with conflicts of interests.

After the independence of the various Soviet republics and the dismantling of COMECON, the national metrology institutes (NMIs) of ECA countries broke their ties to the Soviet Primary Laboratories and the COMECON Primary Etalons. As independent states, the former Soviet republics wanted their own independent quality infrastructure. The former Gosstandart branches of the Soviet republics—with their certification, testing, and metrology centers that were considered secondary laboratories—became, in many cases, the NMIs of the newly established countries. Some of the wealthier economies created new NMIs on top of these structures to replace the old Soviet Union Primary Etalons. The European COMECON countries with prospects of joining the European union (EU) set up their own NMIs as well.

At this point, a rift appeared between countries with aspirations of joining the EU and the former Soviet republics that joined the Commonwealth of Independent States (CIS). In the early days of transition, the new NMIs had little experience in their new functions. Those with EU ambitions joined the European regional metrology organization, European Association of National Metrology Institutes (EURAMET). They became integrated in the European regional metrology system, abandoned the top-down model of metrology, and established their international traceability through the support of this organization. In 1991, due in part to language commonalities, the other Russian-speaking NMIs created their own regional metrology organization, the Euro-Asian Cooperation of National Metrological Institutions (COOMET). The German NMI, Physikalisch-Technische Bundesanstalt, became a strong supporter of COOMET because of the German Democratic Republic's history as a COMECON member country. However, Germany and the Russian Federation are the only NMIs providing resources through expertise, trainings, or organization of regional intercomparisons. Moreover, Germany has been the only country within COOMET with a metrology system fully in line with international best practices.

As a result, while the new EU member states and Balkan NMIs gravitated toward the international system, most CIS NMIs continued to embrace the old model. Almost 20 years after independence, many CIS countries still use the old Gosstandart metrological verification system—Povjerka. The NMIs that did not join EURAMET still send many of their etalons to the former Soviet Primary Laboratories in Russia and Ukraine.

The reasons for this include language, low prices, and lack of awareness. In many respects, little has changed except that Gosstandart branches are now independent NMIs and the countries have the option of using other sources for traceability and metrological exchange.

All ECA countries have public NMIs, but several are experimenting with decentralization to build more efficient systems.

In all ECA countries, as in most countries of the world, the NMI is a publicly owned and publicly managed institution. Exceptions include the United Kingdom, where the NMI is a government-owned contractor-operated organization, and the Netherlands, where the NMI is a private company with a public mandate. However, a number of ECA countries have adopted the decentralized model where a central NMI designates institutions responsible for specific measurement areas (table 7.1). In many countries of the world, there is typically a single designate: the institute responsible for ionizing radiation. This is also the case in ECA countries that have such scientific capabilities, such as Turkey. However, several ECA countries are also adopting more aggressive decentralized models similar to the U.K. and Spanish models, which have three and seven designates, respectively. This strategy is useful when organizations outside of the NMI have already developed expertise in particular metrology areas and the states do not wish to invest in duplicating the same expertise at the NMIs. Several of the Balkan countries, which had to build their NMIs from the ground up after gaining independence in the 1990s, have adopted this approach. These countries include Bosnia and Herzegovina, Croatia (box 7.1), the former Yugoslav Republic of Macedonia, and Slovenia. Slovenia has gone the furthest with 12 designates, one-third of which are private entities. A drawback of this model is that the NMIs lose some of their control over the quality of the designates' services. In small countries, the designates may be monopoly service providers to the NMIs, so contracts may be difficult to enforce.

In most ECA countries, legislation defines relatively autonomous NMIs, but in some cases they are controlled by state policy-making bodies.

The vast majority of NMIs in ECA are part of independent public institutions that do not have policy-making roles, although they typically depend on specific ministries, such as the Ministry of Economy. In this sense, NMIs in ECA are mostly autonomous from the states, notwithstanding conflicts of interest arising from regulatory functions in Central

TABLE 7.1

Organization of National Metrology, 2007–09

	Country	Legal status	Legal and scientific metrology in the same institution	Metrology and technical regulations in the same institutions	Number of designates (decentralized service providers)
EU countries	Bulgaria	Public			
	Hungary	Public	✓		
	Poland	Public	✓		
	Slovenia	Public	✓		4 private, 8 public
	Romania	Public			1 public
Balkan countries and Turkey	Albania	Public	✓		2 public
	Bosnia and Herzegovina	Public	✓		4 private
	Croatia	Public	✓		4 public
	Macedonia, FYR	Public	✓		2 private
	Montenegro	Public	✓		
	Serbia	Public	✓		
	Turkey	Public			1 public
CIS countries and Georgia	Armenia	Public	partly		
	Georgia	Public	✓		
	Kazakhstan	Public		✓	1 public
	Kyrgyz Republic	Public	✓		
	Moldova	Public	✓	✓	
	Tajikistan	Public	✓	✓	
	Ukraine	Public	✓	✓	3 public
	Uzbekistan	Public	✓	✓	1 public
Comparator countries	Germany	Public			3 public
	Ireland	Public	✓		
	Spain	Public	✓		1 private, 6 public
	United Kingdom	Public			2 private, 1 public

Source: World Bank survey of national quality infrastructure institutions.

Asia's NMIs. Figure 7.1 depicts the relative autonomy of the NMIs in different countries, as defined by their legislation. Turkey's NMI, TÜBITAK Ulusal Metroloji Enstitüsü (UME), is the most independent. In fact, UME does not even depend on a ministry but is part of TÜBITAK, Turkey's Scientific and Technological Research Council, which itself does not depend on any ministry. Most of the NMIs in ECA have attained a level of autonomy similar to that of NMIs in Germany. However, autonomy is not necessarily synonymous with good governance; it does not exclude

BOX 7.1

Resource Efficiency Goal of Croatia's Decentralized Metrology System

The State Office for Metrology, DZM, is the national NMI in Croatia but operates only two of the nine national scientific metrology laboratories. Instead of developing completely new fields of metrology in-house, it has chosen to designate a network of external metrology laboratories in universities and research institutions that already possess the technical capacity for innovation. DZM finances the maintenance of reference standards in these laboratories and laboratory inter-comparisons. In some cases, DZM also provides these laboratories with equipment and personnel. However, although not managing these external laboratories directly, DZM must ensure that they provide reliable services and operate at the highest standards. Gaining accreditation for all these laboratories is a challenge. Until now, only two of the external laboratories (for force and length standards) have been accredited by a German body that is a signatory of the European co-operation for Accreditation Multilateral Agreement. Hence, their portion of Croatia's national metrology system is recognized abroad.

Structure of the Croatian Scientific Metrology System

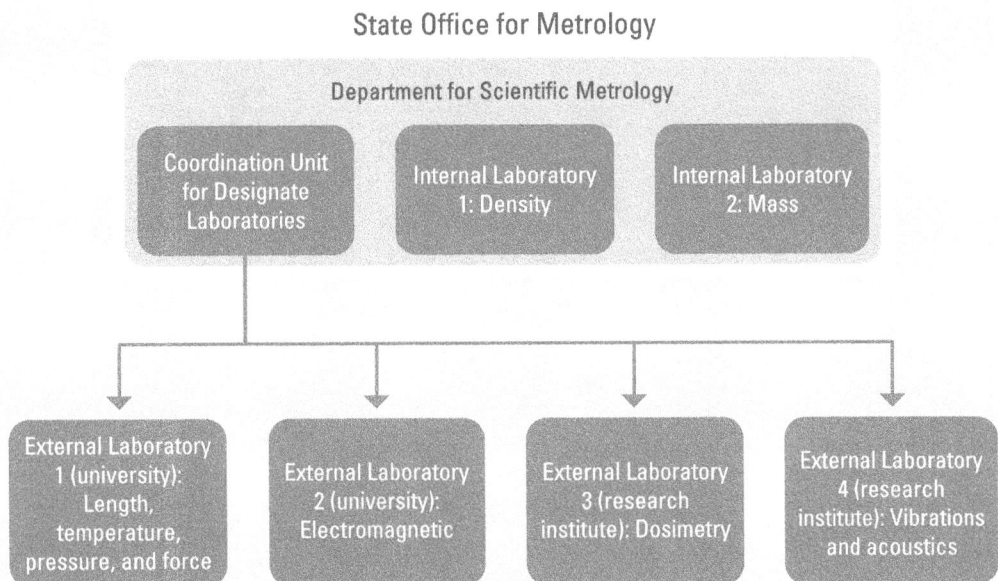

State Office for Metrology

Department for Scientific Metrology

Coordination Unit for Designate Laboratories

Internal Laboratory 1: Density

Internal Laboratory 2: Mass

External Laboratory 1 (university): Length, temperature, pressure, and force

External Laboratory 2 (university): Electromagnetic

External Laboratory 3 (research institute): Dosimetry

External Laboratory 4 (research institute): Vibrations and acoustics

Source: Authors' elaboration based on World Bank 2009.

the management of NMIs from being subject to political influence. Figure 7.1 also shows two NMIs that are still firmly controlled by policy-making bodies. In Armenia, the NMI is a closed-stock company, fully owned by the Ministry of Economy, and does not have the authority to even define the national measurement standards, which is the minimal responsibility of NMIs in most countries.

Metrological Activities in ECA

NMIs in some larger ECA economies are major providers of metrological traceability.

The comparison of the number of annual calibrations across ECA countries (figure 7.2) must be interpreted with care because it mixes routine calibrations that can be extremely simple with sophisticated calibrations.

FIGURE 7.1
Relative Autonomy of Most NMIs in ECA, 2006–09

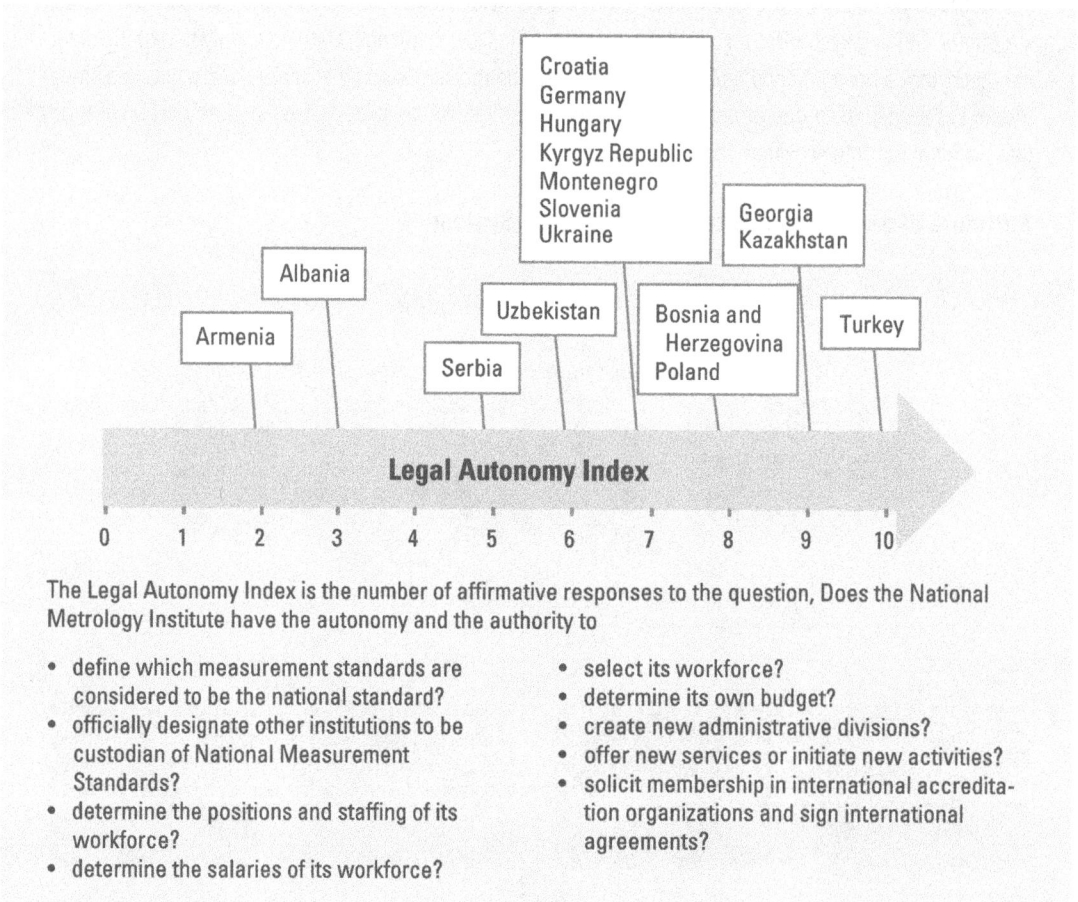

The Legal Autonomy Index is the number of affirmative responses to the question, Does the National Metrology Institute have the autonomy and the authority to

- define which measurement standards are considered to be the national standard?
- officially designate other institutions to be custodian of National Measurement Standards?
- determine the positions and staffing of its workforce?
- determine the salaries of its workforce?

- select its workforce?
- determine its own budget?
- create new administrative divisions?
- offer new services or initiate new activities?
- solicit membership in international accreditation organizations and sign international agreements?

Source: World Bank survey of national quality infrastructure institutions.

FIGURE 7.2
ECA's Larger Countries with NMIs Active in the Calibration Market, 2006–09

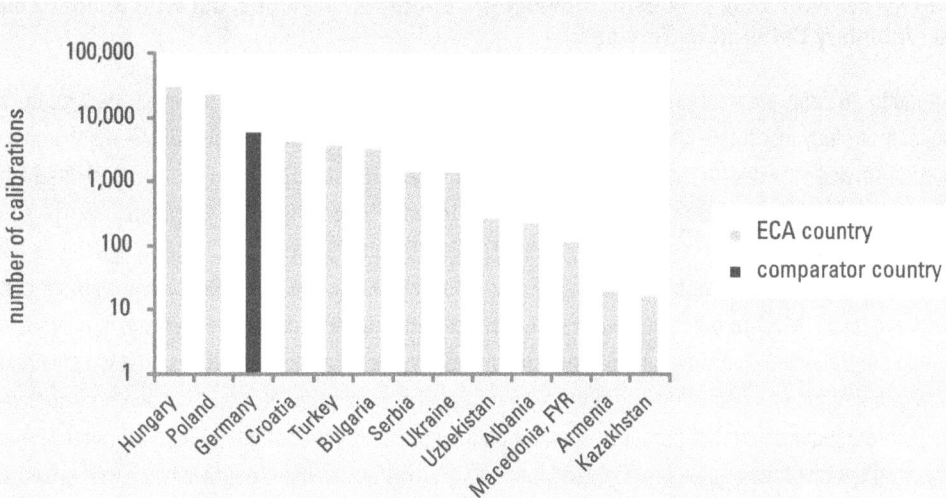

Source: World Bank survey of national quality infrastructure institutions.

The German NMI, Physikalisch-Technische Bundesanstalt, for example, does not provide the types of simple industrial calibrations that one would find in a small ECA economy such as Albania. Moreover, it is also doubtful if the numbers of calibrations listed in some of the CIS countries are actual calibrations or the more straightforward Povjerka (mandatory verification). Nonetheless, based on sheer numbers, the overall picture does show some very active NMIs. Hungary and Poland conduct tens of thousands of calibrations annually, and Croatia, Turkey, and Bulgaria conduct thousands of calibrations. At the other end of the spectrum are Armenia and Kazakhstan, where no more than 20 calibrations are conducted in a single year. In many CIS countries, the demand for traceability is particularly weak because it is not required for the quality of products used in the domestic market or in export markets and there is little awareness in industry of quality management processes (box 7.2). Moreover, in the CIS countries, enterprises are often reluctant to approach the NMIs for voluntary services because they associate the latter with the enforcement of mandatory requirements, fines, and corruption.

Demand for measurement traceability is often limited because of the absence of accreditation.

In many countries, particularly in CIS countries, the accreditation bodies do not conform to international standards—they often provide accreditation without requiring traceability. This practice weakens the demand for traceability from the NMIs. A weak demand for accreditation also reduces

BOX 7.2
The Kyrgyz NMI: Sole Domestic Provider of Calibration Services, but with Scant Demand for Voluntary Calibration Services

Although 28 calibration laboratories are accredited nationally in the Kyrgyz Republic, the country's national metrology institute—the National Institute for Standards and Metrology (NISM)—is the only calibration service provider for the domestic economy at large. This status is because the accredited laboratories are part of large domestic enterprises and are responsible for internal calibration jobs. They do not offer calibration services to the public. These industrial laboratories belong to large companies operating in various sectors—such as electricity, hot water, telecommunications, and agribusiness (soft drinks and dairy products). Most of these companies produce for both internal and export markets, mainly to neighboring Central Asian countries where similar quality requirements apply to products (that is, Gosstandart).

From a regulatory point of view, in the Kyrgyz Republic, calibration is used for mandatory compliance with safety requirements of products. It is Povjerka (mandatory verification) when performed as mandatory verification of the equipment. Demand for *calibrovka* (voluntary calibration) is low. Firms are deterred from seeking calibration from NISM because they associate calibration with mandatory requirements and fines. Firms also have limited market incentives to enhance quality at the enterprise level. Kyrgyz companies export to mainly neighboring CIS countries with similar mandatory standards and requirements, and domestic firms comply with the minimum legal requirements only.

This strategy has its drawbacks for quality. In the case of mandatory verification, firms leave their equipment at NISM but do not have any contact with the technical staff (to avoid corruption). Consequently, there is no knowledge transfer between the two on how to improve the calibration process. Moreover, mandatory verification does not include any information on the reliability of the measurement, nor does it include traceability. However, in the case of voluntary calibration, the technical staff of the NISM meets directly with the clients to discuss the purpose of calibration and the type of accuracy levels required depending on the destination of use of the equipment.

Source: Authors.

incentives for traceability. In many CIS countries, particularly those in the Caucasus and Central Asia, most calibration laboratories are not accredited according to international standards and have limited incentives to seek traceability from the NMIs (figure 7.3)

Public NMIs in ECA often compete in the secondary market for calibration services.

In most high-income countries, the NMIs provide traceability to independent calibration laboratories (the primary calibration market), which then provide calibrations to end users of metrology equipment in industry (the secondary market). For example, in Germany, Physikalisch-Technische Bundesanstalt provides only 20 percent of its calibrations in

FIGURE 7.3

Reduced Demand for NMI's Services in Some Countries That Lack Accredited Laboratories, 2006–09

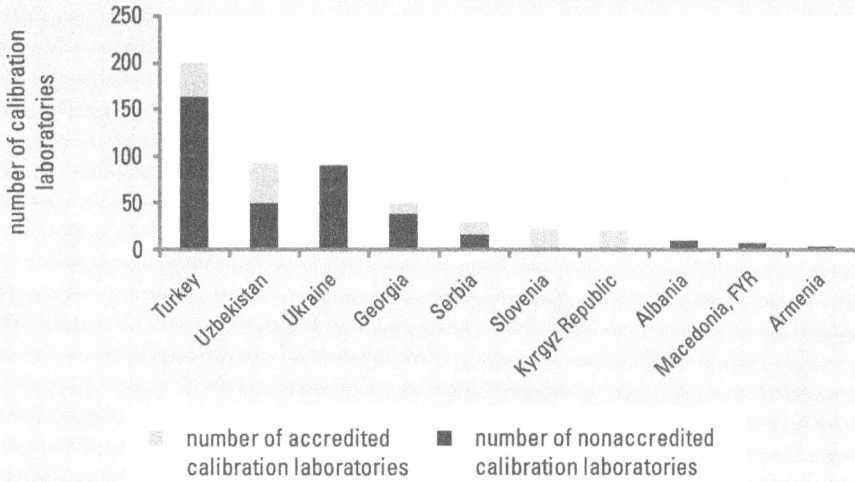

Sources: World Bank survey of national quality infrastructure institutions; ENAC Web site, http://www.enac.es.

the secondary market. In Japan, this figure is closer to 95 percent. In ECA, NMIs provide services in the primary market in countries with developed calibration markets (such as Poland and Slovenia) and in some countries where NMIs are not yet very active in the voluntary calibration area (as in Albania and Kazakhstan). But in a number of ECA countries, NMIs are primarily active in the secondary calibration market and act as either substitutes or competitors to private calibration laboratories. For example, in Bulgaria, Hungary, Turkey, and Ukraine, 75 to 95 percent of calibrations are provided in the secondary market. In Armenia, Georgia, and Montenegro, nearly 100 percent of calibrations are in the secondary market (figure 7.4). In these countries, NMIs are effectively not acting as scientific metrology institutes but as industrial calibration laboratories. This practice can be expected in small economies with low levels of industrial activity such as Armenia, where there are very few commercial calibration laboratories (see figure 7.3). NMIs act as a catalyst for the calibration market in these countries. In larger economies—such as Hungary, Turkey, and Ukraine—the presence of NMIs in the secondary market could be stifling the competitive calibration markets and limiting the diffusion of measurement traceability in the economies. Moreover, it is less efficient for NMIs to provide traceability directly to each end user than to provide it through networks of independent calibration laboratories.

FIGURE 7.4

Service Provision by NMIs in Some ECA Countries to Mostly Industrial End Users, 2006–09

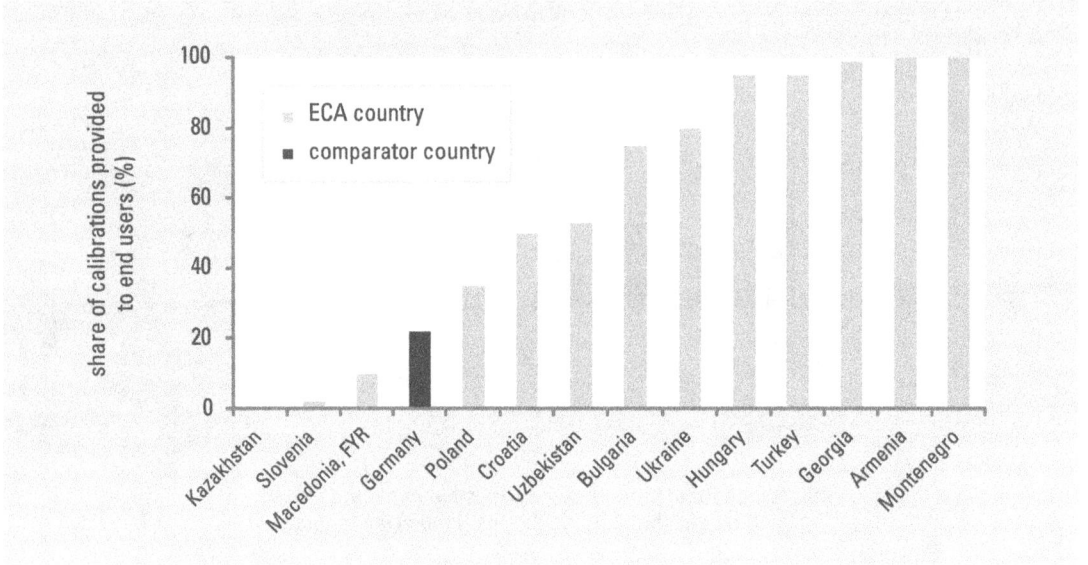

Source: World Bank survey of national quality infrastructure institutions.

NMIs in several CIS countries and some Balkan countries earn their major revenues from the regulatory market.

Revenues from industrial services make up sizable shares of NMI budgets in Georgia and Hungary. In other countries, NMIs survive on government subsidies and regulatory services (figure 7.5). Excessive reliance on government funding and regulatory requirements could limit the incentives NMIs have to market their services in the voluntary calibration market. In fact, most NMIs in countries in Central Asia and the Caucasus almost exclusively serve the mandatory sector. The calibration services in this group of countries are still very poorly developed, mainly because of almost nonexistent demand.

Resources for Metrology

Financing national metrology systems can be expensive for ECA's small economies.

The technical capacity of an NMI is largely driven by its internal management system, the skills and knowledge of its staff, its laboratory equipment and infrastructure, and the international traceability of its measurements. All of these elements make an NMI much more resource

FIGURE 7.5

Limited Industrial Demand for Quality Improvement Related to Metrology in ECA Countries, 2006–09

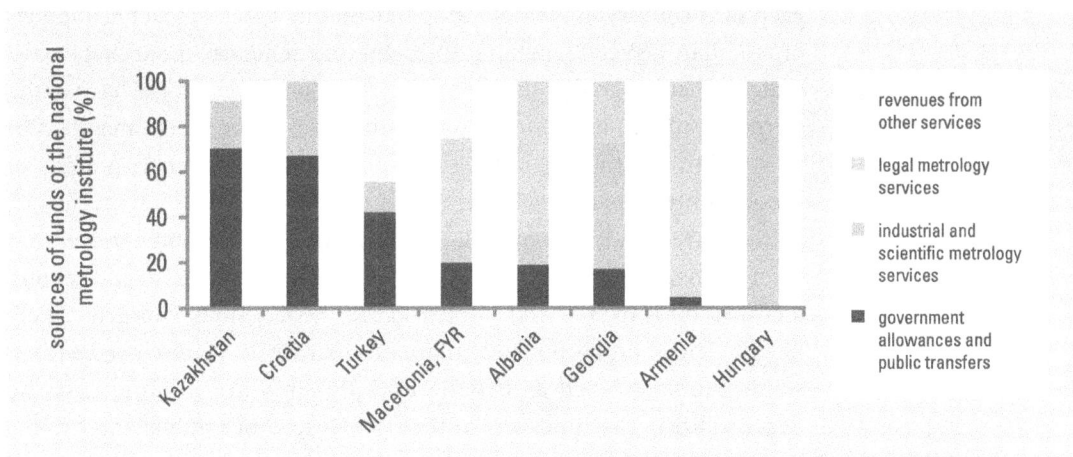

Source: World Bank survey of national quality infrastructure institutions.

intensive than a standardization body or accreditation body. Operating costs, including depreciation of equipment, can easily reach 20 percent per year of investment costs, for example, US$1 million in equipment results in about US$200,000 each year in running costs. The income generated from that equipment, especially in low-cost countries with high personnel turnover, is minimal. Internationally recognized NMI laboratories not only create national costs (personnel, air conditioning, office, and so forth), but also generate expenses in international currency related to traceability, accreditation, intercomparisons, travels, peer evaluations, and so forth, that could easily reach US$20,000 per laboratory and year depending on magnitude, range, and uncertainty.

There are no rules on how much countries should spend on scientific metrology—the expenditure is likely to be dictated by factors such as industrial structure because nations with diversified industry are likely to need a broader range of measurements. The technological sophistication of economies is also a factor to be considered in spending, because NMIs need to stay a step ahead of other users of measurements regarding accuracy and precision. The density of industrial activity also matters—private calibration laboratory markets usually develop in economies where several industrial players require measurement services, whereas states must catalyze the calibration market through investments in NMIs in economies with difficult business environments and limited demand.

Figure 7.6 shows that, on average, the NMI budgets of ECA countries are roughly in line with NMI budgets in high-income countries such as Germany and the Republic of Korea in terms of their gross domestic product (GDP). Yet, the figure also shows minor differences in investment intensity within ECA. The gray line in the figure represents the predicted budgets if the budget-to-GDP ratio of Germany is applied to each ECA country. It is noteworthy that among ECA's smaller economies of less than US$200 billion GDP shown on the figure, 9 out of 11 have budgets that are greater than what would be predicted on the basis of the German ratio. These countries' NMIs have larger budgets than Germany's, relative to the size of their economies. Yet, experience in many of these countries, particularly in the Balkan countries, does not reveal particularly well-endowed or well-staffed NMIs. This evidence shows that even relatively rudimentary NMIs are expensive to maintain and require a critical mass of staff and infrastructure; hence, small countries likely need to spend proportionately more on their NMIs. As discussed earlier, small countries such as Croatia and Slovenia are limiting costs by decentralizing the functions of their NMIs to other public and private institutes.

Several Central Asian NMIs have duplicate NMIs, which create unnecessary strains on the state budgets.

Two different approaches have been used to develop new NMIs in countries in Central Asia. Some states just declared their former Soviet Gosstandart branches (metrology and testing centers) as their new NMIs.

FIGURE 7.6

Disproportionate Expense of Metrology for Small Economies, 2006–09

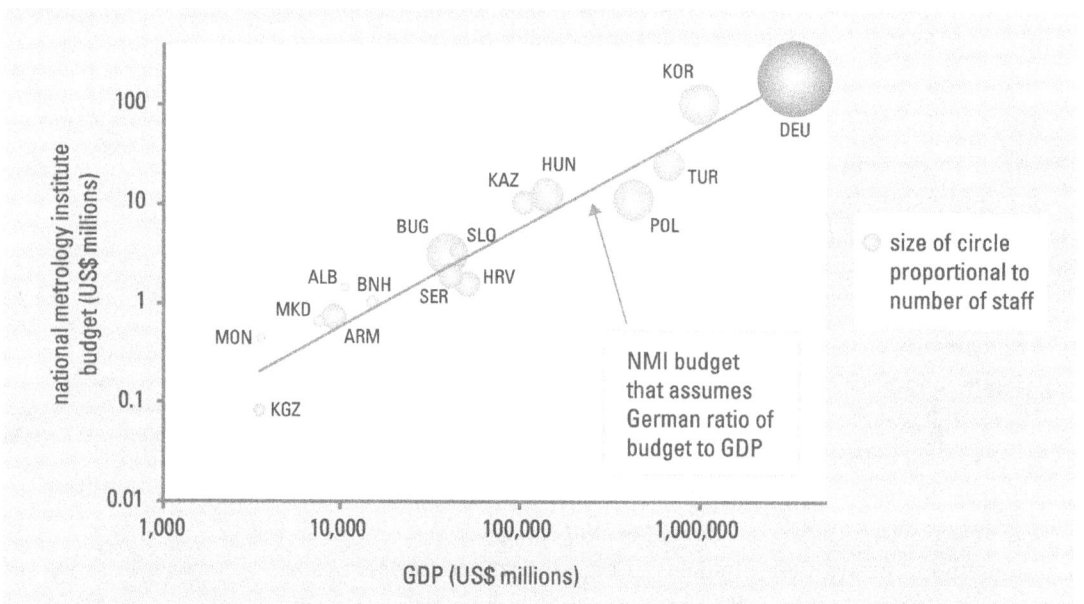

Sources: World Bank survey of national quality infrastructure institutions; World Development Indicators Database.
Note: Gray circle represents Germany. GDP = gross domestic product.

Others, especially those with more financial resources, opted to establish new NMIs on top of the existing centers with the aim of replacing traceability to the Soviet NMIs with their own reference standards (for example, Kazakhstan and Uzbekistan). Additionally, providing internationally recognized traceability for all 80 metrological measures maintained by the Centre for Rendering Metrological Services will be almost impossible in the future. Strengthening the existing metrological infrastructure and reorienting it toward actual demand could, in many cases, prove to be more pragmatic. The latter approach is being implemented in the Kyrgyz metrology institute, the National Institute of Standards and Metrology, by upgrading existing laboratories to comply with calibration and NMI functions. Kazakhstan faces a special situation because the Gosstandart branch was situated in the country's former capital, Almaty. When the capital moved to Astana, the NMI also had to relocate. However, most of the technical competence was still in the Almaty branch.

Staffing is a challenge in ECA's NMIs, particularly those in smaller countries.

Sophisticated measurement equipment is useless unless NMIs have trained staff members who possess the proper skills to operate it. Many ECA countries suffered from a wave of brain drain in the 1990s, when millions of engineers and scientists left the region. There is now a deficiency of engineers and scientists in many ECA countries. Management personnel in NMIs in ECA routinely speak of the difficulty of finding and attracting skilled technical staff, made tougher because NMI staff salaries in most ECA countries are aligned to civil servant salaries that cannot compete with the private sector. In the World Bank's national quality infrastructure survey, 8 out of every 10 NMI respondents reported earning salaries that were only 20 percent to 60 percent of those offered by the private sector for comparable staff. Moreover, limited budgets make it difficult for NMIs to staff their laboratories. Figure 7.6 shows that many NMIs in the Balkan countries have a very limited staff—between 10 and 20 metrologists each—which is not enough for them to reliably offer services in all the required areas of measurement. In other NMIs that have a larger staff, quantity cannot necessarily be equated with quality. In Kazakhstan, for example, which has a relatively large NMI with 136 staff members, only 13 are university-educated technical staff. In Armenia, out of 149 staff members, only 10 are university-educated technical staff. Formal education is an issue, but so is training. Many of ECA's NMIs, particularly in the Balkan and CIS countries, still make use of equipment that is more than 20 years old. Metrologists must receive considerable training to use any newly purchased equipment, which is very different from the old equipment they are used to, and to operate it according to international best practices.

Most NMIs in ECA, except for those in the largest economies, are poorly equipped.

Most of the Balkan and CIS countries did not have NMIs before their independence in the 1990s and had to build them from the ground up. In tumultuous times of independence, when limited fiscal resources were available, space was often allocated for NMIs in administrative buildings where the stringent structural and environmental conditions required for metrology (proper air conditioning and thermal insulation, shielding from external vibration, and so forth) were not available. Many NMIs continue to be located in such buildings today.

In terms of laboratory equipment, ECA's new EU member states and candidate countries have benefited heavily from EU assistance in upgrading their facilities. Some of ECA's larger economies, including Kazakh-

PHOTOGRAPH 7.1

The Kyrgyz NMI relies on outdated equipment for mass measurements.

Source: Authors.

stan and Turkey, have invested heavily in creating state-of-the-art metrology facilities that rival those found in Western Europe. Russia inherited a highly developed metrology infrastructure from the Soviet Union, which remains the strongest in the region. Others still lag significantly, particularly in the CIS (photograph 7.1). In fact, in many CIS countries, although there is equipment, it does not correspond to the needs of the economies but reflects the logic of central planning in which different republics were assigned different areas of specialization under the Soviet Union (box 7.3).

BOX 7.3

Historic Relics of Soviet Central Planning Still Found in the Kyrgyz NMI

During the Soviet era, the enrichment of uranium and heavy weapon manufacturing for military and nuclear energy generation purposes was assigned to Kyrgyz laboratories and domestic state enterprises. As the major supplier of radioactive material in the area of ionizing radiation for the entire Soviet Union, *Kyrgyzstandard*—the predecessor of the National Institute of Standards and Metrology created in 2004—controlled 550 reference measurement standards.

The dissolution of the Soviet Union left the Kyrgyz Republic with a sophisticated measurement infrastructure but no demand for most of its facilities. Potential applications have been identified for the inherited standards (about 70 etalons)—including energy, safety, and medical applications—but these standards lack international traceability, which limits their usability. With little support from the market, these formerly outstanding facilities risk disappearing completely.

Source: National Institute of Standards and Metrology n.d.

NMIs in ECA's smallest Balkan economies offer services in only a few areas of measurement (figure 7.7). For example, while state-of-the-art NMIs such as those in Germany and Turkey offer physical quantities in all 20 measurement areas,[2] NMIs in Moldova and Montenegro offer physical quantities in only 7 measurement areas out of the 20 possible. Although it is probably unnecessary for NMIs in small countries to offer every physical quantity, some key physical quantities are sometimes missing. A number of NMIs in ECA countries—including those in Albania, Croatia, and Georgia—do not operate in the area of flow measurements, which are important for monitoring commerce in water, oil, and gas.

---

2. Measurement areas include dimension, mass, force, electricity, flow, pressure, temperature, volume, acceleration, time and frequency, humidity, roughness, hardness, magnetism, viscosity, acoustics, optics, vibrations, ionizing radiation, and chemistry.

FIGURE 7.7

Broad Range of Measurement Capabilities of NMIs in ECA and Selected Comparator Countries, 2006–09

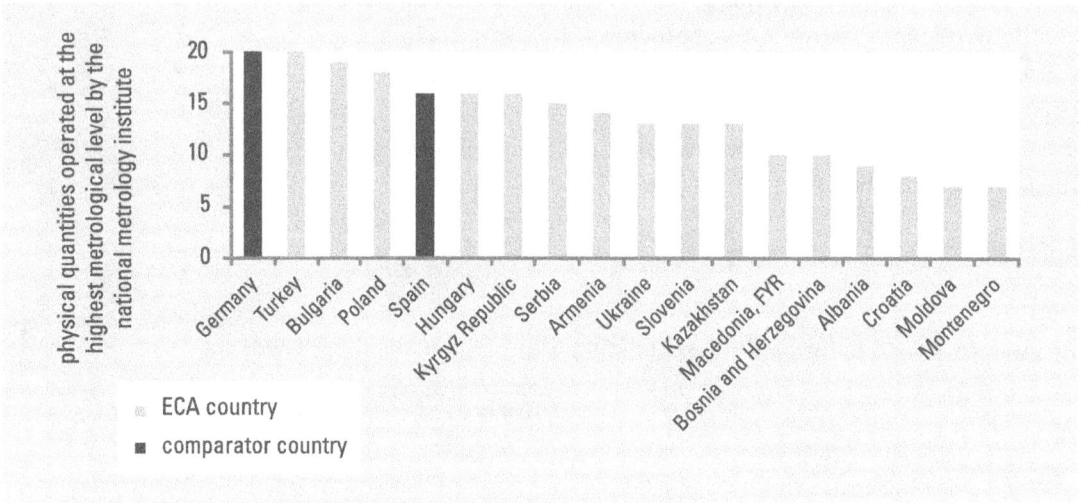

Source: World Bank survey of national quality infrastructure institutions.

Measurement processes of many NMIs in ECA are not credible.

The implementation of a quality system in a metrology laboratory is a minimum requirement for ensuring the reliability and technical competency of measurements. The key issue in most metrology applications is not the accuracy of the measurements but the reliability of the results, particularly in international trade. Although NMIs in all Organisation for Economic Co-operation and Development economies have implemented quality systems, they have traditionally not sought accreditations because they built their reputations over a long period of time and are highly credible in their markets (their existence often predates that of their national accreditation bodies). However, this situation is now changing, and there is a growing trend toward accreditation of NMIs in all countries. Accreditation is most critical for young NMIs that have not yet proven themselves in the market. Although most NMIs in ECA claim to implement quality systems, their assertions are mostly refuted by foreign expert metrologists who visit these NMIs. Moreover, only a few of them are accredited, and even fewer are accredited by signatories of mutual recognition arrangements (MRAs). In the Balkan countries, there is no country where all the laboratories of the NMI are accredited by an MRA signatory. In countries in Central Asia and the Caucasus, not a single NMI has internationally recognized accreditation (table 7.2)

TABLE 7.2

Implementation of a Quality System in NMIs (Self-Declared), 2006–09

	Country	Existing quality systems according to NMI	Accredited quality system	Accreditation from an MRA signatory
EU countries	Slovenia	✓	✓	✓
Balkan countries and Turkey	Albania	✓		
	Bosnia and Herzegovina	✓		
	Croatia	✓	✓	✓
	Macedonia, FYR			
	Montenegro			
	Serbia	✓		
	Turkey	✓	✓	✓
CIS countries and Georgia	Armenia	✓		
	Georgia			
	Kazakhstan	✓	✓	
	Kyrgyz Republic			
	Tajikistan	✓	✓	
	Ukraine	✓	✓	
	Uzbekistan	✓		
Comparator countries	Germany	✓		
	United Kingdom	✓	✓	✓

Source: World Bank survey of national quality infrastructure institutions.

In some Central Asian NMIs, calibration is still performed according to the Povjerka methodology, which does not offer traceability. The NMIs offer traceability services to the Povjerka laboratories that wish to operate as calibration laboratories. While the NMIs continue to issue certificates according to the old Povjerka methodology of verification, the new certificates they issue are now known as calibration certificates.

International Integration

ECA's new EU member states, Balkan countries, and Turkey have integrated Europe's regional metrology system.

Requirements for joining the EU have pushed this group of countries to improve their measurement capabilities and harmonize their systems, procedures, and issued certificates with their peers in the EU. All NMIs from this group of countries have joined Europe's regional metrology organization, EURAMET. EURAMET is technically and organizationally strong and also receives strong financial support from the EU. The new NMIs still have work ahead to develop their metrological capabilities, but they benefit directly from the long metrological history in Europe and from a group of world-class NMIs that are active in EURAMET. Additionally, they easily get traceability (calibration) of their national etalons from the recognized EURAMET members. In fields where no domestic metrological capabilities exist, industries in these countries can easily approach recognized NMIs or calibration laboratories in other EURAMET member states to benefit from the open borders within the EU. For the newcomers from Eastern Europe and the Balkans, it was therefore highly attractive early on to become members of EURAMET and benefit directly from the available European resources. In ECA, only NMIs from four non-CIS countries—Bulgaria, Lithuania, Romania, and the Slovak Republic—remain in the regional metrology organization COOMET, which is centered around CIS countries. But it is clear that these countries' priorities and limited resources are oriented toward EURAMET rather than COOMET.

CIS countries use COOMET to develop their own metrology systems, but it is not as effective as metrology organizations in other regions.

The regional metrology organization COOMET is the platform for developing harmonized metrological capabilities in the CIS. Lesser developed NMIs typically benefit from joining a regional metrology organization, thanks to the mentorship and support provided through more developed NMIs. Russia is the only fully committed global player in COOMET. Although Germany and the Slovak Republic have well-established NMIs, they are mostly active in EURAMET. The vast majority of countries in COOMET have very weak metrology systems that do not operate according to international best practices. In other regions around the world, many "big brothers" are available to support the regional metrology organizations and, especially, newly established developing NMIs. EURAMET naturally benefits from all of Western Europe; the regional Inter-American Metrology Organization relies on the United States, Canada, Mexico, and Brazil; and the Asia-Pacific organization relies on Japan, Australia, and Korea. COOMET is smaller and has only 14 members that are not primarily in other regional organizations; compare this number with the 30 to 40 members in the Inter-American and European organizations. NMIs in COOMET are also isolated by language barriers. They depend on Russian translations of international literature, documents, and procedures and scarcely participate in international technical cooperation projects. This weakness of COOMET may have been one reason why Russia and Kazakhstan recently joined the Asia Pacific Metrology Programme, the regional metrology organization of the Asia-Pacific region. However, neither country is participating in many of the organization's activities. Some NMIs in CIS countries have long been completely internationally isolated. Azerbaijan only recently joined COOMET, and Tajikistan is in the process of doing so. Turkmenistan is still not a member.

CIS countries have two regional organizations active in the area of metrology.

In addition to COOMET, the EuroAsian Interstate Council for Standardization, Metrology, and Certification also plays a role in regional metrology for its 11 CIS members and Georgia. It inherited some of the practices of the old Gosstandardt system, including the political mutual recognition of product certificates. Because the product certification process is based on results from testing laboratories and measurements, there is an indirect mutual recognition of measurement results for this economic trading zone. This system contrasts with typical international mutual recognition systems, such as the International Committee for Weights and Measures Mutual Recognition Arrangement (CIPM MRA), because it does not involve a technical evaluation or comparison of measurement results. In sum, measurements are recognized even if they are not technically credible. In view of this automatic recognition of measurement results, NMIs operating in the region have few incentives to harmonize their systems toward international best practices that demonstrate actual measurement traceability and reliability.

Most ECA countries have moved toward achieving mutual recognition in metrology, but Central Asian and Caucasus countries remain largely isolated.

All EU and most Balkan countries have signed the Metre Convention, the basic international treaty through which countries accept that they will follow the International System of Units. Moreover, all of these countries, apart from Bosnia and Herzegovina and Montenegro, have signed the CIPM MRA for mutual recognition of calibration and measurement capabilities, which plays a critical role in trade relations because many traded goods and commodities are valued through measurement. Membership in the CIPM MRA means that countries can participate in international measurement comparisons to have their calibration and measurement capabilities approved and recognized by every other signatory of the CIPM MRA, which represent the vast majority of world trade. The four CIS countries in proximity to the EU—Belarus, Moldova, Russia, and Ukraine—have also taken the critical steps toward international integration by joining the CIPM MRA. Of the countries in Central Asia and the Caucasus, only Georgia and Kazakhstan have joined either the Metre Convention or the CIPM MRA (table 7.3).

ECA's new EU member states and Russia and Turkey have a competitive number of internationally recognized measurement capabilities, but the remaining ECA countries have none.

Although the CIPM MRA represents a first step toward the harmonization of a country's metrology system, the number of published Calibration and Measurement Capabilities (CMCs) by NMIs in the country reflect the exact scope of measurements in which the country is technically competent. Hence, it is possible for a country to have signed the CIPM MRA but to have not yet demonstrated technical competence in any field. Obtaining CMCs is not easy. It is not simply about purchasing measurement standards and getting them approved; it also requires a demonstration of technical competence during an independent evaluation of the relevant metrology laboratory, including its quality system, traceability, measurement uncertainty, personnel, environmental conditions, and successful intercomparisons. CMCs can also be removed when an NMI cannot prove that it has maintained its capabilities (for example, due to changes in technical personnel, equipment being out of order, or missing traceability). An extreme case was that of Hungary—all CMCs were suspended for almost a year in 2008 because of problems with the quality system.

TABLE 7.3
Country Memberships in International and Regional Metrology Organizations, 2008

	Country	International bodies			Regional bodies		
		Metre Convention	CIPM MRA	OIML	EURAMET	COOMET	WELMEC
EU countries	Bulgaria	✓	✓	✓	✓	✓	✓
	Czech Republic	✓	✓	✓	✓		✓
	Estonia	Assoc.	✓	Corr.	✓		✓
	Hungary	✓	✓	✓	✓		✓
	Latvia	Assoc.	✓	Corr.	✓		✓
	Lithuania	Assoc.	✓	Corr.	✓	✓	✓
	Poland	✓	✓	✓	✓		✓
	Romania	✓	✓	✓	✓	✓	✓
	Slovak Republic	✓	✓	✓	✓	✓	✓
	Slovenia	✓	✓	✓	✓		✓
Balkan countries and Turkey	Albania	Assoc.	✓	✓	Assoc.		
	Bosnia and Herzegovina			Corr.	Assoc.		
	Croatia	Assoc.	✓	✓	✓		Assoc.
	Macedonia, FYR	Assoc.	✓	✓	Assoc.		Assoc.
	Montenegro			Corr.	Assoc.		
	Serbia	✓	✓	✓	✓		Assoc.
	Turkey	✓	✓	✓	✓		Assoc.
CIS countries and Georgia	Belarus	Assoc.	✓	✓		✓	
	Moldova	Assoc.	✓	Corr.		✓	
	Russian Federation	✓	✓	✓		✓	
	Ukraine	Assoc.	✓	Corr.		✓	
	Armenia					✓	
	Azerbaijan					✓	
	Georgia	Assoc.	✓			✓	
	Kazakhstan	Assoc.	✓	✓		✓	
	Kyrgyz Republic			Corr.		✓	
	Tajikistan			Corr.			
	Turkmenistan						
	Uzbekistan			Corr.		✓	
Comparator countries	Brazil	✓	✓	✓			
	China	✓	✓	✓			
	Germany	✓	✓	✓	✓	✓	✓
	Korea, Rep.	✓	✓	✓			
	Spain	✓	✓	✓	✓		✓
	United Kingdom	✓	✓	✓	✓		✓

Sources: Web sites of the metrology organizations.
Note: Assoc. = Associate Member, Corr. = Corresponding Member, OIML = International Organization of Legal Metrology, WELMEC = European Cooperation in Legal Metrology.

FIGURE 7.8

Fewer Internationally Recognized CMCs in Countries in Central Asia, the Caucasus, and the Balkans versus Other ECA Countries and Selected Comparator Countries, 2008

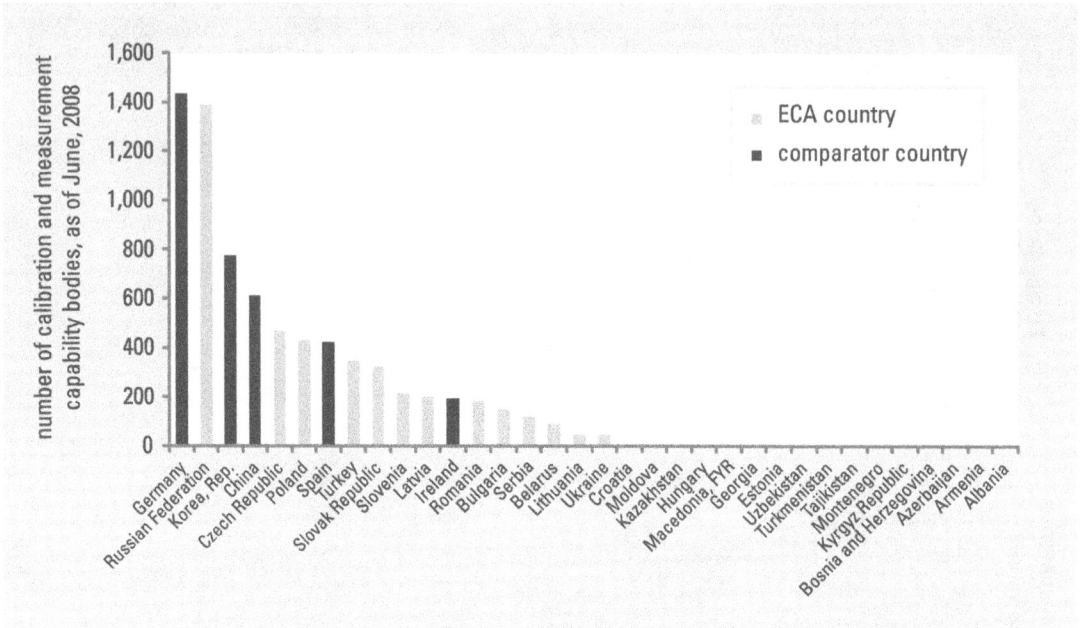

Source: International Bureau of Weights and Measures, http://www.bipm.org.

As seen in figure 7.8, the vast majority of ECA's CMCs are in the hands of Russia. Following far behind are a few EU countries and Turkey. Russia had almost 1,400 of the 4,000 CMCs in ECA in June 2008. In the CIS, apart from Russia, only Belarus and Ukraine have any CMCs. Kazakhstan is actively working on its first CMC claims, the driving force being the oil and gas industry in which Kazakhstan has an interest in developing a reliable measurement system. Without this system, multinational oil and gas companies continue to seek reliable measurements and testing abroad.

ECA countries are divided in the alignment of their legal metrology systems with international practices.

EU member states have all fully aligned their legal metrology systems with European directives, as required by the EU's *acquis communautaire*, and EU candidates such as Turkey have also largely done so. Outside of those groups of countries, ECA countries tend to lag. In CIS countries, verifications of measuring instruments are still carried out according to Gosstandart rules, which are not recognized internationally. And much of the equipment used for legal metrology has no traceability. The legal framework is also not harmonized with international guidelines. In many cases, an excessively broad range of measuring instruments is regulated, even though they do not affect safety, health, or the environment. In other cases, crucial legal metrology activities are missing. In Armenia, for example, there is no inspection of prepackaged goods, so customers cannot know if the amount marked on a food package matches with the contents.

But most ECA countries have taken steps toward international integration by joining international and regional legal metrology organizations. The International Organization of Legal Metrology (OIML) is an intergovernmental treaty organization established in 1955 to promote the global harmonization of legal metrology procedures. Since that time, the OIML has developed a worldwide technical structure that provides its members with metrological guidelines for the elaboration of national and regional requirements concerning the manufacture and use of measuring instruments for legal metrology applications. Apart from the three Caucasian states and Turkmenistan, all ECA countries are members or at least corresponding members with observer status to benefit from metrological guidelines and recommendations to be used for harmonization of national technical regulation in the field of legal metrology. It cannot be expected that the ECA countries, especially those lesser developed, contribute much, but they have at least access to the documents with a relatively low financial input. WELMEC (European Cooperation in Legal Metrology), is the regional organization to harmonize European legal metrology. Apart from Bosnia and Herzegovina, all European countries, including Turkey, are full or associate members.

Upgrading Metrology Systems in ECA

Upgrading of metrology systems can be accomplished through organizational reform, development of infrastructure and skills, and regional and international harmonization and integration.

Reforming Metrology Systems

CIS countries can support industrial competitiveness by refocusing their national metrology systems from verification and legal metrology to scientific and industrial metrology.

In many CIS countries, measurement errors for a large amount of equipment are dictated by the state, and NMIs operate mainly as regulatory control agencies. Their main role is verification of measurement instruments. Although some CIS countries have national measurement standards in the form of etalons, they often have no traceability to international measurements. In this sense, there is no scientific metrology to speak of in those countries. Moreover, few NMIs in countries in the Caucasus and Central Asia actually offer any industrial metrology in the form of commercial calibration services, and when they do, it is only on paper and they have no willing clients.

A first step for those countries is to establish a legal basis to reform NMIs from enforcement bodies to service providers for the economy with official functions in scientific and industrial metrology, with legal metrology responsibilities significantly reduced or separated into another institution. A second step is to transition from the obsolete Povjerka system used by most CIS NMIs to calibration methods that follow international guidelines. Many NMIs already offer calibration on paper, but a closer examination often reveals that the procedure used is based on the Soviet Povjerka system.

Developing National Metrology Institutes

ECA countries establishing or upgrading their NMIs need to start small but with focused long-term development strategies.

NMIs did not exist in each Soviet Republic. The highest metrological level was defined through the Primary Etalons in the Soviet Union and the COMECON member states. After the Soviet breakdown and the subsequent creation of the new states, these states tried to develop independence also in the metrological field by defining their own NMIs. In many cases, this happened only on paper by defining the old existing reference etalons as new national etalons because no resources for an additional infrastructure were available. In former Yugoslavia, the NMI was located in Belgrade, so the newly independent states were faced with building metrology from the ground up. In most countries of the former Yugoslavia and of the Caucasus and Central Asia, NMIs are still in their early stages of development and still lack long-term development strategies for metrology.

NMIs should start small, mastering a few areas before broadening the scope of their activities. Although investing in a wide range of national reference standards and equipment is appealing, it is seldom the critical bottleneck to providing reliable services and achieving measurement traceability. The NMI must first and foremost implement modern laboratory management, develop its human capacity, and participate in international intercomparisons. Most NMIs underestimate the costs and learning curves involved in these processes. Starting small, in a few focused measurement areas; achieving the first international recognitions; learning from these experiences; and replicating them in other areas according to needs are more likely to be beneficial than stockpiling national reference standards, which do not provide services. Another great advantage for economies with limited resources to develop one recognized step (laboratory or calibration service) before the next starts is that they achieve success more quickly, which motivates further action— or opens eyes about wrong assumptions.

In practice, this approach implies selecting one or two basic magnitudes with high economic and social effect (such as mass and temperature measurements) in often-required measurement ranges (such as 1 milligram to 10 kilograms or −30°Celsius to 250°Celsius) and measurement uncertainties that cover industrial and consumer protection needs of the economies. Then develop a manageable scale in the new laboratories (laboratory room, environmental conditions, equipment, accessories, etalons, and so forth), train adequate and sufficient technical staff (at least two to three members per laboratory or calibration service), and develop the quality system according to international standards (ISO/IEC 17025). Before starting, the NMI should do a cost calculation like a private company to get an impression about the operating costs according to international requirements. This exercise could be part of an overall master plan to develop step by step the NMI, in which step one would be the previously mentioned one or two laboratories. The business plan for a period of 10 years with the real operating costs (not only the laboratory running costs, but also the costs related to the NMI functions, such as participation in regional and international activities, travel costs, or conference fees) should be part of the strategy.

A national metrology development plan (strategy), together with a business plan (related costs, incomes, and necessary subsidies by government) and the implementation in small steps (gaining of experience to learn for the next steps and, in parallel, to improve and consolidate the first steps) is a realistic, sustainable approach for economies with limited resources and without a sufficiently great demand to justify and sustain the related costs.

A survey of market needs is a necessary, but often ignored, first step toward a metrology development plan.

The old Soviet Gosstandart system, variations of which are still operating in CIS countries, was a top-down and mandatory system, covering the entire Soviet Union. No demand survey or analysis of metrological needs was necessary because, at least theoretically, each and every measuring instrument and working standard was listed and their accuracies and permissible errors predefined. The approach was crystal clear and the metrological needs predictable.

A new approach for the selection of equipment and reference standards needs to be applied in market economies. Metrological needs should be determined through a thorough and realistic demand survey. Under a voluntary system, customers—in this case, the owners of measuring devices—cannot be forced to bring their equipment to the NMI for calibration. In addition, many types of equipment that need to be verified under the Soviet mandatory system do not actually need to be calibrated if the measuring result has no direct effect on the product quality or on consumer protection. Therefore, the overall demand for the NMI's services after transitioning to a system based on voluntary calibrations is expected to fall. It can be assumed that the quantity (calibration work), the quality (Povjerka versus calibration), and the measurement parameters (equipments and calibration ranges) will change compared to the Soviet system.

Demand from industrial calibration results from the measuring devices that need to be calibrated because of requirements in quality assurance programs or quality systems such as ISO 9001 for companies and ISO/IEC 17025 for laboratories. In the laboratories, the accredited scope clearly indicates which instruments need calibration. Typical tools such as questionnaires or interviews are only partially useful because owners or managers in many CIS countries are often unaware of what needs to be calibrated and what is the difference between calibration and the Povjerka system.

In general, an approximation about the calibration demand could be possible through some statistical methods about, for example, exports, industry visits, and interviews about the applied measuring devices. But, as mentioned before, this approach gives no guarantee of using new installed calibration capabilities, as long as massive awareness campaigns on all levels (end users, calibration laboratories, NMIs, state regulation and inspection bodies, and policy decision makers) are not conducted and respective laws or regulations are changed.

In the field of verification under consumer protection, the analysis is much easier because it is mandatory. National regulations are developed mostly on the basis of international recommendations by OIML. They must be enforced by verification offices. The demand can be derived from the requirements in the regulations, the methods, and reverification periods recommended by OIML and the estimated amount of instruments in the country.

Experience in ECA countries shows that initial demand for calibration services mainly comes from measuring devices in production processes or testing related to export products with high-quality requirements outside the CIS countries' markets. This situation is likely to continue while the regulations and quality standards for the internal markets are not harmonized with international requirements. Therefore, the metrological infrastructure should be developed initially for the lower calibration levels in the basic metrological magnitudes (mass, temperature, pressure, length, and so forth) and with a focus on traceability in chemistry (metrology in chemistry) for the food safety requirements. In this context, the highest accuracy is not as important as a reliable (internationally recognized) accuracy for the industrial reality. An extension to more magnitudes, broader ranges, and smaller measurement uncertainties can be developed when the demand is sufficiently great (critical mass) to justify the additional investment and when the financial commitment and possibilities exist to sustain the investment.

As they develop their services, ECA's NMIs must ensure that they do not compete with the private sector in the industrial calibration market.

NMIs in ECA face a dilemma: if the level of calibrations they offer is too basic, they compete with commercial calibration laboratories of industry equipment and cannot give traceability to these calibration laboratories. If the level of calibrations they offer is too high to serve commercial calibration laboratories, there might be only a few customers coming once a year to the NMI. In this case, one cannot justify sustaining an NMI laboratory with US$20,000 to US$40,000 in operating costs. Thus, a demand survey needs to consider all the different metrological levels of the national metrology infrastructure, from commercial calibration laboratories (the primary calibration market) to industrial equipment (the secondary calibration market) to strike a balance.

NMIs in ECA's more mature quality infrastructures, such as those in Bulgaria and Turkey, need to formulate a strategy for transitioning from the secondary calibration market to the primary calibration market. They should develop a clear strategy to encourage the creation and use of private calibration facilities and to gradually disengage themselves from the secondary calibration market.

The normal development in industrial economies and in many emerging economies has been a bottom-up approach. The NMI starts with low-level, but traceable and recognized, calibrations for industry, and in parallel, it promotes private calibration laboratories by transferring knowledge and procedures and assuring traceability. When the NMI's competence has been demonstrated by successful intercomparison measurements or accreditation, the NMI withdraws its calibration service from the market to concentrate the resources on the development of new services (magnitudes, scopes, and smaller uncertainties). This principle of metrological hierarchy develops according to the demand. A good example is the metrological development in Thailand. When the National Institute of Metrology Thailand was founded in 1998, only a few commercial calibration laboratories with unrecognized services existed. Although it initially had to compete with these calibration laboratories to gain experience, it quickly upgraded to the next higher level. Ten years later, more than 70 calibration laboratories are accredited by ILAC MLA (International Laboratory Accreditation Cooperation Multilateral Recognition Arrangement)–recognized accreditation bodies in Thailand. The National Institute of Metrology Thailand achieved close to 350 CMCs recognized in the International Bureau of Weights and Measures Web site page and does not offer calibration services to the Thai industry in fields covered by calibration laboratories.

ECA countries will need to achieve international traceability for each measurement area developed.

Although ECA's new EU member states and its larger economies are well integrated into the international metrology system, countries in the Balkans, Central Asia, and the Caucasus remain isolated. Their measurements, and all of the tests and certifications that depend on these measurements, are not recognized abroad, posing barriers to trade.

As a first step, every ECA country should join the Metre Convention and the CIPM MRA and be active in the regional organizations COOMET and EURAMET. Active participation in regional and international metrology organizations requires additionally allocated resources from the individual NMIs, but pays back by avoiding reinvention of the wheel in each NMI. Although signing the Metre Convention is straightforward, the CIPM MRA requires that the NMI adhere to some international guidelines in its internal management processes, which it can learn from other institutes. The CIPM MRA opens doors to international traceability through participation in international interlaboratory comparisons. ECA countries in Europe can participate through EURAMET and those in the CIS through COOMET.

As they broaden their measurement capabilities, ECA's NMIs will need to make important investments in upgrading human capacity, equipment, and infrastructure.

Although EU member states and candidate countries have benefited from important equipment investments from EU and other donor projects (box 7.4), this has not been the case in CIS countries. Apart from Kazakhstan, Russia, and Ukraine, much of the equipment in CIS countries is obsolete. Facilities are also an issue. NMIs require specialized facilities to

---

BOX 7.4

World Bank Support for the National Metrology Institute in Turkey

In 1999, the World Bank and the government of Turkey kicked off a US$28 million project to strengthen the country's national metrology institute, Ulusal Metroloji Enstitüsü (UME), over a six-year period. The project would support expansion of UME's facilities to serve a greater portion of the country's metrology needs. The overall strategy for the future development of UME's measurement services involves upgrading (a) the existing measurement services by improving the efficiency with which the measurements are performed and (b) embarking upon measurement services in new areas such as chemical and medical metrology. The project would do so by financing new building, equipment, consultancy, training, and related costs. In addition to expansion of the scope of the metrology institute through investment in its laboratories (photograph 7.2), developing a two-way industrial interface and building up technology transfer are also key elements of the project. A specific program for technology transfer would seek to maximize the benefit of the laboratory's activities through transfer of new measurement technologies to customers, training and advice on best practice in existing technologies, consultancy services, establishment of licensing arrangements, production of newsletters, and development of educational aids.

Strengthening UME's promotional activities would also be supported. These activities would concentrate on increasing awareness in industry of the national measurement system, its structure, and the benefits that a particular company or a particular activity can obtain from proper use of metrology. Technical assistance in the design and delivery of these promotion and outreach activities would form a key part of the project. UME's organizational and management systems would be strengthened to be compatible with the increased coverage of the institute's activities as well as greater interaction with the needs of industry. Technical staff would be trained in the newer areas of metrology, and support would also be provided to the institute for working with other educational and technical institutions to develop metrology-related skills within the country.

Source: World Bank 1999.

PHOTOGRAPH 7.2

UME's electromagnetic compatibility laboratory is state of the art.

Source: Authors

accommodate equipment that is sensitive to temperature, vibrations, humidity, and electromagnetic noise. In many ECA countries, NMIs are housed in administrative buildings that are unfit for metrology even if they are retrofitted.

The next crucial aspect is the technical personnel. Empirically, salaries are very low. The older generation of staff is not enthusiastic to learn about new equipment and new methods (calibration, measurement uncertainty, International Organization for Standardization quality systems, and so forth). The younger staff is using the laboratory work as a springboard for better-paid jobs or further studies while there are no prospects for better payment and responsibilities.

Technical personnel, especially in the highest metrological level of NMIs, need to have career growth prospects. Human resource development, including financially attractive salaries, promotion of English language skills, and access to international exchange activities, is indispensable to guarantee operation. A person who operates equipment costing US$1 million but who earns US$150 per month will not create the results the equipment is worth. Those who become competent to do so will disappear sooner or later to better-paying jobs, and the retraining costs for their successors will be much higher than an adequate salary.

Finally, upgrading management processes is critical to an effective NMI. ECA countries should accredit the laboratories in their NMIs. An internationally recognized laboratory accreditation will increase the quality and credibility of calibration services provided by the NMI. This should be especially useful in countries where the NMI has not established a large customer base or where the country is preparing itself to join the CIPM MRA.

Financing Metrology

Governments must consider that NMIs cannot be self-financing and must include realistic assumptions about public financial commitments in their development plans.

Developing a complete metrology infrastructure is expensive (box 7.5). In addition to equipment and infrastructure costs, NMI operating costs are also extremely high. Operational costs include national costs for personnel, equipment maintenance, and utilities, as well as international costs for traceability, accreditation, intercomparisons, travel, and peer evaluation. If these costs are not adequately budgeted, international recognition will not be granted and investments in equipment and infrastructure will not lead to the expected benefit.

Development of a National Metrology Infrastructure: Expensive and Time Consuming

Typical costs of developing the various elements of a metrology system are shown below. Funds are generally needed for expertise transfer, measurement equipment, and sometimes building of laboratories.

- *Metrology institute:* Funds needed for a metrology institute range between US$5 million and US$200 million, and an institute requires up to 15 years for full development and international recognition.
- *Legal metrology:* Funds needed for legal metrology range between US$0.5 million and US$5.0 million, except for type testing for products, and a system requires up to 5 years for full development and international recognition.
- *Secondary calibration laboratories:* Funds needed for the secondary calibration laboratories range between US$2 million and US$500 million, depending on the needs of the economy and requirements for product testing, and a laboratory takes 2–15 years for full development and international recognition.

Source: Authors.

CIS NMIs will face dramatic increases in their operating costs as they transition from systems based on mandatory verification to a system based on services. Under the Soviet system, NMIs did not face major consequences from the lack of compliance of technical requirements (such as those due to dysfunctional equipment, lack of maintenance, or staff carelessness). Under a globalized metrology system, technical requirements are stricter, and the costs of noncompliance are the loss of international recognition of measurements. As a result, traceability costs could be numerous times higher under a modern metrology system. The same factors apply to the costs of accreditation of the NMI's laboratories by an internationally recognized body. If the overall goal for the metrology is to gain international recognition, CIS NMIs will need to face much greater operating costs for internationally related services (traceability, accreditation, intercomparisons, participation in regional and international organizations, and so forth), whereas the fees that can be charged to customers can only gradually increase. Governments and donors need to be aware of that situation and develop financing models that can guarantee operation for a period of 10–20 years.

ECA countries that make investments in new laboratories and equipment often do not have enough resources to meet annual operating costs. Many of these costs must be covered by the government because NMIs cannot be financially self-sustainable. Metrology development plans must ensure that NMIs are not overdesigned to avoid excessive operational costs. A realistic analysis of actual and potential metrological needs is crucial for the correct selection of metrological infrastructure. This is particularly true in small and less developed economies with very limited fiscal resources. At least a 5-to-10-year business plan with realistic cost calculation and guaranteed incomes (including state subsidies) is required.

Harmonizing Legal Metrology

Although EU and EU candidate countries have harmonized their legal metrology systems with European directives, which meet international norms, such is not the case with many other ECA countries. ECA countries need to ensure that the scope of covered measuring equipment and activities, and procedures used for verification and type approval, follow international guidelines of the OIML. Retaining membership in the OIML is critical, and it can help countries harmonize policies regarding the trade of products and services with a commercial value based on measurements and the trade in measuring instruments.

Legal metrology should be the responsibility of a single public body. Legal metrology institutions in all countries are always public. Legal metrology functions and scientific metrology functions can be performed by a single institution or by two institutions. When they are covered by a single institution, the two functions should be clearly divided to avoid conflicts of interests. In countries where governance is poor and rent-seeking excessive, they should be separated.

Regional and International Integration

Participation in regional metrology organizations is an important channel of knowledge transfer for NMIs and a method to achieve international recognition.

The activities of regional organizations such as EURAMET and COOMET provide opportunities from young or reforming NMIs to learn from the experience of more mature NMIs. EURAMET, in this sense, is most useful because it includes the NMIs of all EU member states. COOMET includes few NMIs with the same depth of experience and technical expertise as EURAMET, but it is the only option for most CIS countries.

The integration in regional and international metrology organizations is also essential for recognition of the national metrology system. This includes not only paying membership fees, but also participating actively in programs or even taking over a leading function to demonstrate competence (for example, working group chairman or pilot laboratory for an intercomparison). An international recognition, as described earlier, is

BOX 7.6

Difficulty in Implementing Shared Metrology Facilities and the Central American Experience

In 1956, six Central American countries signed a treaty establishing the Central American Institute of Research and Industrial Technology (ICAITI). ICAITI was established as a specialized branch of the Secretariat for the Economic Integration of Central America with a board of directors composed of the economy and industry ministers from all Central American countries. Its metrological and testing facilities in Guatemala City would act as a regional resource to promote economic competitiveness and reduce technical barriers to trade. Hundreds of thousands of dollars were invested in its metrology laboratory and staff training, but the institute's capabilities were never used to any great extent by Guatemala's neighbors, and its limited number of clients were almost exclusively from Guatemala. By 1998, ICAITI was no longer functioning.

Sources: ICAITI 1996; World Bank 2000; Organization of American States, http://www.oas.org/juridico/spanish/firmas/f-84.html.

not a political act but requires demonstration of competence face to face with the peers of other NMIs. The related activities bind personnel and resources, which have to be available, do not generate income, and represent additional burdens for NMIs. These need to be considered in an NMI's budget and workplans.

The first priority for ECA should be the strengthening of the regional metrology organization COOMET. Although this plan requires additional resources to be allocated by the individual NMIs, it will pay back in the long run through division of labor and experience exchange that facilitates the development in each NMI.

Small economies can join forces to develop only a few, but complementary, calibration capabilities and to share them in the region to reduce operating costs.

The Balkans, the Caucasus, and Central Asia are three regions in ECA where countries can avoid duplicating expensive metrology facilities by coordinating their investments into complementary capabilities or pooling resources. All three regions have relatively young metrology infrastructure and still have the opportunity to make strategic investment choices. One strategy could be for different countries to specialize in complementary areas of metrology (such as mass, temperature, and chemistry). Another strategy would be for countries to build common regional metrology institutes. Both options are possible if countries can surmount important obstacles. One obstacle is borders: residents of one country must have access to metrology facilities in the other countries and must not pay taxes on equipment crossing borders for calibration purposes. Another obstacle is mutual recognition: for any regional coordination scheme to work, measurements in one country must be recognized in another. This may be easier to achieve among countries that are signatories of the CIPM MRA, but roughly half of the countries in the Balkans, the Caucasus, and Central Asia have not signed this agreement. They would need to implement regional MRA schemes as a starting point. A third important obstacle is geopolitics: a number of countries in those regions do not have good political relationships with their neighbors, and in some cases, there are even frozen conflicts. The failed experience of Central America in a regional metrology illustrates some of the difficulties of regional facilities (box 7.6).

References

ICAITI (Central American Institute of Research and Industrial Technology). 1996. "1996 Strategic Plan: Strategies for Competiveness." ICAITI, Guatemala City.

NISM (National Institute of Standards and Metrology). n.d. "2004–2005 NISM Work Plan." NISM, Bishkek.

World Bank. 1999. "Turkey Industrial Technology Project." Report 18351-TU, Project Appraisal Document, World Bank, Washington, DC.

———. 2000. "The Republic of Guatemala Competitiveness Project." Report 21327-GU, Project Appraisal Document, World Bank, Washington, DC.

———. 2009. "Croatia's EU Convergence Report: Reaching and Sustaining Higher Rates of Economic Growth." Report 48879-HR, World Bank, Washington, DC.

CHAPTER 8

Accreditation: Certified Once—
Accepted Everywhere

*"The world has not to be put in order: the world is order
incarnate. It is for us to put ourselves in unison with this order."*

—Henry Miller, "Paris and Its Suburbs"

‣ After a late start, accreditation is thriving in most countries of Eastern Europe and Central America (ECA).

‣ European Union (EU) countries, Balkan countries, and Turkey have mostly aligned the basic institutional structures of their accreditation systems with international good practices, but accreditation bodies in other ECA countries are often subject to conflicts of interests. Political independence and impartiality provide credibility to an accreditation body.

‣ Although all EU countries, Balkan countries, and Turkey have adopted international accreditation standards, the quality of accreditation is questionable in Commonwealth of Independent States (CIS) countries. Many CIS accreditation bodies offer accreditation based on idiosyncratic national standards or based on international standards without properly trained staff. This practice does little to ensure quality in the conformity assessment market.

265

> **All ECA countries have achieved or are moving toward mutual recognition of their accreditation systems. But some lag significantly, and products must often be retested and recertified when they cross borders—creating unnecessary barriers to trade.**

> **Financing is a challenge for small ECA economies that do not have the critical mass to sustain self-funded accreditation bodies. Countries that have no language or geography barriers can rely on internationally recognized accreditation bodies in neighboring countries.**

> **ECA countries can build solid accreditation systems only through regional cooperation. CIS countries must address the lack of a regional accreditation body.**

Accreditation in Eastern Europe and Central Asia

The accreditation system in Eastern Europe and Central Asia (ECA) as described earlier is relatively new to transition economies. Under central planning and through much of the 1990s, conformity assessment was undertaken and supervised by government ministries and not by an accreditation body. No formal rules were applicable across the spectrum of state conformity assessment bodies to determine whether they were competent in carrying out their tasks. And no politically independent and technically credible body was charged with monitoring these organizations.

Institutional Framework for Accreditation in ECA

All ECA countries have now established national accreditation systems.

ECA countries that are members or prospective members of the European Union (EU) have a clear institutional roadmap to follow for accreditation, spelled out in new EU regulations. In this group, every country has decided to establish a single national accreditation body. This is also the case for all EU countries, where the mutual recognition framework and new regulation on accreditation would make it perfectly feasible for countries to use their neighbors' accreditation system. Nevertheless, small EU countries and candidate countries in the Balkans that have limited economies of scale have established national accreditation bodies. This practice has occurred on the basis of both the political decisions to remain independent from their neighbors and the EU's accession mechanisms, including the Stabilization and Association Agreements, which require membership in the European quality infrastructure organizations. Significant donor support has also facilitated the establishment of national accreditation bodies in accession and candidate countries.

In Commonwealth of Independent States (CIS) countries, accreditation bodies have been created largely in the hope of increasing trade outside the CIS. Mutual acceptance of conformity assessment certificates across CIS countries is mainly undertaken on the basis of political agreements, not on the basis of mutual recognition of the technical aspects of national accreditation systems. This approach means that there are fewer incentives to create national accreditation systems, let alone internationally compatible systems.

EU countries, Balkan countries, and Turkey have mostly aligned the basic institutional structure of their accreditation systems with EU best practices.

In ECA, the most challenging institutional aspect of setting up an accreditation system during the transition period has been to provide complete independence from other elements of the national quality infrastructure and from political influence. Most ECA countries inherited systems in which all functions of the quality infrastructure were centralized and were embedded in political bodies. All EU member states, as well as the candidate and potential candidate countries in the Balkan region and Turkey, have established accreditation structures, largely decoupled from the rest of the national quality infrastructure (table 8.1). All of those

TABLE 8.1

Accreditation Bodies Subject to Conflicts of Interest, 2010

Group	Countries where the accreditation body is involved in standardization, metrology, or conformity assessment
EU and OECD countries	none
Balkan countries and Turkey	none
CIS countries	Azerbaijan, Belarus, Russian Federation, Tajikistan, Turkmenistan, Uzbekistan

Sources: ISO 2006; Web sites of the national standards bodies.
Note: OECD = Organisation for Economic Co-operation and Development.

countries have opted for public institutions, although private institutions do exist in the EU (table 8.2). In the United Kingdom, for example, the accreditation body is a private nonprofit organization operating under a Memorandum of Understanding with the government. ECA's EU and Balkan accreditation bodies are part of a ministry or are a state agency subordinate to a ministry.

TABLE 8.2
Governance of the National Accreditation Bodies, 2006–09

	Country	Legal status	Directive Council elected by a General Assembly of Members	Share of members of the Directive Council designated by the public administration (%)	Consultative council
EU countries	Bulgaria	Public		20	✓
	Hungary	Public	✓	33	✓
	Poland	Public		100	✓
Balkan countries and Turkey	Albania	Public		100	✓
	Croatia	Public		100	✓
	Macedonia, FYR	Public		40	✓
	Serbia	Public		100	✓
	Turkey	Public	✓	—	✓
CIS countries and Georgia	Armenia	Public		70	✓
	Georgia	Public		—	
	Kazakhstan	Public		100	
	Kyrgyz Republic	Public		32	✓
	Moldova	Public	✓	60	✓
	Tajikistan	Public		n.a.	
	Ukraine	Public		—	✓
	Uzbekistan	Public		—	✓
Comparator countries	Spain	Public	✓	n.a.	✓
	United Kingdom	Private		38	✓

Source: World Bank survey of national quality infrastructure institutions.
Note: — = not available, n.a. = not applicable.

Accreditation bodies in ECA's EU countries, Balkan countries, and Turkey have also adopted good governance practices, although the private sector and consumers often have limited influence in governance. As table 8.2 shows, all of those countries have some form of consultative council. In a few cases, a General Assembly of Members elects a Directive (or Executive) Council, although these generally do not go as far as Spain in opening membership to any stakeholder. In Turkey, for example, the members of the General Assembly are representatives of organizations designated by the government, nearly two-thirds of which are public entities.[1] In other cases, the Directive Council itself includes a mix of representatives of the government and representatives of the private sector. This model is used in the United Kingdom, but also in Bulgaria and the former Yugoslav Republic of Macedonia. Each of these countries has gone quite far in providing a voice to the private sector, which holds the majority of the seats of the Executive Council. In other cases, such as Albania, Croatia, Poland, and Serbia, the accreditation body is tightly controlled by the public sector, which nominates all members of the Directive Council. In some cases, even the consultative council is under heavy government influence. In Croatia, for example, the national accreditation body is administered by a Managing Board, appointed by the Croatian government for a period of four years. It also has an Accreditation Board that acts as an advisory body. This board is made up of representatives from government, industrial associations, customers, education institutes, and metrology institutions. However, the members of the Accreditation Board are appointed and revoked by the Managing Board at the proposal of the Chief Executive Officer who is appointed by the government for a period of four years, based on a public tender (World Bank 2009).

Accreditation bodies in ECA's EU countries, Balkan countries and Turkey are largely autonomous and, hence, are shielded from excessive political influence, although there are a few exceptions. An index of institutional autonomy reveals that the sample of accreditation bodies in the EU and Balkan countries appear to have the required flexibility to respond to changing market needs, retain a technically competent workforce, and fulfill their international obligations (figure 8.1). Surprisingly, Bulgaria, although an EU member state, lags in this domain. The Decree for the Structural Regulations of Bulgaria's accreditation body is very constraining and gives the institution very little administrative autonomy. It prescribes the total number of personnel, including their distribution in the different administrative departments, and the description of several employee titles. It also prescribes an administrative structure and accred-

---

1. See Law No. 4457 (1999), *Law on Establishment and Tasks of Turkish Accreditation Agency.*

itation procedure in a level of detail that does not allow the accreditation body to improve the efficiency of its operations. Moreover, the institution's budget must be approved by the government, although the government contributes little to it in net terms, which places further restrictions on the body's autonomy (World Bank 2008).

CIS countries present a different picture, with a mix of institutional structures for accreditation, many of which present serious conflicts of interest.

As has been outlined in previous chapters, EU integration has been a significant driving force for the establishment of a quality infrastructure that complies with international standards. This external driving force does not exist in CIS countries. For these countries, other external factors such as World Trade Organization accession and EU Free Trade Agreement negotiations (in the case of Armenia, Georgia, and Ukraine) have provided moderate driving forces for change. In some countries, such as Georgia, incentives have come from a political will to promote exports to

FIGURE 8.1

Wide Variance of Autonomy of Accreditation Bodies in ECA, 2006–09

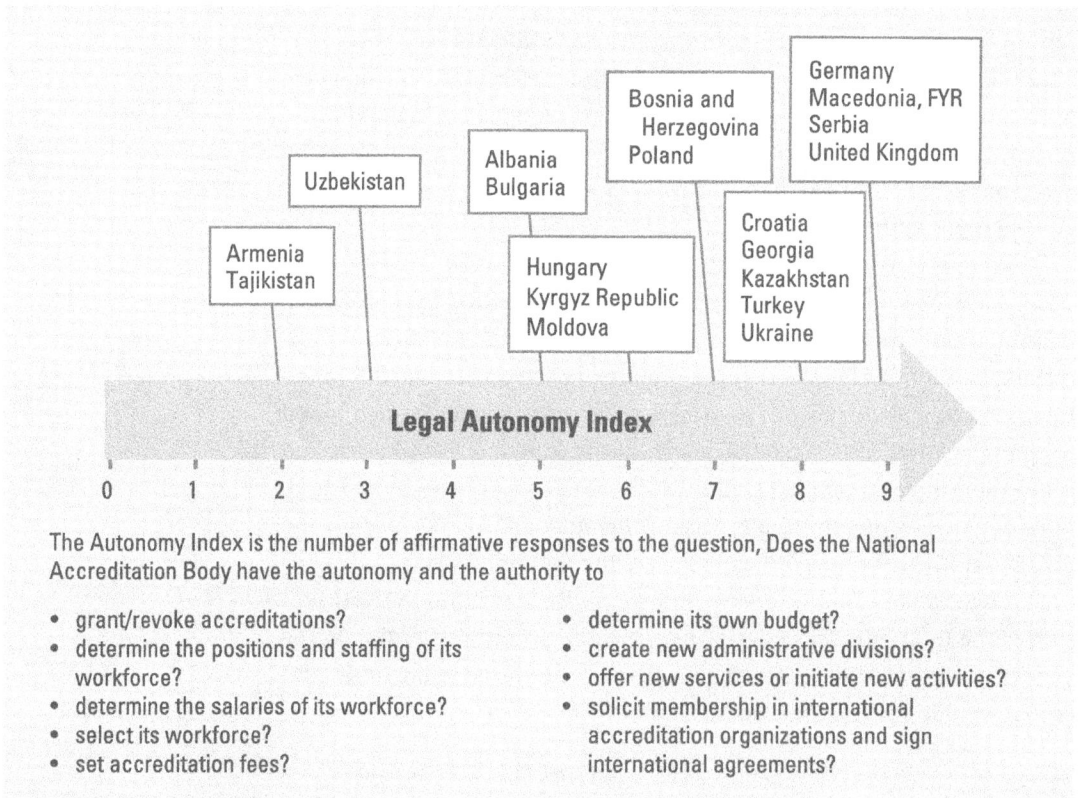

The Autonomy Index is the number of affirmative responses to the question, Does the National Accreditation Body have the autonomy and the authority to

- grant/revoke accreditations?
- determine the positions and staffing of its workforce?
- determine the salaries of its workforce?
- select its workforce?
- set accreditation fees?

- determine its own budget?
- create new administrative divisions?
- offer new services or initiate new activities?
- solicit membership in international accreditation organizations and sign international agreements?

Source: Authors based on the World Bank survey of national quality infrastructure institutions.

regions outside of the CIS, recognizing that an effective accreditation system provides the basis for effective quality assurance services and that international recognition of accreditation facilitates entry of domestic products in foreign markets.

In some CIS countries, accreditation remains locked in the old structures of central planning.

As mentioned in earlier chapters, certification bodies, inspection bodies, and laboratories were assigned or operated by ministries under central planning. A logical consequence was that accreditation was the responsibility of a department of the ministry or the agency responsible for the quality infrastructure or that there was no need for an accreditation function because the government operated all conformity assessment bodies. The legacy of this system is that conformity assessment and accreditation functions remain under one roof.

In a number of CIS countries (see figure 8.2 and table 8.1), a single body is responsible for standardization, calibration, certification, and accreditation. These countries have chosen to stay with the established structures. This is the case of the Russian Federation, where one department of the Federal Agency on Technical Regulations and Metrology is responsible for accreditation, while others are responsible for the remaining functions of the national quality infrastructure. This configuration leads to conflicts of interests because "self-accreditation" of the agencies, laboratories, and certification bodies can be used to compete against laboratories and certification bodies operating outside of this structure. Moreover, self-accreditation is not very credible to consumers and businesses compared to the international practice of third-party accreditation.

FIGURE 8.2

Conflicts of Interest in Functions of Accreditation Agency in Several CIS Countries

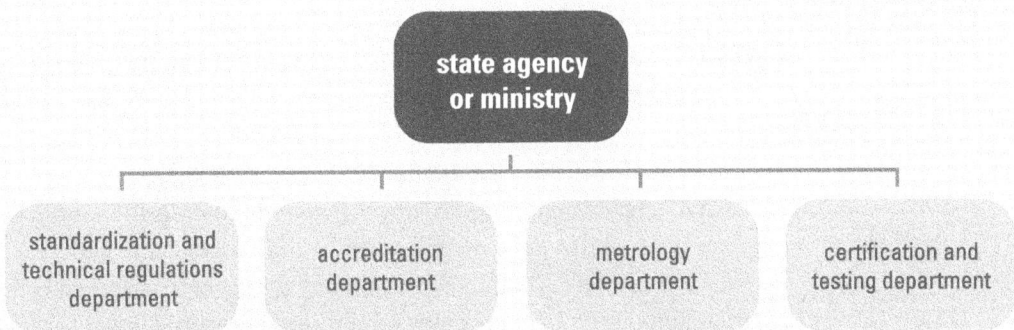

Source: Authors.

Finally, the same agency is developing technical regulations, which may require accreditation from private conformity assessment bodies, and deriving financial benefits from accreditation through services fees.

In many CIS countries, the national accreditation body is subject to political influence and lacks the institutional autonomy to be considered impartial and technically credible. In Tajikistan, accreditation is carried out together with other quality infrastructure functions in a single agency; this agency has very little autonomy to carry out its responsibilities (see figure 8.1); it is governed entirely by government appointees; and in contradiction with international best practice, it has no consultative council or board of appeals. In Armenia, although an Accreditation Agency under the Ministry of Economy undertakes most of the core functions such as evaluation of applications, there is also an Accreditation Board, chaired by the Ministry of Economy, which makes the final decision to grant or revoke accreditations (AEPLAC 2007). Moreover, the Accreditation Agency is not independent from the ministry, on which it depends for virtually all of its internal decisions (see figure 8.1). Other CIS countries have taken incremental steps toward restructuring the accreditation system, but sometimes the separation is not clear. In Kazakhstan, since late 2008, the accreditation body is no longer a department of the Kazakh Committee for Standardization, Certification, and Metrology but is an independent body. However, it is still subordinate to the Kazakh Committee for Standardization, Certification, and Metrology, so the end result is unclear.

Other CIS countries have recently taken bolder steps to restructure their accreditation systems. Over the past seven years, four CIS countries—Georgia, the Kyrgyz Republic, Moldova, and Ukraine—have disposed of the old structures and created new, separate accreditation bodies. The diverse political and economic context of these countries shows that institutional inertia and internal resistance of the incumbent national quality infrastructure agencies can be overcome through political will. In Moldova, pursuant to the Law on Accreditation of 2003, the Moldovan accreditation body, formerly a department of the Moldovan Committee for Standardization, Certification, and Metrology, was separated and placed as a direct subordinate to the Ministry of Economy, as is the case in a number of EU economies. The same was achieved in Ukraine. In both Moldova and the Kyrgyz Republic, the private sector now has a voice in the governance of the accreditation body (see table 8.2).

Finally, one remaining challenge to accreditation in CIS countries is the presence of parallel structures. Although in each country there is, by name, a single accreditation body, in many cases, there is limited coordination among the various public authorities that would benefit from an accreditation function to implement their regulatory functions. As a result, accreditation processes are carried out independently by other ministries (for example, for medical laboratories, food safety testing, and legal metrology) using their own internal processes (box 8.1).

Who Accredits *Povjerka* Laboratories?

In the *Gosstandart* system, the national metrology institute's relationship to industry was not that of a service provider, but of government enforcement of the technical regulations act. It was not tasked with providing calibration services to industry, in the sense of ensuring traceability to the International System of Units and reporting associated measurement uncertainty, but was responsible for implementing metrological verification in the sense of control—*Povjerka*.

A Povjerka laboratory is not a calibration laboratory, but can be considered a legal metrology verification office whose responsibility is the verification of measuring devices defined in a law under consumer protection. These laboratories do not provide industrial calibration services, but are mandated and supervised by a state agency. Although in some cases governments have started requiring their accreditation so that these entities can also serve industry as calibration laboratories, this practice is not yet common. In CIS countries, where Povjerka verification is often still required by a law or technical regulation, accreditation is meeting much resistance because Povjerka laboratories are already considered to be under state control and do not require a second authorization. Resistance is greatest where the competence of the accreditation body is questioned.

In the Kyrgyz Republic, the Kyrgyz Center for Accreditation is accrediting testing laboratories and certification bodies but not calibration laboratories, because the National Metrology Institute under *Kyrgyzstandart* still "authorizes" metrological laboratories for Povjerka verifications. Even though laboratories are free to seek additional accreditation, none is willing to do so because it presents no additional benefit. Povjerka verifications, which probably cover more than 90 percent of their workload, are covered by the official authorization. The Accreditation Body has no power to change the situation, and it remains a dilemma whether to recognize Povjerka certificates as calibration certificates in the accreditation of testing laboratories, although they are not fit for the purpose.

In Uzbekistan, the Department of Accreditation and Inspection of *Uzstandart* is not considered an independent body but fulfills the function of an accreditation body. In Uzbekistan, as well, this department is only accrediting testing laboratories and certification bodies. Calibration laboratories, even though they are performing Povjerka verifications, are accredited by a separate department under the metrology division because of questions about the competence of the accreditation department in metrological matters. In addition, the discrepancies are coming mainly from the different perception about calibration and Povjerka and the different interpretation of the requirements for metrological laboratories.

In Kazakhstan, the situation is different. The independent Kazakh Centre for Accreditation is accrediting calibration laboratories in addition to testing laboratories and certification bodies. But because the laboratories are only permitted by law to issue Povjerka certificates, it is just a clash of terminologies. The temporary solution seems to be to add additional information about the measurement uncertainty into the ordinary Povjerka certificate and treat it as a calibration certificate.

Source: Authors.

Accreditation Activities

Although all EU countries, Balkan countries, and Turkey have now adopted international accreditation standards, the quality of accreditation in CIS countries is questionable.

Accreditation standards provide guidelines for the accreditation procedures to be used for different types of conformity assessment bodies. Unified standards across countries ensure that conformity assessment bodies are accredited according to the same benchmarks in every country. In view of EU accession requirements, EU member, candidate, and potential candidate countries have long disposed of the old incompatible accreditation standards. When EU or Balkan countries such as Croatia or Latvia (table 8.1) do not offer accreditations against the main types of international accreditation standards, it is not because they are using old standards, but rather because they simply do not offer that service, because of either the limited market size or the lack of technical capacity to accredit to the latest international standard. CIS countries, however, have not only adopted fewer international standards, but also continue to accredit according to old standards. Nearly all accreditations in Tajikistan are conducted according to idiosyncratic standards. Although countries such as Armenia have adopted international accreditation standards, this has been in name only, and most of the proper guidelines are not followed (table 8.3).

TABLE 8.3

Adoption of International Standards by Most ECA Countries, 2006–09

Number of the top five most widespread international accreditation standards offered[a]	Country
5	Albania; Bosnia and Herzegovina; Macedonia, FYR; Romania; Serbia; Slovak Republic; Spain; Turkey; Ukraine; United Kingdom
4	Armenia, Croatia, Kyrgyz Republic, Latvia
3	Uzbekistan
2	Georgia, Kazakhstan, Moldova
1	Tajikistan

Sources: World Bank survey of national quality infrastructure institutions; Web sites of the various accreditation bodies.
a. These standards include ISO/IEC 17020:1998 for inspection bodies, ISO/IEC Guide 65 or EN 45011 for product certification bodies, ISO/IEC 17021:2006 for management system certification bodies, ISO/IEC 17024:2003 for personnel certification bodies, and ISO/IEC 17025:2005 for testing and calibration laboratories.

One reason to question the adherence to international accreditation standards in many CIS countries is their limited access to proper metrological traceability. In theory, all testing and calibration laboratories must demonstrate traceability to the International System of Units to be accredited according to international standards.[2] It is questionable whether this can be achieved in a number of ECA countries because the NMI does not offer international traceability to the International System of Units, as demonstrated previously in chapter 7 of this book.

Accreditation has been booming in most ECA countries, but some Balkan and Central Asian countries continue to lag.

Although it must be kept in mind that accreditation—even when performed nominally according to international standards—may mean something very different in Moldova and in Turkey, most ECA countries appear to have no shortage of organizations accredited to international standards (figure 8.3). Because figure 8.3 represents only national accreditations, it excludes local organizations accredited by foreign accreditation bodies—a frequent occurrence in countries such as Serbia and Moldova that lack multilateral recognition arrangements (MLAs)—and, hence, is likely to underrepresent the total number of accreditations. With an economy half of the size of Spain's, Poland harbors more accredited bodies. And accreditations rates have surged in most EU accession countries and in Turkey, partly spurred by the creation of new accreditation bodies and the achievement of mutual recognition in recent years. Turkey was admitted to the European co-operation for Accreditation (EA) MLA in 2006, and the number of its accreditations rose from 15 in 2002 to about 50 in 2005 and to about 300 in 2009. Smaller countries such as Croatia and Latvia now compete well with Ireland in terms of total number of accreditations and outperform it when the size of their gross domestic product (GDP) is taken into account (figure 8.4). Nonetheless, some ECA countries lag. Albania, Bosnia and Herzegovina, and FYR Macedonia have yet to develop their accreditation markets. And as discussed previously, some of the Central Asian economies have not offered any internationally compatible accreditations.

A closer look at the conformity assessment market reveals some gaps in the Balkan and CIS countries. Although countries such as Tajikistan and Uzbekistan display nearly 100 percent accreditation rates in some areas, these are achieved using completely different accreditation practices and, hence, are not comparable to rates achieved in the other coun-

---

2. See ISO/IEC 17025 (ISO and IEC 2005).

FIGURE 8.3

Accreditation to International Standards in ECA, 2006–09

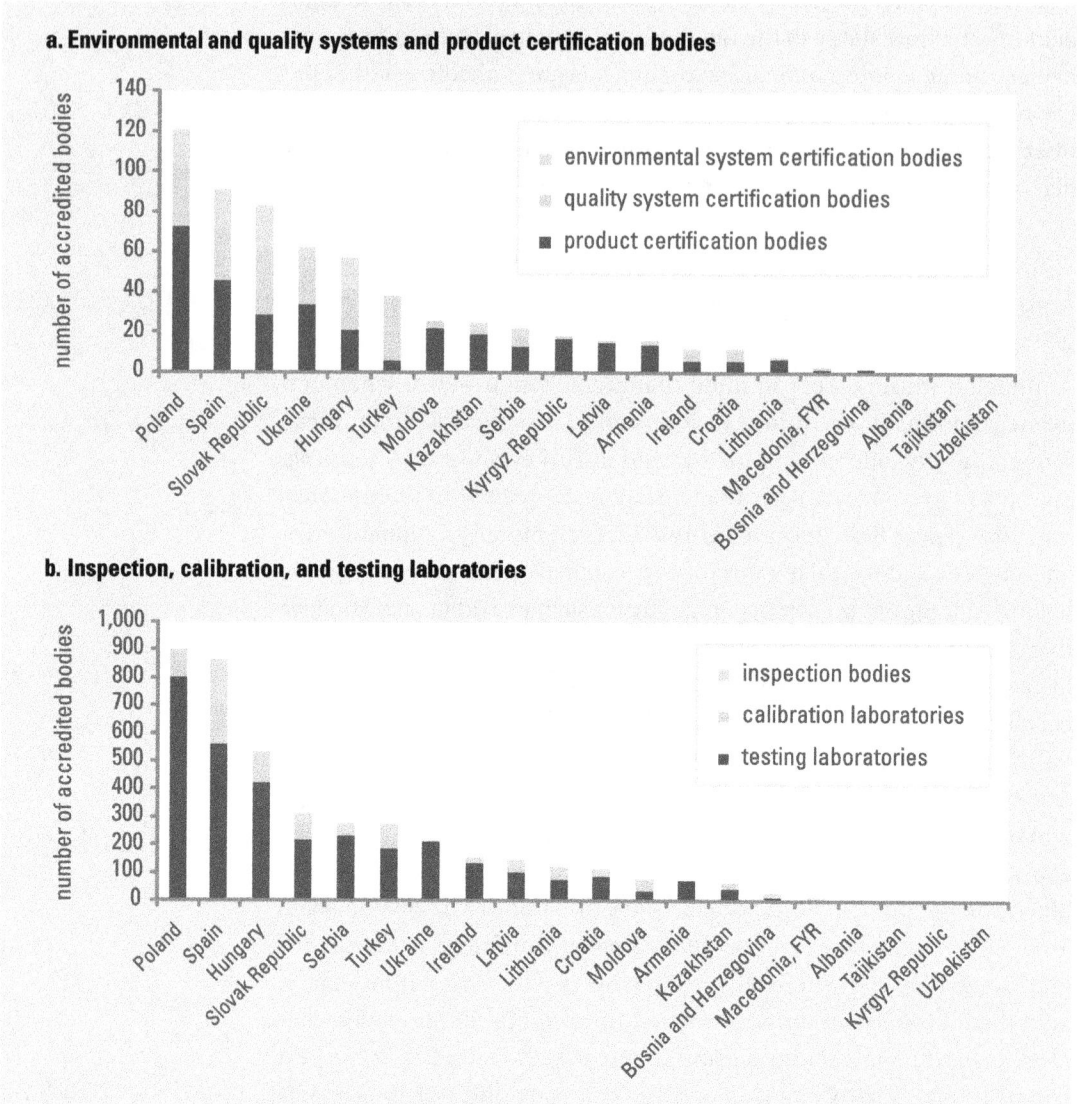

a. Environmental and quality systems and product certification bodies

b. Inspection, calibration, and testing laboratories

Source: World Bank survey of national quality infrastructure institutions.
Note: Only accreditations to internationally compatible standards are considered.

tries, which—at least nominally—have international accreditation standards. In nearly all other Balkan and former Soviet countries for which accreditation market data are available, accreditation rates are low, particularly for laboratories (figure 8.5). This situation is likely due to the limited metrological traceability at the NMI, which makes it impossible to accredit according to international standards in a number of calibration and testing fields.

FIGURE 8.4

Accredited Bodies in ECA Countries and in Selected Comparator Countries, 2006-09

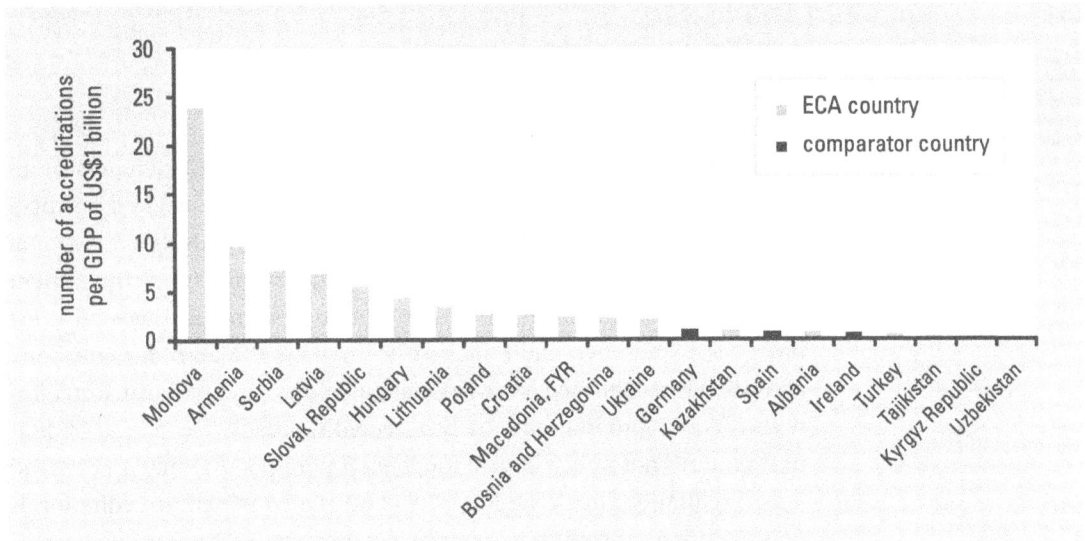

Source: World Bank survey of national quality infrastructure institutions.
Note: Figure includes accreditations for product, personnel, quality systems and environmental systems certification bodies; for inspection bodies; and for calibration and testing laboratories that are officially conducted according to international standards.

FIGURE 8.5

Share of Accredited Laboratories, 2006-09

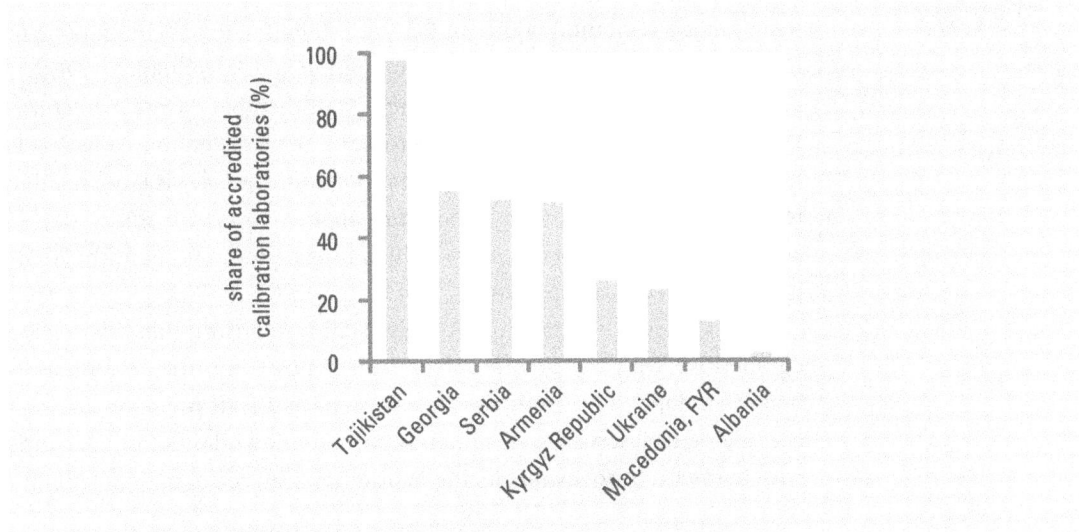

Source: World Bank survey of national quality infrastructure institutions.

Resources for Accreditation

Accreditation bodies in ECA appear to be adequately staffed, but the quality of the personnel is not necessarily up to international levels.

In addition to the basic institutional structure, the effectiveness of an accreditation body and its ability to adhere to international best practices is dependent on the technical capacity of its staff. Unlike a national metrology institute, accreditation bodies do not require much investment in equipment apart from basic information systems. But its staff must have the experience and expertise to manage the accreditation body according to established international guidelines[3] and perform accreditations according to internationally accepted standards.[4] Hence, accreditation requires not only a large enough staff to respond to market demand for accreditation, but also, for ECA countries in which accreditation is new, learning of an entirely new process. In many ECA countries, accreditation bodies functioning according to international guidelines were established in only the past 10 years, so the staff is still learning. Because demand for accreditation depends on much more than the size of the economy, including the level of industrialization, the level of technological sophistication of industry, the demand for regulatory conformity assessment services, and the requirements of export markets, there is no real way to gauge whether any of those accreditation systems has the appropriate number of staff. Nonetheless, figure 8.6 provides a sense that nearly all accreditation bodies in ECA are staffed to levels comparable to their Organisation for Economic Co-operation and Development (OECD) counterparts, with 10 to 30 permanent staff members. Only two countries stand out. Kazakhstan appears to have an accreditation body that is larger than that of most OECD comparator countries and is large relative to its accreditation market. Uzbekistan appears to have a thinly staffed accreditation body—five people—which raises questions about the quality of its accreditation process.

One strategy to attract high-quality staff is to ensure that salaries are competitive with the private sector. This is possible if the accreditation body is independent from the government and staff members are not considered civil servants. Although information on salaries in ECA countries in the EU is not available, the World Bank survey of national quality

---

3. ISO/IEC 17011:2004 (ISO and IEC 2004) specifies general requirements for accreditation bodies assessing and accrediting conformity assessment bodies. It is also appropriate as a requirements document for the peer evaluation process for mutual recognition arrangements between accreditation bodies.
4. See, for example, ISO/IEC 17025 (ISO and IEC 2005).

infrastructure institutions revealed that a number of accreditation bodies in the Balkans and in Central Asia offer salaries that are dramatically lower than in the private sector. In a few cases, the salaries are estimated to be a third of those in the private sector. This is troubling because accreditation bodies need to attract skilled staff and offer compensation that provides disincentives to engage in unethical behavior.

FIGURE 8.6

Critical Mass of Staff Present in Most Accreditation Bodies in ECA, 2006-09

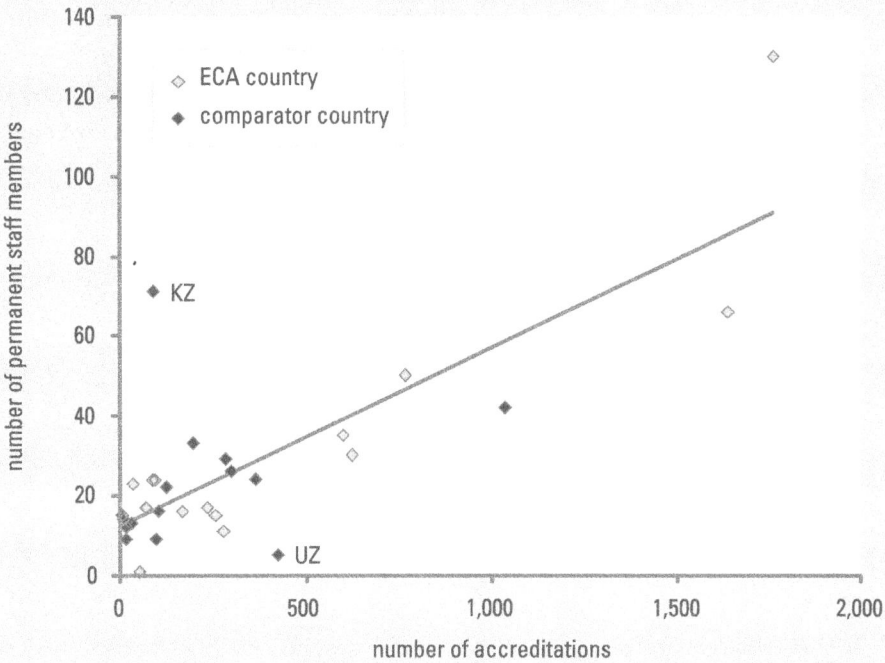

Sources: World Bank survey of national quality infrastructure institutions; Physikalisch Technische Bundesanstalt.
Note: Comparator countries include OECD countries and Hong Kong SAR, China.

Because accreditation can require a technical background for certain scopes of accreditation (such as accreditation of a laboratory with very specialized equipment), accreditation bodies usually rely on a pool of external assessors and external technical experts. Assessors in particular must receive training from the accreditation body. In ECA's EU economies and in many Balkan countries, the general practice is to rely on part-time staff for assessments. In CIS countries, this is not always the case. Some CIS countries—Kazakhstan, the Kyrgyz Republic, Moldova, and Tajikistan—rely entirely on internal permanent staff for this purpose. This practice explains why Kazakhstan has an unusually large accreditation body. All assessors and technical experts are internal. This not only imposes excessive fixed costs on the accreditation body, but also limits the scopes of accreditation that can be offered to areas in which there is internal expertise. Figure 8.7 displays the number of qualified lead assessors in each country, with Spain as a comparator. It is a rough proxy for a country's total capacity for accreditation and ability to serve a wide range of accreditation scopes. One would expect a larger economy to have a greater variety of economic activities and require a larger pool of assessors. Of course, the level of industrialization also influences the degree of specialization of an economy, but this effect is difficult to quantify in a chart. The figure shows that relative to their GDP, ECA countries tend to have sufficient numbers of lead assessors when compared to Spain. The question again is the training received by these assessors. In most Balkan and Central Asian countries, the accreditation body is itself in a learning mode and is unable to offer proper training to assessors. This training must be sought in other countries, which can be expensive and act as a barrier for proper qualification of assessors. As a result, it is not uncommon for accreditation bodies in ECA countries to contract out work to foreign assessors. Additional travel costs and higher fees make this a costly option. Another challenge to impartial accreditation in ECA's small countries is to find technical experts in the local market who are independent of the organization to be accredited.

FIGURE 8.7

Qualified Lead Assessors in ECA and Spain, 2006-09

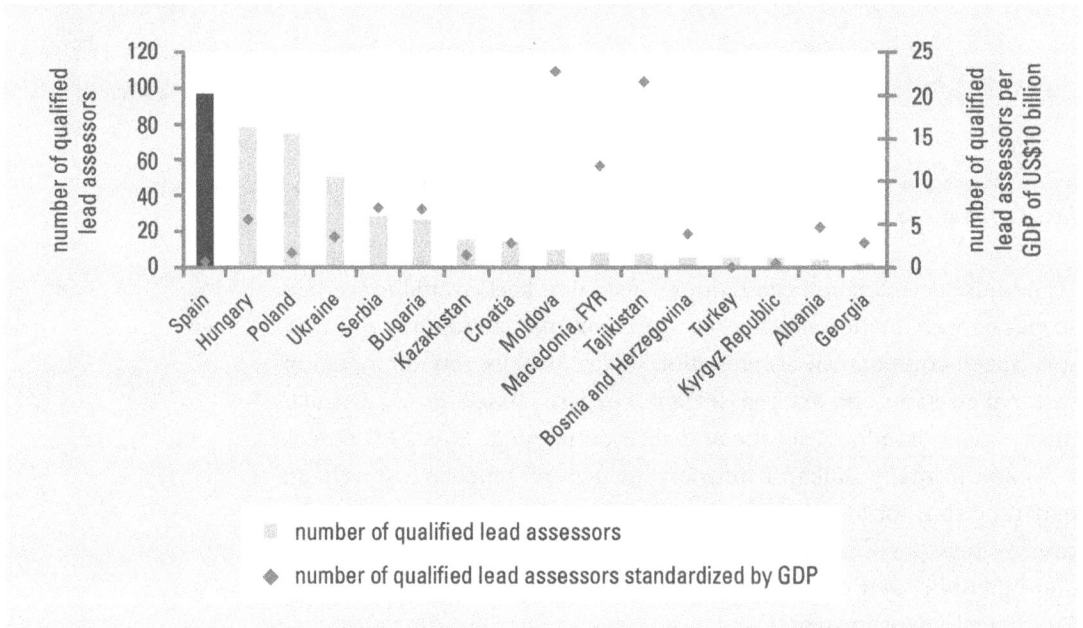

Source: World Bank survey of national quality infrastructure institutions.

Accreditation bodies in some of ECA's smaller countries operate on tight budgets.

Proper financing of the accreditation body is necessary to cover not only staff costs, but also training, much of which must occur overseas in the case of ECA countries; membership fees for international organizations; consultants for establishing a quality management system; information systems; seminars; and awareness campaigns. In the case of centralized quality infrastructure, systems accreditation bodies often do not set their own budgets, so it is difficult to determine whether they are adequately financed. However, data are available for a number of other ECA countries. While ECA's larger economies, such as Poland, Turkey and Ukraine, appear to have sizable annual budgets, ranging from US$500,000 to US$4 million, a number of smaller economies are operating on shoestring budgets, even when taking into account the size of their accreditation market (figure 8.8). Accreditation bodies in Armenia and the Kyrgyz Republic both have budgets of less than US$50,000, far from the critical mass of funding necessary to create an internationally compatible accreditation system. These economies are challenged by both low fiscal resources and small markets that limit the potential for generating revenues.

FIGURE 8.8

Financing of Some Accreditation Bodies in ECA, 2006-09

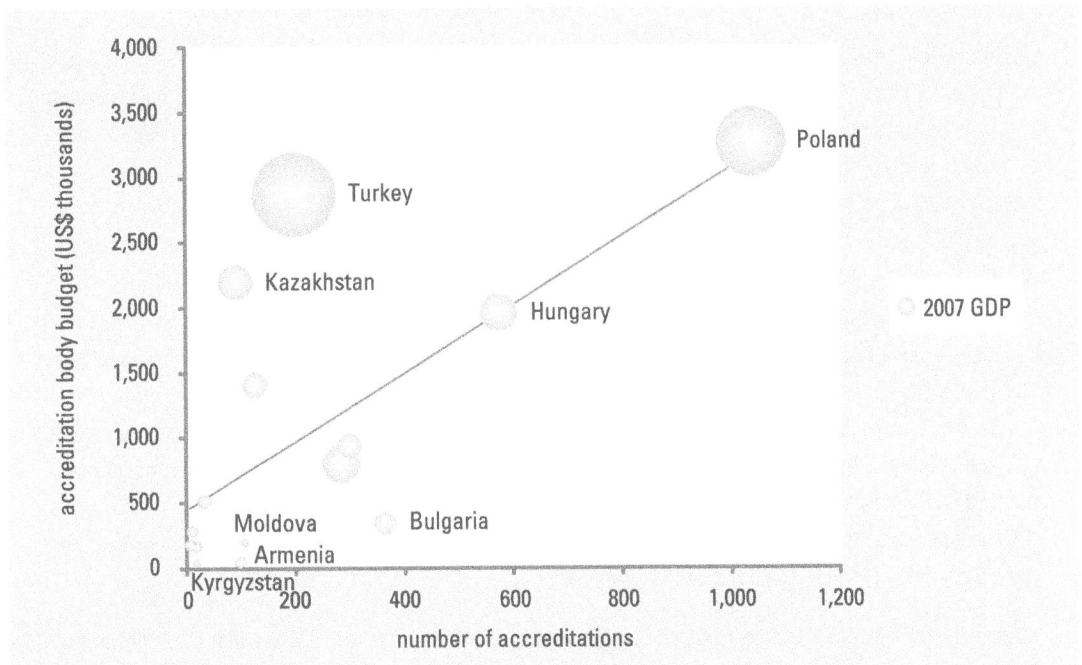

Source: World Bank survey of national quality infrastructure institutions.

In fact, a number of ECA countries are much below the threshold of 100 to 250 accreditations (estimated in chapter 4 of this book) to achieve financial self-sustainability. Albania has 7 accredited bodies, Georgia has 11, and FYR Macedonia has 17. Although some countries, such as Armenia, have more (98), their numbers are likely to fall once the accreditation body adopts more stringent international standards. However, in all ECA countries outside of the EU, accreditation is still in its early stages of development. The conformity assessment bodies to be accredited must comply with new rules and standards as well and must adjust their organization and processes to this process. Therefore, an increase in the number of accredited conformity assessment bodies can be expected. Unfortunately, the potential in the market is not known. Nevertheless, it seems obvious that many of the smaller ECA economies do not require a high number of conformity assessment bodies and that the markets are very limited. If these countries decide to keep an accreditation system, it will need to be subsidized by the state in the short to medium term. Luxembourg, which has a small market for accreditation, aims to achieve administrative economies of scale by consolidating accreditation with other functions of the quality infrastructure, but it has been very cautious to not create conflicts of interest (box 8.2). Cross-

---

BOX 8.2

Ways of Dealing with Luxembourg's Tiny Accreditation Market

Luxembourg is a very small country with a population of 486,000. Its main economic sector is services, which represents 86 percent of GDP and does not create much demand for testing laboratories (the main types of clients of accreditation bodies). In 2008, GDP purchasing power parity was US$42 billion. Luxembourg's accreditation body is part of the Luxembourg Institute for Standardization, Accreditation, and Security (ILNAS), a state agency under the Ministry of Economy and External Trade. ILNAS was founded in June 2008 and is the rare case of an OECD or EU agency that combines standardization, accreditation, legal metrology, market surveillance, and promotion of quality assurance. Luxembourg integrates these various functions under one roof for reasons of efficiency and administrative economies of scale in a tiny economy. It has in its portfolio approximately 30 accredited entities, which is far below the threshold for self-financing.

So, what guarantees the absence of conflicts of interest? First, conformity assessment bodies, potential clients of the accreditation body, have been excluded from ILNAS. The only remaining conflict of interest would be posed if the legal metrology unit sought accreditation from the accreditation unit. To resolve this issue, Luxembourg takes advantage of cross-border accreditation, and the legal metrology unit has been accredited by the Belgian accreditation body.

Sources: World Bank World Development Indicators database; ILNAS Web site, http://www.ilnas.public.lu/fr/index .html.

border accreditation is another option for countries that are too small to sustain an accreditation body, but in some cases there are no immediate neighbors with internationally harmonized accreditation systems or political barriers prevent cooperation.

As shown in figure 8.9, a number of accreditation bodies in ECA remain heavily dependent on government funding, which is to be expected given that the market in those countries is not yet developed. In several of the smaller economies, including Albania, Armenia, Bosnia and Herzegovina, and the Kyrgyz Republic, all accreditation fees are transferred to the state budget. This practice is not common among mature accreditation bodies, because it takes away market incentives. A law on accreditation and government support can promote the public role of accreditation, but accreditation fees are useful to promote its responsiveness to the market. Remarkably, a number of ECA countries are now able to secure most of their funding from accreditation fees alone. In some cases, this is due to high market awareness and trade integration with the EU (for example, Bulgaria, Poland, and Turkey). In others, it is because of policies inherited from central planning that create regulation-driven demand for accreditation (for example, Tajikistan).

FIGURE 8.9

Self-Financing of Some Accreditation Bodies in ECA, 2006-09

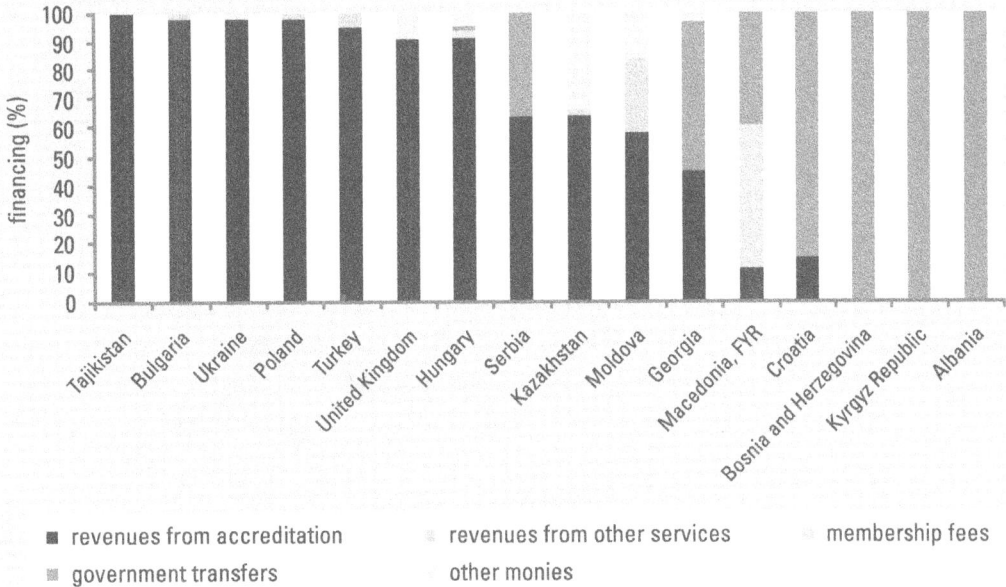

Source: World Bank survey of national quality infrastructure institutions.

Regional and International Integration

While ECA's EU members and Turkey have internationally recognized accreditation systems, Balkan countries are slowly moving in that direction.

Regional and international cooperation in accreditation has two major benefits. First, it allows new accreditation bodies to get up to speed by receiving knowledge, advice, and training from more mature accreditation bodies. Second, it is a gateway to mutual recognition through an international peer review process, the true test of whether an accreditation body is operating according to the highest standards.

All accreditation bodies in the EU are required to be part of the regional body, EA (table 8.4). Most of ECA's EU economies are also members of the International Accreditation Forum (IAF) and International Laboratory Accreditation Cooperation (ILAC), although this is not strictly necessary because the EA is already recognized by IAF and ILAC as one of its three Regional Cooperation Bodies. The EU candidate countries—Croatia, FYR Macedonia, and Turkey—have all recently joined. All of the remaining Balkan countries and some CIS countries have signed contracts of cooperation with the EA. Only some of ECA's EU economies, generally the larger ones, are members of IAF and ILAC. This represents a clear focus of these countries toward Europe and their approach of beginning with regional cooperation before starting international cooperation, if at all.

Almost all of ECA's EU member countries except for Bulgaria, Hungary, and Romania have signed MLAs for all scopes and can provide full service to their economies. This means that all of their accreditations are recognized by all signatories of not only the EA MLA, but also the ILAC Mutual Recognition Arrangement (MRA), the IAF MLA, and all of those of their recognized regional organizations in Asia and the Americas. The 61 countries[5] represented in these MRAs and MLAs represent more than 90 percent of the global economy and of total world merchandise trade in 2008—a huge market opportunity. Table 8.4 highlights how comparator countries from China to Brazil to Germany have now all signed MRAs and MLAs.

The EA MLA requires that accreditation bodies function to the highest standards or impartiality, transparency, and competency. Some EU accession countries have managed to join the EA MLA in a relatively short time after setting up new accreditation bodies. The Czech Republic joined in 1998 and the Slovak Republic in 2001. Others have struggled for a few

---

5. This is the number of countries as of August 1, 2010.

TABLE 8.4

Internationally Isolated Accreditation Systems Outside of the EU and Turkey, 2009

	Country	International bodies		Regional bodies	
		International Accreditation Forum (IAF)	International Laboratory Accreditation Cooperation (ILAC)	European co-operation for Accreditation (EA)	Asia Pacific Laboratory Accreditation Cooperation (APLAC) and Pacific Accreditation Cooperation (PAC)
EU countries	Bulgaria	a	a	partial MLA	
	Czech Republic	partial MLA	MRA	MLA	
	Estonia	a	a	MLA	
	Hungary		associate	member	
	Latvia	a	a	MLA	
	Lithuania	a	a	MLA	
	Poland	MLA	MRA	MLA	
	Romania	member	partial MRA	partial MLA	
	Slovak Republic	MLA	MRA	MLA	
	Slovenia	a	MRA	near total MLA	
Balkan countries and Turkey	Albania	member	associate	cooperation	
	Bosnia and Herzegovina		associate	cooperation	
	Croatia		associate	member	
	Macedonia, FYR		associate	member	
	Montenegro		associate	cooperation	
	Serbia		associate	cooperation	
	Turkey	MLA	MRA	MLA	
CIS countries and Georgia	Armenia				
	Azerbaijan				
	Belarus		affiliate		
	Georgia		affiliate		
	Kazakhstan		associate	cooperation	
	Kyrgyz Republic		associate		
	Moldova		affiliate	cooperation	
	Russian Federation		associate	cooperation	partial MRA (APLAC only)
	Tajikistan				
	Turkmenistan				
	Ukraine		affiliate	cooperation	
	Uzbekistan		affiliate		
Comparator countries	Brazil	partial MLA	MRA	partial MLA	
	China	partial MLA	MRA	partial MLA	MRA
	Germany	MLA	MRA	MLA	
	Korea, Rep.	partial MLA	MRA		MRA
	Spain	a	MRA	near total MLA	
	United Kingdom	MLA	MRA	MLA	

Sources: IAF, http://www.iaf.nu; ILAC, http://www.ilac.org; and EA, http://www.european-accreditation.org.

Note: cooperation = contract of cooperation, MRA = mutual recognition arrangement.

a. EA MLA signatories are recognized by the IAF MLA and the ILAC MRA (Mutual Recognition Agreement). "Partial MLA" implies that the MLA covers less than half of the possible fields of accreditation. "Near total MLA" implies that the MLA covers half or more of the possible fields.

years before being able to join or have not yet succeeded. The scopes of Bulgaria and Romania are limited to one and two fields of accreditation, respectively. In fact, Bulgaria's membership in the EA MLA was suspended in March 2007 because the Accreditation Council was not operational and no procedure existed to appeal against an accreditation decision. The agency was reevaluated by EA and was readmitted to the EA MLA in September 2007. Hungary is a special case and has not yet signed the EA MLA.

Within the Balkans, no country has been able to join the EA MLA as of 2009. Moreover, some EU candidate country governments still do not recognize European accreditations. This imposes additional costs not only on trade, but also on domestic investors (box 8.3). It may take 5 to 10 years for some of the other Balkan countries to achieve this, in light of their still embryonic accreditation systems. As a benchmark, Turkey's accreditation body was launched in 2000, and although it received generous initial support from the government and had a large pool of specialized workforce to choose from and strong market demand, it became a signatory of the EA MLA only in 2006.

BOX 8.3

Lack of Recognition of Foreign Accreditation Systems and Extra Costs for Investors

A company in a Balkan country supplies oil and oil products to more than 100 filling stations all over the country and commercializes bulk metal and metal products. The shortage of oil supply motivated the company to set up a plant to produce biodiesel (processed from rapeseeds), which required a high-quality testing laboratory. To meet demands, the company invested €1 million in laboratory infrastructure to support certification and quality control of the fuel. To meet European standards and to have its testing results internationally recognized, the company's laboratory was accredited under international standard ISO/IEC 17025 (ISO and IEC 2005) by the renowned United Kingdom Accreditation Services (UKAS). The cost of accreditation was over £20,000 (maintenance of accreditation has an annual additional cost of £10,000).

However, the company had to reaccredit its sophisticated (world class) laboratory facility under the same national standard by the domestic accreditation body, whose accreditation scheme is not yet internationally recognized. In other words, the government does not recognize the accreditation issued by a prominent accreditation body that was one of the founding signatories of the EA MLA, the ILAC MRA, and the IAF MRA and is recognized and accepted worldwide. According to best practices, a single internationally recognized accreditation should be adequate to secure national seals of approval in all economies, but the country is not bound by those rules because it has not yet signed any MRA.

Accreditation systems of CIS countries and Georgia remain internationally isolated.

Membership in a regional accreditation organization recognized by the two international organizations ILAC and IAF allows for an accelerated access to international practical experience and information exchange. Because the EA has now been granted an official role by the EU, it is doubtful that non-EU member or candidate countries can be granted full EA membership in the near future. As has been mentioned previously, no regional organization for accreditation exists for CIS countries. Consequently, looking at the participation of CIS countries in regional organizations, one sees a rather different picture emerge.

A few CIS countries have contracts of cooperation with EA, which falls quite short of the benefits of full membership. Russia is the only CIS country that is a member of the regional organization responsible for laboratory accreditation in the Asia-Pacific region (the Asia Pacific Laboratory Accreditation Cooperation, or APLAC). This might also be an avenue for Central Asian countries to join a regional body with experienced members. The Central Asian Cooperation for Metrology, Accreditation, and Standardization was initially created as a donor initiative to fill the gap of a regional accreditation body. However, due to insufficient commitment from the Central Asian member institutions, it has been largely inactive and was suspended as a regional organization by the IAF. In the CIS's regional standardization organization, EuroAsian Interstate Council for Standardization, Metrology, and Certification (EASC), a committee on accreditation exists that has terms of references set up. These terms define for the committee tasks similar to the vision and mission of EA and APLAC. However, anecdotal evidence suggests that the work in the committee is focused more on documents than practical activities. Additionally, here again arises the question of exposure to international experience and expertise because the whole group of EASC countries has a transition background.

In terms of international membership, not a single CIS country is a member of the IAF (table 8.4), which deals with certification and inspection. Although most CIS countries are members of ILAC, which deals with laboratories, many are merely affiliate members.

As a result of this isolation, Russia, having signed the APLAC MRA, which covers only laboratory accreditation, is the only CIS country that has signed any MRA or MLA. In all other CIS countries and in Georgia, none of the certificates, calibration reports, test reports, and inspection reports from bodies accredited nationally are recognized outside the CIS, thereby imposing unnecessary duplicate certification and testing and resulting in lost quality-upgrading opportunities in the enterprise sector (box 8.4).

The absence of a regional organization for accreditation in the CIS region and its consequences are obvious. The affiliation with the international organizations shows that some of the countries might try to gain international recognition directly through the international organizations ILAC and IAF. However, with an increasing number of members, the international organizations are overloaded and shift responsibilities to the regional organizations. Recognition directly through international organizations can hardly be successful. Therefore, the accreditation bodies will need a regional organization.

A major barrier for better implementation of international standards into the working habit of the accreditation bodies of the region and for better international integration is again the lack of use of the English language among the staff of the institutions. Although some of the countries divert from Russian as common language, it remains in use and represents an obstacle to a better exchange of experience and information.

Establishing Credible Accreditation Systems in ECA

Credible accreditation systems can be established through organizational reforms of institutions, international recognition of systems, and enhancement of systems' effectiveness through regional cooperation,

Reforming Institutions

CIS countries aiming to establish internationally recognized accreditation systems must first ensure they are structured and governed according to international norms and have a sound legal basis.

In most CIS countries, the national accreditation body is involved in activities that result in conflicts of interests, such as conformity assessment, or is subject to political interference. Both practices are barriers to an independent and impartial accreditation body. However, resistance to restructuring is often strong because public conformity assessment bodies in CIS countries often use their accreditation functions to limit competition in their conformity assessment market. Accreditation can also be a financially lucrative rent-seeking activity when it is imposed by the state as a condition for entry into the conformity assessment market. Restructuring of accreditation bodies can be achieved only through political will.

Kyrgyz Export Capacity Limited by International Isolation of the Country's Accreditation System

In theory, World Trade Organization membership should have helped open new markets for Kyrgyz producers. Yet, most Kyrgyz companies are severely restricted by technical barriers to trade, which stem from regulatory differences in standards as compared to those of most World Trade Organization members and from nonrecognition of Kyrgyz conformity assessment bodies in the area of product testing and certification. Put simply, beyond CIS trading partners and a handful of neighboring countries, no country recognizes product testing and certification performed in the Kyrgyz Republic. This limitation forces exporting companies to retest their products in accredited foreign laboratories, with evident increases in transaction costs and delays that severely undermine their ability to compete. The following examples highlight how export potential can be hampered by the absence of the international recognition of the Kyrgyz accreditation system.

- A U.S. company was considering the option of importing Kyrgyz canned vegetables, dry fruits, and honey. The company would prefer to run testing locally to save on sampling and U.S. testing costs. International consultants funded by a donor agency carried out a preliminary assessment of laboratories in the Kyrgyz Republic capable of providing the types of testing services required by U.S. importers. Their initial findings revealed major deficiencies in the quality testing infrastructure: only one laboratory in Osh Oblast was able to provide the types of testing and measurements required in the United States. However, this laboratory is accredited according to national standards only. Thus, national certification based on test results performed in this laboratory is not recognized by international markets. As a result of the absence of a recognized accreditation scheme, test results performed and certified in the Kyrgyz Republic are not recognized by most markets outside of the CIS. This nonrecognition considerably increases transaction costs and results in delays, which undermine enterprise competitiveness.

- Another U.S. company interested in buying Kyrgyz honey is facing unnecessarily high transaction costs because of lack of local testing laboratories and internationally accredited certifying bodies. In this specific instance, the Kyrgyz producer was unable to certify the quality of its honey against international standards and had to seek certification abroad. As a result, the U.S. company decided to ship samples of honey from the Kyrgyz Republic for testing in the United States before placing the order. Again, delays and unnecessary duplications of testing and certification procedures increased transaction costs, reducing margins for the Kyrgyz firm and the U.S. company.

In a similar instance, an Italian organization representing some 30 Italian companies that produce furniture is providing training to its local distributors to obtain International Organization for Standardization certification. Its objective is to ensure minimum quality of service in distributing "made in Italy" products in the region to maintain a core clientele of wealthy individuals looking for quality and image through foreign label. The representative firm tried to identify, without success, an internationally accredited certification body in the region to drive down its certification costs. As a result of the unavailability of such internationally accredited bodies capable of providing conformity assessment services at relatively low cost, the distributors are forced to seek certification abroad or obtain certification locally through an internationally accredited certification body that can send a pool of professionals to carry out an International Organization for Standardization assessment of each distributor.

Source: Lorenzo Constantino, personal communication.

Importantly, there must be a single national body with accreditation functions. In a number of ECA countries, there are parallel systems of authorization. Conformity assessment bodies must be authorized by government agencies or ministries to operate in specific areas such as health or the environment. This practice should be abolished, and accreditation should be the only practice used to evaluate the technical competence of conformity assessment bodies.

Good governance is particularly important for accreditation bodies, because their effectiveness depends on transparency and impartiality. Stakeholder participation in formulating a national accreditation strategy, in the governing board of the body and in technical and advisory committees, is important. Particular attention should also be paid to implementing mechanisms to foster impartiality (box 8.5).

Finally, institutional autonomy is important for the development of an effective accreditation body that can respond to market demand and changing international accreditation guidelines. Accreditation legislation should not be too prescriptive in the procedures, workforce, services, and organizational system used in the accreditation body. These constraints make it difficult for accreditation bodies to adapt to changing market requirements and result in inefficiencies. Administrative structure, accreditation processes, and workforce issues should be addressed by the institution's internal regulations instead. The legislation should not reinvent the wheel, but simply make reference to international accreditation guidelines and standards such as ISO/IEC 17011:2004, *Conformity assessment—General requirements for accreditation bodies accrediting conformity assessment bodies*. National accreditation standards should be eliminated to avoid confusion in the market.

Achieving International Recognition of National Accreditation Systems

By joining mutual recognition arrangements, CIS and Balkan countries will be able to expand their trade opportunities.

Most Balkan and CIS countries in ECA have yet to sign an MRA. As a result, none of the tests, certifications, measurements, and inspections covered under the national accreditation system are recognized abroad, and exporters face technical barriers to trade. These countries do not automatically recognize the accreditations of highly reputable signatories of MRAs, meaning that imports from those countries are subject to retesting and recertification, often using less reliable methods than the exporting country.

For Balkan countries, signing the European regional EA MLA should be the priority. This MLA is recognized by signatories of international MRAs. CIS countries can either join the EA MLA, as several countries

---

BOX 8.5

Twelve Ways to Ensure Impartiality in Accreditation Bodies

The twelve ways are as follows:

1. IAF and ILAC undertake international peer evaluation and surveillances to ensure that accreditation standards are followed.

2. The Advisory Board initiates that representatives of all interested parties control the national accreditation body work, and the Steering Board performs the task of financial supervision and monitoring of the business processes to ensure that no corruption will be committed in any step of the process.

3. The Director is permanently contracted and has to be free of conflicts of interests. He or she also has to undertake annual management reviews.

4. The Accreditation Committee makes decisions about findings with experts that are independent of assessments.

5. Independent national accreditation body experts give technical advice to the Technical Committees.

6. The Appeals Board has a problem-solving function. It deals with the solution of appeals, complaints, and disputes by means of mediators.

7. The Quality Manager is responsible for internal audits, done by auditors who are independent of their workplace.

8. The Administration archives all relevant records for traceability of results and decisions, creates data back-up systems, and maintains a controlled quality management system.

9. The Case Manager permanently monitors the performance of assessment teams.

10. Within the training system, it must be ensured that the ISO 19011 requirements are fulfilled.

11. The Assessor team should use the "4-eyes" principle. The assessors themselves will be evaluated by clients and observers (witnessing) and also must create traceability by records of all findings to the data's origin.

12. The certification bodies are checked by a third-party evaluation of competence and by annual surveillance visits. Laboratories are tested by periodic proficiency tests. They all must ensure complete transparency of tests, inspection, and certification reports.

Source: Authors.

outside of Europe have managed to do, or go through international IAF and ILAC MRAs. A first step for CIS countries would be to become members of IAF and ILAC.

CIS and Balkan countries will take several years to develop an internationally harmonized accreditation system, and this process will require government funding.

The process of building up an accreditation system takes time. Organizational structures need to be changed, and personnel need to be trained, gain experience, and develop new working habits. All of these necessities cannot be done through two or three seminars. Although most CIS countries offer accreditation to international standards on paper, a closer examination of accreditation processes often reveals poor interpretations of the standard. The process is complex and should be regarded as a long-term project:

- A first step is to conduct a gap analysis. An example of a gap analysis roadmap that identifies problems linked to technical, administrative, political, and external relations issues can be found in appendix D.

- A strategy and business plan for the national accreditation body should then be developed on the basis of the gap analysis and the national quality infrastructure strategy. The accreditation strategy should be a living document that is regularly adjusted. The business plan should be based on a market analysis for accreditation. The strategy and action plan should be oriented toward the fulfilment of international standards, that is, ISO/IEC 17011. This international standard provides all the requirements for the organizational structure, management, and procedures of an accreditation body.

During its early stages of development, the national accreditation body should receive government support. The funding required to develop a basic internationally recognized accreditation system ranges up to US$2 million over five years. Funds are needed for expertise transfer and development of a pool of assessors and sometimes for information technology equipment and software for databases. International experts are expensive and must be paid in foreign currency. At the same time, participation in regional and international organizations' activities is an absolute necessity, and travel costs are high. Travel is also necessary to attend training sessions offered by foreign accreditation bodies in high-income countries. In the absence of an established customer base, it will be difficult for an accreditation body to be self-sustaining through accreditation fees, and it will require government financial support, particularly to train technical personnel. In the long run, accreditation bodies should be able to cover their costs by their incomes in most markets, although this could still be a challenge in small economies.

ECA's EU member states also need to continue strengthening their national accreditation systems.

All EU member states have internationally recognized accreditation bodies, but there are still possible areas of improvement among accession countries. Multinational certification bodies operating in ECA's EU member states often continued to seek accreditation from EU-15[6] countries long after the national accreditation body was internationally recognized through an MLA. This approach points to certain doubts from the international business community about the quality of the national accreditation systems. Moreover, several of the EU's ECA countries have yet to sign an MLA for all scopes of accreditation.

Building Technical Capacity through Regional Cooperation

There is no substitute to regional cooperation for building technical capacity.

Regional cooperation is the most important step toward the general goal of international recognition. Although accreditation procedures and standards are extensively documented, managing an accreditation body and conducting accreditations cannot be learned from theoretical knowledge only. Regional accreditation organizations allow young accreditation bodies to learn from mature bodies through informal contacts as well as through the capacity-building and knowledge exchange activities typically hosted by these organizations. They can cooperate with other accreditation bodies at similar stages of development to organize joint training activities or to find solutions to common problems. Regional accreditation organizations also provide the framework for monitoring progress in the accreditation system and organize proficiency testing schemes. Joining regional accreditation organizations has important benefits over participating in international organizations such as ILAC and IAF because the latter are focused on political issues related to accreditations rather than the exchange of practical experience.

---

6. These countries are Austria, Belgium, Denmark, Finland, France, Germany, Greece, Ireland, Italy, Luxembourg, the Netherlands, Portugal, Spain, Sweden and the United Kingdom.

Balkan countries can extensively benefit from knowledge transfer by participating in EA.

Membership in EA can allow Balkan countries to benefit from the expertise of the stronger European accreditation bodies as well as the recent experience of accreditation bodies of the EU's accession countries. Although full membership in EA is not possible for non-EU candidate countries, Balkan countries appear to be on their way to eventual EU candidacy status.

The absolute prerequisite for participation in EA is a strong knowledge of the English language. Although much has already been accomplished in the Balkan countries, they and the accreditation bodies should require and support their staff in developing the necessary language skills.

CIS countries must decide on integration with the region or dispersion into other regions.

CIS countries are most in need of knowledge transfer. Their accreditation systems are the least developed and they have had relatively less exposure to other accreditation bodies in regional and international organizations.

The lack of a regional accreditation organization is the most significant obstacle to the development of the accreditation systems in CIS countries. In contrast to the Balkan countries, CIS countries cannot rely on an organization like EA that covers their geographic area. Some of the Central Asian countries have started to meet regularly to exchange their experience and conduct joint activities such as proficiency testing schemes. But these activities are being coordinated by foreign experts and cannot be a substitute to an internationally recognized regional organization formed through the political will of its members.

There are two strategic options for CIS countries: (a) establishment of a new regional organization or (b) membership in existing organizations outside of their region (APLAC and EA). Both options have their advantages and disadvantages:

1. Establishment of a new regional organization:

• Advantages:

   ▷ Geographic proximity would enable dynamic participation.

   ▷ The use of Russian as a common first or second language would also enhance participation.

▷ The EASC already exists as a suborganization to the CIS and could be used for such an initiative.

▷ A regional organization could be used not only for knowledge transfer, but also for better leverage of complementary regional accreditation resources (see the following section, titled "Enhancing the System's Effectiveness through Regional Cooperation").

• Disadvantages:

▷ There is a risk of failure. The unsuccessful experience of Central Asia's recent attempt at creating a regional organization, Central Asian Cooperation for Metrology, Accreditation, and Standardization, shows that the political willingness to integrate among certain CIS countries is rather low. When foreign donor funding ran out, cooperation almost stopped.

▷ The resources and the network externalities from a regional organization with a very small number of member countries might be limited. There are only 12 EASC members. Regional accreditation organizations in Europe, the Americas, and East Asia all have more than 20 members.

▷ A new regional organization would lack a well-integrated stronger partner that could deliver necessary expertise and methodology. Such an organization would require outside support. The situation would be aggravated by the different paces of reform toward the international standards system in the region. Behind the different paces stand different goals, intentions, and political support. The different goals could negatively influence international cooperation.

2. Membership in an existing regional organization:

• Advantages:

▷ CIS countries would benefit from the experience of a large pool of strong, well-integrated accreditation bodies and from a plethora of capacity-building activities.

• Disadvantages:

▷ CIS countries may not be able to ever gain full membership in EA or APLAC. EA has been given an official function by the EU, so it is unlikely to allow non-EU member or candidate countries to gain full membership. APLAC is open to Asia Pacific Economic Cooperation (APEC) members and grants membership to non-APEC countries only on an exceptional basis. Within ECA, only Russia is a member of APEC.

▷ English is the lingua franca of existing regional accreditation organizations, and yet, its use is often lacking among accreditation staff
and management in CIS countries.

Enhancing the System's Effectiveness through Regional Cooperation

ECA countries can also cooperate on a regional accreditation to complement each others' capabilities. A self-contained accreditation system is
not feasible in a small economy. When the market for accreditation is
limited, it is not financially sustainable and, thus, is expensive to run for
the government. Another bottleneck is the availability of independent
technical experts for the audits. In small markets, it is difficult to find
experts as assessors that are independent of the organizations to be
accredited. Furthermore, the accreditation bodies must conduct proficiency tests. Given a small number of conformity assessment bodies, the
implementation of these activities could become a difficulty. Most countries of the Balkans, the Caucasus, and Central Asia face these difficulties.

Regional cooperation can help address these challenges. Options
range from relying entirely on foreign accreditation to sharing accreditation resources:

- A first, rather radical option is for small countries to forgo a national
accreditation body and to rely on accreditation from internationally
recognized bodies in neighbouring countries. This option is possible
under EU regulations on accreditation and market surveillance and
could be an effective solution for small Balkan countries that could
rely on Austria, Greece, Slovenia, or Turkey. The main challenge
would be the language barrier. Although theoretically possible, this
option is unlikely. For reasons of national pride and national independence, countries are unlikely to decide to abandon their national
accreditation bodies altogether.

- A second option is a regional accreditation body, such as the Joint
Accreditation System of Australia and New Zealand. A regional body,
in which each country would retain national representatives, could
pool expertise and resources of neighboring countries. A regional body
could face significant political obstacles.

- A third option could be based on the exchange of technical experts.
Technical experts having received specialized training in one country
could join an assessment team in another.

- A fourth option could be the coordinated specialization of accreditation bodies. An accreditation body could subcontract some or most activities of the accreditation process to another stronger, more recognized body.

References

AEPLAC (Armenian-European Policy and Legal Advice Centre). 2007. "Assessment of Institutional Standing in the Fields of Standardisation, Accreditation, Conformity Assessment, Metrology, and Market Surveillance." Report, AEPLAC, Yerevan.

ISO (International Organization for Standardization). 2006. *ISO Members 2005.* Geneva: ISO.

ISO (International Organization for Standardization) and IEC (International Electrotechnical Commission). 2004. *ISO/IEC 17011:2004: Conformity assessment—General requirements for accreditation bodies accrediting conformity assessment bodies.* Geneva: ISO and IEC

———. 2005. *ISO/IEC 17025:2005 (E): General requirements for the competence of testing and calibration laboratories.* Geneva: ISO and IEC.

World Bank. 2008. *Bulgaria Investment Climate Assessment.* Washington, DC: World Bank.

———. 2009. "Croatia's EU Convergence Report: Reaching and Sustaining Higher Rates of Economic Growth." Report 48879-HR, World Bank, Washington, DC.

CHAPTER 9

Conclusion: Moving Forward

"Your task is not to foresee the future, but to enable it."

—Antoine de Saint-Exupéry, *The Wisdom of the Sands* (1948)

▷ **Good governance and institutions—lacking conflicts of interest—are essential for an effective, internationally recognized national quality infrastructure (NQI).**

▷ **Countries in Eastern Europe and Central Asia (ECA) can become more competitive by abolishing mandatory standards developed by national standards bodies, adopting a system of technical regulations developed by policy-making bodies with relevant areas of responsibility, and harmonizing standards with regional and international trade partners.**

▷ **ECA's metrology systems desperately need better equipment and infrastructure, but such efforts must be accompanied by upgrading human resources, implementing quality systems, and achieving international traceability. An incremental approach—one laboratory at a time—avoids repetition of mistakes.**

▷ **ECA countries can build solid accreditation systems only through regional cooperation. Members of the Commonwealth of Independent States (CIS) must address their lack of a regional accreditation body.**

> **Government financial and technical support can help small and medium enterprises (SMEs) upgrade quality but must be carefully designed and delivered.**

> **ECA countries can leverage support from a number of international institutions, including the World Bank, but this is best achieved when national quality strategies put stakeholders in the driver's seat.**

Incentives for Reform in Eastern Europe and Central Asia

Every country in Eastern Europe and Central Asia (ECA) except Turkmenistan has varying degrees of incentives to adopt international standards for national quality infrastructure (NQI):

- Many are already European Union (EU) members.

- Several aim to join the EU or to negotiate free trade agreements with it.

- Others have only recently joined the World Trade Organization (WTO).

- Many are engaged in WTO accession talks (map 9.1).

With a few exceptions, these four groups roughly correspond to the extent of reform in ECA countries. All of ECA's EU members have replaced *Gosstandart* systems with the international model. Some, such as Bulgaria and Romania, have not yet fully harmonized their NQI with EU standards, but their goals are clear and well within reach. Among the three EU candidate countries, Croatia and the former Yugoslav Republic of Macedonia are implementing serious reforms as part of accession efforts, which require harmonizing NQI. The third country, Turkey, has already completed most NQI reforms (box 9.1).

Outside these two EU-oriented groupings, ECA's WTO members are at various stages of reform, with latecomers such as Ukraine still having a long way to go. WTO observer countries, on the road to WTO accession negotiations, are a mixed bag. Some, such as Uzbekistan, have undertaken almost no reforms. Others, such as Albania and Serbia, have moved further ahead with a clear eye on greater trade integration with the EU. Turkmenistan remains in its own category, with no near-term prospects of joining the WTO and, hence, few external incentives for reform.

MAP 9.1

Incentives for Most ECA Countries to Reform Their Infrastructure for Quality, 2011

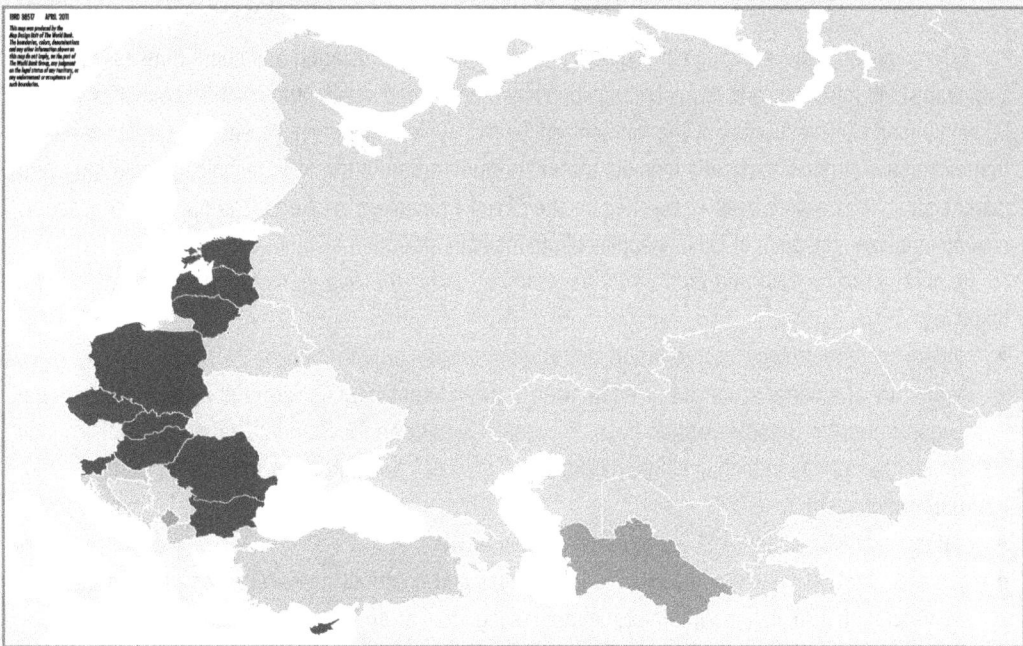

■ EU member   ▨ EU candidate   WTO member only   ▨ WTO observer only   ▨ no EU or WTO affiliation

Sources: World Trade Organization, http://www.wto.org; European Union, http://europa.eu.

Improving Governance for National Quality Infrastructure

A number of ECA countries—most EU members—have harmonized their NQI with international norms. But 20 years after the breakup of the former Soviet Union, others continue to operate much closer to the model developed under central planning based on top-down decision making, limited stakeholder involvement, technological rigidity, and mandatory technical regulations. NQI can benefit from sound governance and institutions and from organization and coordination.

Sound Governance and Institutions for Modern, Effective National Quality Infrastructure.

An effective NQI rests on principles of transparency, openness, consensus, impartiality, and technical credibility. These principles depend on institutional rather than technical factors—and if they are ignored, no

EU Accession Requirement of Harmonizing of NQI

The EU's so-called *New Approach* and *Global Approach* to standardization and conformity assessment, European standardization, and mutual recognition have contributed significantly to the development of the EU single market. The success of the harmonized EU NQI system has played a vital role in ensuring the free movement of goods between member states. Harmonization of the NQI, technical regulations, and market surveillance activities is codified in the "Free Movement of Goods" chapter of the *acquis communautaire*—the body of EU law applicable to member states.

Requirements for NQI and conformity assessment under the *acquis communautaire* include the following:

- Independent metrology, accreditation, and standardization organizations
- Voluntary standards prepared or adapted in a transparent way as required by the International Organization for Standardization (ISO), European Committee for Standardization (CEN), European Committee for Electrotechnical Standardization (CENELEC), and European Telecommunications Standardization Institute (ETSI).
- Adoption of 85 percent of EU harmonized standards
- An accreditation system compatible with the rules and practices of the European co-operation for Accreditation (EA), in line with the EA mutual recognition arrangement
- A metrology system compatible with the rules and practices of the European Association of National Metrology Institutes (EURAMET) and the European Cooperation in Legal Metrology (WELMEC)
- A national metrology institute that has signed the International Bureau of Weights and Measures (BIPM) mutual recognition agreement and that has entries in the Calibration and Measurement Capabilities (CMCs) tables
- A policy on traceability compatible with the International Laboratory Accreditation Cooperation (ILAC) guidelines
- Metrological inspection and market surveillance systems compatible with rules defined by the International Organization of Legal Metrology (OIML)

Source: Authors.

amount of staff training or technological investment can create a modern NQI. They depend on the overall structure and governance of the NQI.

For EU members as well as Turkey, high-quality governance and legislation for NQI have been established and mostly implemented. Many EU candidate and potential candidate countries have made good progress in improving the governance of their NQI. They have restructured institutional setups and reoriented them to meet the requirements of EU and international standards. But the situation is very different in CIS countries. Some are adapting the governance of their NQI according to international rules, while others are basically maintaining systems established in the Soviet era.

*As a first step, many CIS countries need to restructure their
national quality infrastructure.*

Most CIS countries have either a monolithic NQI or an NQI integrated
with political institutions. Removing political interference and conflicts of
interests requires providing more autonomy to NQI institutions—a goal
best achieved by establishing independent institutions. For an effective
NQI, countries should adhere to the following steps at the very least:

- The accreditation body must be independent from other NQI institutions.

- Scientific metrology, accreditation, and standardization bodies should
  not be involved in developing technical regulations, mandatory standards, or other regulatory activities.

- These bodies should be free from political interference and have the
  autonomy to respond to market needs and represent their countries in
  relevant international organizations.

- In countries with limited histories of good governance and public
  management, standardization should be independent from certification, testing, and scientific metrology.

*As a second step, principles of good governance
must be applied.*

Though upgrading the NQI requires addressing technical gaps linked to
technology and worker skills, that action alone will not create an effective
NQI capable of achieving international recognition. Nor is there a technocratic solution to developing an NQI over time that responds to economic and social needs. Involving a broad range of stakeholders in
decision making about the NQI and providing them with some degree of
political autonomy is a first step at achieving good governance. Coordinating the infrastructure for quality at the national level is also important
in countries where market demand is too underdeveloped and civil society too weak to articulate the needs of the economy. Coordination is
especially important at the early stages of NQI development and when
critical decisions need to be made. An NQI's structure, governance, and
functions must be reflected in national legislation—with the legislation
reflecting WTO principles to reduce technical barriers to trade, guidelines
for major international NQI bodies, and the main elements of a national
NQI strategy.

In Armenia, in 2010 the government, together with the World Bank
and other donors (the European Commission and the German agency

Physikalisch-Technische Bundesanstalt), organized a workshop so that stakeholders in the NQI and international experts could discuss the differences between the Armenian system and international best practices and could identify options for convergence. The workshop led to a Quality Infrastructure Reform Strategy that defines clear timelines, reforms, and investments.

Involving the main private and public stakeholders in the governance of national quality infrastructure institutions generates more demand-oriented institutions.

The composition and terms of reference for boards or councils of scientific metrology, accreditation, and standardization institutions should reflect the need for stakeholder involvement. Too often, as shown in this book, the boards or councils of these institutions—especially if they are government institutions—include only representatives of ministries. Because these institutions are generally established by legislation, it follows that the legislation governing such institutions should be reviewed and aligned with international best practices.[1] Such reviews should take into account the following issues:

- The composition of the board or council should reflect the beneficiaries of the outputs of the NQI institution. For example, if industry is the main beneficiary of standards, most board or council members should come from industry. They should not be mere representatives but, rather, captains of industry—individuals with an important power base in the country's relevant industries who know how industry functions. They should explain to the board or council the needs of industry and promote the NQI institution's role and services in industry at a high level—that is, in their own boardrooms. Board or council members can be appointed by the relevant minister, but only after proper consultations with stakeholders. The number of members should be manageable—preferably 10 to 16—to optimize the board or council's effectiveness. The relevant minister can appoint the chair of the board or council, but the chief executive of the NQI institution should not hold an office on the board or council even though he or she should be a full member.

- The board or council should have the authority to determine the strategy of the NQI institution. Checks and balances can easily be included to ensure that this strategy is aligned with relevant government policies, such as trade policy. The board or council will usually be account-

1. See, for example, OIML (2004).

able to the relevant minister or even to parliament. If the board or council does not directly appoint the director of the institution, it should have a major say in who is chosen. Moreover, the director should have a mandate and should not be susceptible to changes in government administrations. Given the learning curve involved in managing an NQI institution, frequent changes in leadership reduce technical capacity and institutional memory.

- For regional and international recognition and for correct understanding and implementation of international standards, NQI management should have good knowledge of the English language. Language barriers have been a huge obstacle to the development of internationally harmonized NQI. They hamper participation in regional and international events and make it difficult to understand international standards, thereby undermining their implementation.

- Boards and councils should be given fiduciary responsibility for the NQI institution, preferably within the framework of an approved government policy if it remains a government institution. It should not be necessary to obtain approval from ministry officials for normal expenditures. When an annual budget has been approved by government, the board or council should be allowed to exercise full fiduciary control.

- Legislation should be enabling, relegating technical details to a lower-level or secondary legislation. Examples include legal metrology legislation that authorizes the relevant minister to promulgate regulations or decrees for specific measuring equipment to be used in trade, health, or law enforcement that would contain the technical details with which such equipment must comply. This relegation allows for more rapid updating of technical requirements, while enabling legislation does not do so.

- International best practice often requires an NQI institution to establish a forum where stakeholders can provide input and recommendations for the government and the board or council to consider about the institution's outputs and operations. Forum members may include representatives of industry, importers, academia, authorities, buyers, and consumer organizations. Such a forum should not have any governance authority over the NQI institution, but should provide its board or council and the relevant minister with appropriate advice on policy and process.

Such reforms are important even if the funding for NQI institutions is largely provided by government. The reforms give the main stakeholders of NQI institutions a strong say in their activities and, thus, are much more likely to ensure that the institutions attain their proper place in industry and among the authorities. Following these recommendations will ensure that the board or council is effective and that the institution operates in accordance with sound business principles and meets the needs of its stakeholders.

Organization and Coordination for Quality Infrastructure

A national coordination framework can help ECA countries develop infrastructure for quality.

Many ECA countries have developed or reformed their NQI in unplanned or uncoordinated ways, leading to imbalances in the system. For example, some established large metrology institutes with capacities that did not correspond to the demand from testing and calibration laboratories. In some cases, there was no demand for the institutes' new calibration services because technical regulations still required Povjerka (the Soviet era mandatory metrological verification system).

The web of relationships between NQI institutions and policy making bodies makes it difficult to operate without coordination. Laws point out what area is regulated by whom through technical regulations. Markets are regulated from a technical point of view by technical regulations prepared and enforced by regulating bodies. In turn, regulators prepare technical regulations using standards prepared by standardization organizations. But most of these regulations depend on measurements performed by testing or calibration laboratories. Hence, trained and certified inspectors are needed to implement technical regulations. Both measurement laboratories and inspection bodies must be accredited by the accreditation institute. In addition, the accuracy and international acceptance of the measurements performed by testing and analysis laboratories must be guaranteed by the metrology institute, whose staff members also generally serve as technical assessors during the laboratory accreditation process. This system is rather complicated and sophisticated.

In high-income economies, all coordination is performed by interest groups representing industry. These groups form technical committees for standardization, prepare draft regulations, identify available measurement infrastructure (including universities), and establish needed testing facilities if none exist in the country. Such groups stay in touch with all elements of the conformity assessment system because they need these activities to be competitive and survive.

In many ECA countries, particularly in the Balkan and CIS countries, quality awareness is developing slowly. Neither business associations nor consumer protection organizations are established in a way that allows enterprises or consumers to adequately express their interests. As long as these actors do not demand improvements in NQI services, the institutions have no motivation to change. The only such incentive could arise from government decisions.

Though coordination could be left to government, most ECA countries would benefit from formal structures to receive stakeholder inputs.

ECA countries typically have a ministry or department responsible for funding and overseeing the NQI. Processes should be established to involve stakeholders in an NQI strategy. They can take the form of a national quality council that identifies needs and articulates a response strategy. This council could also provide a platform for gathering and disseminating information and for discussing and solving problems related to the preparation and implementation of technical regulations and standards.

   Such a coordinating body should ideally be in the private sector, but in many countries, this is not possible because industry is underdeveloped and does not have the resources needed to develop one. The government can fulfill the coordination role until industry is mature enough to sustain it, but doing so requires considerable expertise and continuity. Stakeholders in a national quality council should include industry (especially clients of the NQI), consumers, universities, NQI institutions, and policy-making bodies and agencies (figure 9.1).

FIGURE 9.1

One Approach to Coordinating the National Quality Infrastructure

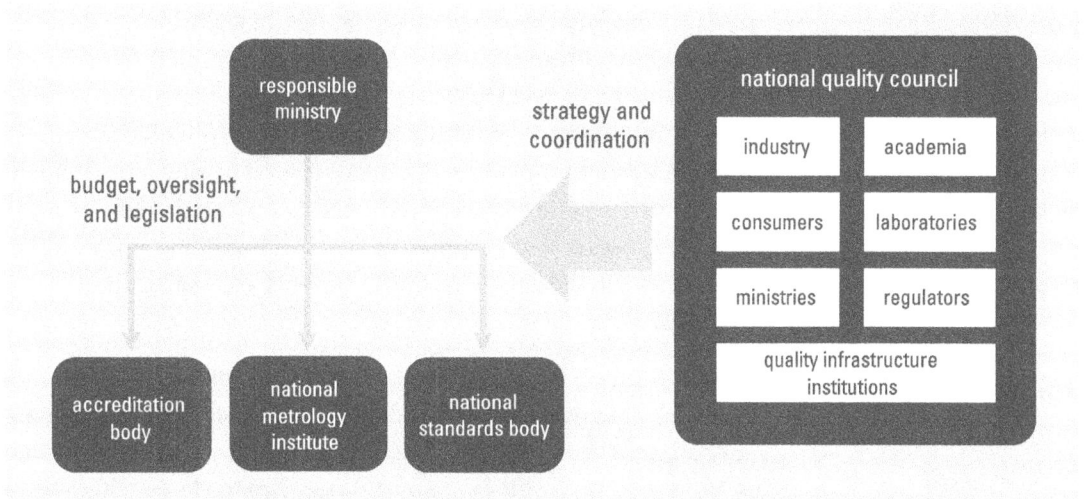

Source: Authors.

Georgia's recently formed quality council has 28 members, including the minister of economic development and several other high-level officials from the ministry responsible for the NQI. The council also includes high-level representatives from other ministries, such as the ministry of energy and ministry of agriculture, as well as heads of various NQI institutions, consumer groups, and private sector representatives.

The tasks of a national quality board or council should be defined by the stakeholders, but should include coordinating and maintaining implementation of a national strategy for the NQI. Strategies for individual NQI institutions can then be derived from this national strategy and be translated into specific plans or programs. In addition, a national quality board or council can be used to coordinate and facilitate cooperation and integration among regional organizations.

Investing in the National Quality Infrastructure

Investments include those in infrastructure and skills and World Bank projects.

Investments in Infrastructure and Skills

Investments in infrastructure and skills are often needed when a strategy for quality reform and upgrading has been developed. In ECA, there are four main sources of funding for NQI upgrading:

- *National budget support*. Few countries provide such funding, and it tends to be limited and short lived.

- *Projects prepared and implemented by donor countries* (such as those sponsored by Germany through its national metrology institute, Physikalisch-Technische Bundesanstalt). Most of these projects have small budgets (less than US$1 million) and are used to transfer expertise through training and consulting programs. Such projects sometimes provide needed, useful funds for calibrating or repairing measurement equipment. These funds are rarely used to buy equipment or build laboratories—except when projects focus on building up a specific aspect of the NQI, such as technical capacity in a particular field of metrology.

- *EU projects*. These projects generally cost several millions of dollars and provide considerable expertise and, often, EU-made equipment to the beneficiaries. The EU also sponsors twinning projects, in which its NQI institutions partner with their non-EU counterparts in ECA, providing them with ongoing technical assistance.

- *World Bank projects.* These are typically lending projects with multiple components in which the NQI component can range from US$5 million–US$40 million. Recent examples include projects in Albania, the Kyrgyz Republic, FYR Macedonia, Moldova, and Turkey. These projects provide equipment, expertise, specialized premises, and public awareness campaigns.

The budgets of these projects should be viewed in perspective of the total costs of developing an internationally harmonized NQI (table 9.1). In FYR Macedonia, a key benefit has been to help meet the requirements of the EU *acquis communautaire* (box 9.2).

World Bank Projects to Strengthen National Quality Infrastructure

World Bank projects to strengthen NQI generally cover metrology, standardization, and accreditation. Some include financing for programs to stimulate demand for certification among SMEs. Metrology is usually supported by financing calibration; expertise transfer; and procurement of equipment, software, books, repairs, specialized laboratory furniture, and new premises for laboratories. Similarly, standardization is supported by providing funds for expertise transfer and procurement of information technology equipment, software, books, and translation of standards. The main areas of accreditation support include expertise transfer, procurement of information technology and training equipment, software, and books, as well as activities to expand the pool of assessors. Most of the

TABLE 9.1

Approximate Costs and Time for Developing a National Quality Infrastructure

Component	Investment cost range (US$ millions)	Development time range for international harmonization (years)
National metrology institute	5–200	15
Legal metrology	0.5–5.0	5
Secondary calibration and testing laboratories	2–500	2–15
National accreditation body	0.5–2.0	5
National standards body	0.5–2.0	5

Source: Authors.

projects include public awareness campaigns to increase stakeholders' knowledge about the infrastructure for quality. Some projects also support country project implementation units by providing funds for expertise transfer and procurement of information technology and office equipment, software, and books.

These Bank projects provide major direct benefits, including establishing needed infrastructure, expertise, strategies, policies, action plans, visions, long-term sustainability, international recognition, contacts, and project implementation experience. There are also indirect benefits. Most important are coordination among NQI institutions, increased awareness and coordination in relevant ministries and regulatory bodies, capacity building, and accelerated development.

BOX 9.2

Bringing FYR Macedonia Closer to EU Membership by Upgrading Its National Quality Infrastructure

The October 2009 EU Progress Report (Commission of the European Communities 2009) highlights gaps in FYR Macedonia's quality infrastructure. The chapter on the free movement of goods under the *acquis communautaire* states that "administrative infrastructure and capacity are still inadequate for full and efficient implementation and enforcement of the legislation" (Commission of the European Communities 2009, 32). In particular, the report states that the national Bureau of Metrology "does not have enough laboratory equipment or trained staff to function efficiently" (Commission of the European Communities 2009, 32) and refers to the limited progress made by the national standards body toward full membership in the European Committee for Standardization (CEN) and European Committee for Electrotechnical Standardization (CENELEC).

The World Bank's Business Environment Reform and Institutional Strengthening (BERIS) project provides financing for equipment, training, and expertise transfer services. Many of these efforts are linked to the requirements for EU accession listed in the EU Progress Report. Fulfilling these obligations requires establishing standardization, metrology, and accreditation institutions that function according to principles spelled out by EU organizations in these fields—CEN and CENELEC, together with the European Association of National Metrology Institutes (EURAMET) and European Co-operation for Accreditation (EA).

For example, FYR Macedonia's national standards body must fulfill the membership requirements of the European Committee for Standardization, including a document management system provided under BERIS. The committee is scheduled to conduct a preappraisal of the standards body in October 2010. BERIS also provides support to train assessors of FYR Macedonia's accreditation institute based on EU guidelines. Without trained assessors, the institute's accreditations cannot be recognized in the EU—a condition for EU accession.

Source: Authors.

Project Implementation Challenges

Although each country has its own ecosystem for the NQI, many common challenges arise when implementing NQI projects. The main challenges are a lack of properly maintained laboratories, land for new premises, appropriate staff, foreign language skills, and procurement experience.

External problems also occur, including shortages in metrology in terms of measurement equipment, number and adequacy of producers, suitable training organizations, and availability of good consultants. When these problems are overcome—including solving potential problems with customs for equipment and installing it in appropriate laboratories—a third set of problems emerges. These are operational problems related to the maintenance, repair, and traceability (calibrations, international comparisons, and proficiency testing) of delicate measurement equipment.

Though not directly related to NQI projects, another set of challenges includes corruption, weak governance, lack of awareness about international projects, favoritism, and internal politics—especially for coalition governments.

The Way Forward

ECA countries can reform their national quality infrastructure by moving from

- Systems based on technical regulations to systems based on voluntary standards

- Systems based on state ownership and control of NQI to systems based on public and private ownership

- Systems operating in isolation to regionally and internationally integrated systems and reliance on foreign services when possible

The first step toward establishing an internationally recognized NQI that supports industrial competitiveness is ensuring good governance and creating institutions that lack conflicts of interest. To achieve this, some ECA countries will need to restructure their NQI and create independent, transparent institutions that hear the voices of all stakeholders in the system. An NQI cannot exist without government support. ECA countries can take several approaches to upgrading their NQI and so enhance their products, processes, and services and ease technical barriers to trade.

A national coordination framework can help all ECA countries develop their NQI. Many countries in the region have developed or reformed their NQI in an unplanned, uncoordinated way—resulting in imbalances in the system. Although coordination could be left to government, most ECA countries could also benefit from formal structures to receive input from stakeholders.

A second condition for an NQI that both serves economic growth and provides useful services is to abolish mandatory standards developed by a national standards body and streamline technical regulations. When mandatory standards have been abolished and technical regulations minimized, NQI institutions can support business competitiveness in ECA. Harmonizing national standards with regional and international trade partners is the next step toward supporting global market integration, though such efforts are usually highly technical and do not happen overnight. Still, improving trade opportunities and knowledge inflows requires adopting regional and international standards over national standards.

Many CIS countries are particularly in need of restructuring their NQI. Removing political interference and conflicts of interests requires providing more autonomy to institutions that support this infrastructure. These countries should, at minimum, do the following:

- Accreditation bodies must be independent from all other NQI institutions.

- Metrology, accreditation, and standardization bodies should not be involved in the development of technical regulations, mandatory standards, or other regulatory activities.

- Metrology, accreditation, and standardization bodies should be free from political interference and be able to respond to market needs and to represent their countries in relevant international organizations.

To strengthen metrology, countries will need to upgrade equipment and infrastructure. But such efforts will be fruitless unless human resources are improved, quality control systems are implemented, and international traceability is achieved. An incremental approach, working with one laboratory at a time in the national metrology institute, avoids repetition of mistakes. Accreditation bodies can also be modernized, particularly if Caucasus and Central Asian countries cooperate.

A survey of market needs is an essential but often ignored first step toward developing a metrology plan. As they broaden their measurement capabilities, ECA's national metrology institutes will need to invest in upgrading human capacity, equipment, and infrastructure. Any upgrading should be done in the context of harmonization with international norms for NQI, including the adoption of relevant management processes.

Still, across ECA countries, expensive equipment operated by the most scientifically advanced personnel is useless unless it is operated under international quality assurance guidelines. When institutions have been reformed on the basis of international norms, capacity building and technological upgrading can be targeted to individual aspects of NQI to achieve quick wins and exhibit demonstrable effects. The end goal should be an internationally harmonized NQI that responds to the needs of society without duplicating the role of the private sector.

Most ECA countries can build solid accreditation systems only through regional cooperation. But CIS countries must address their lack of a regional accreditation body. To reduce operating costs, small ECA economies can join forces to develop and share complementary calibration capabilities. ECA's EU member states also need to continue strengthening their national accreditation systems while supporting regional collaboration.

In many ECA countries, a supply-side approach alone is insufficient for developing a market for quality services. Many firms in the region are unaware of their quality needs, face financial barriers, and are reluctant to approach NQI institutions because, for decades, they have associated them with state control, rent-seeking, and corruption. So, for systems to be sustainable, governments can support the demand for quality services by SMEs by providing financial and technical assistance—though this will require carefully designed delivery mechanisms.

ECA countries can leverage support for these efforts from a number of international institutions, including the World Bank. But these goals are best achieved when they are part of national quality strategies that put stakeholders in the driver's seat.

As ECA countries implement and upgrade their NQI, they must decide how to cater to technological needs; mitigate environmental, health, and safety concerns; and avoid unnecessary technical barriers to trade. The road to an internationally recognized NQI is long, but the experiences of new EU members show that no obstacle is too large.

ECA policy makers face decisions about what type of NQI will best enable their countries' further engagement with the globally integrated economy. Policy makers also face challenges about both how and how quickly to transform the systems they have inherited and about how to restructure conformity assessment infrastructure. These efforts must reflect the varying economic, political, and historical contexts of ECA countries.

References

Commission of the European Communities. 2009. "The Former Yugoslav Republic of Macedonia 2009 Progress Report." Commission of the European Communities, Luxembourg.

OIML (International Organization of Legal Metrology). 2004. *Elements for a Law on Metrology*. International Document OIML D 1:2004 E, OIML, Paris.

Industry Classification According to the Revealed Quality Elasticity

NACE	Industry	RQE
155	Dairy products; ice cream	1
159	Beverages	1
160	Tobacco products	1
172	Textile weaving	1
176	Knitted and crocheted fabrics	1
182	Other wearing apparel and accessories	1
191	Tanning and dressing of leather	1
192	Luggage, handbags, saddlery, and harness	1
193	Footwear	1
242	Pesticides, other agro-chemical products	1
243	Paints, coatings, printing ink	1
244	Pharmaceuticals	1
246	Other chemical products	1
282	Tanks, reservoirs, central heating radiators, boilers	1
292	Other general purpose machinery	1
293	Agricultural and forestry machinery	1
294	Machine-tools	1
295	Other special purpose machinery	1
312	Electricity distribution and control apparatus	1
322	TV, and radio transmitters, apparatus for line telephony	1
331	Medical equipment	1
332	Instruments for measuring, checking, testing, navigating	1
334	Optical instruments and photographic equipment	1
335	Watches and clocks	1
341	Motor vehicles	1
342	Bodies for motor vehicles, trailers	1
343	Parts and accessories for motor vehicles	1

NACE	Industry	RQE
352	Railway locomotives and rolling stock	1
353	Aircraft and spacecraft	1
362	Jewelry and related articles	1
365	Games and toys	1
151	Meat products	2
152	Fish and fish products	2
156	Grain mill products and starches	2
157	Prepared animal feeds	2
158	Other food products	2
171	Textile fibers	2
175	Other textiles	2
177	Knitted and crocheted articles	2
181	Leather clothes	2
183	Dressing and dyeing of fur; articles of fur	2
203	Builders' carpentry and joinery	2
222	Printing	2
230	Coke, refined petroleum, and nuclear fuel	2
245	Detergents, cleaning and polishing, perfumes	2
247	Man-made fibers	2
252	Plastic products	2
262	Ceramic goods	2
263	Ceramic tiles and flags	2
273	Other first processing of iron and steel	2
281	Structural metal products	2
286	Cutlery, tools, and general hardware	2
291	Machinery for production, use of mechanical power	2
300	Office machinery and computers	2
315	Lighting equipment and electric lamps	2
316	Electrical equipment n. e. c.	2
321	Electronic valves and tubes, other electronic comp.	2
351	Ships and boats	2
355	Other transport equipment n. e. c.	2
361	Furniture	2
363	Musical instruments	2
364	Sports goods	2
153	Fruits and vegetables	3
154	Vegetable and animal oils and fats	3
174	Made-up textile articles	3
201	Sawmilling, planing, and impregnation of wood	3
202	Panels and boards of wood	3
204	Wooden containers	3
205	Other products of wood	3
211	Pulp, paper, and paperboard	3
212	Articles of paper and paperboard	3

NACE	Industry	RQE
221	Publishing	3
241	Basic chemicals	3
251	Rubber products	3
261	Glass and glass products	3
264	Bricks, tiles, and construction products	3
265	Cement, lime, and plaster	3
266	Articles of concrete, plaster, and cement	3
267	Cutting, shaping, finishing of stone	3
268	Other nonmetallic mineral products	3
271	Basic iron and steel, ferro-alloys (ECSC)	3
272	Tubes	3
274	Basic precious and nonferrous metals	3
283	Steam generators	3
287	Other fabricated metal products	3
296	Weapons and ammunition	3
297	Domestic appliances n. e. c.	3
311	Electric motors, generators, and transformers	3
313	Isolated wire and cable	3
314	Accumulators, primary cells, and primary batteries	3
323	TV, radio, and recording apparatus	3
354	Motorcycles and bicycles	3
366	Miscellaneous manufacturing n. e. c.	3

Source: Aiginger (2000).
Note: NACE = Nomenclature Statistique des Activités Économiques dans la Communauté Européenne (Statistical Classification of Economic Activities in the European Community). n. e. c. = not elsewhere classified. RQE = Revealed Quality Elasticity. The RQE scores are as follows: 1 = high RQE; 2 = medium RQE; 3 = low RQE.

Reference

Aiginger, K. 2000. "Europe's Position in Quality Competition." Background Report for "The European Competitiveness Report 2000." Enterprise DG Working Paper (September 2000), European Commission, Brussels.

Quality Indicators in Eastern Europe and Central Asia

Unit Values

Computing Unit Values

Unit values form the basis of the indicators used to measure quality. Unit values normally are defined as nominal sales divided by quantity, and export unit values are therefore defined as export values (sales) divided by an export quantity measured in kilograms. Import unit values are import values divided by imported quantities. In this study, we use detailed data on the four-digit NACE (Nomenclature Statistique des Activités Économiques dans la Communauté Européenne, or Statistical Classification of Economic Activities in the European Community) level.

Unit values are calculated on the four-digit NACE level. Denoting the value of exports[1] (VX) of the product class i to the European Union by country c in year t—for which export quantity (QX) information in kilograms is available—by values for quantity (VQX_{ict}), the export unit value (UVX_{ict}) is defined as follows:

$$UVX_{ict} = VQX_{ict} / QX_{ict}$$

Advantages and Limitations of the Unit Value Approach

In many instances, higher prices for a given product from different suppliers reflect higher quality. Unit values therefore can be interpreted as an indicator of the consumer's evaluation of product quality. In the absence of inelastic supply, higher prices reflect higher quality. In models of

---

1. The same procedure applies to the calculation of import unit values.

imperfect competition, increases in unit values in heterogeneous markets signal quality improvements, together with growing product differentiation. Therefore, under a broad set of circumstances, unit values can be used to measure the degree of quality of a product (Greenaway, Hine, and Milner 1994).

In several empirical studies, unit values have been used as a proxy of quality, although the methodologies applied to calculate these quality indicators based on unit values have varied (for example, Aiginger 1997, 1998, 2000; Dulleck and others 2003; Kandogan 2004; Hallak 2005; Fabrizio, Igan, and Mody 2007). The wide use of unit values as a measure of product quality goes back to their multiple advantages. First, quantity information is available at disaggregated levels of industry aggregation, the country and time availability is rich, and the information is a useful indicator for comparing quality levels across different countries. Moreover, Aiginger (2000) reveals that unit values reflect most of the components that add value to a product. Generally, capital-intensive industries depict lower unit values than skill- and technology-intensive industries. Skills and technology are important determinants of quality.

Like other quality indicators, unit values have both advantages and disadvantages. The composition problem is a shortcoming of using unit values. Product categories usually include different goods, so differences in unit values can reflect not only differences in the quality of goods, but also differences in the export composition within a product category.

Various Indicators Based on Unit Values

The most basic indicator that can be created from unit values is the aggregate relative unit value, which is defined as the ratio between the export unit value and the import unit value. More precisely, it is calculated from the ratio between the average price per kilogram of total manufacturing exports and the average price per kilogram of total imports. An important limitation of this indicator is that it is influenced by a country's export and import structure.

To overcome this shortcoming, one can calculate the relative unit value on the disaggregated level. For the calculation of this relative unit value 2 (RUV2), we divide the export unit value by the import unit value on the four-digit NACE industry level instead of calculating these divisions on the total manufacturing level (see table B.1). The advantage of this relative unit value is that it allows us to compare exports and imports directly at the product class level.[2] The RUV2 can be aggregated by means

---

2. From this, it follows that only industries for which export unit values and import unit values exist simultaneously are taken into consideration.

TABLE B.1
Relative Unit Values

Indicator (abbreviation)	Description
Unit value	Nominal sales divided by a quantity unit (usually kilograms or tons)
Export unit value (XUV)	Export value divided by an export quantity measured in kilograms calculated per country c (XUV_c) or calculated per country c and 4-digit NACE industry i (XUV_{ci})
Import unit value (MUV)	Import value divided by an import quantity measured in kilograms calculated per country c (MUV_c) or calculated per country c and 4-digit NACE industry i (MUV_{ci})
Relative unit value 2 (RUV2)	Export unit value relative to import unit value at the disaggregated 4-digit NACE industry level (XUV_{ci}/MUV_{ci}) and then aggregated by quantity weights
Relative unit value 3 (RUV3)	Export unit value relative to a benchmark (benchmark is the export unit value of the world exports w to the EU) at the disaggregated 4-digit NACE industry level (XUV_{ci}/XUV_{wi}) and then aggregated by quantity weights

Source: Authors' calculations based on Eurostat Database.

of quantity weights. The share of the quantity of the individual four-digit product classes in the total quantity exported is used as a weight.[3]

One disadvantage of the RUV2 indicator is that the comparison between export and import unit values is subject to potential biases, because exports include insurance and freight costs (due to the use of mirror statistics), whereas imports do not. We therefore calculated the relative unit value 3 (RUV3) indicator, which relates the export unit value of individual countries to a benchmark. In our case, the benchmark is the export unit value of world exports to the European Union (EU). Analyzing this indicator on the disaggregated level has the advantage that the quality of every country's exported products is then compared with the same benchmark, namely, the quality of the world's exports to the EU in the same industry. When analyzing this indicator on the total manufacturing level, however, remember that the industries included may vary across countries. For a reduction of the effect of trade structure,

---

3. These weights change when the export structure of the country changes, and the aggregate unit value ratio therefore is influenced not only by the quality of the products themselves, but also by the composition of total exports.

industries with the highest effect on unit value indicators are not considered for the computation of the unit value indicators. These are the textile, textile product, leather, and leather product sectors.

The Grubel-Lloyd Index

Grubel-Lloyd (GL) indexes measure the amount of intraindustry trade between countries or country groups (Grubel and Lloyd 1975). The Grubel-Lloyd index is equal to 100 if all trade is the intraindustry type, which is the case when the export and import structures of a country or country group are identical, and zero if all trade is the interindustry type. One disadvantage of the Grubel-Lloyd index is that it is sensitive to the industry or country aggregation level. However, according to the literature, the 4-digit NACE industry level should be sufficiently disaggregated for intraindustry trade calculations. Detailed Grubel-Lloyd indexes for each product group at the 4-digit NACE industry level are calculated using the following formula:[4]

$$GL_i = 100 - \frac{|X_i - M_i|}{(X_i + M_i)} * 100$$

This observed intraindustry trade (IIT) at the 4-digit NACE industry level is further classified into vertical (VGLi) and horizontal (HGLi) intraindustry trade. Vertical IIT measures the share of IIT with goods of different qualities, whereas horizontal IIT measures the share of IIT with goods of similar qualities. Put differently, horizontal product differentiation refers to varieties of products of the same quality level and approximately the same price, while vertical product differentiation constitutes different varieties of products of different qualities, often in different price segments. In this context, horizontal IIT is defined as simultaneous export and import and is identified by a range of relative export and import unit values of about 15 percent.

For analysis of the differences in the quality and technology content of products, the share of vertical IIT is further divided into two different types of vertical IIT—high quality and low quality. This methodology was introduced by Greenaway, Hine, and Milner (1994, 1995). It is based on the use of unit value information: a spread between export and import unit values of more than 15 percent is used to divide between horizontal and vertical IIT. When this relative unit value indicator lies below 0.85, IIT is defined as low-quality vertical IIT.

---

4. The following labeling and subscripts will be used: X = export; M = import; i = sector.

References

Aiginger, K. 1997. "The Use of Unit Values to Discriminate between Price and Quality Competition." *Cambridge Journal of Economics* 21 (5): 571–92.

———. 1998. "Unit Values to Signal the Quality Position of CEECs." In *The Competitiveness of Transition Economies*, Austrian Institute of Economic Research (WIFO), Vienna Institute for Comparative Economic Studies (WIIW), and Organisation for Economic Co-operation and Development (OECD), 93–121. OECD Proceedings Series. Paris: OECD.

———. 2000. "Europe's Position in Quality Competition." Background Report for "The European Competitiveness Report 2000." Enterprise DG Working Paper (September 2000), European Commission, Brussels.

Dulleck, U., N. Foster, R. Stehrer, and J. Wörz. 2003. "Dimensions of Quality Upgrading: Evidence for CEEC's." Working Paper 0314, Department of Economics, University of Vienna.

Fabrizio, S., D. Igan, and A. Mody. 2007. "The Dynamics of Product Quality and International Competitiveness." IMF Working Paper 07/97, International Monetary Fund, Washington, DC.

Greenaway, D., R. Hine, and C. Milner. 1994. "Country-Specific Factors and the Pattern of Horizontal and Vertical Intra-Industry Trade in the UK." *Review of World Economics (Weltwirtschaftliches Archiv)* 130 (1): 77–100.

———. 1995. "Vertical and Horizontal Intra-industry Trade: A Cross Industry Analysis for the United Kingdom." *The Economic Journal* 105 (433): 1505–18.

Grubel, H., and P. J. Lloyd. 1975. *Intra-Industry Trade.* London: Macmillan.

Hallak, J. C. 2005. "Product Quality and the Direction of Trade." University of Michigan, April.

Kandogan, Y. 2004. "How Much Restructuring Did the Transition Countries Experience? Evidence from Quality of Their Exports." Working Paper 637, William Davidson Institute, University of Michigan, Ann Arbor.

Copyright Issues

An issue that invariably surfaces in the debates regarding standards in developing economies is copyright. In developed countries, it is common practice that national standards enjoy copyright, because the national standards bodies derive the bulk of their income from the sale of standards. International Organization for Standardization (ISO) and International Electrotechnical Commission (IEC) international standards likewise are protected by international copyright. This means that no organization or person is entitled to obtain the text of an ISO or IEC standard and to publish it under their own name or provide it free of charge to industry. The copyright of ISO and IEC standards is ceded to the national standards body when it becomes a full member of ISO or IEC. But then the national member body is expected to vigorously protect the copyright of the international standard. National standards that are adoptions of international standards must be sold for a specified minimum price; they cannot be given away free of charge.[1] However, many of the standards of the intergovernmental standards bodies such as the International Telecommunication Union, Codex Alimentarius Commission, and others are provided free of charge. Hence, adopting them as national standards does not involve any copyright issues.

Another limiting factor is that *associate* members, *corresponding* members, or *developing country* members often have only limited access to the international standards and, therefore, cannot adopt any amount of international standards as national standards. Details vary and change from time to time among the international bodies. This is probably the most compelling reason for the national standards body to become a full member of these organizations, because the cost of purchasing a full set

---

1. In the case of ISO, these arrangements are contained in their POCOSA agreement (ISO 2005). The IEC has a similar system in place.

of the international standards from, for example, ISO or IEC is far more than the annual membership fee.[2]

Another issue that often leads to much debate is whether national standards should retain their copyright when they are referenced in technical regulations or other national legislation. In general, it is accepted that national standards bodies should be paid for the standards they publish, and hence, even in the case of standards being referenced in national legislation, their copyright remains. This policy should, however, be made clear in their own legislation. Many developing economies have adopted a policy of providing national standards to the industry at the lowest-level prices, but just high enough to comply with ISO or IEC regulations, making them more readily available to industry that is not as affluent as in industrialized countries.

Reference

ISO (International Organization for Standardization). 2005. "POCOSA 2005: ISO Policies and Procedures for Copyright, Copyright Exploitation Rights, and Sales of ISO Publications." ISO, Geneva.

---

2. The membership fee of ISO, for example, is calculated in accordance with per capita gross national product, value of exports and imports, and involvement in standardization and is fixed by a number of units on these factors. A unit is approximately US$6000. Member bodies pay typically between 5 and 170 units, corresponding members 2 to 4 units, and subscriber members as little as half a unit. A national standards body of a developing economy can therefore be paying about 10 units (US$60,000) for full membership and gain unlimited access to all 16,000 ISO standards, whereas purchasing them would cost at least US$2.4 million (at an estimated average price of US$150).

Accreditation Gap Analysis

In the framework of the European Phare Programme, the European Union provided Central and Eastern European countries with technical assistance for the national quality infrastructure. One objective was to help the national accreditation bodies reach a level of competence required to become signatories to the European co-operation for Accreditation Multilateral Agreement on the accreditation of laboratories, certification bodies, and inspection bodies. This objective was achieved through annual assessment visits to investigate the present level of competence of the national accreditation body as a way to decide if further supporting activities were necessary. A 30 Milestones Analysis was developed in 1995. Six peer evaluator teams assessed the MSTQ (metrology, standards, testing, and quality) infrastructure in 13 Central and Eastern European countries yearly until the year 2000. After its successful implementation in accession countries, this roadmap was used as a Physikalisch-Technische Bundesanstalt planning and monitoring tool for setting up accreditation schemes in more than 20 projects around the world.

Figure D.1 shows a network plan describing the relation of each milestone to the others. The dark gold boxes represent political aspects, dark gray boxes are related to the administration, light gold boxes deal with technical aspects, and light gray boxes represent external relations.

The problems identified through this approach can be categorized into four main groups: political problems, administrative problems, technical problems, or problems with external relations. Following is an overview of the possible and frequent difficulties:

Political Problems

1.   National policy: missing legislation, change of ministers or government policies

FIGURE D.1

Gap Analysis Schematic for a National Accreditation Body

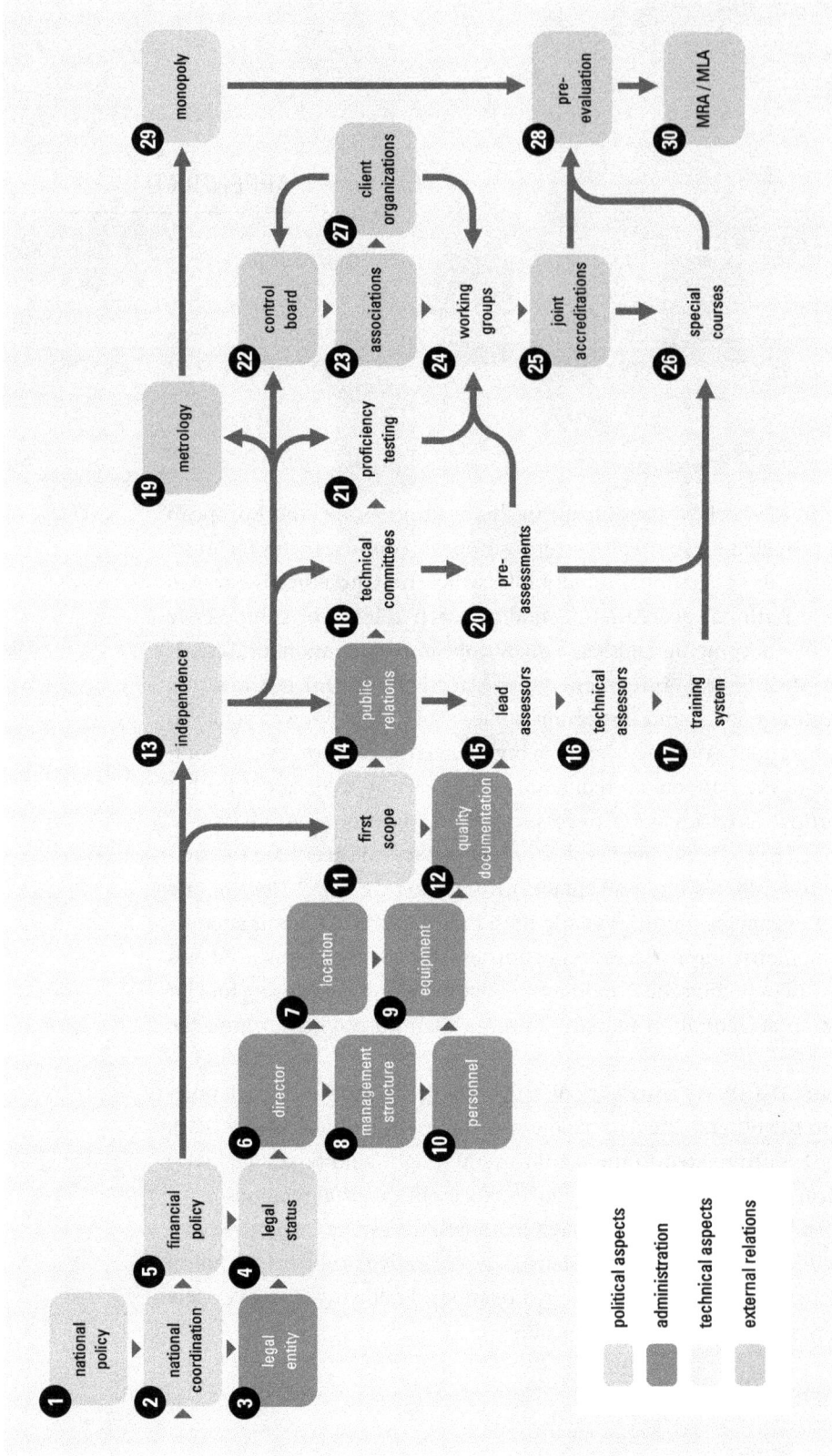

Source: Authors' elaboration.

Note: MLA = multilateral recognition arrangement, MRA = mutual recognition arrangement.

2. National coordination: missing cooperation with involved ministries or authorities

4. Legal status: juridical problems to designate a national institution

5. Financial policy: insufficient financial resources, no business plan, no costs awareness

13. Independency: too much political influence, no anticorruption measures

11. First scope: no clear decision about scope of activities, no limits of activities

29. Monopoly: no arrangements with national ministries; for example, health care, agriculture

Problems with Administration

3. Legal entity: no registration as a legal entity, liability not defined, no assurance

6. Director: director not designated, no permanent work contract

7. Location: selection by political aspects, no focus on customer needs

8. Management structure: no delegation of responsibilities, no modern management

9. Equipment: poor conditions for confidentiality; common use of phones, fax, computer, copy machines

10. Personnel: poorly qualified staff, low salaries, corruption

12. Quality documentation: too much bureaucracy, no lean management, no quality improvement

14. Public relations: poor marketing, only one language (no English skills)

Technical Problems

15. Lead assessors: poor qualification, experience, leadership; high workload

16. Technical assessors: conflicts of interests, wide scope, poor qualification

17. Training system: poor trainer qualification, no adequate training plans, poor effectiveness

18. Technical committees: poor access to resource persons, low outcome quality

19. Metrology: no international traceability, poor cooperation, no chemical metrology, no delegation of calibration services

20. Pre-assessments: costs, poor resources, lack of experts, poor requests, low outcome quality

21. Proficiency testing: no local services, high costs, no follow-up services, poorly qualified proficiency testing provider

24. Working groups: poor access to experts, poor language skills, low outcome quality

26. Special courses: no qualified provider, no systematic qualification, no analysis of needs, low effectiveness, no follow-up activities

Problems with External Relations

22. Control board: interested parties missing, dominance of power, poor outcome quality

23. Associations: high costs, poor language skills, no designation of qualified delegates

25. Joint accreditations: poor contacts, high costs, no awareness for regional cooperation

27. Client organizations: poor reputation of accreditation body, no national associations, poor access to main players

28. Pre-evaluation: inexperienced peer evaluators, high costs, poor understanding of culture and history

30. Mutual recognition arrangement/multilateral recognition arrangement: partly no acceptance on global markets, poor anticorruption measures